NUMBER TWO HUNDRED AND TWENTY-THREE

The Old Farmer's Almanac

CALCULATED ON A NEW AND IMPROVED PLAN FOR THE YEAR OF OUR LORD

2015

BEING 3RD AFTER LEAP YEAR AND (UNTIL JULY 4) 239TH YEAR OF AMERICAN INDEPENDENCE

Fitted for Boston and the New England states, with special corrections and calculations to answer for all the United States.

Containing, besides the large number of Astronomical Calculations and the Farmer's Calendar for every month in the year, a variety of

NEW, USEFUL, & ENTERTAINING MATTER.

Established in 1792 by Robert B. Thomas (1766–1846)

Nature is whole and yet never finished.
–Johann Wolfgang von Goethe, German writer (1749–1832)

Cover T.M. registered in U.S. Patent Office

Copyright © 2014 by Yankee Publishing Incorporated
ISSN 0078-4516

Library of Congress Card No. 56-29681

Original wood engraving by Randy Miller

THE OLD FARMER'S ALMANAC • DUBLIN, NH 03444 • 603-563-8111 • ALMANAC.COM

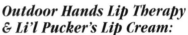

Contents

(continued on page 6)

Contents

(continued from page 4)

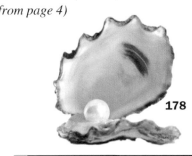

178

There's more of everything at Almanac.com.

Three Cheers!

This year, dear reader, marks a variety of historic records set by this modest annual and its related endeavors. As your humble servants, we recognize and proclaim that for all of our successes—great or small, in print or electronic technology—we are indebted to each and every one of you. We salute and thank you!

Your enthusiasm for and loyalty to this calendar of the heavens and yearly time capsule has, with this edition, once again solidified its standing as "the oldest continuously published periodical in North America." Yet it is not this Almanac's longevity that we honor foremost; rather, it is you, for procuring the previous edition in such record numbers that its presence in hands and homes across the continent has scarcely ever been exceeded. We hope that the information in this edition similarly meets (dare we say "exceeds"?) your expectations, and we eagerly await your comments and observations.

Many of you rejoiced at the debut this year of our annual *All-Seasons Garden Guide* as a full-size (no longer digest) magazine, with its mesmerizing displays of blooms and edibles. We thank you from our roots. Next March's edition promises more beautiful and delicious garden delights.

We would also like to high-five the youngsters—and teachers and parents—who read and rave about our biannual Almanac for Kids. Your fun is our fulfillment. Send us your ideas!

Being of a modern mind, this Almanac is fully engaged in popular media and social networking. In these means, you have also demonstrated unprecedented interest, for which we are also grateful. To wit:

■ In March 2014, the volume of new visitors to and viewers of pages on Almanac.com surpassed all previous monthly tallies, with 4.4 million and 11+ million, respectively.

■ Our number of Facebook friends hovers at about 550,000. One post about the lunar eclipse on April 14–15 was read by some 5.8 million people.

■ Your use of reading devices to engage with Almanac offerings—apps, the digital Almanac, and the Almanac Monthly magazine—encourages us to produce more, an opportunity that we welcome. About these and any other of our endeavors, we welcome you to contact us at Almanac.com/Feedback.

Finally, in closing this passage and beginning a new Almanac, we offer three cheers, each with heartfelt appreciation: one for you, one for the years we have enjoyed together, and one for the new year that unfolds before us all.

–J. S., June 2014

However, it is by our works and not our words that we would be judged. These, we hope, will sustain us in the humble though proud station we have so long held in the name of

Your obedient servant,

Explore Almanac.com

Almanac.com/Weather
Get daily forecasts, folklore, blogs, history, and detailed reference materials.

Almanac.com/Gardening
Grow more, better, right now!

Almanac.com/Astronomy
Everything under the Sun, including the Moon, every day (and night).

Almanac.com/Mobile
Experience Almanac.com, created for a smaller screen, on your iPhone and get companion apps at iTunes.

Almanac.com/Cooking
Make meals easy and delicious with thousands of free recipes.

Almanac.com/Newsletters
Keep in touch. Subscribe to our free e-newsletters:
Almanac Companion: Timely new ideas and special offers.
Recipe Box: Seasonal recipes, contests, blogs, and more.

Almanac.com/Videos
Learn how-to or get a giggle with us in the garden and kitchen, on full Moon days, and more!

Almanac.com/Shop
Discover unique collections of made-in-the-USA weather, gardening, and cooking products, plus a whole lot more!

Almanac.com/Feedback
Got a question? A comment? We love to hear from you!

Almanac.com/Contests
Win fabulous prizes! Share photos or recipes, test your trivia knowledge, enter our drawings—have fun!

FOLLOW US!
Facebook.com/theoldfarmersalmanac

 PIN US!
Pinterest.com/Almanac

TWEET US!
Twitter.com/Almanac

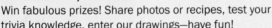

2015   THE OLD FARMER'S ALMANAC   11

ON THE FARM

As people become more concerned about the quality of the food they eat and the environment in which they live, urban farms will continue to grow in number.

–Michael Levenston, City Farmer Society, Vancouver, British Columbia

SOME URBAN FARMERS are renting space on front lawns to grow crops. Others are growing produce hydroponically in greenhouses on rooftops.

FARMERS EVERYWHERE are renting pollinating bee hives from hobby beekeepers; creating free apps, kids' books, and lesson plans to teach kids where food comes from; grazing their goats in parks and woodlands to reduce feed cost and clear land.

PEOPLE ARE TALKING ABOUT
- Farmers posting their surplus produce on Web sites, deeply discounted, so that it can be bought and used by restaurants and home cooks.

- Restaurants and caterers creating dishes from food waste.

- Companies buying bruised, misshapen produce rejected by supermarkets and using it to make low-cost meals for people in need.

WE'RE SAVING WATER
- growing drought-resistant edibles such as prickly pear cactus

- relying on satellite imagery to predict drought and crop yields

BY THE NUMBERS
38,629: schools participating in a USDA program to teach kids about agriculture

- using plastic barriers to hold water in the root zones of plants

EVERYBODY'S DOING IT
- "aquafarming" at home: growing leafy greens or herbs over fishbowls (the roots keep the water clean and fish waste feeds the plants)

FARMS OVER FAIRWAYS

We will be seeing more residential developments with farms on the property. Farms are the new golf courses.

–Ann Marie Gardner, editor, Modern Farmer

Photos, from top: Zoey Kroll/Wikimedia; Mark Byzewski/Wikimedia

GOOD EATS

Home cooks will explore global cuisines.
–Maile Carpenter, editor in chief,
Food Network Magazine

EVERYBODY'S DOING IT

• paying attention to specific regional flavors and cooking styles, such as Greek, Korean, and Vietnamese

• making desserts in oversize pie dishes and cooking two roasts at once in large Dutch ovens

• using phone apps to know when foods in the fridge are about to expire

OUR FAVE CRAVES:

chocolate teas, seaweed chips, truffle ketchup

DINERS ARE DEMANDING . . .

• menus that carry the names of the farms that produced their food

• meats in season from small farm producers

• "meaterys" that put every part of the animal on the menu

• to see food being made, e.g., cheese in big vats

PEOPLE ARE TALKING ABOUT

• hamburgers made from laboratory-grown meat

WORD TO THE WISE

Za'atar: a mix of sumac berries, sesame seed, thyme, and other herbs used in Middle Eastern dishes

WORKPLACE CAFÉS

are labeling dishes with "traffic light" colors (red, yellow, green), based on nutrition levels and/or placing healthy food at eye level and unhealthy food out of reach.

WEIGHTY RESEARCH

• Dieters who had a bit of sweets per day shed 15 additional pounds, on average.

• Putting foods on a "Do Not Eat" list makes us crave them more.

BY THE NUMBERS

64% of food shoppers buy organic occasionally

31: average number of pounds of fresh and processed tomatoes eaten by an adult annually

825: number of licensed U.S. artisan cheese producers

75% of families eat most meals in the kitchen (18% munch on the couch)

34% of families typically eat together seven nights a week

193: number of restaurant meals the average person eats annually *(continued)*

IN THE GARDEN

More home gardeners are looking to their gardens as an oasis for providing backyard habitat, food for themselves, and beauty.

–Maree Gaetani, spokesperson, Gardener's Supply Company

EVERYBODY'S DOING IT

- swapping seeds
- building cold rooms or root cellars
- grafting different varieties on one plant (e.g., tomatoes with potatoes; multiple apples on a single tree)
- growing "micro-greens": spinach, pea,

Mantis Does It All!
- Speed Weeds In Minutes
- Tills New Garden Beds
- Digs Planting Holes
- And Much More...

Precision Cultivator!

One Year RISK-FREE Trial

Easy-to-Use Tiller!

Busts Tough Sod!

This 20 lb Wonder Will Cut Your Garden Chores...*In Half!*

Discover The Mantis Difference...In Your Own Garden!

The Mantis Tiller is the lightest weight, easy-to-use gardening powerhouse that makes back-breaking hand tools...*OBSOLETE!* Sod bust a new garden, weed around delicate plants, or dig a hole for a new shrub...the *Mantis can do it all!*

- Powerful enough for big gardens ...nimble enough for small.
- Turns even tough, hard clay soil into rich, crumbly loam.

- So lightweight that it's a breeze to handle in the garden.
- Cuts through tough soil and roots like a chainsaw through wood!

- Create and maintain beautiful planting beds all season long.

SAVE $30 Plus FREE SHIPPING!
(on selected models)
Call for complete details.

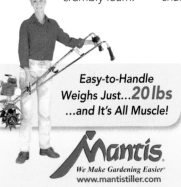

Easy-to-Handle Weighs Just...20 lbs ...and It's All Muscle!

Mantis®
We Make Gardening Easier®
www.mantistiller.com

© 2014, Schiller Grounds Care, Inc.

Call Toll-Free For Your FREE Catalog and DVD...TODAY!

1-888-240-4556 Dept: MT141034

YES! Please rush my **FREE Catalog and DVD** plus details on your one year NO-RISK Trial, $30 Savings (on selected models) and FREE Shipping.

NAME_____

ADDRESS_____

CITY_____ STATE _____ ZIP _____

Mail to: Mantis, 1028 Street Rd, Dept. MT141034
Southampton, PA 18966

beet, or purple mustard seedlings for use in salads, soups, and sandwiches

Microgreens salad

MORE HOME GROWERS are leaving some harvestable vegetables for foraging pollinators and/or creating "bee hotels" with dead trees or limbs to increase the number of nesting habitats for bees.

(continued)

BY THE NUMBERS

1.7 million:
home owners with newly purchased greenhouses

$29.1 billion:
spent by households on lawns and gardens

$347:
spent, on average, annually by home gardeners; young males spend about $100 more, with many growing hops for beer brewing or grapes for winemaking

---

COLORFUL COMBOS

FOR THE EYE, FOR POLLINATORS, AND FOR BOUQUETS . . .

- 'Sonnet Orange Scarlet' snapdragons, 'Red Salad Bowl' lettuce, and 'Triple Curled' parsley

- red giant mustard, 'Orange Fantasia' Swiss chard, and Shungiku greens

- 'Rosa Bianca' eggplant with 'French Vanilla' marigolds

- 'Green Envy' zinnia, 'Limelight Spray' millet, and 'Green Ball' dianthus

- 'Redbor' kale and 'Bull's Blood' beet

'Rosa Bianca' eggplant and 'French Vanilla' marigolds

FAVORITE FRESH PICKS . . .

- kale, beets, and turnips to make healthy chips

- colorful varieties: blue-green 'Savoy Express' cabbage, 'Blue Solaise' leek, 'Black Seeded Simpson' lettuce, and purple pea pods 'Shiraz'

- drought-tolerant varieties: 'Zapotec' pleated tomato, 'Rutgers' tomato, 'Painted Mountain' corn

- long-producing heirlooms: 'Glass Gem' corn, 'Green Zebra', and 'Amana Orange' tomatoes

—Lisa Hilgenberg, fruit and vegetable garden horticulturist, Chicago Botanic Garden

'Glass Gem' corn

Photos: microgreens, www.jolleyfarms.com; eggplant, National Garden Bureau; marigolds, W. Atlee Burpee & Co.; corn, Greg Shoen/nativeseeds.org

OUR HEALTH & WELLNESS

Much of health care currently taking place within hospitals and clinics will be shifted to the home or corner drugstore.

–Dr. Steven Steinhubl, director of digital medicine, Scripps Health, San Diego, California

THE DOCTOR IS IN . . . our pockets, with wearable sensors that diagnose viral and bacterial infections and track our stress, sleep, heart rhythm, and blood pressure.

MEDICAL MIRACLES COMING SOON

- capsules in the body that take and transmit pictures to doctors

BY THE NUMBERS

367,000: robot-aided surgeries performed in the U.S. in 2012

34% of adults nap on a typical day

78 fewer calories are consumed daily, compared to previous years

$28 million: spent by consumers on vitamins annually

EVERYBODY'S DOING IT

looking for balance in their lives: Just a change in mind-set can turn a task like weeding into an opportunity to meditate.

–Suzi McCoy, Garden Media, Kennett Square, Pennsylvania

- wheelchairs that turn in the direction in which the user thinks about moving his or her hands

SECRETS OF A HEALTHY LIFE

- **Giving of yourself:** The mortality rate of volunteers is 22 percent lower than that of nonvolunteers.

- **Berries:** Women who ate three or more servings of blueberries and strawberries per week were 34 percent less likely to have a heart attack.

PEOPLE ARE TALKING ABOUT

- wandering around in silence in public parks for mindfulness training

- relaxation coaches who improve our slumber

- spray-on caffeine to keep us alert

LIFE IS GOOD . . . for spouses, in beds with snore features that allow a snorer's headrest to be raised; bicyclists, with scarves that inflate automatically in an accident; poor posture sufferers, with belts that vibrate if they slouch.

(continued)

Herbal Formula Eases Aches And Pains

Barbara Burke, Crown Point, IN: "My husband was waking up 2 to 3 times a night with knee pain. On day 2 of using Steuart's Pain Formula he slept all night long."

Steuart Laboratories originally developed Steuart's Pain Formula for race horses. "People now use the product to relieve joint and muscle pain associated with arthritis and injuries," Steuart says. The cream contains extracts of the herbs Comfrey and Arnica in a liposome base that penetrates the skin rapidly.

5 oz. Airless Pump
$29.90 + S&H

Also Available

2 oz. for
$14.95 + S&H

Steuart Laboratories
203 N. Main Street, P.O. Box 306,
Mabel, Minn. 55954
507-493-5585 toll free: 877-210-9664
www.steuartlaboratories.com

Mike Marsden, Mabel, Minn: "I keep a jar of Steuart's Pain Formula by my bed and reach for it at night when my knee pain flares up. It knocks the pain right out."

OUR ANIMAL FRIENDS

As the economy improves, people are turning back to the big dogs they love, which cost more to feed and care for than the smaller breeds.

–Lisa Peterson, spokesperson, American Kennel Club

PEOPLE ARE TALKING ABOUT
- chickens, diapered and running around the house
- subscriptions for pet treats and toys
- pets using electronic devices to entertain themselves while home alone

DOMESTIC DELIGHTS INCLUDE grooming stations; pet-size furniture, pet-height windows, and heated window seats; overhead catwalks; and entry tunnels with paw wash-and-dry systems so that pets don't track dirt on carpets

TO TRACK ACTIVITY, pets are wearing collar pedometers.

(continued)

BY THE NUMBERS

68%
of households have at least one pet

$330 million:
spent on Halloween outfits for pets in 2013

AROUND THE HOUSE

With more people . . . making do with less square footage, there is a growing trend of furniture that does double duty. *–Amanda Dameron, editor in chief,* Dwell

OUR DREAM HOME IS
• a historical house, but not an exact replica; e.g., vintage exterior, with open interior

• a lighthouse renovated for living space

• a classic barn dismantled, moved, and rebuilt

• less than 500 square feet in a "micro-neighborhood"

• one with a small front yard setback and sidewalks

NEW HOME WISH LIST
• his-and-her master bathrooms

• ventless, smoke-free fireplaces on a wall or counter or midroom

• floor tiles that kill bacteria and improve air quality

• windows coated to repel stains and grime

HOME BUYERS' BARGAINING CHIPS:
the seller's possessions, e.g., houseplants, bed linens, pots, pans, and alarm clocks: We want it all!

PEOPLE ARE TALKING ABOUT
• bright walls in mint greens, turquoises, pale yellows, and oranges

• freestanding walls of water, illuminated by colored lights

• wider, thinner handmade bricks in a variety of colors

WE'RE ADAPTING TO CLIMATE CHANGE,
with accommodation architecture that lets seawater in during storm surges; by moving utility controls from basements to attics; by installing moss roofs—their insulation effects cut heating and cooling costs; with "performance dashboards" that track energy and water use, indoor air cleanliness, and our recycling habits.

STUFF WE LOVE
• corduroy upholstery

• macramé and fiber art wall decor

• baby-changing tables that become bookcases

• crystal tables, lamps, and bowls

• smoke alarms that can be silenced with a wave of the hand

(continued)

HELP PLACE WREATHS ON THE GRAVES OF THE AMERICAN HEROES WHO PLACED THEIR LIVES ON THE LINE FOR YOU...

TECH TALK

Technology is democratizing landscape design. People are taking mobile devices in[to] their yards for access to expertise that can save them time and money.
–Julie Moir Messervy, author, landscape designer, and creator of the Home Outside Palette app

THE LATEST FROM THE LAB . . .

• cars that park themselves and come when called with a phone app

• plants that glow in the dark, with genes from bioluminescent bacteria and fireflies

• cars powered by solar panels that fit into the trunk

• DNA-driven regeneration of extinct frogs and other animals.

BEEN WHERE, DONE WHAT?

Space tourists will board pressurized 4-ton capsules that are lifted 20 miles up by giant helium-filled balloons to get a view of Earth. Ticket price: $75,000.

(continued)

OUR PASSION FOR FASHION

This will be the year of the mash-up . . .
a return to the exuberant, free spirit of the 1970s,
with the structured tailoring and subdued color
palette of the 1940s.
–*Dyanna Dawson, blog author,* Street Fashion Style

NEWS TO DYE FOR

"Colors in menswear will be much more daring and vibrant. It's going to be acceptable, rather than astonishing, to see men wearing color," says Scott F. Stoddart, dean of Liberal Arts, Fashion Institute of Technology.

WEAR IT, WEATHER OR NOT!

The former rules of season-appropriate colors, patterns, and prints will be disregarded as an outcome of unpredictable climatic conditions.
–*Steven Faerm, professor of fashion design, Parsons The New School for Design, New York City*

THE LOOK FOR LADIES
- "regal," with embroidery, emblems, and crests; hues of teal blue, deep red, honey, and reddish brown; and fabrics in luxurious mohair, shearling, and silk

- slim pants with high waistlines

- faux fur backpacks

- leather in sweatpants and square-cut sweatshirts

- motorcycle jackets in colorful hues

HUES FOR GALS:
gold, royal blue, navy, tomato red, and tan, as well as floral patterns

CLOTHES THAT MAKE THE MAN
- double-breasted suits

- pleats and cuffs on pants

- fur trim on hats, boots, and parkas

- plaids reminiscent of the 1920s

TONES FOR GUYS:
sage, purple, indigo, and burgundy suits, slacks, and sport coats,

COMING SOON TO CLOSETS
- clothing that changes color with the wearer's mood
- clothing that flashes in synch with music
- fabric that is both printed and sewn into a garment at home
–*William C. Perrine, School of Fashion Design and Merchandising, Kent State University*

plus flowery, geometric-pattern sport shirts

THE HIP MAN
will have short and slicked-back hair, plus a full beard.

PEOPLE ARE TALKING ABOUT

• T-shirts, socks, and underwear that deodorize by neutralizing smells at the molecular level

• purses with solar panels that recharge devices

• botanical dyes and fabric that depict the source plant

CULTURE CUES

The "makers" movement will continue . . . as consumers grow more and more interested in all things small-batch and handcrafted.
—Rachel Hardage Barrett, editor in chief, Country Living

THE PACE OF OUR PASTTIMES
We're racing modified lawn mowers and riding with "slow bike" clubs that pedal at a snail's pace and celebrate the last cyclist to finish.

PEOPLE ARE TALKING ABOUT

• turning parking spaces into mini parks for a day

• "slow TV," e.g., knitting and chess programs

• taking "shelfies"—photos of our books

IN PURSUIT OF FUN

• We're teaming up to take turns throwing axes.

• We're searching for antique commodes, sinks, and toilet paper.

BY THE NUMBERS
214,000: dads who are at-home fathers (up 46 percent in 10 years)

75%
of commuters travel alone by car

• Adults are taking classes in double Dutch jump roping.

• Metal detectorists are competing to find "treasures" set out the night before. *(continued)*

MONEY MATTERS

Crowd-funding is taking a giant leap forward.
–*Daniel Levine, director,*
The Avant-Guide Institute,
New York City

WE'RE HOOKED ON HAGGLING

Forty-eight percent of shoppers bargained for a better deal at least once in the past 3 years. Each saved, on average:

- $100 on collectibles and antiques
- $200 on appliances
- $300 on furniture

COLLECTORS' CORNER

Collecting will be driven by the millennial generation. The goal is to repurpose, reinvent, and reevaluate items from the past—all the time knowing that buying vintage is a green activity.
–*Gary Piattoni, appraiser, Evanston, Illinois*

TAKE IT . . .
- pillows and purses in vintage fabrics
- early cameras and typewriters (as decorative objects)
- early–20th-century enamel-on-steel advertising signs

LEAVE IT . . .
Movie star autographs; most are by secretaries or assistants. "Even the legit ones have dropped in value because of a glut flooding the market," says appraiser Rudy Franchi.

WATCH IT GO . . .
Sports items representing historic feats by great athletes are bringing record prices:

- $1.4 million for one of Jesse Owens's 1936 Olympic gold medals
- $717,000 for a Lou Gehrig New York Yankees game-used uniform from 1927

BEST BUY: CHRISTMAS ORNAMENTS
Those from 19th-century Germany are top-of-the-market, but values are also high for any made up through the 1950s. ∎

Stacey Kusterbeck, a frequent contributor to *The Old Farmer's Almanac,* writes about popular culture from New York State.

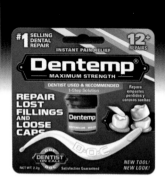

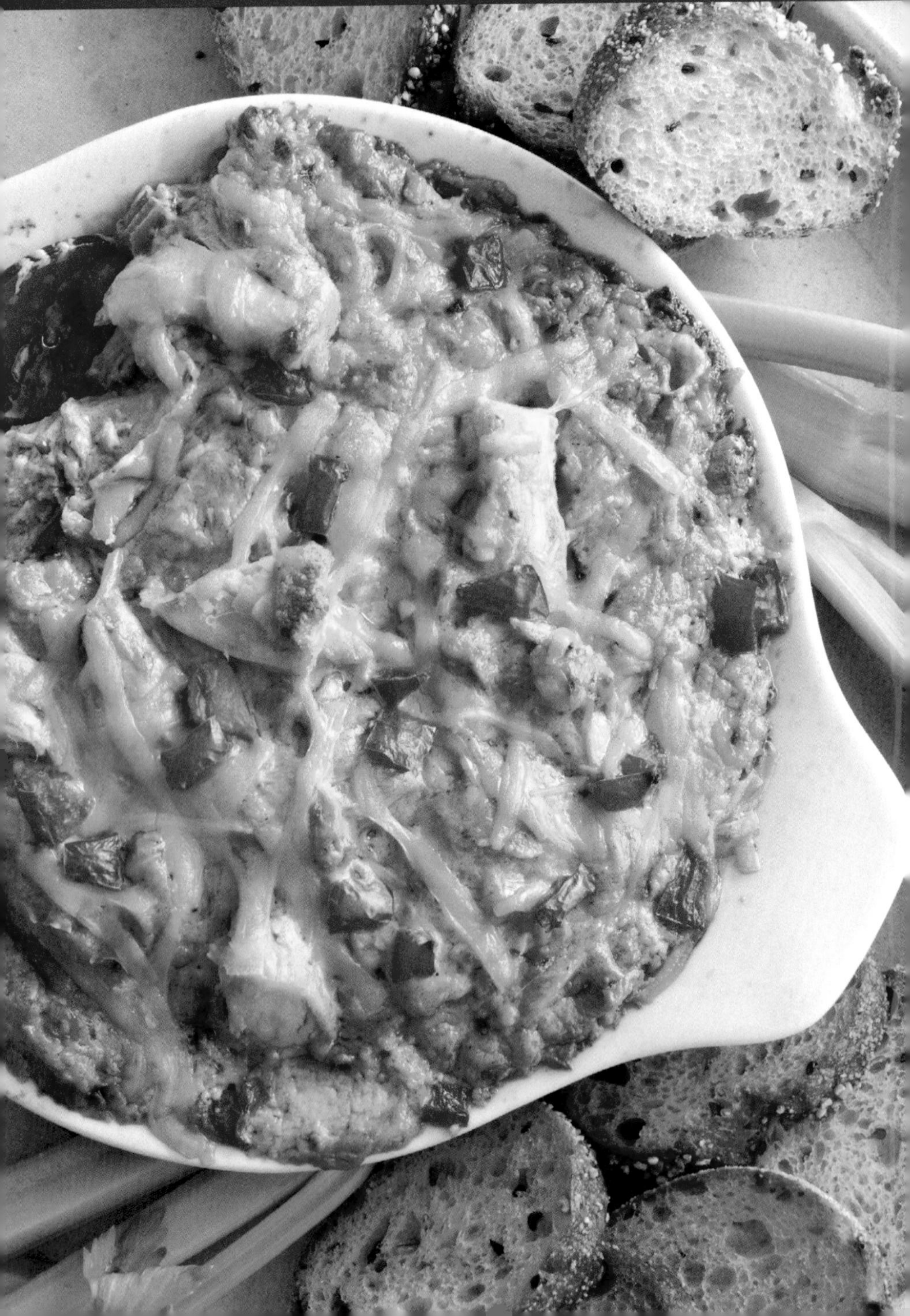

Cook Up Some Comfort!

America's most trusted Almanac brings you America's tastiest *Comfort Food:* our brand-new cookbook with over 200 recipes. Sample one or all of these recipes. Once you try *Comfort Food,* you'll want to buy it for yourself or a friend—which is quick and easy at **Almanac.com/ComfortFood.**

Hot Buffalo Chicken and Cheese Dip

2 tablespoons (¼ stick) unsalted butter

½ cup finely chopped onion

2 cloves garlic, minced

1 cup frozen corn kernels, slightly thawed

2½ cups finely chopped rotisserie chicken meat

⅔ cup prepared Buffalo wing sauce

12 ounces cream cheese, softened

⅔ cup mayonnaise

1 packet (1 ounce) ranch dressing mix

½ cup crumbled blue cheese

1 ripe tomato, halved, seeded, and finely diced

3 cups shredded sharp cheddar cheese

■ Preheat the oven to 350°F. Butter three or four shallow gratin dishes or one or two deep ones.

■ Melt the butter in a skillet over medium heat. Add the onion and cook for 4 minutes, stirring often. Add the garlic and corn and cook for 3 to 4 minutes. Add the chicken and Buffalo wing sauce. Simmer for 3 minutes, stirring often. Remove from the heat and set aside.

■ Combine the cream cheese, mayonnaise, and ranch dressing mix in a large bowl. Beat with an electric mixer for about 1 minute, or until soft and fluffy. Add the blue cheese and chicken mixture. Blend evenly with a wooden spoon.

■ Divide the mixture among the prepared dishes. Sprinkle diced tomato and cheddar cheese evenly over the portions. Bake on the center oven rack for 25 to 30 minutes, or until bubbly and golden. **Makes 8 to 10 servings.** *(continued)*

Photography: Becky Luigart-Stayner; food styling, Anna Kelly; prop styling, Jan Guatro

Super-Creamy Mac and Cheese

½ pound elbow noodles

1 teaspoon olive oil

6 tablespoons (¾ stick) unsalted butter, divided

1 medium onion, finely chopped

3 tablespoons all-purpose flour

2 cups milk, divided

1 cup chicken stock

1 tablespoon Dijon-style mustard

1 teaspoon salt

freshly ground black pepper, to taste

3 cups shredded extra sharp cheddar cheese

3 ounces cream cheese, in pieces, softened

¾ to 1 cup fine cracker crumbs or panko bread crumbs

■ Preheat the oven to 350°F. Butter a large, shallow casserole.

■ Prepare the noodles according to the package directions. Drain, transfer to a large bowl, drizzle with oil, and toss to avoid clumping.

■ Melt 3 tablespoons of the butter in a large saucepan over medium heat, add the onion, and cook for 5 minutes, or until soft. Add the flour and cook for 1 minute more, stirring. Add 1 cup of milk and stir. As the sauce thickens, add the remaining 1 cup of milk. Bring to a simmer. Add the chicken stock and heat gently for 3 to 4 minutes, stirring constantly. Add the mustard, salt, and pepper, to taste. Add the cheddar cheese, 1 cup at a time, and stir. Add more as it melts. Add the cream cheese and stir until melted.

■ Pour the sauce over the noodles and stir to coat. Transfer the mixture to the casserole. Sprinkle with cracker crumbs to cover evenly.

■ Melt the remaining 3 tablespoons of butter in a pan over low heat and drizzle over the crumbs. Bake for 30 to 35 minutes, or until bubbly.

Makes 6 servings.

(continued)

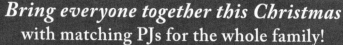

Southwestern Pumpkin Burgers

3 tablespoons vegetable oil, divided

½ cup finely chopped onion

½ cup frozen corn kernels, thawed

¼ cup finely chopped green bell pepper

1 clove garlic, minced

1 teaspoon cumin

1 teaspoon chili powder

½ teaspoon smoked paprika

¾ cup fine-curd cottage cheese

½ cup canned pumpkin

1 egg yolk

2 tablespoons chopped fresh Italian parsley

scant ½ teaspoon salt

freshly ground black pepper, to taste

1¼ cups panko bread crumbs

1 cup shredded pepper jack or sharp cheddar cheese

ranch dressing (optional)

■ Heat 2 tablespoons of the oil in a skillet over medium heat; add the onion, corn, and bell pepper; and cook for 5 minutes, or until soft. Add the garlic, cumin, chili powder, and smoked paprika and cook for 30 seconds more, stirring constantly. Remove from the heat.

■ In a large bowl, combine the cottage cheese, pumpkin, and egg yolk and mix with a wooden spoon. Add the onion–corn–pepper mixture, parsley, salt, and black pepper, to taste. Stir and add the bread crumbs and cheese. Stir until combined. Cover and refrigerate for at least 2 hours, or overnight.

■ Heat 1 tablespoon of oil in a nonstick skillet over medium heat. Shape the pumpkin mixture into six ¾-inch-thick patties. Place them in the skillet and cook, in batches, if necessary, for 3 minutes on each side, or until lightly browned, turning once. Serve with or without buns, passing the ranch dressing at the table, if desired.

Makes 6 servings.   *(continued)*

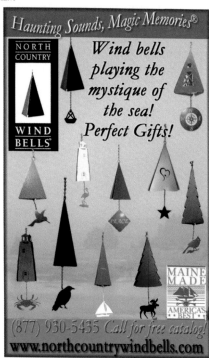

Roasted Autumn Vegetables

- 1 pound small red-skinned potatoes, quartered, or whole creamer potatoes
- 2 cups peeled butternut squash, cut into ½-inch dice
- 2 large carrots, peeled and cut into ½-inch-thick diagonal slices
- 2 parsnips, peeled and cut into ½-inch-thick diagonal slices
- 2 to 3 cups packed kale, rinsed and chopped
- 3 tablespoons olive oil
- 1 tablespoon chopped fresh rosemary or 1 teaspoon dried rosemary
- 2 cloves garlic, minced
- salt and freshly ground black pepper, to taste

■ Preheat the oven to 450°F. Lightly oil two large, rimmed baking sheets.

■ Combine the vegetables, olive oil, rosemary, garlic, salt, and pepper, to taste, in a large bowl and toss by hand to coat. Spread the mixture evenly onto the baking sheets and bake for 15 minutes on separate oven racks. After 15 minutes, stir the vegetables with a spatula and return to the oven, switching the rack position of the sheets. Bake for 15 minutes more, or until the vegetables are tender and browned.

Makes 6 servings.

38

Slow Cooker Barbecue Brisket

3 tablespoons vegetable oil
2 large onions, halved and thinly sliced
3 cloves garlic, minced
2 teaspoons smoked paprika
1 teaspoon chili powder
1 bottle (12 ounces) beer
1½ cups tomato-based chili sauce
¾ cup packed light-brown sugar
1 tablespoon Worcestershire sauce
1 teaspoon salt
1 teaspoon onion salt
1 teaspoon dried thyme
½ teaspoon freshly ground black pepper
1 beef brisket (3½ to 4 pounds), trimmed of fat

■ Heat the oil in a large, nonreactive skillet over medium heat, add the onions, and cook for 10 minutes, or until soft. Add the garlic, paprika, and chili powder and cook for 30 seconds, stirring. Add the remaining ingredients, except for the brisket, and cook until heated through. Remove the skillet from the heat.

■ Pour half of the sauce into a large slow cooker. Add the brisket and cover with the remaining sauce. Cover and cook on low for 8 hours.

■ Transfer the brisket to a large casserole and ladle all of the remaining sauce over it. Cool to room temperature. Cover with plastic wrap and refrigerate overnight.

■ Preheat the oven to 350°F. Transfer the meat to a cutting board. Cut the meat across the grain into ⅓-inch-thick slices.

■ Pour the sauce into a large saucepan and bring to a simmer. Return the sauce to the casserole and add the sliced meat. Bake for 30 minutes, uncovered. Transfer the meat slices to a platter and spoon the sauce over the meat. **Makes 8 to 10 servings.** *(continued)*

39

Warm Brownie Pie

your favorite piecrust

Filling:

½ cup (1 stick)
unsalted butter

1⅓ cups chocolate
chips, divided

2 large eggs, at room
temperature

½ cup packed
light-brown sugar

⅓ cup sugar

1½ teaspoons vanilla
extract

½ cup all-purpose
flour

¼ teaspoon salt

1 cup chopped
walnuts, preferably
toasted

■ Roll the pastry into a 12-inch circle and line a 9-inch (not deep-dish) pie plate with it. Pinch the overhanging pastry into an upstanding rim or trim to be flush with the side of the pan and crimp the edge with a fork. Refrigerate for 15 minutes.

■ Preheat the oven to 350°F.

For filling:

■ Melt the butter in a saucepan over medium heat. Add 1 cup of the chocolate chips and heat for a few seconds more, then remove from the heat. Tilt the pan to make the butter run over the chips. Set aside for 5 minutes. Whisk to smooth the chips.

■ In a large bowl, combine the eggs, sugars, and vanilla and whisk until evenly blended. Add the melted chocolate and whisk to blend. Add the flour and salt and stir until combined. Add the nuts and the remaining ⅓ cup of chocolate chips. Scrape the filling into the piecrust and smooth the top.

■ Bake on the center oven rack for 30 to 35 minutes, or until a crust develops and the pie rises slightly. (A toothpick inserted into the center will not come out clean.)

■ Transfer to a cooling rack. Serve warm.

Makes 8 to 10 servings. ■

FREE Report

$15.00 Value

Scams Exposed

Learn the truth about distilled, mineral, tap, spring, filtered, bottled, well, alkalized, reverse osmosis... Which one is best for you?

Call for FREE Report & Catalog

800-874-9028 Ext 675

Or visit: waterwise.com/ofa

Waterwise Inc
PO Box 494000 Leesburg FL 34749-4000

© 2014 Waterwise Inc

Cook Up Some Comfort!

Our newest cookbook is guaranteed to keep family and friends coming back for more. Over 200 recipes, with color photos and 140 timesaving tips.

Comfort Food

By Ken Haedrich and the Almanac editors

Only $19.95
plus shipping & handling

GET YOURS TODAY AT:
Almanac.com/ComfortFood
or call 1-800-ALMANAC

Also available for purchase as an eBook or wherever books are sold.

The #1 Stairlift in the World...
JUST GOT BETTER!

INTRODUCING THE NEW & IMPROVED ACORN STAIRLIFT

THE PERFECT SOLUTION FOR ANYONE WHO STRUGGLES ON THE STAIRS!

NEW & IMPROVED FEATURES

- More comfortable, padded seat
- Easier to use paddle switches on each arm
- Slimmer design, takes up less space
- New, more attractive look

 The only stairlift to earn the Ease-of-Use commendation from the Arthritis Foundation.

 **CALL TODAY!** FOR YOUR FREE, LIFE-CHANGING INFORMATION KIT AND DVD!

CALL NOW TOLL-FREE
1-877-865-0461

 **ACORN STAIRLIFTS**

Winners in the 2014 Carrot Recipe Contest

*Thanks to the hundreds of entrants who made choosing the
prize recipients another delicious dilemma. Try these recipes and tell
us at Almanac.com/Feedback if you think that they're winners!*

FIRST PRIZE: $250

Carrot Ginger Soup

2 tablespoons (¼ stick) butter or margarine

2 leeks, chopped

1 pound carrots, peeled and diced

1 pound potatoes, peeled and diced

1 orange, zest and juice

1 teaspoon chopped ginger

1 teaspoon brown sugar

4 cups vegetable broth

1 cup milk

salt, to taste

dash of dry sherry, to taste

dash of nutmeg, to taste

chopped fresh parsley or cilantro, for garnish

■ In a large soup pot, melt the butter. Add the leeks and sauté until they are soft. Add the carrot, potato, zest and juice of the orange, ginger, and brown sugar. Cook for 5 to 7 minutes, or until softened.

■ Add the broth and milk and simmer for 20 minutes.

■ Transfer the soup to a blender or food processor and purée in batches. Return to the soup pot.

■ Season with salt, sherry, and nutmeg, to taste. Serve garnished with chopped fresh parsley. **Makes 4 to 6 servings.**

–*Ann Fine, Kansas City, Missouri*
(continued)

Photography: Becky Luigart-Stayner; food styling, Anna Kelly; prop styling, Jan Guatro

SECOND PRIZE: $150

Apple Cider Risotto With Carrot Confetti

2 cups carrot pieces in a variety of colors (e.g., orange, yellow, purple), plus some rounds, or "coins," for garnish

1½ teaspoons olive oil

1 medium apple, pared, cored, and cut into ½-inch pieces

1 cup apple cider

½ cup dry white wine

5 cups vegetable stock

1½ tablespoons butter

½ cup minced shallots

2 cups Arborio rice

2 tablespoons minced fresh sage leaves, plus whole leaves, for garnish

¾ cup shredded Asiago cheese

salt and freshly ground black pepper, to taste

■ Preheat the oven to 350°F.

■ Spread the carrot pieces and coins on a baking sheet in a single layer, drizzle with the olive oil, and toss to coat. Roast for 10 to 15 minutes, or until lightly browned but not crisp. Set aside, reserving the coins in a separate bowl.

■ Put the apple pieces into a bowl.

■ In a pan, bring the apple cider just to a boil, then pour it over the apple pieces and set aside for 3 minutes. Strain the apple pieces, reserve the cider, and add the apple pieces to the carrot pieces.

■ Add the wine to the reserved cider.

■ In a large pan, bring the stock to a boil, then reduce the heat to low.

■ Melt the butter in a soup pot over medium heat. Add the shallots and cook until translucent. Add the rice and stir to coat each grain with butter. Add the cider–wine mixture and cook, stirring frequently, until all of the liquid is absorbed. Add the warm stock, 1 cup at a time, stirring constantly, until the rice absorbs most of the liquid before adding more. Allow 25 to 30 minutes. Add the sage, carrot and apple pieces, cheese, and salt and pepper, to taste. Stir until the cheese melts.

■ Transfer to a serving bowl and garnish with carrot coins and sage leaves. **Makes 6 to 8 servings.**

–*Mona Grandbois, Biddeford, Maine*

(continued)

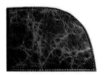

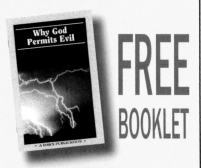

Spiced Carrot Biscuits With Salted Caramel Butter

- 3½ cups all-purpose flour
- ½ cup packed light-brown sugar
- 1 tablespoon plus 2 teaspoons baking powder
- ½ teaspoon plus 1 pinch salt, divided
- 1 teaspoon pumpkin pie spice
- 1 cup (2 sticks) cold butter
- 1½ cups puréed cooked carrots (about 2 pounds fresh)
- ⅔ cup plus 1 tablespoon buttermilk, divided
- ⅓ cup golden raisins
- ½ cup (1 stick) butter, softened
- ¼ cup thick caramel sauce (store-bought or homemade)

■ Preheat the oven to 425°F. Lightly grease a large baking sheet.

■ In a large bowl, stir together the flour, sugar, baking powder, ½ teaspoon of salt, and pumpkin pie spice. Cut in the cold butter with a fork or pastry tool until the mixture resembles coarse crumbs. Add the carrots and ⅔ cup of buttermilk and stir just until combined.

■ Turn the dough out onto a lightly floured surface. Sprinkle the dough with the raisins. Knead 10 times. Roll the dough to approximately a 1-inch thickness. Using a 2½-inch round cutter, press out biscuits, rerolling the dough as necessary.

■ Place the biscuits on the prepared baking sheet at least 1 inch apart. Bake for 20 minutes, or until golden brown. Brush the tops with the remaining buttermilk. Set aside.

■ In a bowl, beat together the softened butter, caramel sauce, and remaining salt until combined. Serve with the biscuits. **Makes 12 biscuits.**

–*Crystal Schlueter, Northglenn, Colorado*

Mrs. Nelson's
CANDY HOUSE
"Your house for all occasions"

Candies! For over 50 years we have
used only the finest ingredients in
our candies—cream, butter, honey,
and special blends of chocolates.
Call for a FREE brochure. Long famous
for quality candies mailed all over the
world. Treat yourself or someone
special today.

Come visit us today!

292 Chelmsford Street
Chelmsford, MA 01824
For Free Brochure Call:

978-256-4061

Jingle all the way!

*Now you can have
your own festive sleigh
bells hanging on the
door to welcome guests
at the holidays or
all–year–round!
Handcrafted in
New Hampshire
using only the finest
leather and solid
brass sleigh bells.*

Photo courtesy of Country Sampler

New England Bells

46 Lempster Street • Lempster, NH • 03605
Order online or call:
www.newenglandbells.com
603-863-3800

Harris Tweed
paired with
Viyella

... an intimate blend of natural fibers is soft, warm, light,
and supremely comfortable. Its fine blend of 80% long
staple cotton and 20% merino wool affords the unique
combination of luxury and practicality. Produced solely by
William Hollins & Company Ltd., Viyella's been world-
famous for superb British textile craftsmanship since 1784.
Reg. sizes Small-XXL. Tall sizes L-3XL. Robes also available.

MILLER BROS·NEWTON
Fine Men's Clothier Since 1844

www.mbnmenswear.com
105 Main Street • Keene, NH • 888-256-1170

Leo's Soap
All Natural Laundry Powder

Designed to save you money and
provide you with the cleanest,
softest clothes you've ever had!
No Chemicals • Fragrance-Free
Whiter, brighter clothes with only
One Tablespoon per Load!

1-866-755-0334
www.leossoap.com

 MADE IN THE USA

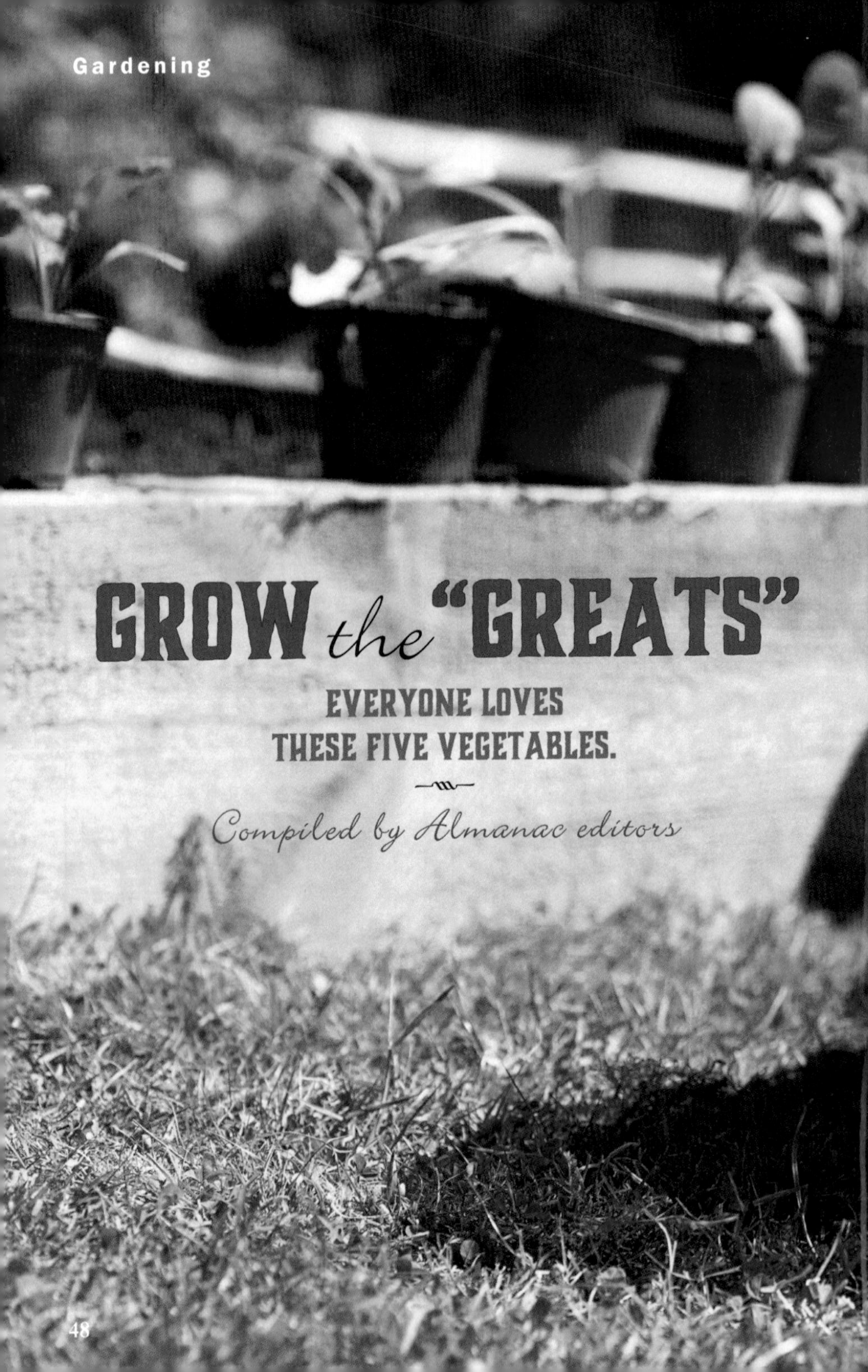

GROW *the* "GREATS"

EVERYONE LOVES
THESE FIVE VEGETABLES.

—m—

Compiled by Almanac editors

'Yellow Pear'

'Green Zebra'

SOW GOOD

Plant basil near tomatoes; the herb repels whiteflies and mosquitoes and attracts pollinators.

Water regularly. Inconsistent soil moisture causes blossom-end rot.

Store tomatoes with their stem ends pointing down; they will stay fresh longer.

'Early Girl'

Gardening

I never yet ate any [vegetables] that so well suited my palate, as those taken immediately from my own garden.

–Robert B. Thomas, founder and editor,
The Old Farmer's Almanac (1766–1846)

—⁓—

According to a variety of sources, one or more of these vegetables appears on everyone's "favorite vegetable" list. Whether you are a beginning gardener or a seasoned master, apply this time-tested advice for a tasty bounty.

—⁓— SHOW TOMATOES LOVE —⁓—

Ask neighbors and your local nursery for recommendations, especially for disease-resistant strains, or try heirlooms such as 'Brandywine' and 'Green Zebra', hybrids 'Early Girl' and All-America winner 'Celebrity', and quick-maturing cherries such as 'Super Sweet 100', 'Sweet Million', 'Yellow Pear', and 'Jasper' F1.

Start tomato seeds indoors about 6 weeks before planting time. Fill the containers just half full of soil. Once the seedlings emerge, fill in around the stems to encourage good roots.

Plant seedlings outside when evening temperatures are above 55°F. Tomatoes like warm weather.

If you purchase lanky seedlings, bury the stems horizontally up to the first two leaves when you plant them. Set the seedlings in a circle (like a wagon wheel). Then you can water and fertilize them through the center.

Water tomatoes at least once a week; keep the supply of moisture even. Just before harvesttime, reduce watering to boost the flavor intensity.

Tomatoes are heavy feeders and like rich soil, but too much fertilizer results in lots of leaves and no fruit. Fertilize with liquid seaweed or fish emulsion during the growing season.

Heirloom tomatoes need less fertilizer than hybrids. Instead, use a slow-release fertilizer or cottonseed meal.

Several weeks into the growing season, mulch the

Photos, from top: Laura Berman; Laura Berman; Burpee.com

2015

THE OLD FARMER'S ALMANAC

'Irish Cobbler'

area around tomatoes with a thick layer of well-rotted hay, black plastic, or mulch. Thoroughly cover all of the soil between the plants to prevent soilborne diseases from splashing up onto the leaves during rainstorms.

When plants are about a foot tall, support them with stakes or cages. (Cages can be covered with clear plastic to add warmth in cold regions.)

For a bumper crop, remove suckers that form between the main branches and pinch off all late blossoms that will not have a chance to mature.

―⁓― KEEP AN EYE ON POTATOES ―⁓―

Buy certified seed potatoes. Popular backyard varieties include 'Red Norland', 'Kennebec', heirloom 'Irish Cobbler', yellow-flesh 'Yukon Gold' and 'Yellow Finn', and fingerling-type 'Russian Banana'. Just before planting, carefully cut the bigger potatoes with a clean knife into 1½- to 2-inch pieces with one or two eyes on each piece.

Presprout seed potatoes indoors to get a jump on planting. Lay cut-up pieces and small whole potatoes in a single layer (space widely) on a tray or in a shallow box. Place near a sunny window where the temperature is 60°F or warmer day and night. Three to 10 days later, when the sprouts are 1 inch long, they are ready to plant.

Plant seed potatoes in loose, fertile, well-draining soil in full sun as soon as the soil is about 45° to 55°F and can be turned over without clumping. With a hoe or round-point shovel, dig a trench about 6 inches wide and 8 inches deep, tapering the bottom to about 3 inches wide. Put a seed potato piece, cut side down, every 14 inches and cover with 3 to 4 inches of soil.

In 12 to 16 days, when sprouts appear, use a hoe to gently fill in the trench with another 3 to 4 inches of soil, leaving a few inches of the plants exposed. Repeat in several weeks, leaving the soil mounded up 4 to 5 inches above ground level.

Do not allow sunlight to fall on the potatoes, which develop under the surface of the soil, or they will turn green. Do the hilling in the morning, when plants are at their tallest. During the heat of the day,

Pepper seedlings

SOW GOOD

Before planting, soak the seeds overnight in warm water for a head start.

Place a book of matches or a teaspoon of sulfur in the bottom of each planting hole when setting out pepper transplants. Sulfur acidifies the soil slightly, allowing the plants to use fertilizer more efficiently.

Bell peppers

Gardening

plants start drooping.

If your garden soil is very rocky, put the seed potato pieces directly on the ground and cover with straw or leaves, hilling the material up as the potatoes grow.

Maintain even moisture, especially from the time sprouts appear until several weeks after they blossom. If you water too much right after planting and not enough as the potatoes begin to form, they can become misshapen.

Harvest baby potatoes 2 to 3 weeks after the plants stop flowering. For mature potatoes, wait 2 to 3 weeks after the foliage has died. On a day when the soil is dry, dig potatoes carefully to avoid cutting or bruising their skins. If the soil is very wet, let the potatoes air-dry as much as possible before putting them in bags or baskets.

⎯ PAMPER PEPPERS ⎯

Select early-maturing pepper varieties (55 to 60 days) and start seeds indoors 8 to 10 weeks before the last frost date. Maintain the seeds at 75°F under fluorescent light for 10 to 12 hours per day. Two weeks before planting, cover the pepper plot with clear plastic to warm the soil.

Harden off the seedlings for at least 2 weeks by leaving them outdoors for longer periods of time each day.

Peppers like full sun and well-draining, composted soil with a pH between 6 and 8. However, peppers deplete the soil: Do not plant them in the same place (or the same soil, if in pots) 2 years in a row.

Temperature is important for peppers. A short growing season, low nighttime temperatures (regularly below 55°F), unexpected frosts, and high sunlight intensity from longer days create problems. So does too much water: Peppers easily succumb to wet feet.

Plant when nights remain above 55°F and daytime temperatures average 70°F. To protect plants from chilly nights and/or blustery winds, cover them. Row covers or plastic jugs with the bottom cut out (remove the cap for ventilation) work well.

(continued)

Photos, from top: Alexander Podshivalov/Media Bakery; Visions/GAP photos

'Superstar'

Summer savory

SOW GOOD

Plant summer savory with onions to improve growth and flavor.

Once or twice during the growing season, brew a strong tea from burdock leaves and apply it to the base of each onion plant to discourage onion maggots.

'Red Wethersfield'

Gardening

Protect pepper plants from cutworms with cardboard collars around the stems.

Water at least 2 inches per week during dry spells. Sweet peppers need a steady supply of water up to harvesttime. Hot peppers develop more heat if water is withheld right before the harvest.

Use a balanced fertilizer. Too much nitrogen can produce lush foliage but also blossom failure and/or no fruit.

After blossoms have set, spray the pepper plants with a magnesium solution (1 tablespoon of Epsom salts in 1 quart of water) or scratch 1 tablespoon of Epsom salts into the soil around each plant. More blossoms will appear and fruit will be bigger.

Harvest peppers when the fruit feels firm and separates easily from the plant. Do not twist the stem; use a knife or scissors to cut it.

—⁓— EASE INTO ONIONS —⁓—

Onions respond to length of day when forming bulbs, and some southern favorites won't mature quickly enough in northern climates. Figure out how many days are in your growing season and find varieties that will mature in that time. (See the Frost and Growing Seasons chart.) Favorites include heirloom 'Red Wethersfield', sweet 'Walla Walla', and All-America winner 'Superstar'.

If you are starting from seeds indoors, plant 8 to 12 weeks before the last frost.

If you are starting seeds in the garden, sow them ½-inch deep. Maintain even moisture; if the soil dries out, the seeds won't germinate. Thin emerging seedlings to 3 inches apart.

If you are planting onion sets, plant them 2 to 6 inches apart, gently pressing them into loose soil as soon as the ground can be worked. (Use the closer spacing if you want to pull immature onions as scallions.)

Onions prefer temperatures of 55° to 75°F to form bulbs. Keep onions evenly moist and make sure that they receive 1 inch of water per week. Once established, mulch to suppress weeds and conserve soil moisture.

(continued)

GARDEN DEFENDERS

www.GardenDefenders.com
(855) 692 - 4727

DEFEND *YOUR* **GARDEN** *WITH*

Special internet price: Take more than **50% OFF** when you use offer code **"OFA2015AC"** at checkout on **GardenDefenders.com**

$229.00 Retail Price
$99.00 Sale Price

AirCrow **Little Crow** Inflatable Scarecrow

$279.00 Retail Price
$139.00 Sale Price

AirCrow **Blackbird** Inflatable Scarecrow

GARDENDEFENDERS.COM

Over 26,000 Items for FARM•SHOP•HOME

AGRI SUPPLY®
"Since 1962"

- **Cooking Supplies**
- **Lawn & Garden**
- **Shop Supplies**
- **Sporting Goods**
- **Trailer Supplies**
- **Livestock Supplies**
- **Truck Accessories**
- **Disc/Tillage**

CALL 800-345-0169
TODAY FOR A
FREE CATALOG

SHOP ONLINE OR FIND A STORE NEAR YOU
WWW.AGRISUPPLY.COM

Burn *SAFELY* with the Stainless Steel

Portable Burn-Cage™

Perfect For: Old Leaves and Branches
Sensitive Financial Documents
Burnable Household Waste

CLEANER MORE EFFICIENT FIRES. Perforated lid and sidewalls maximize airflow and trap burning embers. High burn temperatures mean thorough incineration with less residue and ash.

LIGHT-WEIGHT and portable.

PEACE OF MIND. It's the SAFE way to burn.

84038X © 2014

Burncage.com

No more rusty barrel!

- Folds for easy storage.
- Optional Ash Catcher available.

NEW XL MODEL AVAILABLE!

CALL TODAY for FREE Information Kit, Pricing and Factory Direct Coupon.

TOLL FREE **800-731-0493**

Rosemary

SOW GOOD

To help you spot the row where tiny carrot leaves first appear, mix carrot seeds with radish seeds when you sow them. The radishes sprout more quickly and can be harvested before the later-developing carrots.

To deter bean beetles and carrot flies, plant rosemary in the garden.

Wash freshly harvested carrots, cut off the green tops, and store the carrots in plastic bags in the refrigerator. Leaving the tops on will make the carrots limp.

'Chantenay'

Gardening

Harvest onions when the tops fall over and dry. Leave the onions on top of the soil for 1 to 2 days during clear weather and then spread them out in a warm, well-ventilated area until the necks are dry. Put them in large-mesh citrus bags or wrap them individually in newspaper and store in a cool (35° to 45°F), dark place. Do not store potatoes and onions together. Onions release a gas that can spoil potatoes.

KEEP CARROTS HAPPY

Carrot flavor can vary depending on the type of soil. Experiment with different varieties, including heirloom 'Chantenay' and the unusually coral-hued 'Atomic Red'. If you are growing carrots in containers, look for the round All-America winner 'Thumbelina' or the tiny 'Little Finger'.

Prepare the soil by turning it over to a depth of at least 1 foot before planting carrots. If your soil is heavy clay or very rocky, plant carrots in a 12-inch-deep raised bed filled with fluffy, rich soil.

Keep carrots away from soil that has recently had manure added into it, or they may grow "legs" and appear forked. Work used coffee grounds into the soil as fertilizer.

Plant carrot seeds ¼-inch deep. Cover with a layer of vermiculite or fine compost to prevent a crust from forming and slowing germination.

After the leafy seedlings emerge and you can see them, thin to 3 to 4 inches apart. When thinning carrots, pinch off the tops of unwanted plants rather than pull them out, to prevent uprooting the plants that you want to keep.

If you see orange crowns emerging at soil level, cover them with soil or compost to keep them from turning green and becoming bitter.

As a general rule, the smaller the carrot, the better it will taste. Begin harvesting carrots when they are the size of your finger. Baby carrots are ready for eating 45 to 55 days after planting. Mature carrots need 70 to 90 days. You can also mulch them heavily with well-rotted hay in the fall and leave them in the soil until early winter. ■

Photos, from top: Thinkstock; Maxine Adcock/GAP photos

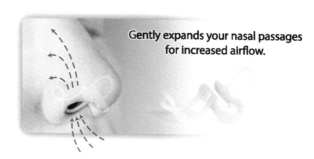

Make a
Cultivated
Exchange

Lettuce is luscious and kale is comforting, but to put some pizzazz into your garden, grow Asian greens.

Asian greens are easily grown in garden beds. In fact, these lush leaves deserve a place alongside the ornamental plants before they go into your salad bowl. Use them in borders, alongside pathways, and in the front yard. Mix colors and textures to create eye-catching impact.

Here are a few to try in containers or beds.

(continued)

Two varieties of Amaranth greens, *Amaranthus tricolor*

Photos: Laura Berman

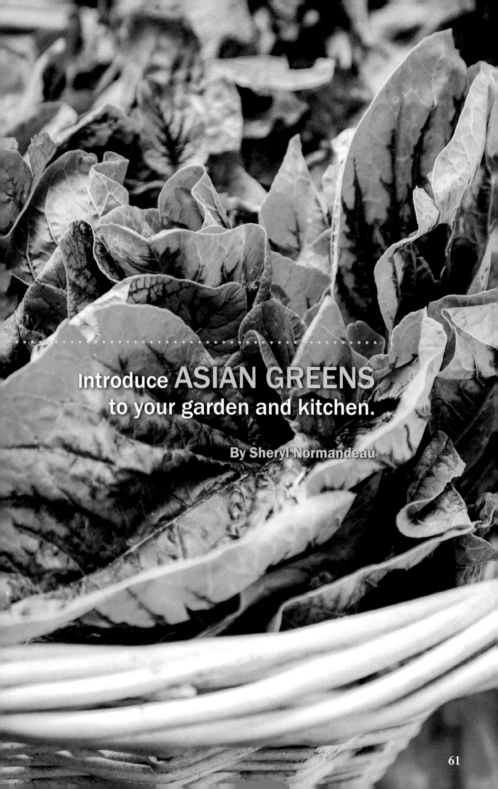

Introduce ASIAN GREENS
to your garden and kitchen.

By Sheryl Normandeau

Amaranth

(aka Chinese Spinach, Hiyu, Callaloo), *Amaranthus tricolor*

Highly decorative red, green, or striped foliage makes amaranth stand out in any garden. Some species are strictly ornamental; look for edible types for culinary use. Amaranth is typically known as a grain crop; its seeds have been harvested for centuries in Asia, Europe, and Central and South America. The plant is heat and drought tolerant, not prone to bolting, and disease and pest resistant. Substitute its tasty leaves in any recipe that calls for cooked spinach, such as stir-fries, soups, and pastas.

Garland chrysanthemum

(aka Shungiku), *Chrysanthemum coronarium*

Not all garden 'mums are edible, but this one is! Native to the Mediterranean, garland chrysanthemum is gorgeous and tasty. Both the greens and cheerful yellow flowers can be eaten. Plant this cool-weather crop in full sun or partial shade. Prolonged heat will cause the greens to become bitter, so sow seeds in early spring and late summer for best flavor. Harvest leaves when they are young and tender and add to salads, soups, and stir-fries. Allow some plants to flower for a decorative addition to your garden—and your salad bowl. *(continued)*

Photos, from top: Laura Berman; Pat Tuson/GAP Photos

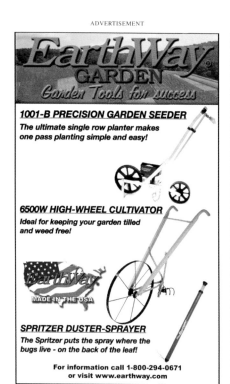

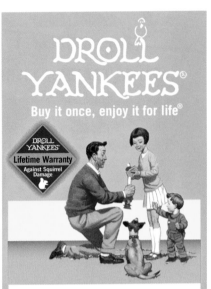
Gardening

....

Komatsuna

(aka mustard spinach),
Brassica rapa var. *perviridis,* syn.
Brassica rapa var. *komatsuna*

A Japanese green with a mustardy bite, komatsuna has round, slightly savoyed (crinkled), dark green leaves borne on sturdy stalks. Komatsuna is best harvested at the baby green stage (4 to 6 inches tall): Remove the entire plant and then reseed (in the same spot, if desired) for another crop later on. You can eat the stems, leaves, and yellow flowers. Leaves are often pickled, but they can be eaten raw in salads or cooked into a quiche or scrambled eggs.

(continued)

Photo: Carole Drake/GAP Photos

Mibuna

Brassica rapa var. *japonica*

Another green that can tolerate partial shade, hardy mibuna can be sown successively from late spring through late autumn. Its narrow, rounded, green leaves offer an attractive contrast when planted alongside mustards. Harvest mibuna at the baby greens stage for a mild, slightly peppery taste. The flavor intensifies as plants mature. Mibuna is a good cut-and-come-again crop and will regrow several times over the season. Its leaves can be pickled or eaten raw in mixed greens salads. Chop and add some to soups or potato salads.

(continued)

Photo: Jo Whitworth/GAP Photos

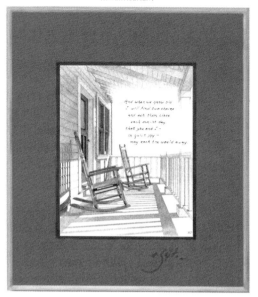

A Most Unusual Gift of Love

THE POEM READS:

*"...And when we grow old I will find two chairs
and set them close each sun-lit day,
that you and I – in quiet joy –
may rock the world away."*

Dear Reader,

The drawing you see above is called *In Our Time*. I created this in honor of two of my dearest friends. After writing the poem, I worked with a quill pen and placed thousands of these dots, one at a time, to create this gift for someone who is very much part of my life.

Now, I have decided to offer *In Our Time* to those who share and value its sentiment. Each litho is numbered and signed by hand and precisely captures the detail of the drawing. As a wedding, anniversary or Christmas gift for your husband or wife or a particularly dear friend, I believe you will find it most appropriate.

Measuring 14" by 16", it is available either fully framed in a subtle copper tone with hand-cut mats: outside mat is medium beige and the inside mat is burgundy, at $135, or in the mats alone at $95. Please add $14.50 for insured shipping and packaging. Either way, your satisfaction is completely guaranteed.

My best wishes are with you.

The Art of Robert Sexton • P.O. 581 • Rutherford, CA 94573

All major credit cards are welcome. Order online or call us at (415) 989-1630 between between 10 and 6 P.M. PST. Checks are also accepted. *Please allow 3 weeks for delivery.*

Please visit my Web site at

www.robertsexton.com

Mizuna

(aka Chinese potherb mustard, Japanese salad green), *Brassica rapa* var. *nipposinica*

Although mizuna is closely related to mustard, it doesn't deliver the same fiery kick to the taste buds; instead, its flavor is similar to that of cabbage. This cool-weather crop will germinate at low temperatures and can tolerate light frost. In addition, mizuna performs very well in the heat of summer and will not readily bolt.

Harvest the feathery green or purple leaves as you would for any cut-and-come-again crop, allowing the center rosette to continue to grow, or harvest entire mizuna plants at once and immediately reseed for successive crops, in the same spot or elsewhere. Use mizuna fresh in mixed greens salads or wilted in potato or pasta salads. Add it to chicken soups or stir-fry it with noodles or rice.

Don't stop with these delicious varieties! Experiment with other Japanese greens, Oriental spinaches, baby leaf greens, the spicy and frilly Asian mustards, and colorful Asian lettuces. *(continued)*

Put Up a Pot

To maximize your harvest in a small space, grow Asian greens in a container. Experiment with different varieties for a pleasing color palette as well as fresh, new culinary ingredients.

Select containers with adequate drainage and add a generous handful of compost to your potting soil. Position the container in sun, protected from wind. Add edible flowers or herbs to complement the greens' bright foliage. Greens in containers have a tendency to dry out faster than those planted in beds, and wind and hot sun will increase their thirst, so water accordingly.

Photos, from top: Laura Berman; Jo Whitworth/GAP Photos

Mixed salad greens,
including mizuna

Tips for Growing the Best Greens

Asian greens like well-draining soil that is rich in organic matter. Fertilize with light feedings of diluted liquid kelp. Stick to a regular watering schedule; most greens will not tolerate drought, and their flavor may be affected. Water deeply and at the base of the plants, not from above.

Some greens will bolt (go to seed) in sustained heat. To ensure a midsummer harvest, select varieties that are bred for bolt resistance. (Check seed catalogs and packets for details.) To stave off bolting, sow crops in late spring and late summer or early autumn. To extend the growing season, plant cool-weather greens in a cold frame or use cloches as protection during cold nights.

Because Asian greens can go quickly from seed to table—most burst into life within a week or two of planting—sow them successively over the entire growing season. Not all varieties will mature at the same time, ensuring continuous color and texture. Some crops will take longer than others; garland chrysanthemum and amaranth, for example, need time to show off their pretty flowers.

Many Asian greens are "cut-and-come-again" crops: Pick the outermost leaves first; allow the plants to keep growing for a continuous supply of fresh greens. Plants may be harvested before they reach maturity, at the "baby" stage of development (at least 4 inches tall), when the leaves are at their most tender. When you thin plants, eat the thinnings! Just trim off the roots, wash, and add them to salads or sandwiches. ■

Sheryl Normandeau is an avid gardener, writer, and blogger in Calgary, Alberta.

Choose Life
Grow Young with HGH

From the landmark book Grow Young with HGH comes the most powerful, over-the-counter health supplement in the history of man. Human growth hormone was first discovered in 1920 and has long been thought by the medical community to be necessary only to stimulate the body to full adult size and therefore unnecessary past the age of 20. Recent studies, however, have overturned this notion completely, discovering instead that the natural decline of Human Growth Hormone (HGH), from ages 21 to 61 (the average age at which there is only a trace left in the body) and is the main reason why the body ages and fails to regenerate itself to its 25 year-old biological age.

Like a picked flower cut from the source, we gradually wilt physically and mentally and become vulnerable to a host of degenerative diseases, that we simply weren't susceptible to in our early adult years.

Modern medical science now regards aging as a disease that is treatable and preventable and that "aging", the disease, is actually a compilation of various diseases and pathologies, from everything, like a rise in blood glucose and pressure to diabetes, skin wrinkling and so on. All of these aging symptoms can be stopped and rolled back by maintaining Growth Hormone levels in the blood at the same levels HGH existed in the blood when we were 25 years old.

There is a receptor site in almost every

Have Your Own Walden

*It's more of a puddle
than a pond,
but the effect is transcendental.*

BY MARTHA DEERINGER • ILLUSTRATION BY KIM KURKI

There is something about a body of water that
breeds a calm state of mind. Yet most of us don't
have 2 years, 2 months, and 2 days to sit beside
one and ponder the world and our place in it, as
writer Henry David Thoreau did at Walden Pond
in Concord, Massachusetts, starting in 1845.

However, if your heart yearns for the contem-
plative influence of a pond, you can build your
own, right next to your favorite lawn chair.

(continued)

That man is the richest whose
pleasures are the cheapest.

–Henry David Thoreau, American writer (1817–62)

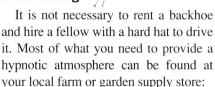

Gardening

It is not necessary to rent a backhoe and hire a fellow with a hard hat to drive it. Most of what you need to provide a hypnotic atmosphere can be found at your local farm or garden supply store:

• a round, galvanized stock tank (4 feet in diameter and 2 feet deep, if possible)
• a bag of sand
• three or four concrete blocks
• water cleansing agents
• four or five common goldfish
• water plants
• rocks

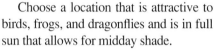

Choose a location that is attractive to birds, frogs, and dragonflies and is in full sun that allows for midday shade.

Spread the sand on the ground and use it to level the tank. Check the level with a straight board and a carpenter's level. A lopsided water garden will interfere with the serenity.

Place the tank on top of the level sand. Fill it with water to within a few inches of the top and, for the health of the fish that you will introduce into it, treat the water with drops of a cleaning agent that removes chlorine and chloramine. The fish will add a flash of color and feast on mosquito larvae, thus keeping these pests at bay, which will also enhance your serenity.

Stand a concrete block on end in the water near one side of the pond and arrange the rocks atop it in such a way that they protrude from the water. This will enable any creatures that are unfortunate enough to fall into the water to climb out, as well as give birds a secure platform for drinking and bathing.

Choose water plants that suit your locality. Hardy water lilies sport astonishing flowers, will bloom until the water freezes, and survive winter in all

Psoriasis? Dermatitis? Dandruff? Dry, Itchy Skin?

Now you can relieve the itching and restore your skin to its clear healthy state!

Introducing Soravil™, the scientifically advanced skin therapy system whose active ingredients are clinically proven to provide immediate relief from Psoriasis, Dermatitis, Dandruff, and other bothersome skin disorders.

If you suffer from an irritating skin disorder, you must try Soravil™! Unlike anything you may have tried in the past, Soravil™ is guaranteed to provide immediate relief from the redness and irritation associated with chronic skin disorders. Our clinically tested formulas soothe, moisturize and heal dry, damaged skin...leaving it feeling smooth, supple, and healthy again! Even better, the power of Soravil™ is available in the form of Shampoo and Body Wash, so you can treat your condition as part of your daily routine. There is also easy to apply (and invisible) Body Gel and Skin Spray to take care of those stubborn flare ups. Soravil™ makes it easy for you to relieve yourself from that bothersome skin disorder.

What are you waiting for? If you want to relieve yourself from the suffering and rejuvenate your dry, itchy skin, it's time you tried Soravil™! This highly effective formula is guaranteed to work for you. So don't suffer any longer, call today for your risk-free trial, 1-800-711-0719, Offer # 909.

Success Stories:

*"Right away it cleared my arms up.
I think your product is wonderful.
Thanks so much!"*
-Judy K.

*"I am amazed at the improvement that
Soravil has made to my scalp! To say
I'm delighted would be putting it lightly."*
-David L.

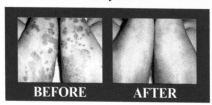

BEFORE **AFTER**

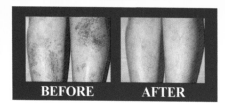

BEFORE **AFTER**

Call now and get your risk-free trial!
1-800-711-0719

Mention Offer # 909 and ask how you can get a **FREE SUPPLY** of our Soravil Skin Hydration Formula.

**Active Ingredient FDA Approved • Results Guaranteed
Steroid-Free Formula • Provides Immediate Relief
Works On All Skin Types • Easy Application-No Mess**

Gardening

PUDDLE MAINTENANCE

The upkeep of a stock tank water garden is minimal. Feed the fish daily with common goldfish food and push fertilizer pellets made for aquatic plants into the soil of the water lily once a month. If evaporation gets ahead of rainfall, add treated water.

In the coldest regions, an inexpensive tank heater will create an opening in the ice in winter so that the fish can breathe.

planting zones. Put a layer of gravel on top of the soil in the pot that contains your aquatic plants to discourage soil from floating out into the water.

Bog plants grow with their roots in the water and leaves above the surface. They provide upright areas of interest and resting places for butterflies and dragonflies. Curly rush, dwarf cattails, and papyrus are bog plants that thrive in a water garden. Underwater grasses such as anacharis and hornwort float below the surface, help to remove phosphates from the water, and give the fish something yummy to graze on.

Set another concrete block on its side in the tank. Put a potted water lily on it in such a way that the top of the pot is at least a foot below the water surface. The leaves of the lily will spread to shade most of the water in the pond and keep algae to a minimum.

Acclimate the goldfish, then add them to the tank. Take a seat within arm's reach, relax, and contemplate the simple life, as Thoreau did. Perhaps you will also discover that the laws of the universe begin to seem less complex. ∎

Martha Deeringer writes for children and adults from her home on a central Texas cattle ranch. Visit her at www.marthadeeringer.com.

What's Happened to All the

Quail?

by Karen L. Kirsch

The songbirds leave us at the summer's close,
Only the empty nests are left behind,
And pipings of the quail among the sheaves.

–Henry Wadsworth Longfellow, American poet (1807–82)

"I used to hear them all the time," people would wistfully recall, often following this with their rendition of the distinctive call: "bob*white,* bob-bob*white.*"

In many areas, the once plentiful game bird is little more than a memory. In the late 1990s, studies to monitor the status of northern bobwhite quail were initiated throughout its native range (roughly the eastern two-thirds of the United States, plus extreme southern Ontario). The northern bobwhite is the most widespread of six quail species and one of the most studied game birds. Collected data revealed an 87 percent decline in population over the previous four decades. This coincided with the agricultural revolution that brought monoculture, herbicide and pesticide use, and forestry management, among other factors. However, thanks to coordinated conservation efforts that began in 2002, habitat is being reestablished, and northern bobwhite quail, with their plaintive calls, are returning.

These shy and elusive birds are ground foragers that thrive in native grasslands and open woodlands and at forest edges. They are nonmigratory, with a natural life span of 2 years, on average (80 percent live less than 1 year). In springtime, hens settle onto grass- or pine needle–lined shallow bowls in the earth, preferably with a canopy of tall

(continued on page 86)

LORE AND MORE

- Ancient Egyptians considered quail a culinary delicacy. The birds were bred on large farms as food for workers and, separately, prepared for the deceased. The quail is a common figure in hieroglyphics.
- Quail meat is low in fat, high in protein, and slightly sweet-tasting. Relative to their weight, the eggs are more nutritious than chicken eggs.
- Quail eggs are the smallest commercially available.
- Research has shown that quail eggs may aid in relief from allergies and asthma.
- *When quail are heard in the evening, expect fair conditions tomorrow.*
- To "quail" means to show fear or cower—not what the birds do when startled.
- In Austria's Tyrol region, the number of a quail's cries is thought to indicate the number of years the hearer will remain unmarried.

Don't Buy Survival Food... Until You Read This!

Bad news...

Sooner or later, a crisis will hit you like a locomotive. The evidence is everywhere – storms, wars, terrorism – the list goes on. When a disaster strikes, you have to be ready. You need to make darn sure your family is prepared.

Well, I decided to stop worrying and do something about it. So I got in touch with my buddy Frank Bates and put my order in for his Food4Patriots survival food kits.

This is Frank's new line of survival food and there are 4 reasons why it's literally flying off the shelves:

Food4Patriots is an incredible value. This high quality survival food contains no fillers and is made in the U.S.A. And the price? As low as $1.39 per serving!

Military-grade packaging and 25 year shelf-life. Food4Patriots is sealed in Mylar and comes in compact, air-tight containers you can stack and store anywhere – basement, garage, cabin, or RV. And "rotating" your food? Forget about that! With Food4Patriots, you don't need to!

Delicious meals ready in just minutes. You get a wide variety of mouth-watering favorites for breakfast, lunch, and dinner.

Free bonuses! My 3-month kit came with 5,400+ heirloom survival seeds, 4 hard copy books, an 11-in-1 survival tool, and some other cool stuff.

Don't let a crisis totally knock you off your guard. Get the same peace of mind I have now by making sure your family has enough survival food on hand – just in case. You'll be glad you did.

P.S. Got a call from Frank and guess who just tried to buy up his entire supply of food? The answer is shocking...

LOG-ON NOW TO GETFOOD60.COM

SOCIALITE PROVES QUAIL FOLKLORE IS FOR THE BIRDS

Quail appear as sustenance in biblical accounts, and some believe that one of those incidents gave rise to a supposedly unwinnable bet: that nobody could eat quail for 30 consecutive days because it is too rich.

The annals of history suggest otherwise: Many have tried and a few have succeeded. The first woman to consume 30 quail in 30 days may have been Mrs. George B. Titus of Chicago. On December 25, 1888, the *Sacramento* [Calif.] *Daily Union* reported that Mrs. Titus had consumed her 30th bird ("Always broiled") on the previous day. Her husband, a jeweler, had wagered $200 and a diamond ring against her. According to the article, she had not yet collected her due.

Painting: Louis Agassiz Fuertes

We set out to build the best leaf vacuum, *EVER!*

NEW MODELS
LOWEST PRICES EVER!

☑ **Maximum Vacuum Force**
☑ **Easy, 1-Hand, 1-Step Dumping**
☑ **Collection Bag Stores Flat**
☑ **Converts to an All-Season Utility Trailer**

We started with the most powerful engines...but we didn't stop there. The NEW DR® Leaf Vacuum is designed from the top down to make yard clean up easier, faster, more thorough and more satisfying than ever before. Try one for six months and see for yourself!

Unload with just one hand!

Doubles as a utility trailer!

84584X © 2014

DRleafvac.com

Mow Fence Lines 3X FASTER!

with the 3-POINT HITCH DR® TRIMMER MOWER!

MOW FENCE LINES FAST! Spring-loaded mowing arm automatically deflects around fence posts.

MOW ROUGH GROUND! Deck pivots up and down to mow ditches and roadsides without scalping.

NO STEEL BLADES! Commercial-duty, 175 mil cutting line is flexible and durable. Goes where a bladed mower can't.

NEW FOR 2014!

NOW FOR ATVS
or any other vehicle with a pin hitch (UTV, Riding Mower, Compact Tractor). Clean up all the hard-to-reach corners of your property!

TRIM AND MOW WHILE YOU RIDE!

84583X © 2014

Plus!

BEST DEAL EVER!
on Walk-Behind Models.

DRtrimmer.com

Try a DR® at Home for 6 Months!
Call for details.

Call for a FREE DVD and Catalog!
Includes product specifications and factory-direct offers.

TOLL FREE 800-731-0493

PROFESSIONAL POWER
DR
DONE RIGHT

grasses or forbs (nonwoody, broadleaf plants) for protection. One hen can incubate 12 to 20 eggs for 23 days, but only about 25 percent of a clutch will be successful, so hens frequently try for a second or third brood.

Chicks leave the nest shortly after hatching and take their first flight at just 2 weeks. They must have access

vival of at least some. They reassemble by issuing a special call. When mortality significantly decreases a covey size, the remaining birds join up with another. Spring signals mating season and the cycle begins anew.

Tromping through fields and flushing a covey is a rare thrill. We may never see the rich populations of years past, but

A northern bobwhite covey drinks at a pond in southern Texas.

to bare ground where they can move about easily and catch insects. Adult quail consume the seeds of over 1,000 different weeds, as well as a variety of small bugs.

By late summer, as many as two dozen birds gather in coveys of two or more families, in brushy areas such as hedgerows or forest edges that are usually near a food source such as a post-harvest grainfield. The covey roosts in a circle with heads pointing outward to conserve heat and to keep watch. If disturbed, the birds flush, breaking skyward in different directions to ensure the sur-

by restoring their habitat we can make sure that "bob*white,* bob-bob*white*" will never be just a memory.

WHAT YOU CAN DO

To learn more about northern bobwhite quail in your area, contact your local Division of Fish & Wildlife or the National Bobwhite Conservation Initiative (NBCI): bringbackbobwhites.org. ∎

Karen L. Kirsch lives in Louisville, Ohio, with three dogs, eight cats, two donkeys, a flock of geriatric free-range chickens, and the occasional opossum. She writes about environmental issues for numerous publications and in her blog at mysmallcountrylife.com.

Frozen lighthouse, St. Joseph,
Michigan, Dec. 20, 2010

WHEN
AND WHY
WIND
Chills

There's no such thing
as bad weather—
just bad clothing.

BY WILLIAM L. FARRELL

Many of us decide how to dress or
go outdoors based on information we
receive through our meteorologists.
Every once in a while in winter in
northern states and southern Canada,
the local meteorologist's forecast will
sound something like this: "Northwest winds gusting to nearly 30 miles
per hour will combine with temperatures near 20 below zero tonight to

Weather

create windchill values of 50 below."

Wow! Does this really mean that our faces will freeze in minutes while walking the dog? What *does* it mean?

The Windchill Temperature Index (we'll just call it "windchill") is an important piece of information that can come in handy for your comfort, health, and even survival. When a low temperature and high wind speed indicate a windchill at or below –25°F, the National Weather Service (NWS) issues a windchill warning. The dangers are real: Your appendages can freeze and your chance for survival is reduced, if you are not properly prepared. People are advised to bring pets indoors, children are not allowed outside during school recess, and the homeless are advised to seek shelter. Dangerously low windchill readings, especially when the ambient air temperature is below 32°F, can result in permanent injury from frostbitten skin and, when the body's core temperature falls below 95°F, death from hypothermia.

COLDLY CALCULATING

Windchill is not measured with an instrument; it is a calculated value based on temperature and wind speed. According to the NWS, the measurements for calculating windchill were originally, and for years, based on the research of Antarctic explorers Paul Siple and Charles Passel in 1940. Their findings were published in 1945. They measured the cooling rate of water in a small plastic cylinder attached to the top of a 33-foot-high pole. Because Siple and Passel's results underestimated the time necessary to freeze human flesh, a new index designed to more accurately

reflect how cold air feels on human skin
was developed in 2001.

This calculation, still in use today, is
based on the results of trials conducted
by the Defence and Civil Institute of Environmental Medicine in Toronto, Canada. Six men and six women, with ther-
mal transducers attached to their faces to
measure the heat flow from their cheeks,
forehead, nose, and chin, were placed in
a chilled wind tunnel. Skin temperature
readings were obtained at an average
height of 5 feet—the typical height of
the adult human face.

Temperatures used to calculate windchill are now taken at or below 50°F.
Wind speed measurements are taken
above 3 miles per hour.

GETTING **UNDER** YOUR **SKIN**

Our bodies radiate heat and generate a
thin layer of warm air a few millimeters
thick on the surface of our skin. When
left undisturbed in low temperatures and
no wind, this thin layer of air protects
and insulates us from the cold. If we
disturb this layer of air—for example,
by blowing on a small portion of our
skin—this area quickly falls to the ambient air temperature. Conversely, in warm
(or hot) temperatures, such as in a sauna,
blowing on the skin will disturb the pro-
tective layer of air and we will become
uncomfortably warm, even hot.

Since cold is what matters most here,
if you were to stand outside in a bathing suit when the temperature is 30°F
(as I did in research for this article, but
do not recommend), it would take a certain amount of time to lower your body
temperature. If you set up a fan that
moved the ambient air across your skin

Mother Nature's Insect Control

MOSQUITO DUNKS®
MOSQUITO BITS®

Kills mosquitoes before they're old enough to bite! ®

- The #1 biological mosquito killer—100% natural and biodegradable. *Kills mosquito larvae and nothing else!*
- Use in bird baths, planters, potted plants—in any standing water.
- Controls larvae within 24 hours—will not harm animals, fish, birds, honey bees or plants. Works for 30 days or more.
- Mosquito Bits®—a versatile granular application with a spice shaker top — easily broadcasts over treatment area.

Caterpillar & Webworm Control

- 100% natural alternative. Contains no synthetic toxins.
- Controls caterpillars and worms on fruit trees, vegetables, ornamentals, and shade trees in and around the home and garden.
- *USE UP TO THE DAY OF HARVEST.*

Year-Round® Spray Oil

- Apply early in the growing season to prevent insect and fungal damage.
- Protection for your garden, vegetables, house plants, fruit trees, and ornamentals—both indoors and out.
- Recommended by top growers and agricultural experts — *USE UP TO THE DAY OF HARVEST.*

FOR ORGANIC PRODUCTION

OMRI Listed

Summit *...responsible solutions.*
800.227.8664 SummitResponsibleSolutions.com

Summit ... *responsible solutions*®, Year Round® Spray Oil, Mosquito Dunks®, and Mosquito Bits® are registered trademarks of Summit Chemical Company.

HOW **ABOVE FREEZING** FEELS LIKE **BELOW FREEZING**

In this example, with a constant temperature of 40°F, the windchill temperature index goes down as the wind speed picks up. At a 40°F actual temperature, you can not get frostbite, but you can get hypothermia.

Actual Temperature	Wind Speed	Windchill Temperature Index
40°F	4 mph	37°F
40°F	10 mph	34°F
40°F	20 mph	30°F
40°F	30 mph	28°F
40°F	40 mph	27°F

You can explore these and other calculations with an online windchill calculator at www.weather.gov/os/windchill. View the Canadian windchill chart at Almanac.com/content/windchill-chart-Canada.

at 20 mph, the wind would increase your body's rate (or speed) of cooling as if you were standing in still air at 17°F.

Here's why this phenomenon is called the windchill *effect:* As the wind speed increases in cold air, it effectively increases the rate at which you lose heat from exposed skin. The wind has the effect only of cooling the skin quickly; with no wind, the skin would cool to the ambient temperature more slowly. In both calm and windy conditions, the skin's surface temperature would never fall lower than the ambient temperature—in this case, 30°F.

It is worth pointing out that although the skin temperatures would never fall below the ambient temperature, when this temperature is below freezing, your skin would become frostbitten and eventually you would die from hypothermia.

This brought to mind my years growing up in the Berkshire Hills of Massachusetts. For several days during February 1958, when I was a third grader, the temperature fell to –10°F. Yet I vividly remember skiing on our local rope tow after school every day (and all day during school vacation) and walking home in the dark carrying my skis on my shoulder. My mother dressed me in two pairs of socks, two sets of long underwear, a sweater, a jacket, ski pants, insulated mittens, a trooper hat, a face mask, and a wool neck gaiter. (When I peeled off the last layers, I found that I was drenched in sweat.)

Nowadays, these conditions would require a warning from the National Weather Service. While a warning should be taken seriously, it should not be an excuse to cower from winter. While I am not suggesting that you don what I wore as an 8-year-old, if you know how to dress accordingly, you can enjoy the outdoors. With careful preparation, we should all be able to get outside and embrace the cold. ∎

William L. Farrell, a retired mathematics teacher, writes from Dublin, New Hampshire.

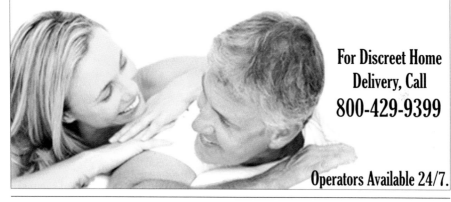

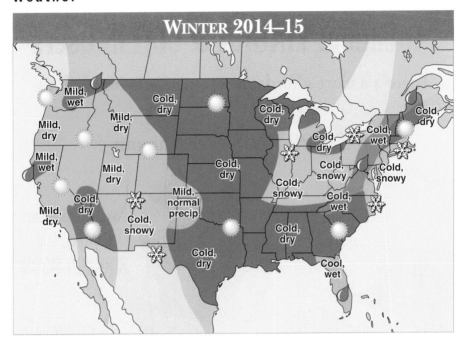

WINTER 2014–15

These weather maps correspond to the winter (November through March) and summer (June through August) predictions in the General Weather Forecast (opposite). Forecast terms here represent deviations from the normals; learn more on page 194.

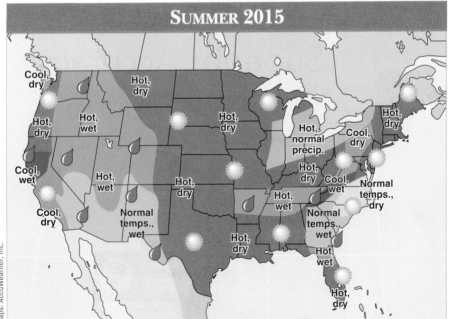

SUMMER 2015

Maps: AccuWeather, Inc.

The General Weather Report and Forecast

For regional forecasts, see pages 196–213.

What's shaping the weather? Solar Cycle 24 officially began on January 4, 2008, but there was minimal activity until early 2010. While activity has picked up since then, this cycle is the smallest in more than 100 years. As solar activity continues to decline from a low peak, we expect temperatures in much of the nation to be below normal this winter and above normal next summer. While Winter 2014–15 will not be as snowy as last winter, much of the northeastern quarter of the country still will have above-normal snowfall.

Other key factors in coming weather patterns include a continued warm phase in the Atlantic Multidecadal Oscillation (AMO), a cold phase in the North Atlantic Oscillation (NAO) during most of the winter, and the long-term cool phase of the Pacific Decadal Oscillation (PDO), despite some warm-phase intervals. Oscillations are linked ocean–atmosphere patterns that influence the weather over periods of weeks to years.

One of the keys to the upcoming winter will be the El Niño Southern Oscillation (ENSO), which many are forecasting to be in its warm El Niño phase. If this occurs, then winter will likely be much rainier than we are forecasting in California and the Southwest. We believe it more likely that El Niño will be in a weak to neutral phase.

Winter is expected to be another cold one in the eastern half to two-thirds of the nation, with above-normal temperatures, on average, in the West. Snowfall will be above normal in most of the Northeast, although below normal in much of New England. Florida will have above-normal rainfall, while most of the southeastern and central states will have below-normal precipitation. We expect above-normal snowfall from eastern Arizona into the Big Bend of Texas and above-normal rainfall from parts of inland Washington into the northwest corner of Montana and just north of California's Bay region. Other areas in the western third of the country, including most of California, should have below-normal precipitation.

Spring will bring above-normal temperatures to the eastern half of the nation from late March through early May; temperatures will be below normal, generally, in the West. Precipitation will be below normal in most states near the Atlantic and Pacific coasts, but above normal in most spots in the central two-thirds of the nation.

Summer temperatures will be above normal in most places, the main exceptions being the mid-Atlantic and southwestern states. Rainfall will be below normal in most of the nation's midsection, which may reduce yields of corn, wheat, soybeans, and other crops grown within this area. The drought in much of California will likely continue as well, putting additional stress on our food supply.

The hurricane season will not be particularly active. Storms that do arrive will threaten the Gulf states much more than the Atlantic coast. A major hurricane strike is most likely to occur in late August in the area from Louisiana into eastern Texas.

Autumn temperatures will be above normal in most of the eastern half of the nation and below in the West. Precipitation will be below normal in most of the southeastern and western states and above normal elsewhere.

To learn how we make our weather predictions and to get a summary of the results of our forecast for last winter, turn to page 194.

The Old Farmer's Almanac

Established in 1792 and published every year thereafter

ROBERT B. THOMAS, *founder* (1766–1846)

YANKEE PUBLISHING INC.

EDITORIAL AND PUBLISHING OFFICES

P.O. Box 520, 1121 Main Street, Dublin, NH 03444

Phone: 603-563-8111 • Fax: 603-563-8252

EDITOR *(13th since 1792)*: Janice Stillman
ART DIRECTOR: Colleen Quinnell
COPY EDITOR: Jack Burnett
SENIOR RESEARCH EDITOR: Mare-Anne Jarvela
SENIOR EDITOR: Heidi Stonehill
SENIOR ASSOCIATE EDITOR: Sarah Perreault
EDITORIAL ASSISTANCE: Tim Clark
INTERN: Sarah Drory
WEATHER GRAPHICS AND CONSULTATION:
AccuWeather, Inc.

V.P., NEW MEDIA AND PRODUCTION:
Paul Belliveau
PRODUCTION DIRECTORS:
Susan Gross, David Ziarnowski
SENIOR PRODUCTION ARTISTS:
Rachel Kipka, Lucille Rines

WEB SITE: ALMANAC.COM

NEW MEDIA EDITOR: Catherine Boeckmann
WEB DESIGNERS: Lou S. Eastman, Amy O'Brien
E-COMMERCE MANAGER: Alan Henning
PROGRAMMING: Reinvented, Inc.

CONTACT US

We welcome your questions and comments about articles in and topics for this Almanac. Mail all editorial correspondence to Editor, The Old Farmer's Almanac, P.O. Box 520, Dublin, NH 03444-0520; fax us at 603-563-8252; or contact us through Almanac.com/Feedback. *The Old Farmer's Almanac* can not accept responsibility for unsolicited manuscripts and will not acknowledge any hard-copy queries or manuscripts that do not include a stamped and addressed return envelope.

Thank you for buying this Almanac! We hope that you find it "useful, with a pleasant degree of humor." Thanks, too, to everyone who had a hand in it, including advertisers, distributors, printers, and sales and delivery people.

OUR CONTRIBUTORS

Bob Berman, our astronomy editor, is the director of Overlook Observatory in Woodstock and Storm King Observatory in Cornwall, both in New York. In 1976, he founded the Catskill Astronomical Society. Bob has led many aurora and eclipse expeditions, venturing as far as the Arctic and Antarctic.

Tim Clark, a retired high school English teacher from New Hampshire, wrote the Farmer's Calendar essays that appear in this edition. His recordings of them are available free at Almanac.com/Multimedia. He has composed the weather doggerel on the Calendar pages since 1980.

Bethany E. Cobb, our astronomer, earned a Ph.D. in astronomy at Yale University and is an Assistant Professor of Honors and Physics at George Washington University. She also conducts research on gamma-ray bursts and follows numerous astronomy pursuits, including teaching astronomy to adults at the Osher Lifelong Learning Institute at UC Berkeley. When she is not scanning the sky, she enjoys playing the violin, figure skating, and reading science fiction.

Celeste Longacre, our astrologer, often refers to astrology as "a study of timing, and timing is everything." A New Hampshire native, she has been a practicing astrologer for more than 25 years. Her book, *Love Signs* (Sweet Fern Publications, 1999), is available for sale on her Web site, www .yourlovesigns.com.

Michael Steinberg, our meteorologist, has been forecasting weather for the Almanac since 1996. In addition to college degrees in atmospheric science and meteorology, he brings a lifetime of experience to the task: He began predicting weather when he attended the only high school in the world with weather Teletypes and radar.

Free Heirloom Seeds!

Small Seed Company Offering $20.00 In Free Heirloom Seeds Just To Get The Word Out About How Delicious Old Time Varieties Taste!

By Mike Walters
Staff Writer

If you want to grow better tasting vegetables, this will be the most important message you will read this year. Here's why:

Heirloom Solutions in Thomson, Illinois is celebrating the 2015 gardening season by actually giving away $20.00 in free heirloom seeds to readers of the *Old Farmer's Almanac*.

Better yet, after you receive your catalog, you get to pick which free seeds they'll send you. (Most companies won't let you do that.)

Why would they do that?

The answer is simple. To prove to the world that old time heirloom varieties just plain taste better! The world's become a pretty crazy place these days, but there's one thing you can depend on year after year... and that's the extraordinary taste of the old time varieties. You know the ones I'm talking about... the ones Grandma and Grandpa used to grow.

The folks at Heirloom Solutions are so confident that you'll love the old time heirloom vegetable varieties that they are willing to "go the extra mile" to convince *Old Farmer's Almanac* readers with this unusual offer.

Here's how to get your free seeds:

If you have a computer you can go watch a special video about this free heirloom seeds offer by going to:

www.FreeHeirloomSeeds.com

If you don't have a computer, you can simply send $2.00 to cover some of the shipping and handling for the new 2015 catalog. Be sure to include your address so they'll know where to send your catalog as well as your phone number so one of the guys can call and tell you how to get the seeds you want. Don't worry, no one will pressure you into ordering anything you don't want. They simply don't allow that.

To get your new 2015 catalog and $20.00 in free heirloom seeds, please send $2.00 to:

Heirloom Solutions
2200 Illinois Route 84
P.O. Box 487
Thomson, IL 61285

Or call the toll-free number: 800-280-3465 to have one of our Heirloom Seed Consultants help you set up your account.

THE 2015 EDITION OF

The Old Farmer's Almanac
Established in 1792 and published every year thereafter
ROBERT B. THOMAS, *founder* (1766–1846)

YANKEE PUBLISHING INC.
P.O. Box 520, 1121 Main Street, Dublin, NH 03444
Phone: 603-563-8111 • Fax: 603-563-8252

PUBLISHER *(23rd since 1792):* Sherin Pierce
EDITOR IN CHIEF: Judson D. Hale Sr.

FOR DISPLAY ADVERTISING RATES
Go to Almanac.com/AdvertisingInfo or
Call 800-895-9265, ext. 149

Stephanie Bernbach-Crowe • 914-827-0015
Brenda Escalante • 785-274-4404
Steve Hall • 800-736-1100, ext. 320
Susan Lyman • 646-221-4169

FOR CLASSIFIED ADVERTISING
Call Gallagher Group • 203-263-7171

AD PRODUCTION COORDINATOR: Janet Grant

PUBLIC RELATIONS
Quinn/Brein • 206-842-8922
ginger@quinnbrein.com

CONSUMER MAIL ORDERS
Call 800-ALMANAC (800-256-2622)
or go to Almanac.com/Shop

CONSUMER MARKETING MANAGER:
Kate McPherson • 800-895-9265, ext. 188

RETAIL SALES
Stacey Korpi, 800-895-9265, ext. 160

ALMANAC FUND-RAISING
ofafundraising@yankeepub.com
Carlene McCarty • vtbooklady@gmail.com

DISTRIBUTORS
NATIONAL: Curtis Circulation Company
New Milford, NJ
BOOKSTORE: Houghton Mifflin Harcourt
Boston, MA

The Old Farmer's Almanac publications are available for sales promotions or premiums. Contact Beacon Promotions, info@beaconpromotions.com.

YANKEE PUBLISHING INCORPORATED
Jamie Trowbridge, *President;* Judson D. Hale Sr., *Senior Vice President;* Paul Belliveau, Jody Bugbee, Judson D. Hale Jr., Brook Holmberg, Sherin Pierce, *Vice Presidents.*

The Old Farmer's Almanac/Yankee Publishing Inc. assumes no responsibility for claims made by advertisers or failure by its advertisers to deliver any goods or services advertised herein. Publication of any advertisement by The Old Farmer's Almanac/ Yankee Publishing Inc. is not an endorsement of the product or service advertised therein.

PRINTED IN U.S.A.

"My friends all hate their cell phones... I love mine!"
Here's why.

Say good-bye to everything you hate about cell phones. Say hello to Jitterbug.

"Cell phones have gotten so small, I can barely dial mine"
Not Jitterbug®, it features a larger keypad for easier dialing. It even has an oversized display so you can actually see it.

"I had to get my son to program it"
Your Jitterbug set-up process is simple. We'll even pre-program it with your favorite numbers.

Available in Blue, Red and White.

"I tried my sister's cell phone... I couldn't hear it"
Jitterbug is designed with an improved speaker. There's an adjustable volume control, and Jitterbug is hearing-aid compatible

Why pay for minutes you'll never use!

	Basic 14	Basic 19
Monthly Minutes	50	was ~~100~~ NOW 200
Monthly Rate	$14.99	$19.99
Operator Assistance	24/7	24/7
911 Access	FREE	FREE
Long Distance Calls	No add'l charge	No add'l charge
Voice Dial	FREE	FREE
Nationwide Coverage	YES	YES
Friendly Return Policy[1]	30 days	30 days

More minute plans available.
Ask your Jitterbug expert for details.

Order now
and receive
a Car Charger
for your Jitterbug
– a $24.99 value.
Call now!

Enough talk. Isn't it time you found out more about the cell phone that's changing all the rules? Call now, Jitterbug product experts are standing by.

1998 Ruffin Mill Road
Colonial Heights, VA 23834

Jitterbug5 Cell Phone
Call toll free today to get
your own Jitterbug5 phone.
Please mention promotional code 48058.
1-877-513-8982
www.jitterbugdirect.com

47616

Eclipses

■ There will be four eclipses in 2015, two of the Sun and two of the Moon. Solar eclipses are visible only in certain areas and require eye protection to be viewed safely. Lunar eclipses are technically visible from the entire night side of Earth, but during a penumbral eclipse, the dimming of the Moon's illumination is slight.

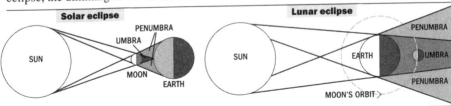

March 20: Total eclipse of the Sun. This eclipse will not be visible from North America but will be visible from Greenland, Iceland, Europe, North Africa, and northwestern Asia.

April 4: Total eclipse of the Moon. This eclipse will be visible from North America. The eclipse will be best observed from the western states and provinces. The Moon will set during the eclipse for observers in the eastern regions. It will enter the penumbra at 5:00 A.M. EDT and the umbra at 6:15 A.M. The Moon will leave the umbra at 9:45 A.M. and the penumbra at 11:01 A.M.

September 13: Partial eclipse of the Sun. This partial eclipse will not be visible from North America but will be visible from parts of southern Africa, the southern half of Madagascar, the southern Indian Ocean, and the eastern part of Antarctica.

September 27–28: Total eclipse of the Moon. This eclipse will be visible from North America. The eclipse will be best viewed from the eastern half of North America. The Moon will be rising during the eclipse for western regions. The Moon will enter the penumbra at 8:10 P.M. EDT and the umbra at 9:07 P.M. on September 27; totality begins at 10:11 P.M.

Full-Moon Dates (Eastern Time)

	2015	2016	2017	2018	2019
Jan.	4	23	12	1 & 31	21
Feb.	3	22	10	–	19
Mar.	5	23	12	1 & 31	20
Apr.	4	22	11	29	19
May	3	21	10	29	18
June	2	20	9	28	17
July	1 & 31	19	9	27	16
Aug.	29	18	7	26	15
Sept.	27	16	6	24	14
Oct.	27	16	5	24	13
Nov.	25	14	4	23	12
Dec.	25	13	3	22	12

On September 28, the Moon will leave the umbra at 12:27 A.M. and the penumbra at 1:24 A.M.

The Moon's Path

The Moon's path across the sky changes with the seasons. Full Moons are very high in the sky (at midnight) between November and February and very low in the sky between May and July.

Next Total Eclipse of the Sun

March 9, 2016: visible from Indonesia and the North Pacific Ocean.

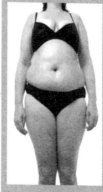

Bright Stars

Transit Times

■ This table shows the time (EST or EDT) and altitude of a star as it transits the meridian (i.e., reaches its highest elevation while passing over the horizon's south point) at Boston on the dates shown. The transit time on any other date differs from that of the nearest date listed by approximately 4 minutes per day. To find the time of a star's transit for your location, convert its time at Boston using Key letter C **(see Time Corrections, page 252).**

–Beth Krommes

Star	Constellation	Magnitude	Time of Transit (EST/EDT) Bold = P.M. Light = A.M.						Altitude (degrees)
			Jan. 1	Mar. 1	May 1	July 1	Sept. 1	Nov. 1	
Altair	Aquila	0.8	**12:51**	8:59	6:00	2:00	**9:52**	**4:52**	56.3
Deneb	Cygnus	1.3	**1:42**	9:50	6:50	2:50	**10:42**	**5:43**	92.8
Fomalhaut	Psc. Aus.	1.2	**3:58**	**12:06**	9:06	5:06	1:03	**7:59**	17.8
Algol	Perseus	2.2	**8:08**	**4:16**	**1:16**	9:16	5:13	1:13	88.5
Aldebaran	Taurus	0.9	**9:35**	**5:43**	**2:43**	10:44	6:40	1:40	64.1
Rigel	Orion	0.1	**10:14**	**6:22**	**3:22**	11:22	7:18	2:18	39.4
Capella	Auriga	0.1	**10:16**	**6:24**	**3:24**	11:25	7:21	2:21	93.6
Bellatrix	Orion	1.6	**10:24**	**6:32**	**3:33**	11:33	7:29	2:29	54.0
Betelgeuse	Orion	var. 0.4	**10:54**	**7:02**	**4:02**	**12:03**	7:59	2:59	55.0
Sirius	Can. Maj.	−1.4	**11:44**	**7:52**	**4:52**	**12:52**	8:49	3:49	31.0
Procyon	Can. Min.	0.4	12:42	**8:46**	**5:46**	**1:46**	9:43	4:43	52.9
Pollux	Gemini	1.2	12:48	**8:52**	**5:52**	**1:53**	9:49	4:49	75.7
Regulus	Leo	1.4	**3:11**	**11:15**	**8:15**	**4:15**	**12:11**	7:12	59.7
Spica	Virgo	var. 1.0	6:27	2:35	**11:31**	**7:31**	**3:28**	10:28	36.6
Arcturus	Boötes	−0.1	7:17	3:25	**12:25**	**8:22**	**4:18**	11:18	66.9
Antares	Scorpius	var. 0.9	9:31	5:39	2:39	**10:35**	6:32	**1:32**	21.3
Vega	Lyra	0	11:38	7:46	4:46	12:46	**8:38**	3:38	86.4

Rise and Set Times

■ To find the time of a star's rising at Boston on any date, subtract the interval shown at right from the star's transit time on that date; add the interval to find the star's setting time. To find the rising and setting times for your city, convert the Boston transit times above using the Key letter shown at right before applying the interval **(see Time Corrections, page 252).** The directions in which the stars rise and set, shown for Boston, are generally useful throughout the United States. Deneb, Algol, Capella, and Vega are circumpolar stars—they never set but appear to circle the celestial north pole.

Star	Interval (h. m.)	Rising Key	Rising Dir.*	Setting Key	Setting Dir.*
Altair	6 36	B	EbN	E	WbN
Fomalhaut	3 59	E	SE	D	SW
Aldebaran	7 06	B	ENE	D	WNW
Rigel	5 33	D	EbS	B	WbS
Bellatrix	6 27	B	EbN	D	WbN
Betelgeuse	6 31	B	EbN	D	WbN
Sirius	5 00	D	ESE	B	WSW
Procyon	6 23	B	EbN	D	WbN
Pollux	8 01	A	NE	E	NW
Regulus	6 49	B	EbN	D	WbN
Spica	5 23	D	EbS	B	WbS
Arcturus	7 19	A	ENE	E	WNW
Antares	4 17	E	SEbE	A	SWbW

*b = "by"

The Twilight Zone

Twilight is the time when the sky is partially illuminated preceding sunrise and again following sunset. The ranges of twilight are defined according to the Sun's position below the horizon. **Civil twilight** occurs when the Sun's center is between the horizon and 6 degrees below the horizon (visually, the horizon is clearly defined). **Nautical twilight** occurs when the center is between 6 and 12 degrees below the horizon (the horizon is distinct). **Astronomical twilight** occurs when the center is between 12 and 18 degrees below the horizon (sky illumination is imperceptible). When the center is at 18 degrees (**dawn** or **dark**) or below, there is no illumination.

Length of Astronomical Twilight (hours and minutes)

LATITUDE	Jan. 1 to Apr. 10	Apr. 11 to May 2	May 3 to May 14	May 15 to May 25	May 26 to July 22	July 23 to Aug. 3	Aug. 4 to Aug. 14	Aug. 15 to Sept. 5	Sept. 6 to Dec. 31
25°N to 30°N	1 20	1 23	1 26	1 29	1 32	1 29	1 26	1 23	1 20
31°N to 36°N	1 26	1 28	1 34	1 38	1 43	1 38	1 34	1 28	1 26
37°N to 42°N	1 33	1 39	1 47	1 52	1 59	1 52	1 47	1 39	1 33
43°N to 47°N	1 42	1 51	2 02	2 13	2 27	2 13	2 02	1 51	1 42
48°N to 49°N	1 50	2 04	2 22	2 42	—	2 42	2 22	2 04	1 50

TO DETERMINE THE LENGTH OF TWILIGHT: The length of twilight changes with latitude and the time of year. Use the **Time Corrections** table, **page 252,** to find the latitude of your city or the city nearest you. Use that figure in the chart above with the appropriate date to calculate the length of twilight in your area.

TO DETERMINE WHEN DAWN OR DARK WILL OCCUR: Calculate the sunrise/sunset times for your locality using the instructions in **How to Use This Almanac, page 124.** Subtract the length of twilight from the time of sunrise to determine when dawn breaks. Add the length of twilight to the time of sunset to determine when dark descends.

E X A M P L E :

Boston, Mass. (latitude 42°22')

Sunrise, August 1	5:36 A.M. EDT
Length of twilight	− 1 52
Dawn breaks	3:44 A.M.
Sunset, August 1	8:04 P.M. EDT
Length of twilight	+1 52
Dark descends	9:56 P.M.

Principal Meteor Showers

SHOWER	BEST VIEWING	POINT OF ORIGIN	DATE OF MAXIMUM*	NO. PER HOUR**	ASSOCIATED COMET
Quadrantid . . . .**Predawn**		N	**Jan. 4**	25	—
Lyrid . . . . .Predawn		S	Apr. 22	10	Thatcher
Eta Aquarid. . . . . .Predawn		SE	May 4	10	Halley
Delta Aquarid . . . . . . .Predawn		S	July 30	10	—
Perseid . . . .**Predawn**		NE	**Aug. 11–13**	50	**Swift-Tuttle**
Draconid . . . . .Late evening		NW	Oct. 9	6	Giacobini-Zinner
Orionid . . . . .Predawn		S	Oct. 21–22	15	Halley
Taurid . . . . .Late evening		S	Nov. 9	3	Encke
Leonid. . . . . .Predawn		S	Nov. 17–18	10	Tempel-Tuttle
Andromedid . . . . .Late evening		S	Nov. 25–27	5	Biela
Geminid . . . .**All night**		NE	**Dec. 13–14**	75	—
Ursid . . . . .Predawn		N	Dec. 22	5	Tuttle

May vary by one or two days   **Moonless, rural sky*   **Bold = most prominent**

NEUROPATHY FOOT PAIN?

If you suffer from neuropathy, or pain in your feet due to nerve damage, you should know that help is available. 20 million Americans suffer from neuropathy and put up with the pain because they are not aware of this proven treatment.

MagniLife® Pain Relieving Foot Cream contains eucalyptus oil and yellow jasmine, which relieve pain, tingling, and numbness, while natural moisturizers restore cracked, damaged, and itchy skin to help protect against infection. Results are so fantastic, long-time sufferers are finally getting relief. *"I tried it on both heels that have been aching me for months. I loved it, both my heels have been happy and so am I. I thank you for this foot cream it works wonders." – Paulette S., CA.*

MagniLife® Pain Relieving Foot Cream is **available at Walgreens, CVS/pharmacy, Rite Aid Pharmacy and Walmart,** located in the foot care and diabetes sections. Order risk free for $19.99 ($5.95 S&H) for a 4 oz jar. Get a **FREE** jar when you order two for $39.98 ($9.95 S&H). Send payment to: MagniLife PC-FA3, PO Box 6789, McKinney, TX 75071 or call **1-800-515-1815**. Guaranteed results, or return the jars within 90 days for a full refund. Order now at **www.PRFootCream.com**.

RESTLESS LEGS SYNDROME?

If uncomfortable sensations in your legs accompanied by an irresistible urge to move are keeping you from falling asleep, you may have Restless Legs Syndrome (RLS). Affecting more than 30 million Americans, RLS causes symptoms such as creepy, crawly, tingling and pulling sensations that urge you to move your legs when resting.

MagniLife® Restless Legs Cream allows you to rest comfortably again. Massage it into your legs and feet to relieve and soothe the symptoms of RLS. Formulated to allow for absorption of specific vitamins and minerals that provide relief from those painful and annoying sensations. Infused with Lavandula Angustifolia and other essential oils for relaxation so you can get a good night's sleep. *"Your Restless Legs Cream is wonderful! It has helped me so much in getting a decent night's sleep." – M. Segal, CA.*

MagniLife® Restless Legs Cream is **available at Walgreens, CVS/pharmacy and Rite Aid Pharmacy**. Order risk free for $19.99 ($5.95 S&H) for a 4 oz jar. Get a **FREE** jar when you order two for $39.98 ($9.95 S&H). Send payment to: MagniLife RC-FA3, PO Box 6789, McKinney, TX 75071 or call **1-800-515-1815**. Guaranteed results, or return the jars within 90 days for a full refund. Order now at **www.RLScream.com**.

SHINGLES PAIN OR ITCH?

If you suffer from shingles outbreaks and experience pain, tingling, burning, or a blistering skin rash that often results in long-term pain even after the rash is gone, you should know that help is available. Many people are putting up with the discomfort and itching because they are not aware of this new advancement in shingles care.

MagniLife® Shingles Recovery Cream contains 16 powerful ingredients such as arnica and tea tree oil that help restore the skin and relieve the itching and discomfort. *"I have been using your product for my rash and saw results almost immediately. The MagniLife Shingles Recovery Cream helped soothe the pain, itching and redness. This is the only product I've found that really helps." - H Reaves, Huntington Beach, CA.*

MagniLife® Shingles Recovery Cream is **available at CVS/pharmacy and Rite Aid Pharmacy**. Order risk free for $19.99 ($5.95 S&H) for a 1.8 oz jar. Get a **FREE** jar when you order two for $39.98 ($9.95 S&H). Send payment to: MagniLife SH-FA3, PO Box 6789, McKinney, TX 75071 or call **1-800-515-1815**. Guaranteed results, or return the jars within 90 days for a full refund. Order now at **www.ShinglesRecovery.com**.

The Visible Planets

■ Listed here for Boston are viewing suggestions for and the rise and set times (EST/EDT) of Venus, Mars, Jupiter, and Saturn on specific days each month, as well as when it is best to view Mercury. Approximate rise and set times for other days can be found by interpolation. Use the Key letters at the right of each listing to convert the times for other localities **(see pages 124 and 252)**. *For all planet rise and set times by zip code, visit* **Almanac.com/Astronomy.**

Venus

Venus's apparition cycle repeats every 8 years. This year offers a reprise of its wonderful 2007 appearance. Venus is bright and obvious as soon as the year begins, a brilliant evening star low in the west after sunset. It stands higher and brighter at dusk through the winter and reaches its highest point in April and May, when it sets 3½ hours after sunset. Lower but even brighter in June, Venus vanishes behind the Sun in a conjunction on August 15 before quickly reappearing as a morning star in the predawn east in late August and standing spectacularly high and dazzling in September. Venus slowly fades for the rest of the year.

Jan. 1	set	5:38	A	Apr. 1	set	10:22	E	July 1	set	10:41	D
Jan. 11	set	6:03	B	Apr. 11	set	10:45	E	July 11	set	10:09	D
Jan. 21	set	6:29	B	Apr. 21	set	11:07	E	July 21	set	9:27	D
Feb. 1	set	6:57	B	May 1	set	11:24	E	Aug. 1	set	8:29	D
Feb. 11	set	7:22	C	May 11	set	11:36	E	Aug. 11	set	7:29	D
Feb. 21	set	7:47	C	May 21	set	11:40	E	Aug. 21	rise	5:33	B
Mar. 1	set	8:06	D	June 1	set	11:36	E	Sept. 1	rise	4:27	B
Mar. 11	set	9:30	D	June 11	set	11:25	E	Sept. 11	rise	3:44	B
Mar. 21	set	9:55	D	June 21	set	11:07	E	Sept. 21	rise	3:18	B

Oct. 1	rise	3:06	B
Oct. 11	rise	3:03	B
Oct. 21	rise	3:08	C
Nov. 1	rise	2:19	C
Nov. 11	rise	2:33	C
Nov. 21	rise	2:50	C
Dec. 1	rise	3:08	D
Dec. 11	rise	3:29	D
Dec. 21	rise	3:50	E
Dec. 31	rise	4:12	E

Mars

Mars becomes brilliant and ventures close to Earth every other year. This is a Martian "off" year. The planet starts the year dim and low in the west at dusk and meets blue Neptune telescopically on January 18 and 19, and then the crescent Moon on January 22. Faint in the southwest at nightfall, Mars closely meets Venus from February 19 to 21. The crescent Moon spectacularly joins this tight but low conjunction on February 20. Mars vanishes in the Sun's glare in March. It reappears in August in Cancer, low and faint, and finishes the year near Virgo's blue star Spica, rising at around 2:00 A.M.

Jan. 1	set	7:43	B	Apr. 1	set	8:46	D	July 1	rise	4:48	A
Jan. 11	set	7:44	B	Apr. 11	set	8:45	E	July 11	rise	4:39	A
Jan. 21	set	7:46	B	Apr. 21	set	8:44	E	July 21	rise	4:32	A
Feb. 1	set	7:47	C	May 1	set	8:42	E	Aug. 1	rise	4:24	A
Feb. 11	set	7:48	C	May 11	set	8:40	E	Aug. 11	rise	4:18	A
Feb. 21	set	7:48	C	May 21	set	8:37	E	Aug. 21	rise	4:12	A
Mar. 1	set	7:48	C	June 1	set	8:31	E	Sept. 1	rise	4:05	B
Mar. 11	set	8:48	D	June 11	set	8:25	E	Sept. 11	rise	3:59	B
Mar. 21	set	8:47	D	June 21	rise	4:58	A	Sept. 21	rise	3:52	B

Oct. 1	rise	3:45	B
Oct. 11	rise	3:38	B
Oct. 21	rise	3:30	C
Nov. 1	rise	2:22	C
Nov. 11	rise	2:13	C
Nov. 21	rise	2:04	C
Dec. 1	rise	1:55	C
Dec. 11	rise	1:46	C
Dec. 21	rise	1:36	D
Dec. 31	rise	1:25	D

☞ **Bold = P.M.** ☞ Light = A.M.

–illustrations, Beth Krommes

Find more heavenly details at Almanac.com/Astronomy. **2015**

Jupiter

♃ **The largest planet begins the year conspicuously in Leo,** rising after nightfall. Retrograding into Cancer in February, Jupiter has its opposition on the 6th, when it is out all night. Jupiter remains an evening star through June, when it returns to Leo and spectacularly stands near Venus and the Moon on the 19th and 20th. June 29 starts a beautifully tight 5-day meeting with Venus, low in the west at dusk. It remains visible for July 4 revelers but sinks into the solar glare by month's end. Jupiter strikingly reappears in October as a morning star in the predawn east. By year's end, it rises before midnight.

Jan. 1	rise	**7:36**	B	Apr. 1	set	4:20	E	July 1	set	**10:43**	D
Jan. 11	rise	**6:52**	B	Apr. 11	set	3:41	E	July 11	set	**10:08**	D
Jan. 21	rise	**6:07**	B	Apr. 21	set	3:02	E	July 21	set	**9:34**	D
Feb. 1	rise	**5:16**	B	May 1	set	2:24	E	Aug. 1	set	**8:57**	D
Feb. 11	set	6:45	E	May 11	set	1:47	E	Aug. 11	set	**8:23**	D
Feb. 21	set	6:02	E	May 21	set	1:11	E	Aug. 21	set	**7:49**	D
Mar. 1	set	5:28	E	June 1	set	12:31	E	Sept. 1	rise	5:47	B
Mar. 11	set	5:46	E	June 11	set	**11:52**	E	Sept. 11	rise	5:19	B
Mar. 21	set	5:05	E	June 21	set	**11:17**	E	Sept. 21	rise	4:51	B
								Oct. 1	rise	4:22	B
								Oct. 11	rise	3:53	B
								Oct. 21	rise	3:24	B
								Nov. 1	rise	1:50	C
								Nov. 11	rise	1:19	C
								Nov. 21	rise	12:47	C
								Dec. 1	rise	12:14	C
								Dec. 11	rise	**11:36**	C
								Dec. 21	rise	**11:00**	C
								Dec. 31	rise	**10:23**	C

Saturn

♄ **Saturn begins 2015 in Libra, rising just before dawn. This** year, its famous ice rings are nearly fully "open," making the planet brighter than it has appeared in more than a decade. In mid-March, in Scorpius, Saturn starts rising at around midnight. It rises before 11:00 P.M. in mid-April and at nightfall in mid-May. At opposition on May 22, Saturn is out all night and remains a bright evening star through August. Gorgeous through backyard telescopes, Saturn starts sinking lower in the southwest at nightfall in early autumn. It becomes too low to observe by mid-October and hovers behind the Sun in a conjunction on November 29.

Jan. 1	rise	4:06	E	Apr. 1	rise	**11:26**	E	July 1	set	2:52	B
Jan. 11	rise	3:31	E	Apr. 11	rise	**10:44**	E	July 11	set	2:12	B
Jan. 21	rise	2:56	E	Apr. 21	rise	**10:02**	E	July 21	set	1:31	B
Feb. 1	rise	2:16	E	May 1	rise	**9:20**	E	Aug. 1	set	12:47	B
Feb. 11	rise	1:40	E	May 11	rise	**8:37**	E	Aug. 11	set	12:08	B
Feb. 21	rise	1:03	E	May 21	rise	**7:54**	E	Aug. 21	set	**11:25**	B
Mar. 1	rise	12:32	E	June 1	set	4:57	B	Sept. 1	set	**10:43**	B
Mar. 11	rise	12:54	E	June 11	set	4:15	B	Sept. 11	set	**10:06**	B
Mar. 21	rise	12:14	E	June 21	set	3:34	B	Sept. 21	set	**9:28**	B
								Oct. 1	set	**8:52**	B
								Oct. 11	set	**8:15**	B
								Oct. 21	set	**7:39**	B
								Nov. 1	set	**6:00**	B
								Nov. 11	set	**5:24**	B
								Nov. 21	set	**4:49**	B
								Dec. 1	rise	6:43	E
								Dec. 11	rise	6:09	E
								Dec. 21	rise	5:35	E
								Dec. 31	rise	5:01	E

Mercury

☿ **Mercury alternately darts above the eastern and western horizons roughly every 2 months. Observers can see this** tiny world when it's at least 5 degrees above the horizon and when it exceeds magnitude 0.5. This year, such favorable conditions occur in the western sky at dusk during the first half of January and from April 23 to May 7. In the predawn eastern sky, Mercury puts in a marginal appearance from February 20 to 26 and a much better one from October 8 to 27. Mercury forms a close conjunction with Venus from January 7 to 12.

DO NOT CONFUSE ■ *Venus and Jupiter in late June and early July. Venus is brighter.* ■ *Jupiter, Mars, Regulus, and Venus vertically aligned in early October. They appear as given in order here, from lowest to highest.* ■ *Mars and Virgo's star Spica at year's end. Spica is brighter and blue.*

Astronomical Glossary

Aphelion (Aph.): The point in a planet's orbit that is farthest from the Sun.

Apogee (Apo.): The point in the Moon's orbit that is farthest from Earth.

Celestial Equator (Eq.): The imaginary circle around the celestial sphere that can be thought of as the plane of Earth's equator projected out onto the sphere.

Celestial Sphere: An imaginary sphere projected into space that represents the entire sky, with an observer on Earth at its center. All celestial bodies other than Earth are imagined as being on its inside surface.

Circumpolar: Always visible above the horizon, such as a circumpolar star.

Conjunction: The time at which two or more celestial bodies appear closest in the sky. **Inferior (Inf.):** Mercury or Venus is between the Sun and Earth. **Superior (Sup.):** The Sun is between a planet and Earth. Actual dates for conjunctions are given on the **Right-Hand Calendar Pages, 129–155;** the best times for viewing the closely aligned bodies are given in **Sky Watch** on the **Left-Hand Calendar Pages, 128–154.**

Declination: The celestial latitude of an object in the sky, measured in degrees north or south of the celestial equator; analogous to latitude on Earth. This Almanac gives the Sun's declination at noon.

Eclipse, Lunar: The full Moon enters the shadow of Earth, which cuts off all or part of the sunlight reflected off the Moon. **Total:** The Moon passes completely through the **umbra** (central dark part) of Earth's shadow. **Partial:** Only part of the Moon passes through the umbra. **Penumbral:** The Moon passes through only the **penumbra** (area of partial darkness surrounding the umbra). **See page 102** for more information about eclipses.

Eclipse, Solar: Earth enters the shadow of the new Moon, which cuts off all or part of the Sun's light. **Total:** Earth passes through the umbra (central dark part) of the Moon's shadow, resulting in totality for observers within a narrow band on Earth. **Annular:** The

Moon appears silhouetted against the Sun, with a ring of sunlight showing around it. **Partial:** The Moon blocks only part of the Sun.

Ecliptic: The apparent annual path of the Sun around the celestial sphere. The plane of the ecliptic is tipped 23½° from the celestial equator.

Elongation: The difference in degrees between the celestial longitudes of a planet and the Sun. **Greatest Elongation (Gr. Elong.):** The greatest apparent distance of a planet from the Sun, as seen from Earth.

Epact: A number from 1 to 30 that indicates the Moon's age on January 1 at Greenwich, England; used in calculations for determining the date of Easter.

Equinox: When the Sun crosses the celestial equator. This event occurs two times each year: **Vernal** is around March 20 and **Autumnal** is around September 22.

Evening Star: A planet that is above the western horizon at sunset and less than 180° east of the Sun in right ascension.

Golden Number: A number in the 19-year cycle of the Moon, used in calculations for determining the date of Easter. (Approximately every 19 years, the Moon's phases occur on the same dates.) Add 1 to any given year and divide by 19; the remainder is the Golden Number. If there is no remainder, use 19.

Greatest Illuminated Extent (Gr. Illum. Ext.): When the maximum surface area of a planet is illuminated as seen from Earth.

Magnitude: A measure of a celestial object's brightness. **Apparent** magnitude measures the brightness of an object as seen from Earth.

(continued)

NEW PROSTATE PILL HELPS RELIEVE SYMPTOMS WITHOUT DRUGS OR SURGERY

Combats all-night bathroom urges and embarrassment... *Yet most doctors don't even know about it!*

By Health Writer, Peter Metler

Thanks to a brand new discovery made from a rare prostate relief plant; thousands of men across America are taking their lives back from "prostate hell". This remarkable new natural supplement helps you:

- **MINIMIZE** constant urges to urinate
- **END** embarrassing sexual "let-downs"
- **SUPPORT** a strong, healthy urine flow
- **GET** a restful night of uninterrupted sleep
- **STOP** false alarms, dribbles
- **ENJOY** a truly empty bladder

More men than ever before are dealing with prostate problems that range from annoying to downright EMBARRASSING! But now, research has discovered a new solution so remarkable that helps alleviate symptoms associated with an enlarged prostate (sexual failure, lost sleep, bladder discomfort and urgent runs to the bathroom). Like nothing before!

Yet 9 out of 10 doctors don't know about it! Here's why: Due to strict managed health care constrictions, many MD's are struggling to keep their practices afloat. "Unfortunately, there's no money in prescribing natural products. They aren't nearly as profitable," says a confidential source. Instead, doctors rely on toxic drugs that help, but could leave you sexually "powerless" (or a lot worse)!

On a CNN Special, Medical Correspondent Dr. Steve Salvatore shocked America by quoting a statistic from the prestigious Journal of American Medical Association that stated, "... about 60% of men who go under the knife for a prostatectomy are left UNABLE to perform sexually!"

PROSTATE PROBLEM SOLVED!

But now you can now beat the odds. And enjoy better sleep, a powerful urine stream and a long and healthy love life. The secret? You need to load your diet with essential Phyto-Nutrients, (traditionally found in certain fruits, vegetables and grains).

The problem is, most Phyto-Nutrients never get into your bloodstream. They're destroyed

HERE ARE 6 WARNING SIGNS YOU BETTER NOT IGNORE

✓ Waking up 2 to 6 times a night to urinate
✓ A constant feeling that you have to "go"... but can't
✓ A burning sensation when you do go
✓ A weak urine stream
✓ A feeling that your bladder is never completely empty
✓ Embarrassing sputtering, dripping & staining

by today's food preparation methods (cooking, long storage times and food additives).

YEARS OF RESEARCH

Thankfully, a small company (Wellness Logix™) out of Maine, is on a mission to change that. They've created a product that arms men who suffer with prostate inflammation with new hope. And it's fast becoming the #1 Prostate formula in America.

Prostate IQ™ gives men the super-concentrated dose of Phyto-Nutrients they need to beat prostate symptoms. "You just can't get them from your regular diet" say Daniel. It's taken a long time to understand how to capture the prostate relieving power of this amazing botanical. But their hard work paid off. *Prostate IQ*™ is different than any other prostate supplement on the market...

DON'T BE FOOLED BY CHEAP FORMULATIONS!

Many hope you won't notice, but a lot of prostate supplements fall embarrassingly short with their dosages. The formulas may be okay, but they won't do a darn thing for you unless you take 10 or more tablets a day. *Prostate IQ*™ contains a whopping 300mg of this special "Smart Prostate Plant". So it's loaded with Phyto-Nutrients. Plus, it gets inside your bloodstream faster and stays inside for maximum results!

TRY IT RISK-FREE

SPECIAL OPPORTUNITY

Get a risk-free trial supply of *Prostate IQ*™ today - just for asking. But you must act now, supplies are limited!

Call Now, Toll-Free at:

1-800-380-0925

THESE STATEMENTS HAVE NOT BEEN EVALUATED BY THE FDA. THESE PRODUCTS ARE NOT INTENDED TO DIAGNOSE, TREAT, CURE OR PREVENT ANY DISEASE.

Objects with an apparent magnitude of 6 or less are observable to the naked eye. The lower the magnitude, the greater the brightness. An object with a magnitude of –1, for example, is brighter than an object with a magnitude of +1. **Absolute** magnitude expresses how bright objects would appear if they were all the same distance (about 33 light-years) from Earth.

Midnight: Astronomically, the time when the Sun is opposite its highest point in the sky. Both 12 hours before and after noon (so, technically, both A.M. and P.M.), midnight in civil time is usually treated as the beginning of the day, rather than the end. It is typically displayed as 12:00 A.M. on 12-hour digital clocks. On a 24-hour time cycle, 00:00, rather than 24:00, usually indicates midnight.

Moon on Equator: The Moon is on the celestial equator.

Moon Rides High/Runs Low: The Moon is highest above or farthest below the celestial equator.

Moonrise/Moonset: When the Moon rises above or sets below the horizon.

Moon's Phases: The changing appearance of the Moon, caused by the different angles at which it is illuminated by the Sun. **First Quarter:** Right half of the Moon is illuminated. **Full:** The Sun and the Moon are in opposition; the entire disk of the Moon is illuminated. **Last Quarter:** Left half of the Moon is illuminated. **New:** The Sun and the Moon are in conjunction; the Moon is darkened because it lines up between Earth and the Sun.

Moon's Place, Astronomical: The position of the Moon within the constellations on the celestial sphere. **Astrological:** The position of the Moon within the tropical zodiac, whose twelve 30° segments (signs) along the ecliptic were named more than 2,000 years ago after constellations within each area. Because of precession and other factors, the zodiac signs no longer match actual constellation positions.

Morning Star: A planet that is above the eastern horizon at sunrise and less than 180° west of the Sun in right ascension.

Node: Either of the two points where a celestial body's orbit intersects the ecliptic. **Ascending:** When the body is moving from south to north of the ecliptic. **Descending:** When the body is moving from north to south of the ecliptic.

Opposition: The Moon or a planet appears on the opposite side of the sky from the Sun (elongation 180°).

Perigee (Perig.): The point in the Moon's orbit that is closest to Earth.

Perihelion (Perih.): The point in a planet's orbit that is closest to the Sun.

Precession: The slowly changing position of the stars and equinoxes in the sky caused by a slight wobble as Earth rotates around its axis.

Right Ascension (R.A.): The celestial longitude of an object in the sky, measured eastward along the celestial equator in hours of time from the vernal equinox; analogous to longitude on Earth.

Solar Cycle: In the Julian calendar, a period of 28 years, at the end of which the days of the month return to the same days of the week.

Solstice, Summer: When the Sun reaches its greatest declination (23½°) north of the celestial equator, around June 21. **Winter:** When the Sun reaches its greatest declination (23½°) south of the celestial equator, around December 21.

Stationary (Stat.): The brief period of apparent halted movement of a planet against the background of the stars shortly before it appears to move backward/westward (retrograde motion) or forward/eastward (direct motion).

Sun Fast/Slow: When a sundial reading is ahead of (fast) or behind (slow) clock time.

Sunrise/Sunset: The visible rising and setting of the upper edge of the Sun's disk across the unobstructed horizon of an observer whose eyes are 15 feet above ground level.

Twilight: For definitions of civil, nautical, and astronomical twilight, **see page 106.** ∎

24

STRANGE
THINGS
ABOUT THE
UNIVERSE

COMPILED BY BOB BERMAN

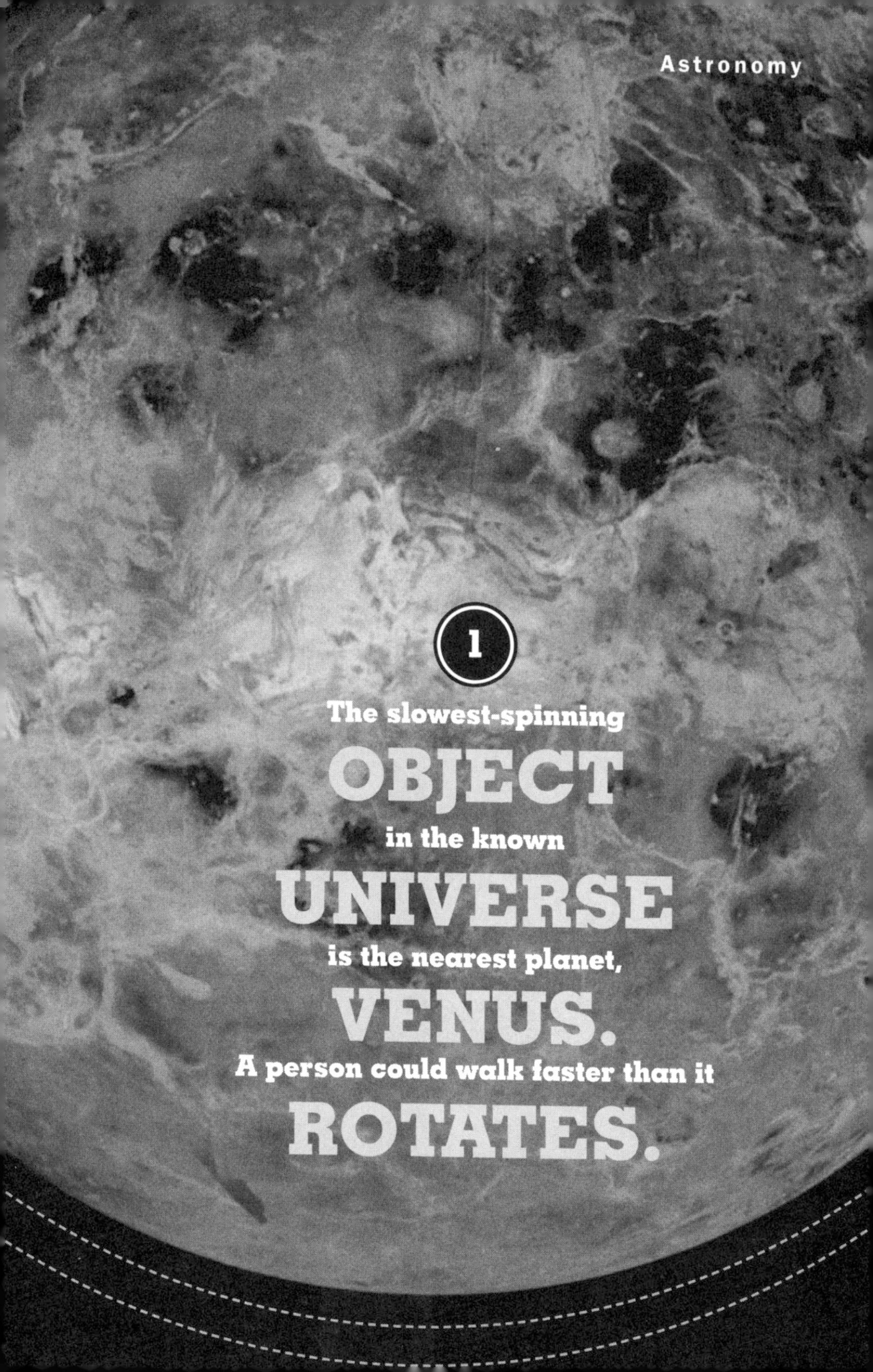

1

The slowest-spinning
OBJECT
in the known
UNIVERSE
is the nearest planet,
VENUS.
A person could walk faster than it
ROTATES.

The **density** of every neutron star is equivalent to what you would have after crushing a cruise ship until it's the size of the ball in a ballpoint pen.

The longest star name still in common usage is Libra's **Zubeneschamali.** The shortest is **Sun.**

Mid–19th century scientists found that **sunspots** increase and then fade out in an 11-year cycle. Other scientists knew that earthly compasses strangely fluctuate in the same 11-year period. Yet it was years before anyone put these ideas together and realized that the Sun intimately affects our world through magnetism.

The large dark blotches on the
MOON,
called mares or seas,
are all named for
WEATHER
events (Ocean of Storms) or
EMOTIONS
(Sea of Tranquility).

There's a separate "Earth" inside our planet: **Earth's core** is not liquid iron as was once believed, but a solid ball the size of Pluto—and it spins faster than the rest of our world.

The Sun's energy output is equivalent to the explosion of **91 billion 1-megaton** hydrogen bombs each second.

8

Astronomer **Percival Lowell** obsessively hunted for a ninth planet, "Planet X," in vain. However, it was discovered from his observatory in 1930 by **Clyde Tombaugh,** and this is one reason that the name Pluto was chosen to honor Lowell. The first two letters are his initials.

9

The rocky celestial body with the shortest life span is Mars's moon

PHOBOS.

The closest moon to any planet, it will crash into the Martian surface in

10 MILLION YEARS.

10

The first person who said that our planet moves was not Copernicus or Galileo. It was **Aristarchus of Samos.** This bearded genius was ignored for 18 centuries.

11

On a scale model in which Earth is a **dust mote,** the Sun would be one inch away and the size of the period at the end of this sentence. The nearest star would be another period 4¼ miles distant.

12

The most common object in the universe (possessing mass) is the **neutrino.** These tiny particles are more numerous than anything else by far. A trillion neutrinos fly through each of your fingernails every second.

(continued)   117

13

The universe is expanding, but no one knows how far. It has no outside or edge. The extent of the known **universe** is 38 to 47 billion light-years in every direction.

14

When observed in desert skies far from any city, there seem to be millions of **stars** visible to the naked eye. (The naked eye limit is about magnitude 5.8.) However, the actual number is about 2,600. You could count every star in 20 minutes at a leisurely rate of about two per second.

15

The **nuclear fusion** that produces the Sun's heat and light occurs in its innermost quarter, a tiny "sun within the Sun." The surface we see is merely where the energy escapes.

16

The largest storm in the known universe is Jupiter's **Great Red Spot,** a hurricane that is three times the width of Earth and floats 5 miles above Jupiter's surface.

17

Galileo was the first person to see

SATURN'S RINGS,

but his telescopes were so poor that he believed to his dying day that the rings were attached

HANDLES,

like those on a teacup.

18

In addition to white, stars are colored red, orange, blue, violet, yellow, brown, even black. The single missing hue is **green.**

(continued)

TECHNOLOGY SIMPLIFIED – BIGGER AND BETTER

Wow! A Simple to Use Computer Designed Especially for Seniors!

Easy to read. Easy to see. Easy to use. Just plug it in!

FREE Automatic Software Updates

There is finally a computer that's designed for simplicity and ease of use. It's the WOW Computer, and it was designed with you in mind. This computer is easy-to-use, worry-free and literally puts the world at your fingertips. From the moment you open the box, you'll realize how different the WOW Computer is. The components are all connected; all you do is plug it into an outlet and your high-speed Internet connection. Then you'll see the screen – it's now 22 inches. This is a completely new touch screen system, without the cluttered look of the normal computer screen. The "buttons" on the screen are easy to see and easy to understand. All you do is touch one of them, from the Web, Email, Calendar to Games– you name it… and a new screen opens up. It's so easy to use you won't have to ask your children or grandchildren for help. Until now the very people who could benefit most from E-mail and the Internet are the ones that have had the hardest time accessing it. Now, thanks to the WOW Computer, countless older Americans are discovering the wonderful world of the Internet every day. Isn't it time you took part? Call now, and a patient, knowledgeable product expert will tell you how you can try it in your home for 30 days. If you are not totally satisfied, simply return it within 30 days for a refund of the product purchase price. Call today.

Call now toll free and find out how you can get the new WOW! Computer.

Mention promotional code 48057 for special introductory pricing.

1-877-794-5386

80992

19

The fastest twirling objects in the universe are **pulsars** (tiny stars). Since 1982, some 200 have been discovered. The fastest-spinning of these turns 716 times per second. (The second fastest spins 641 times per second.) From a pulsar's surface, other stars would appear not as dots but as white lines in the sky.

20

The first of a new type of celestial object—**asteroids**—was discovered on January 1, 1801.

23

Half of the

MOON

is composed of a single element, the same one that makes up two-thirds of your body weight:

OXYGEN.

21

Neptune has the strongest **winds** in the solar system. Its air howls at 1,300 miles per hour, four times faster than Earth's fiercest tornadoes.

24

After the Moon is struck by a **meteoroid** or falling spacecraft, it vibrates for hours. ∎

22

The universe's second most abundant element, **helium,** is the only one that never freezes solid.

Bob Berman is the director of Overlook Obervatory in Woodstock and Storm King Observatory in Cornwall, both in New York.

Teach Your Brain How to Remember Again – with Just a Simple Pill

Are you tired of feeling "foggy"... absent-minded... or confused? Find out how some people stay sharp and mentally focused - even at age 90!

By Steven Wuzubia, Health Correspondent;

Clearwater, Florida:

Nothing's more frustrating than when you forget names... misplace your keys... or just feel "a little confused". And even though your foggy memory gets laughed off as just another "senior moment", it's not very funny when it keeps happening to you. Like gray hair and reading glasses... some people accept their memory loss as just a part of getting older. But it doesn't have to be that way.

Today, people in their 70's, 80's even their 90's... are staying mentally fit, focused and "fog-free". So what do they know that you don't?

THE SECRET TO UNLOCK YOUR BRAIN

A tiny pill called Lipogen PS Plus, made exclusively in Israel, is an incredible supplement that feeds your brain the nutrients it needs to stay healthy. Developed by Dr. Meir Shinitzky, Ph.D., former visiting professor at Duke University, and recipient of the prestigious J.F. Kennedy Prize.

Dr. Shinitzky explains: "Science has shown, when your brain nutrient levels drop, you can start to experience memory problems. Your ability to concentrate and stay focused becomes compromised. And gradually, a "mental fog" sets in. It can damage every aspect of your life".

In recent years, researchers identified the importance of a remarkable compound called phosphatidylserine (PS). It's the key ingredient in Lipogen. And crucial to your ability to learn and remember things as you age.

OFFICIALLY REVIEWED BY THE U.S. FOOD AND DRUG ADMINISTRATION:

Lipogen safety has been reviewed by the Food & Drug Administration. Lipogen is the **ONLY** Health Supplement that has a "Qualified Health Claim for both **Cognitive Dysfunction** and **Dementia**".

SIGNIFICANT IMPROVEMENTS

In 1992, doctors tested phosphatidylserine on a select group of people aged 60-80 years old. Their test scores showed impressive memory

MY MEMORY WAS STARTING TO FAIL ME.

I'd forget all kinds of things and my memory was becoming pretty unreliable. Something I just said would completely slip my mind and I was worried about it. I read about Lipogen and wanted to try it. After a few weeks, I noticed I wasn't forgetting things anymore. It's great! I have actual recall, which is super! Thanks Lipogen for giving me my memory back.
- *Ethel Macagnoney*

improvement. Test subjects could remember more and were more mentally alert. But doctors noticed something else. The group taking phosphatidylserine, not only enjoyed sharper memory, but were also more upbeat and remarkably happy.

YOUR MEMORY UNLEASHED!

Lipogen is an impressive fusion of the most powerful, natural memory compounds on Earth. It produces amazing results, especially for people who have tried everything to improve their memory before, but failed. Lipogen gives your brain the vital boost it needs to jump-start your focus and mental clarity. "It truly is a godsend!" says Shinitzky.

"SEE FOR YOURSELF" RISK-FREE SUPPLY

We've made special arrangements with the distributor of Lipogen PS Plus to offer you a "Readers Only Discount". This trial is 100% Risk-Free. It's a terrific deal. If Lipogen PS Plus doesn't help you think better, remember more, and improve your mind, clarity and mood – you won't pay a penny! (less S&H).

So don't wait. Now you can join the thousands of people who think better, remember more, and enjoy clear, "fog-free" memory. Think of it as making a "wake-up call" to your brain.

Call Now, Toll-Free!
1-800-609-3558

2014

January
S	M	T	W	T	F	S
			1	2	3	4
5	6	7	8	9	10	11
12	13	14	15	16	17	18
19	20	21	22	23	24	25
26	27	28	29	30	31	

February
S	M	T	W	T	F	S
						1
2	3	4	5	6	7	8
9	10	11	12	13	14	15
16	17	18	19	20	21	22
23	24	25	26	27	28	

March
S	M	T	W	T	F	S
						1
2	3	4	5	6	7	8
9	10	11	12	13	14	15
16	17	18	19	20	21	22
23	24	25	26	27	28	29
30	31					

April
S	M	T	W	T	F	S
		1	2	3	4	5
6	7	8	9	10	11	12
13	14	15	16	17	18	19
20	21	22	23	24	25	26
27	28	29	30			

May
S	M	T	W	T	F	S
				1	2	3
4	5	6	7	8	9	10
11	12	13	14	15	16	17
18	19	20	21	22	23	24
25	26	27	28	29	30	31

June
S	M	T	W	T	F	S
1	2	3	4	5	6	7
8	9	10	11	12	13	14
15	16	17	18	19	20	21
22	23	24	25	26	27	28
29	30					

July
S	M	T	W	T	F	S
		1	2	3	4	5
6	7	8	9	10	11	12
13	14	15	16	17	18	19
20	21	22	23	24	25	26
27	28	29	30	31		

August
S	M	T	W	T	F	S
					1	2
3	4	5	6	7	8	9
10	11	12	13	14	15	16
17	18	19	20	21	22	23
24	25	26	27	28	29	30
31						

September
S	M	T	W	T	F	S
	1	2	3	4	5	6
7	8	9	10	11	12	13
14	15	16	17	18	19	20
21	22	23	24	25	26	27
28	29	30				

October
S	M	T	W	T	F	S
			1	2	3	4
5	6	7	8	9	10	11
12	13	14	15	16	17	18
19	20	21	22	23	24	25
26	27	28	29	30	31	

November
S	M	T	W	T	F	S
						1
2	3	4	5	6	7	8
9	10	11	12	13	14	15
16	17	18	19	20	21	22
23	24	25	26	27	28	29
30						

December
S	M	T	W	T	F	S
	1	2	3	4	5	6
7	8	9	10	11	12	13
14	15	16	17	18	19	20
21	22	23	24	25	26	27
28	29	30	31			

2015

January
S	M	T	W	T	F	S
				1	2	3
4	5	6	7	8	9	10
11	12	13	14	15	16	17
18	19	20	21	22	23	24
25	26	27	28	29	30	31

February
S	M	T	W	T	F	S
1	2	3	4	5	6	7
8	9	10	11	12	13	14
15	16	17	18	19	20	21
22	23	24	25	26	27	28

March
S	M	T	W	T	F	S
1	2	3	4	5	6	7
8	9	10	11	12	13	14
15	16	17	18	19	20	21
22	23	24	25	26	27	28
29	30	31				

April
S	M	T	W	T	F	S
			1	2	3	4
5	6	7	8	9	10	11
12	13	14	15	16	17	18
19	20	21	22	23	24	25
26	27	28	29	30		

May
S	M	T	W	T	F	S
					1	2
3	4	5	6	7	8	9
10	11	12	13	14	15	16
17	18	19	20	21	22	23
24	25	26	27	28	29	30
31						

June
S	M	T	W	T	F	S
	1	2	3	4	5	6
7	8	9	10	11	12	13
14	15	16	17	18	19	20
21	22	23	24	25	26	27
28	29	30				

July
S	M	T	W	T	F	S
			1	2	3	4
5	6	7	8	9	10	11
12	13	14	15	16	17	18
19	20	21	22	23	24	25
26	27	28	29	30	31	

August
S	M	T	W	T	F	S
						1
2	3	4	5	6	7	8
9	10	11	12	13	14	15
16	17	18	19	20	21	22
23	24	25	26	27	28	29
30	31					

September
S	M	T	W	T	F	S
		1	2	3	4	5
6	7	8	9	10	11	12
13	14	15	16	17	18	19
20	21	22	23	24	25	26
27	28	29	30			

October
S	M	T	W	T	F	S
				1	2	3
4	5	6	7	8	9	10
11	12	13	14	15	16	17
18	19	20	21	22	23	24
25	26	27	28	29	30	31

November
S	M	T	W	T	F	S
1	2	3	4	5	6	7
8	9	10	11	12	13	14
15	16	17	18	19	20	21
22	23	24	25	26	27	28
29	30					

December
S	M	T	W	T	F	S
		1	2	3	4	5
6	7	8	9	10	11	12
13	14	15	16	17	18	19
20	21	22	23	24	25	26
27	28	29	30	31		

2016

January
S	M	T	W	T	F	S
					1	2
3	4	5	6	7	8	9
10	11	12	13	14	15	16
17	18	19	20	21	22	23
24	25	26	27	28	29	30
31						

February
S	M	T	W	T	F	S
	1	2	3	4	5	6
7	8	9	10	11	12	13
14	15	16	17	18	19	20
21	22	23	24	25	26	27
28	29					

March
S	M	T	W	T	F	S
		1	2	3	4	5
6	7	8	9	10	11	12
13	14	15	16	17	18	19
20	21	22	23	24	25	26
27	28	29	30	31		

April
S	M	T	W	T	F	S
					1	2
3	4	5	6	7	8	9
10	11	12	13	14	15	16
17	18	19	20	21	22	23
24	25	26	27	28	29	30

May
S	M	T	W	T	F	S
1	2	3	4	5	6	7
8	9	10	11	12	13	14
15	16	17	18	19	20	21
22	23	24	25	26	27	28
29	30	31				

June
S	M	T	W	T	F	S
			1	2	3	4
5	6	7	8	9	10	11
12	13	14	15	16	17	18
19	20	21	22	23	24	25
26	27	28	29	30		

July
S	M	T	W	T	F	S
					1	2
3	4	5	6	7	8	9
10	11	12	13	14	15	16
17	18	19	20	21	22	23
24	25	26	27	28	29	30
31						

August
S	M	T	W	T	F	S
	1	2	3	4	5	6
7	8	9	10	11	12	13
14	15	16	17	18	19	20
21	22	23	24	25	26	27
28	29	30	31			

September
S	M	T	W	T	F	S
				1	2	3
4	5	6	7	8	9	10
11	12	13	14	15	16	17
18	19	20	21	22	23	24
25	26	27	28	29	30	

October
S	M	T	W	T	F	S
						1
2	3	4	5	6	7	8
9	10	11	12	13	14	15
16	17	18	19	20	21	22
23	24	25	26	27	28	29
30	31					

November
S	M	T	W	T	F	S
		1	2	3	4	5
6	7	8	9	10	11	12
13	14	15	16	17	18	19
20	21	22	23	24	25	26
27	28	29	30			

December
S	M	T	W	T	F	S
				1	2	3
4	5	6	7	8	9	10
11	12	13	14	15	16	17
18	19	20	21	22	23	24
25	26	27	28	29	30	31

Love calendar lore? Find more at Almanac.com.

How to Use This Almanac

The Calendar Pages (128–155) are the heart of *The Old Farmer's Almanac*. They present sky sightings and astronomical data for the entire year and are what make this book a true almanac, a "calendar of the heavens." In essence, these pages are unchanged since 1792, when Robert B. Thomas published his first edition. The long columns of numbers and symbols reveal all of nature's precision, rhythm, and glory, providing an astronomical look at the year 2015.

–Beth Krommes

Why We Have Seasons

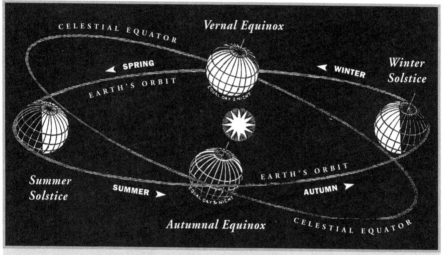

THE SEASONS OF 2015

Vernal equinox ... March 20, 6:45 P.M. EDT
Summer solstice .. June 21, 12:38 P.M. EDT

Autumnal equinox .. Sept. 23, 4:21 A.M. EDT
Winter solstice .... Dec. 21, 11:48 P.M. EST

■ The seasons occur because as Earth revolves around the Sun, its axis remains tilted at 23.5 degrees from the perpendicular. This tilt causes different latitudes on Earth to receive varying amounts of sunlight throughout the year.

In the Northern Hemisphere, the summer solstice marks the beginning of summer and occurs when the North Pole is tilted toward the Sun. The winter solstice marks the beginning of winter and occurs when the North Pole is tilted away from the Sun.

The equinoxes occur when the hemispheres equally face the Sun. At this time, the Sun rises due east and sets due west. The vernal equinox marks the beginning of spring; the autumnal equinox marks the beginning of autumn.

In the Southern Hemisphere, the seasons are the reverse of those in the Northern Hemisphere. **(continued)**

The Left-Hand Calendar Pages • 128–154

The **Left-Hand Calendar Pages** contain sky highlights, daily Sun and Moon rise and set times, the length of day, high tide times, the Moon's astronomical place and age, and more for Boston. Examples of how to calculate astronomical times for your location are shown below.

A SAMPLE MONTH

SKY WATCH ☆ *The box at the top of each Left-Hand Calendar Page describes the best times to view celestial highlights, including conjunctions, meteor showers, and planets. The dates on which select astronomical events occur appear on the Right-Hand Calendar Pages.*

1 2 3 4 5 6 7 8

Get these pages with times set to your zip code at Almanac.com/Access.

Day of Year	Day of Month	Day of Week	☼ Rises h. m.	Rise Key	☼ Sets h. m.	Set Key	Length of Day h. m.	Sun Fast m.	Declination of Sun ° '	High Tide Times Boston	☾ Rises h. m.	Rise Key	☾ Sets h. m.	Set Key	☾ Astron. Place	Age
1	1	Th.	7:13	E	4:22	A	9 09	12	22 s.58	7¾ 8½	1:54	B	3:36	E	TAU	11
2	2	Fr.	7:13	E	4:23	A	9 10	12	22 53	8¾ 9½	2:40	B	4:36	E	TAU	12
3	3	Sa.	7:13	E	4:23	A	9 10	11	22 48	9½ 10¾	3:30	B	5:31	E	TAU	13

1 To calculate the sunrise time for your locale: Note the Sun Rise Key letter on the chosen day. In the **Time Corrections** table on **page 252**, find your city or the city nearest you. Add or subtract the minutes that correspond to the Sun Rise Key letter to/from the sunrise time given for Boston.

EXAMPLE:

■ To calculate the time of sunrise in Denver, Colorado, on the first day of the month:

Sunrise, Boston, with Key letter E (above)	7:13 A.M. EST
Value of Key letter E for Denver (p. 252)	+ 7 minutes
Sunrise, Denver	7:20 A.M. MST

Use the same procedure with Boston's sunset time and the Sun Set Key letter value to calculate the time of sunset in your locale.

2 To calculate the length of day for your locale: Note the Sun Rise and Sun Set Key letters on the chosen day. In the **Time Corrections** table on **page 252**, find your city. Add or subtract the minutes that correspond to the Sun Set Key letter to/from Boston's length of day. *Reverse* the sign (minus to plus, or plus to minus) of the Sun Rise Key letter minutes. Add or subtract it to/from the first result.

EXAMPLE:

■ To calculate the length of day in Richmond, Virginia, on the first day of the month:

Length of day, Boston (above)	9h. 09m.
Sunset Key letter A for Richmond (p. 256)	+ 41m.
	9h. 50m.
Reverse sunrise Key letter E for Richmond (p. 256, +11 to −11)	− 11m.
Length of day, Richmond	9h. 39m.

3 Use the Sun Fast column to change sundial time to clock time. A sundial reads natural, or Sun, time, which is neither Standard nor Daylight time. To calculate clock time on a sundial in Boston, subtract the minutes given in this column; add the minutes when preceded by an asterisk [*]. To convert the time to your city, use Key letter C in the table on **page 252**.

ATTENTION, READERS: *All times given in this edition of the Almanac are for Boston, Massachusetts, and are in Eastern Standard Time (EST), except from 2:00 A.M., March 8, until 2:00 A.M., November 1, when Eastern Daylight Time (EDT) is given.*

E X A M P L E :

■ To change sundial time to clock time in Boston, or, for example, in Salem, Oregon:

Sundial reading (Boston or Salem)	12:00 noon
Subtract Sun Fast (p. 124)	– 12 minutes
Clock time, Boston	**11:48 A.M. EST**
Use Key letter C for Salem (p. 255)	+ 27 minutes
Clock time, Salem	**12:15 P.M. PST**

4 This column gives the degrees and minutes of the Sun from the celestial equator at noon EST or EDT.

5 This column gives the approximate times of high tides in Boston. For example, the first high tide occurs at 7:45 A.M. and the second occurs at 8:30 P.M. the same day. (A dash indicates that high tide occurs on or after midnight and is recorded on the next day.) Figures for calculating high tide times and heights for localities other than Boston are given in the **Tide Corrections** table on **page 250**.

6 To calculate the moonrise time for your locale: Note the Moon Rise Key letter on the chosen day. Find your city on **page 252**. Add or subtract the minutes that correspond to the Moon Rise Key letter to/from the moonrise time given for Boston. (A dash indicates that the moonrise occurs on or after midnight and is recorded on the next day.) Find the longitude of your city on **page 252**. Add a correction in minutes for your city's longitude (see table, above right).

–Beth Krommes

➡ Get the Left-Hand Calendar Pages with times set to your zip code at **Almanac.com/Access**.

Longitude of city	Correction minutes
58°–76°	0
77°–89°	+1
90°–102°	+2
103°–115°	+3
116°–127°	+4
128°–141°	+5
142°–155°	+6

E X A M P L E :

■ To calculate the time of moonrise in Lansing, Michigan, on the first day of the month:

Moonrise, Boston, with Key letter B (p. 124)	1:54 P.M. EST
Value of Key letter B for Lansing (p. 254)	+ 53 minutes
Correction for Lansing longitude, 84° 33'	+ 1 minute
Moonrise, Lansing	**2:48 P.M. EST**

Use the same procedure with Boston's moonset time and the Moon Set Key letter value to calculate the time of moonset in your locale.

7 The Moon's Place is its *astronomical* placement in the heavens at midnight. Do not confuse this with the Moon's *astrological* place in the zodiac. All calculations in this Almanac are based on astronomy, not astrology, except for those on **pages 244, 246–247**.

In addition to the 12 constellations of the zodiac, this column may indicate these: Auriga **(AUR)**, a northern constellation between Perseus and Gemini; Cetus **(CET)**, which lies south of the zodiac, just south of Pisces and Aries; Ophiuchus **(OPH)**, a constellation primarily north of the zodiac but with a small corner between Scorpius and Sagittarius; Orion **(ORI)**, a constellation whose northern limit first reaches the zodiac between Taurus and Gemini; and Sextans **(SEX)**, which lies south of the zodiac except for a corner that just touches it near Leo.

8 The last column gives the Moon's Age, which is the number of days since the previous new Moon. (The average length of the lunar month is 29.53 days.) **(continued)**

THE OLD FARMER'S ALMANAC

The Right-Hand Calendar Pages • 129–155

A SAMPLE MONTH

- Weather prediction rhyme.
- Symbols for notable celestial events. (See opposite page for explanations.)
- Proverbs, poems, and adages generally appear in this font.
- Sundays and special holy days generally appear in this font.
- The bold letter is the Dominical Letter (from A to G), a traditional ecclesiastical designation for Sunday determined by the date on which the first Sunday falls. For 2015, the Dominical Letter is **D**.
- Noteworthy historical events, folklore, and legends appear in this font.
- High tide heights, in feet, at Boston, Massachusetts.
- Civil holidays and astronomical events appear in this font.
- Religious feasts generally appear in this font. A [T] indicates a major feast that the church has this year temporarily transferred to a date other than its usual one.

Day of Month	Day of Week	Dates, Feasts, Fasts, Aspects, Tide Heights	Weather
1	Th.	New Year's Day • Holy Name • First Rose Bowl football game, 1902	*Hours*
2	Fr.	Kenneth Brugger and Cathy Aguado discovered first winter refuge of monarch butterflies, Mexico, 1975 • {10.6 / 9.3	*and*
3	Sa.	☾ RIDES HIGH • ☌♇☉ • First covered skating rink in Canada opened, Halifax, N.S., 1863	*hours*
4	**D**	2nd S. af. Ch. • Full Wolf ○ • ⊕ AT PERIHELION • {10.6 / 9.4	*of*
5	M.	Twelfth Night • First successful photo of aurora, by physicist Martin Brendel, 1892 • Tides {10.6 / 9.4	*snow*
6	Tu.	Epiphany • George Washington married Martha Dandridge Custis, 1759 • {10.5 / —	*showers;*
7	W.	Distaff Day • *Partly work and partly play, Ye must on St Distaff's Day.* • Tides {9.4 / 10.3	*feeling*
8	Th.	☌♃☾ • First U.S. State of the Union address, 1790	*more*
9	Fr.	☾ AT APO. • Geneticist Sir Alec Jeffreys born, 1950 • {9.2 / 9.7	*like*
10	Sa.	☾ ON EQ. • RCA introduced 45-rpm vinyl record format, 1949 • {9.1 / 9.4	*Labrador!*
11	**D**	1st S. af. Ep. • Canadian prime minister Sir John A. Macdonald born, 1815	*High*
12	M.	Plough Monday • ☾ AT ☊ • French haute cuisine founder Marie-Antoine Carême died, 1833	*times*
13	Tu.	St. Hilary • Mickey Mouse comic strip debuted in newspapers, 1930 • {9.0 / 8.4	*for*
14	W.	☿ GR. ELONG. (19° EAST) • Rare black rhino born, St. Louis Zoo, Mo., 2011 • Tides {9.1 / 8.3	*snow-*
15	Th.	First U.S. all-glass windowless structure completed, Toledo, Ohio, 1936 • Tides {9.3 / 8.4	*drifts*
16	Fr.	☌♄☾ • 121.5-lb. blue catfish caught, Lake Texoma, Tex., 2004 • Tides {9.6 / 8.6	*and*
17	Sa.	U.S. statesman Benjamin Franklin born, 1706 • Tides {10.1 / 9.0	*ski*
18	**D**	2nd S. af. Ep. • ☾ RUNS LOW • Meteorite fell into doctor's office, Lorton, Va., 2010	*lifts.*
19	M.	**Martin Luther King Jr.'s Birthday (observed)** • ☌♂♆ • ☌♇☾	*Raining,*
20	Tu.	New ● • ☿ STAT. • *A north wind with new Moon will hold until the full.*	*temperatures*
21	W.	☾ AT PERIG. • ☌☿☾ • ☌♀☾ • {11.9 / —	*gaining.*
22	Th.	St. Vincent • ☌♂☾ • ☌♆☾ • Tides {10.8 / 12.0	*Mercy's*
23	Fr.	Envelope machine patented, 1849 • 13.4" snow, Boston, 2005 • Tides {11.0 / 11.8	*sakes:*
24	Sa.	☾ ON EQ. • U.S. Supreme Court justice Thurgood Marshall died, 1993 • Tides {11.1 / 11.4	*Sunny*
25	**D**	3rd S. af. Ep. • ☾ AT ☋ • ☌⛢☾ • {11.0 / 10.8	*breaks*
26	M.	Conversion of Paul[T] • *It's no use boiling your cabbage twice.* • Tides {10.8 / 10.1	*make*

☞ **For explanations of Almanac terms, see the glossaries on pages 110, 157, and 158.**

Predicting Earthquakes

■ Note the dates in the **Right-Hand Calendar Pages** when the Moon rides high or runs low. The date of the high begins the most likely 5-day period of earthquakes in the Northern Hemisphere; the date of the low indicates a similar 5-day period in the Southern Hemisphere. Also noted are the 2 days each month when the Moon is on the celestial equator, indicating the most likely time for earthquakes in either hemisphere.

–Beth Krommes

■ Throughout the **Right-Hand Calendar Pages** are groups of symbols that represent notable celestial events. The symbols and names of the principal planets and aspects are:

☉	**Sun**	♆	**Neptune**
○●☾	**Moon**	♇	**Pluto**
☿	**Mercury**	☌	**Conjunction (on the same celestial longitude)**
♀	**Venus**		
⊕	**Earth**		
♂	**Mars**	☊	**Ascending node**
♃	**Jupiter**	☋	**Descending node**
♄	**Saturn**	☍	**Opposition (180 degrees from Sun)**
⛢	**Uranus**		

EXAMPLE:

☌♇☉ on the 3rd day of the month (see opposite page) means that on that date a conjunction (☌) of Pluto (♇) and the Sun (☉) occurs: They are aligned along the same celestial longitude and appear to be closest together in the sky.

EARTH AT PERIHELION AND APHELION

■ Perihelion: January 4, 2015. Earth will be 91,401,423 miles from the Sun. Aphelion: July 6, 2015. Earth will be 94,506,589 miles from the Sun.

2015 Calendar Highlights

MOVABLE RELIGIOUS OBSERVANCES

Septuagesima Sunday	**February 1**
Shrove Tuesday	**February 17**
Ash Wednesday	**February 18**
Palm Sunday	**March 29**
Good Friday	**April 3**
First day of Passover	**April 4**
Easter	**April 5**
Orthodox Easter	**April 12**
Rogation Sunday	**May 10**
Ascension Day	**May 14**
Whitsunday–Pentecost	**May 24**
Trinity Sunday	**May 31**
Corpus Christi	**June 7**
First day of Ramadan	**June 18**
Rosh Hashanah	**September 14**
Yom Kippur	**September 23**
First Sunday of Advent	**November 29**
First day of Chanukah	**December 7**

CHRONOLOGICAL CYCLES

Dominical Letter	**D**
Epact	**10**
Golden Number (Lunar Cycle)	**2**
Roman Indiction	**8**
Solar Cycle	**8**
Year of Julian Period	**6728**

–Beth Krommes

ERAS

Era	Year	Begins
Byzantine	**7524**	September 14
Jewish (A.M.)*	**5776**	September 14
Chinese (Lunar) [Year of the Sheep or Goat]	**4713**	February 19
Roman (A.U.C.)	**2768**	January 14
Nabonassar	**2764**	April 20
Japanese	**2675**	January 1
Grecian (Seleucidae)	**2327**	September 14 (or October 14)
Indian (Saka)	**1937**	March 22
Diocletian	**1732**	September 12
Islamic (Hegira)*	**1437**	October 15

**Year begins at sunset the evening before.*

THE ELEVENTH MONTH • 2014

SKY WATCH ☆ *Mercury has its best morning star apparition during the first 10 days of the month, 10 degrees above the eastern horizon 40 minutes before sunrise. With Venus and Saturn gone and Mars dim and low in Sagittarius, the action shifts to reappearing, brightening Jupiter, now in Leo, where the planet rises at around 11:00 P.M. in midmonth and is visible for more than half the night. The Moon is to its right on the 13th. Also at midmonth, Orion rises by 9:00 P.M., with Sirius, the Dog Star, up an hour later, introducing the brilliant stars of the cold season. A crowd surrounds the Sun on the 22nd: the Moon, Saturn, Mercury, and Venus, all tightly clustered but unseen in the solar glare.*

○	**Full Moon**	6th day	17th hour	23rd minute
◑	**Last Quarter**	14th day	10th hour	15th minute
●	**New Moon**	22nd day	7th hour	32nd minute
◐	**First Quarter**	29th day	5th hour	6th minute

After 2:00 A.M. on November 2, Eastern Standard Time is given.

Get these pages with times set to your zip code at Almanac.com/Access.

Day of Year	Day of Month	Day of Week	☼ Rises h. m.	Rise Key	☼ Sets h. m.	Set Key	Length of Day h. m.	Sun Fast m.	Declination of Sun ° '	High Tide Times Boston		☾ Rises h. m.	Rise Key	☾ Sets h. m.	Set Key	☾ Astron. Place	☾ Age
305	1	Sa.	7:17	D	**5:37**	B	10 20	32	14 s. 33	6½	**6¾**	**2:35**	D	1:01	C	CAP	9
306	2	**E**	6:18	D	**4:36**	B	10 18	32	14 52	6½	**7**	**2:11**	D	1:11	D	AQU	10
307	3	M.	6:19	D	**4:35**	B	10 16	32	15 11	7½	**8**	**2:45**	C	2:22	D	PSC	11
308	4	Tu.	6:21	E	**4:33**	B	10 12	32	15 29	8½	**9**	**3:21**	C	3:32	E	PSC	12
309	5	W.	6:22	E	**4:32**	B	10 10	32	15 47	9¼	**9¾**	**3:57**	C	4:42	E	PSC	13
310	6	Th.	6:23	E	**4:31**	B	10 08	32	16 05	10	**10¾**	**4:37**	C	5:51	E	ARI	14
311	7	Fr.	6:24	E	**4:30**	B	10 06	32	16 23	11	**11½**	**5:20**	B	6:58	E	ARI	15
312	8	Sa.	6:26	E	**4:29**	B	10 03	32	16 41	11¾	—	**6:07**	B	8:00	E	TAU	16
313	9	**E**	6:27	E	**4:28**	B	10 01	32	16 58	12¼	**12½**	**6:57**	B	8:57	E	TAU	17
314	10	M.	6:28	E	**4:27**	B	9 59	32	17 15	1	**1¼**	**7:51**	B	9:49	E	ORI	18
315	11	Tu.	6:29	E	**4:26**	B	9 57	32	17 31	1¾	**2**	**8:46**	C	10:34	E	GEM	19
316	12	W.	6:31	E	**4:25**	B	9 54	32	17 47	2¾	**2¾**	**9:42**	C	11:14	E	GEM	20
317	13	Th.	6:32	E	**4:24**	B	9 52	31	18 03	3½	**3¾**	**10:39**	C	11:49	E	CAN	21
318	14	Fr.	6:33	E	**4:23**	B	9 50	31	18 19	4¼	**4½**	**11:35**	C	**12:21**	D	CAN	22
319	15	Sa.	6:34	E	**4:22**	B	9 48	31	18 34	5¼	**5½**	—	–	**12:50**	D	LEO	23
320	16	**E**	6:36	E	**4:21**	B	9 45	31	18 49	6	**6½**	12:32	D	**1:19**	D	SEX	24
321	17	M.	6:37	E	**4:20**	B	9 43	31	19 04	7	**7¼**	1:30	D	**1:47**	D	LEO	25
322	18	Tu.	6:38	E	**4:19**	B	9 41	31	19 18	7¾	**8¼**	2:28	D	**2:16**	C	VIR	26
323	19	W.	6:39	E	**4:18**	B	9 39	30	19 32	8½	**9**	3:28	E	**2:47**	C	VIR	27
324	20	Th.	6:41	E	**4:18**	B	9 37	30	19 46	9¼	**9¾**	4:30	E	**3:22**	C	VIR	28
325	21	Fr.	6:42	E	**4:17**	A	9 35	30	19 59	10	**10½**	5:32	E	**4:01**	B	LIB	29
326	22	Sa.	6:43	E	**4:16**	A	9 33	30	20 12	10½	**11¼**	6:35	E	**4:45**	B	LIB	0
327	23	**E**	6:44	E	**4:16**	A	9 32	29	20 25	11¼	12	7:37	E	**5:37**	B	OPH	1
328	24	M.	6:45	E	**4:15**	A	9 30	29	20 37	**12**	—	8:35	E	**6:34**	B	OPH	2
329	25	Tu.	6:46	E	**4:15**	A	9 29	29	20 49	12¾	**12¾**	9:28	E	**7:37**	C	SAG	3
330	26	W.	6:48	E	**4:14**	A	9 26	28	21 00	1½	**1¾**	10:16	E	**8:44**	C	SAG	4
331	27	Th.	6:49	E	**4:14**	A	9 25	28	21 11	2¼	**2½**	10:59	E	**9:53**	C	CAP	5
332	28	Fr.	6:50	E	**4:13**	A	9 23	28	21 22	3¼	**3½**	11:37	D	**11:02**	D	AQU	6
333	29	Sa.	6:51	E	**4:13**	A	9 22	27	21 32	4¼	**4½**	**12:13**	D	—	–	AQU	7
334	30	**E**	6:52	E	**4:12**	A	9 20	27	21 s. 42	5¼	**5½**	**12:47**	D	12:12	D	PSC	8

 To use this page, see p. 124; for Key letters, see p. 252. ☞ **Bold = P.M.** ☞ Light = A.M.

NOVEMBER HATH 30 DAYS • 2014

November, month of mornings misty-bright
With golden light. –Mortimer Collins

Day of Month	Day of Week	Dates, Feasts, Fasts, Aspects, Tide Heights	Weather
1	Sa.	All Saints' • Sadie Hawkins Day • ☌♆☾ • ☿ GR. ELONG. (19° WEST)	*Mild*
2	E	21st S. af. P. • Daylight Saving Time ends, 2:00 A.M. • ☾ AT PERIG.	*retreat*
3	M.	All Souls'[T] • ☾ ON EQ. • Mary Jacob received patent for a brassiere, 1914 • {10.6 / 10.5	*means*
4	Tu.	Election Day • ☾ AT ☋ • ☌♅☾ • Tides {11.0 / 10.6	*muddy*
5	W.	U.S. president Franklin D. Roosevelt reelected to third term in office, 1940 • Tides {11.4 / 10.7	*feet.*
6	Th.	Full Beaver ○ • Black bears head to winter dens now. • {11.6 / 10.7	*Enjoy*
7	Fr.	98-mph winds, Block Island, R.I., 1953 • Tides {11.7 / 10.5	*the*
8	Sa.	Royal Canadian Mint ordered to change 12-sided nickel back to round shape, 1962 • Tides {11.5 / —	*sunshine*
9	E	22nd S. af. P. • ☾ RIDES HIGH • Abolitionist Elijah Parish Lovejoy born, 1802	*while*
10	M.	☌♂♇ • Jeweler Harry Winston donated Hope Diamond to Smithsonian, D.C., 1958 • {9.9 / 10.8	*it*
11	Tu.	St. Martin of Tours • Veterans Day • 83°F day/17°F night, Oklahoma City, Okla., 1911	*lasts:*
12	W.	Indian Summer • Lobsters move to offshore waters. • {9.2 / 9.8	*piles of*
13	Th.	☌♀♄ • Thousands of meteors fell per hour, eastern U.S., 1833 • Tides {8.9 / 9.4	*snow*
14	Fr.	☾ AT APO. • ☌♃☾ • Jean Drapeau became mayor of Montreal for 8th time, 1982	*and*
15	Sa.	*When wild geese soar overhead, even terrapins stamp their feet on the ground.* • Tides {8.7 / 8.8	*blustery*
16	E	23rd S. af. P. • ♆ STAT. • Crab apples are ripe now.	*blasts!*
17	M.	St. Hugh of Lincoln • ☾ ON EQ. • Baseball player Roger Peckinpaugh died, 1977	*Don't*
18	Tu.	☌♄☉ • Comic strip *Calvin and Hobbes* debuted, 1985 • Tides {9.4 / 9.0	*be*
19	W.	☾ AT ☊ • Columbus first sighted Puerto Rico, 1493 • Tides {9.8 / 9.2	*ungrateful;*
20	Th.	Astronomer Edwin P. Hubble born, 1889 • {10.1 / 9.4	*give*
21	Fr.	☌☿☾ • 3.8 earthquake near Northglenn, Colo., 1965 • Tides {10.5 / 9.6	*thanks*
22	Sa.	New ● • ☌♀☾ • ☌♄☾ • Pirate Blackbeard died, 1718 • {10.8 / 9.8	*for*
23	E	24th S. af. P. • U.S. Coast Guard Women's Reserve (SPARs) authorized, 1942	*every*
24	M.	☾ RUNS LOW • Cape Breton Railway opened, N.S., 1890 • Tides {11.2 / —	*plateful.*
25	Tu.	☌♇☾ • *The sun at home warms better than the sun elsewhere.* • Tides {9.9 / 11.2	*Snow's*
26	W.	☌☿♄ • ☌♂☾ • Comedian Milton Berle married Lorna Adams, 1991	*hateful,*
27	Th.	Thanksgiving Day • ☾ AT PERIG. • Tides {10.0 / 10.9	*but*
28	Fr.	Tennis player Dwight Davis died, 1945 • Tides {10.0 / 10.6	*removal*
29	Sa.	☌♆☾ • Fire destroyed much of Maryland Agricultural College, College Park, Md., 1912	*wins*
30	E	1st S. of Advent • ☾ ON EQ. • Tides {10.1 / 10.0	*approval.*

He travels best that knows when to return. –Thomas Middleton

Farmer's Calendar

■ The old New England saying, "Chop your own wood and it will warm you twice," is definitely an understatement. As anyone who has processed their own firewood knows, the activity warms you many more times than that: Once the tree is felled, it must be cut to length, split, stacked, covered, and then carried into the house daily. Certainly with chainsaws and power splitters, today's woodcutters have it easier than their ancestors, but they still work hard.

Putting up your own firewood saves money, but as most wood enthusiasts will tell you, it is rewarding in other ways, too. Many folks enjoy cutting wood for the exercise and the chance to spend time outdoors. Some do it to help the environment: Not only is wood a renewable energy source, but also burning it responsibly may contribute less to global warming than using oil, coal, or natural gas. Woody plants take in carbon dioxide from the air, thereby recycling the gas that was released from decaying or burning logs.

Of course, wood supplies a soothing warmth that no other fuel can provide, encouraging family and friends to gather around a roaring fire for pleasant conversation. Many romances have blossomed in front of a flickering fireplace—just one more wonderful way that wood warms you.

Listen to the Farmer's Calendar at Almanac.com/Multimedia.

DECEMBER

THE TWELFTH MONTH • 2014

SKY WATCH ☆ *The Moon hovers just above greenish Uranus at nightfall on the 1st. Use binoculars. The Moon visits the Hyades star cluster in Taurus on the 5th. The 13th brings the year's best meteor shower, the Geminids. A meteor every minute or two should appear in dark rural skies between 8:00 and 11:00 P.M. After 11:30, the unwelcome Moon will rise to brighten the heavens. Winter begins with the solstice on the 21st, at 6:03 P.M. After that date, Jupiter starts rising by 8:30 P.M. and is nicely high after 10:00 P.M. Venus might be glimpsed low in the west at dusk by month's end—a harbinger of its superb evening star apparition this coming spring. Saturn can be seen low in the east before dawn.*

○ **Full Moon**	6th day	7th hour	27th minute
◑ **Last Quarter**	14th day	7th hour	51st minute
● **New Moon**	21st day	20th hour	36th minute
◐ **First Quarter**	28th day	13th hour	31st minute

All times are given in Eastern Standard Time.

Get these pages with times set to your zip code at Almanac.com/Access.

Day of Year	Day of Month	Day of Week	☼ Rises h. m.	Rise Key	☼ Sets h. m.	Set Key	Length of Day h.	Length of Day m.	Sun Fast m.	Declination of Sun °	Declination of Sun '	High Tide Times Boston		☾ Rises h. m.	Rise Key	☾ Sets h. m.	Set Key	☾ Astron. Place	☾ Age
335	1	M.	6:53	E	**4:12**	A	9	19	27	21 s.	51	6¼	**6¾**	**1:21**	C	1:20	D	PSC	9
336	2	Tu.	6:54	E	**4:12**	A	9	18	26	22	00	7¼	**7¾**	**1:56**	C	2:29	E	PSC	10
337	3	W.	6:55	E	**4:12**	A	9	17	26	22	09	8	**8¾**	**2:33**	C	3:36	E	PSC	11
338	4	Th.	6:56	E	**4:11**	A	9	15	25	22	17	9	**9½**	**3:13**	B	4:42	E	ARI	12
339	5	Fr.	6:57	E	**4:11**	A	9	14	25	22	24	9¾	**10½**	**3:57**	B	5:45	E	TAU	13
340	6	Sa.	6:58	E	**4:11**	A	9	13	25	22	32	10½	**11¼**	**4:46**	B	6:45	E	TAU	14
341	7	**E**	6:59	E	**4:11**	A	9	12	24	22	38	11¼	12	**5:38**	B	7:39	E	TAU	15
342	8	M.	7:00	E	**4:11**	A	9	11	24	22	45	**12**	—	**6:33**	B	8:27	E	GEM	16
343	9	Tu.	7:01	E	**4:11**	A	9	10	23	22	51	12¾	**12¾**	**7:29**	C	9:10	E	GEM	17
344	10	W.	7:02	E	**4:11**	A	9	09	23	22	56	1½	**1½**	**8:26**	C	9:47	E	CAN	18
345	11	Th.	7:03	E	**4:11**	A	9	08	22	23	01	2¼	**2¼**	**9:23**	C	10:21	E	CAN	19
346	12	Fr.	7:04	E	**4:11**	A	9	07	22	23	06	3	**3**	**10:20**	C	10:51	D	LEO	20
347	13	Sa.	7:04	E	**4:11**	A	9	07	22	23	10	3¾	**3¾**	**11:17**	D	11:20	D	SEX	21
348	14	**E**	7:05	E	**4:12**	A	9	07	21	23	13	4½	**4¾**	—	–	11:48	C	LEO	22
349	15	M.	7:06	E	**4:12**	A	9	06	21	23	16	5¼	**5¾**	12:15	D	**12:16**	C	VIR	23
350	16	Tu.	7:06	E	**4:12**	A	9	06	20	23	19	6¼	**6½**	1:13	E	**12:46**	C	VIR	24
351	17	W.	7:07	E	**4:12**	A	9	05	20	23	21	7	**7½**	2:13	E	**1:18**	C	VIR	25
352	18	Th.	7:08	E	**4:13**	A	9	05	19	23	23	7¾	**8¼**	3:14	E	**1:54**	B	LIB	26
353	19	Fr.	7:08	E	**4:13**	A	9	05	19	23	24	8½	**9¼**	4:17	E	**2:36**	B	LIB	27
354	20	Sa.	7:09	E	**4:14**	A	9	05	18	23	25	9¼	**10**	5:20	E	**3:24**	B	SCO	28
355	21	**E**	7:09	E	**4:14**	A	9	05	18	23	26	10	**10¾**	6:21	E	**4:19**	B	OPH	0
356	22	M.	7:10	E	**4:15**	A	9	05	17	23	25	11	**11½**	7:18	E	**5:22**	C	SAG	1
357	23	Tu.	7:10	E	**4:15**	A	9	05	17	23	25	11¾	—	8:11	E	**6:30**	C	SAG	2
358	24	W.	7:11	E	**4:16**	A	9	05	16	23	24	12¼	**12½**	8:57	E	**7:40**	C	CAP	3
359	25	Th.	7:11	E	**4:16**	A	9	05	16	23	22	1¼	**1¼**	9:38	E	**8:52**	D	AQU	4
360	26	Fr.	7:12	E	**4:17**	A	9	05	15	23	20	2	**2¼**	10:16	D	**10:02**	D	AQU	5
361	27	Sa.	7:12	E	**4:18**	A	9	06	15	23	18	3	**3¼**	10:51	D	**11:12**	D	AQU	6
362	28	**E**	7:12	E	**4:19**	A	9	07	14	23	15	3¾	**4¼**	11:25	C	—	–	PSC	7
363	29	M.	7:12	E	**4:19**	A	9	07	14	23	11	4¾	**5¼**	11:59	C	12:21	E	PSC	8
364	30	Tu.	7:13	E	**4:20**	A	9	07	13	23	08	5¾	**6¼**	**12:34**	C	1:28	E	PSC	9
365	31	W.	7:13	E	**4:21**	A	9	08	13	23 s.	03	6¾	**7½**	**1:13**	B	2:33	E	ARI	10

 To use this page, see p. 124; for Key letters, see p. 252. ☞ **Bold = P.M.** ☞ Light = A.M.

CALENDAR

There he stands in the foul weather,
The foolish, fond Old Year. –Henry Wadsworth Longfellow

Day of Month	Day of Week	Dates, Feasts, Fasts, Aspects, Tide Heights	Weather
1	M.	St. Andrew[T] • ☾☉☽ • Tom Brokaw signed off as anchor of *NBC Nightly News*, 2004	Wintry
2	Tu.	St. Viviana • ☾ AT ☋ • Napoleon Bonaparte crowned Emperor of France, 1804	it
3	W.	*Search others for their virtues, thyself for thy vices.*	ain't—
4	Th.	Astronaut Roberta Lynn Bondar born, 1945 • { 11.1 / 9.9	no
5	Fr.	Deadly F5 tornado struck Vicksburg, Miss., 1953	complaints!
6	Sa.	St. Nicholas • Full Cold ○ • Rankin/Bass's *Rudolph* debuted on TV, 1964	Snowier:
7	E	2nd Sunday of Advent • National Pearl Harbor Remembrance Day • ☾ RIDES HIGH	Storefronts
8	M.	☿ IN SUP. ☾ • Winterberry fruit especially showy now. • Tides { 10.8	are
9	Tu.	♃ STAT. • Robert Cushman gave first known sermon in "U.S.," Plymouth Colony, Mass., 1621	showery,
10	W.	St. Eulalia • Col. John P. Stapp attained 632 mph on rocket sled, 1954 • Tides { 9.4 / 10.2	light
11	Th.	☾♃ • First dental use of nitrous oxide, 1844 • { 9.2 / 9.8	displays
12	Fr.	Our Lady of Guadalupe • ☾ AT APO. • Singer Connie Francis born, 1938	glowier.
13	Sa.	St. Lucia • *Lucy light, Lucy light, Shortest day and longest night.* • { 8.9 / 9.0	Shoppers
14	E	3rd ☉. of Advent • Halcyon Days begin. • ☾ ON EQ. • { 8.8 / 8.7	are
15	M.	*Gone With the Wind* premiered, Loew's Grand Theater, Atlanta, Ga., 1939 • { 8.9 / 8.5	prowling,
16	Tu.	☾ AT ☋ • Hiram W. Hayden patented machine to make brass kettles, 1851	blizzard
17	W.	Ember Day • First day of Chanukah • Tides { 9.3 / 8.6	howling!
18	Th.	John William Draper took first photo of Moon, 1839	Drifts
19	Fr.	Ember Day • ☾♄☾ • Beware the Pogonip. • { 10.1 / 9.1	a-heaping,
20	Sa.	Ember Day • ☾♀♇ • Pianist Arthur Rubenstein died, 1982 • { 10.6 / 9.4	lords
21	E	4th S. of Advent • Winter Solstice • New ● • ☾ RUNS LOW	a-leaping,
22	M.	St. Thomas[T] • ☾♀☾ • ☾♀☾ • ☾♇☾ • ☿ STAT.	Yule
23	Tu.	*Better the cold blast of winter than the hot breath of a pursuing elephant.* • Tides { 11.6	logs
24	W.	☾ AT PERIG. • ☾♀♇ • Unofficial Christmas truce began in areas of Western Front, WWI, 1914	burning,
25	Th.	**Christmas** • ☾☉☾ • 1.3" snow, Atlanta, Ga., 2010	gifts
26	Fr.	St. Stephen • Boxing Day (Canada) • First day of Kwanzaa • ☾♅☾	returning.
27	Sa.	St. John • ☾ ON EQ. • Steve Largent's 752nd career catch set NFL record, 1987 • { 10.5 / 10.7	Winds
28	E	1st ☉. af. Ch. • ☾☉☾ • 83" snow on ground, Bathurst, N.B., 1978 • { 10.4 / 10.2	are
29	M.	Holy Innocents[T] • ☾ AT ☋ • U.S. president Andrew Johnson born, 1808 • { 10.4 / 9.7	keen
30	Tu.	*True happiness is in a contented mind.* • Tides { 10.4 / 9.4	for
31	W.	St. Sylvester • Entertainer Roy Rogers married actress Dale Evans, 1947 • { 10.4 / 9.3	2015!

Farmer's Calendar

■ The year went by in the blink of an eye. Soon, the holidays will be over and a new year will be upon us. Now is the time to look back and reflect on the past months to see what we have accomplished—or tried to accomplish. There are some who say, "Take off the rearview mirror and drive on," but reviewing the past is a valuable learning tool that keeps us from repeating mistakes and reminds us of the things that worked, helping us to make better choices now and in the future.

Journaling is a wonderful way to keep track of the past. Write in your journal every day, even if it is just a sentence, and date your entries. This will allow you to revisit the progression of your thoughts and actions over the past year.

A journal is a practical way of keeping track of things like weather events and planting dates, but, more important, it allows you to think about your life. Did you do something that you came to regret? What things did you do that made you proud? Could you have done something differently that may have resulted in a different outcome? Do you have any habits or behaviors that you'd like to improve? In what ways have you become a better person?

Moving forward into the new year should be easier if we remember to keep the rearview mirror in adjustment.

2015

Listen to the Farmer's Calendar at Almanac.com/Multimedia.

131

THE FIRST MONTH • 2015

SKY WATCH ☆ *Earth reaches perihelion, its annual point closest to the Sun, on the 4th. All of the planets are visible as the year begins. The innermost duo—Mercury and Venus—has a lovely tight conjunction from the 7th to the 12th, standing 10 degrees high half an hour after sunset, in the southwest. Dim Mars hovers above them, in Aquarius. Saturn appears before dawn, in the east, as it crosses Libra into Scorpius. It hovers next to the waning crescent Moon on the 16th. The Moon forms a close triangle with Venus and Mercury on the 21st and meets Mars and Neptune the next night. Brilliant Jupiter, in Leo, rises by 6:00 P.M. at month's end.*

○ **Full Moon**	4th day	23rd hour	53rd minute
◑ **Last Quarter**	13th day	4th hour	46th minute
● **New Moon**	20th day	8th hour	14th minute
◐ **First Quarter**	26th day	23rd hour	48th minute

All times are given in Eastern Standard Time.

Get these pages with times set to your zip code at Almanac.com/Access.

Day of Year	Day of Month	Day of Week	☼ Rises h. m.	Rise Key	☼ Sets h. m.	Set Key	Length of Day h. m.	Sun Fast m.	Declination of Sun ° '	High Tide Times Boston		☾ Rises h. m.	Rise Key	☾ Sets h. m.	Set Key	☾ Astron. Place	☾ Age
1	1	Th.	7:13	E	**4:22**	A	9 09	12	22 s.58	7¾	**8½**	**1:54**	B	3:36	E	TAU	11
2	2	Fr.	7:13	E	**4:23**	A	9 10	12	22 53	8¾	**9½**	**2:40**	B	4:36	E	TAU	12
3	3	Sa.	7:13	E	**4:23**	A	9 10	11	22 48	9½	**10¼**	**3:30**	B	5:31	E	TAU	13
4	4	**D**	7:13	E	**4:24**	A	9 11	11	22 41	10¼	**11**	**4:23**	B	6:21	E	ORI	14
5	5	M.	7:13	E	**4:25**	A	9 12	10	22 35	11	**11¾**	**5:19**	C	7:06	E	GEM	15
6	6	Tu.	7:13	E	**4:26**	A	9 13	10	22 28	11¾	—	**6:15**	C	7:46	E	GEM	16
7	7	W.	7:13	E	**4:27**	A	9 14	10	22 20	12¼	**12½**	**7:13**	C	8:21	E	CAN	17
8	8	Th.	7:13	E	**4:28**	A	9 15	9	22 12	1	**1**	**8:10**	C	8:53	D	LEO	18
9	9	Fr.	7:12	E	**4:29**	A	9 17	9	22 04	1½	**1¾**	**9:06**	D	9:23	D	LEO	19
10	10	Sa.	7:12	E	**4:30**	A	9 18	8	21 55	2¼	**2½**	**10:03**	D	9:51	D	LEO	20
11	11	**D**	7:12	E	**4:32**	A	9 20	8	21 46	3	**3¼**	**11:00**	D	10:18	C	VIR	21
12	12	M.	7:12	E	**4:33**	A	9 21	8	21 36	3¾	**4**	**11:59**	E	10:47	C	VIR	22
13	13	Tu.	7:11	E	**4:34**	A	9 23	7	21 26	4½	**5**	—	–	11:17	C	VIR	23
14	14	W.	7:11	E	**4:35**	A	9 24	7	21 16	5½	**5¾**	12:58	E	11:50	C	VIR	24
15	15	Th.	7:10	E	**4:36**	A	9 26	6	21 05	6¼	**6¾**	1:59	E	**12:28**	B	LIB	25
16	16	Fr.	7:10	E	**4:37**	A	9 27	6	20 53	7¼	**7¾**	3:00	E	**1:11**	B	LIB	26
17	17	Sa.	7:09	E	**4:38**	A	9 29	6	20 42	8	**8¾**	4:01	E	**2:02**	B	OPH	27
18	18	**D**	7:09	E	**4:40**	B	9 31	5	20 30	9	**9½**	5:01	E	**3:01**	B	SAG	28
19	19	M.	7:08	E	**4:41**	B	9 33	5	20 17	9¾	**10¼**	5:56	E	**4:06**	C	SAG	29
20	20	Tu.	7:08	E	**4:42**	B	9 34	5	20 04	10½	**11¼**	6:47	E	**5:17**	C	SAG	0
21	21	W.	7:07	E	**4:43**	B	9 36	5	19 51	11½	—	7:32	E	**6:31**	C	AQU	1
22	22	Th.	7:06	E	**4:45**	B	9 39	4	19 37	12	**12¼**	8:13	D	**7:45**	D	CAP	2
23	23	Fr.	7:06	E	**4:46**	B	9 40	4	19 24	12¾	**1¼**	8:51	D	**8:58**	D	AQU	3
24	24	Sa.	7:05	E	**4:47**	B	9 42	4	19 09	1¾	**2**	9:26	D	**10:09**	E	PSC	4
25	25	**D**	7:04	E	**4:48**	B	9 44	4	18 55	2½	**3**	10:01	C	**11:18**	E	PSC	5
26	26	M.	7:03	E	**4:50**	B	9 47	3	18 39	3½	**4**	10:37	C	—	–	PSC	6
27	27	Tu.	7:02	E	**4:51**	B	9 49	3	18 24	4½	**5**	11:15	C	12:25	E	ARI	7
28	28	W.	7:01	E	**4:52**	B	9 51	3	18 08	5½	**6**	11:55	B	1:29	E	ARI	8
29	29	Th.	7:00	E	**4:54**	B	9 54	3	17 52	6½	**7¼**	**12:39**	B	2:30	E	TAU	9
30	30	Fr.	6:59	E	**4:55**	B	9 56	3	17 36	7½	**8¼**	**1:27**	B	3:26	E	TAU	10
31	31	Sa.	6:58	E	**4:56**	B	9 58	2	17 s.19	8½	**9¼**	**2:18**	B	4:18	E	ORI	11

 To use this page, see p. 124; for Key letters, see p. 252. ☞ **Bold = P.M.** ☞ Light = A.M.

JANUARY HATH 31 DAYS • 2015

Just listen to the merry New Year's bells!
All hearts rejoice and catch the cheerful tone. –M. A. Baines

Day of Month	Day of Week	Dates, Feasts, Fasts, Aspects, Tide Heights	Weather
1	Th.	**New Year's Day** • **Holy Name** • First Rose Bowl football game, 1902	*Hours*
2	Fr.	Kenneth Brugger and Cathy Aguado discovered first winter refuge of monarch butterflies, Mexico, 1975 • {10.6/9.3	*and*
3	Sa.	☾ RIDES HIGH • ☌♇☉ • First covered skating rink in Canada opened, Halifax, N.S., 1863	*hours*
4	**D**	**2nd S. af. Ch.** • **Full Wolf** ○ • ⊕ AT PERIHELION • {10.6/9.4	*of*
5	M.	Twelfth Night • First successful photo of aurora, by physicist Martin Brendel, 1892 • Tides {10.6/9.4	*snow*
6	Tu.	**Epiphany** • George Washington married Martha Dandridge Custis, 1759 • {10.5/—	*showers;*
7	W.	Distaff Day • *Partly work and partly play, Ye must on St Distaff's Day.* • Tides {9.4/10.3	*feeling*
8	Th.	☌♃☾ • First U.S. State of the Union address, 1790	*more*
9	Fr.	☾ AT APO. • Geneticist Sir Alec Jeffreys born, 1950 • {9.2/9.7	*like*
10	Sa.	☾ ON EQ. • RCA introduced 45-rpm vinyl record format, 1949 • {9.1/9.4	*Labrador!*
11	**D**	**1st S. af. Ep.** • Canadian prime minister Sir John A. Macdonald born, 1815	*High*
12	M.	Plough Monday • ☾ AT ☊ • French haute cuisine founder Marie-Antoine Carême died, 1833	*times*
13	Tu.	**St. Hilary** • Mickey Mouse comic strip debuted in newspapers, 1930 • {9.0/8.4	*for*
14	W.	☿ GR. ELONG. (19° EAST) • Rare black rhino born, St. Louis Zoo, Mo., 2011 • Tides {9.1/8.3	*snow-*
15	Th.	First U.S. all-glass windowless structure completed, Toledo, Ohio, 1936 • Tides {9.3/8.4	*drifts*
16	Fr.	☌♄☾ • 121.5-lb. blue catfish caught, Lake Texoma, Tex., 2004 • Tides {9.6/8.6	*and*
17	Sa.	U.S. statesman Benjamin Franklin born, 1706 • Tides {10.1/9.0	*ski*
18	**D**	**2nd S. af. Ep.** • ☾ RUNS LOW • Meteorite fell into doctor's office, Lorton, Va., 2010	*lifts.*
19	M.	**Martin Luther King Jr.'s Birthday (observed)** • ☌♂♆ • ☌♇☾	*Raining,*
20	Tu.	**New** ● • ☿ STAT. • *A north wind with new Moon will hold until the full.*	*temperatures*
21	W.	☾ AT PERIG. • ☌☿☾ • ☌♀☾ • {11.9/—	*gaining.*
22	Th.	**St. Vincent** • ☌♂☾ • ☌♆☾ • Tides {10.8/12.0	*Mercy's*
23	Fr.	Envelope machine patented, 1849 • 13.4" snow, Boston, 2005 • Tides {11.0/11.8	*sakes:*
24	Sa.	☾ ON EQ. • U.S. Supreme Court justice Thurgood Marshall died, 1993 • Tides {11.1/11.4	*Sunny*
25	**D**	**3rd S. af. Ep.** • ☾ AT ☋ • ☌♅☾ • {11.0/10.8	*breaks*
26	M.	**Conversion of Paul** • *It's no use boiling your cabbage twice.* • Tides {10.8/10.1	*make*
27	Tu.	Raccoons mate now. • Astronomer Beatrice Tinsley born, 1941 • Tides {10.5/9.5	*lakes.*
28	W.	**St. Thomas Aquinas** • U.S. Coast Guard established, 1915 • Tides {10.2/9.1	*More*
29	Th.	Actor Paul Newman married Joanne Woodward, 1958	*flaking—*
30	Fr.	☾ RIDES HIGH • ☿ IN INF. ☌ • Tides {10.0/8.8	*practically*
31	Sa.	*The wise man has long ears and a short tongue.*	*baking!*

Farmer's Calendar

■ For the past several days, the temperature has been at or below zero at 5:00 A.M., when we take the dogs out for their walk. We rarely see or hear traffic at this hour. No jets fly overhead, and no one else is walking. The absence of such ordinary sounds allows us to hear noises that we'd miss in the daylight.

To the Cree of Canada, now was the time of the Moon of Popping Trees. As the water in trees' sap freezes and expands, the crack of the wood sounds like cap pistols or firecrackers. It is not loud, but it startles us as we walk up the dark road.

Passing the frozen pond, we occasionally hear a louder, deeper boom as its frozen water expands, too. In 1795, Charles Hutton, a Fellow of Britain's Royal Society, wrote of "sudden cracks or rifts in the ice of the lakes of Sweden, 9 or 10 feet deep, and many leagues long; the rupture being made with a noise not less loud than if many guns were discharged together."

The strangest sound always comes from exactly the same place in the woods, but only in the very early morning and only on the coldest days of the year. The first time we heard it, it sounded like the barking of a seal, so every time we hear it now, we say, "There's the seal." It's just two tree limbs rubbing against each other. We hope.

SKY WATCH ☆ *Venus appears higher up each evening and stands next to Neptune on the 1st. Jupiter, retrograding into Cancer, has its opposition on the 6th; it is then at its closest, biggest, and brightest of the year and is out all night long. Dazzling Venus hovers very close to faint orange Mars from the 19th to the 21st, low in the southwest at nightfall. On the 20th, the crescent Moon joins this conjunction—a don't-miss event 18 degrees high in deepening dusk. Binoculars will reveal green Uranus right next to the crescent Moon on the 21st. Meanwhile, in the predawn eastern sky, Saturn in Scorpius is now high enough for telescopic observation.*

○	**Full Moon**	3rd day	18th hour	9th minute
◑	**Last Quarter**	11th day	22nd hour	50th minute
●	**New Moon**	18th day	18th hour	47th minute
◐	**First Quarter**	25th day	12th hour	14th minute

All times are given in Eastern Standard Time.

Get these pages with times set to your zip code at Almanac.com/Access.

Day of Year	Day of Month	Day of Week	Rises h. m.	Rise Key	Sets h. m.	Set Key	Length of Day h. m.	Sun Fast m.	Declination of Sun ° ′	High Tide Times Boston		Rises h. m.	Rise Key	Sets h. m.	Set Key	Astron. Place	Age
32	1	**D**	6:57	E	**4:58**	B	10 01	2	17 s.02	9¼	**10**	**3:12**	C	5:04	E	GEM	12
33	2	M.	6:56	E	**4:59**	B	10 03	2	16 45	10	**10¾**	**4:08**	C	5:45	E	GEM	13
34	3	Tu.	6:55	E	**5:00**	B	10 05	2	16 28	10¾	**11¼**	**5:04**	C	6:22	E	CAN	14
35	4	W.	6:54	D	**5:01**	B	10 07	2	16 10	11½	**12**	**6:01**	C	6:55	E	CAN	15
36	5	Th.	6:53	D	**5:03**	B	10 10	2	15 52	**12**	—	**6:58**	D	7:25	D	LEO	16
37	6	Fr.	6:52	D	**5:04**	B	10 12	2	15 33	12½	**12¾**	**7:55**	D	7:54	D	SEX	17
38	7	Sa.	6:51	D	**5:05**	B	10 14	2	15 15	1	**1¼**	**8:52**	D	8:22	D	LEO	18
39	8	**D**	6:50	D	**5:07**	B	10 17	2	14 56	1¾	**2**	**9:49**	D	8:50	C	VIR	19
40	9	M.	6:48	D	**5:08**	B	10 20	2	14 37	2¼	**2¾**	**10:47**	E	9:19	C	VIR	20
41	10	Tu.	6:47	D	**5:09**	B	10 22	2	14 17	3	**3½**	**11:46**	E	9:51	C	VIR	21
42	11	W.	6:46	D	**5:11**	B	10 25	2	13 57	3¾	**4¼**	—	–	10:25	B	LIB	22
43	12	Th.	6:44	D	**5:12**	B	10 28	2	13 38	4¾	**5¼**	12:45	E	11:05	B	LIB	23
44	13	Fr.	6:43	D	**5:13**	B	10 30	2	13 17	5½	**6¼**	1:45	E	11:50	B	OPH	24
45	14	Sa.	6:42	D	**5:14**	B	10 32	2	12 57	6½	**7¼**	2:43	E	**12:43**	B	OPH	25
46	15	**D**	6:40	D	**5:16**	B	10 36	2	12 37	7½	**8¼**	3:39	E	**1:43**	B	SAG	26
47	16	M.	6:39	D	**5:17**	B	10 38	2	12 16	8½	**9**	4:32	E	**2:50**	C	SAG	27
48	17	Tu.	6:38	D	**5:18**	B	10 40	2	11 55	9¼	**10**	5:20	E	**4:02**	C	CAP	28
49	18	W.	6:36	D	**5:20**	B	10 44	2	11 34	10¼	**10¾**	6:03	E	**5:17**	D	AQU	0
50	19	Th.	6:35	D	**5:21**	B	10 46	2	11 12	11	**11¾**	6:43	D	**6:32**	D	AQU	1
51	20	Fr.	6:33	D	**5:22**	B	10 49	2	10 51	**12**	—	7:21	D	**7:47**	D	PSC	2
52	21	Sa.	6:32	D	**5:23**	B	10 51	2	10 29	12½	**12¾**	7:58	C	**9:00**	E	PSC	3
53	22	**D**	6:30	D	**5:25**	B	10 55	2	10 07	1¼	**1¾**	8:35	C	**10:11**	E	PSC	4
54	23	M.	6:29	D	**5:26**	B	10 57	3	9 45	2¼	**2¾**	9:14	C	**11:18**	E	CET	5
55	24	Tu.	6:27	D	**5:27**	B	11 00	3	9 23	3	**3½**	9:54	B	—	–	ARI	6
56	25	W.	6:26	D	**5:28**	B	11 02	3	9 01	4	**4½**	10:38	B	12:22	E	TAU	7
57	26	Th.	6:24	D	**5:30**	B	11 06	3	8 39	5	**5¾**	11:25	B	1:21	E	TAU	8
58	27	Fr.	6:23	D	**5:31**	B	11 08	3	8 16	6	**6¾**	**12:15**	B	2:14	E	TAU	9
59	28	Sa.	6:21	D	**5:32**	B	11 11	3	7 s.54	7	**7¾**	**1:08**	B	3:02	E	GEM	10

FEBRUARY HATH 28 DAYS • 2015

Then come the wild weather—come sleet or come snow,
We will stand by each other, however it blow. –H. W. Longfellow

Day of Month	Day of Week	Dates, Feasts, Fasts, Aspects, Tide Heights	Weather
1	D	**Septuagesima** • ☌♀♆ • –45°F, Pittsburg, N.H., 1920	*Groundhog*
2	M.	**Candlemas** • Groundhog Day • *At Candlemas, Cold come to us.* • Tides {10.2 9.2	*found*
3	Tu.	**Full Snow** ○ • Col. Eileen Collins became first woman in U.S. to pilot space shuttle *(Discovery)*, 1995	*fog.*
4	W.	☌♃☾ • Entertainer Liberace died, 1987 • Tides {10.2 9.4	*New*
5	Th.	**St. Agatha** • Edwin Prescott patented a centrifugal railway, 1901 • Tides {10.1 —	*snows*
6	Fr.	☾ at apo. • ♃ at ☍ • Robert E. Lee named Confederate general in chief, 1865	*and*
7	Sa.	☾ on eq. • American Guernsey Cattle Club founded, N.Y.C., 1877 • Tides {9.5 9.8	*blue*
8	D	**Sexagesima** • ☾ at ☊ • Naturalist Henry Walter Bates born, 1825	*toes.*
9	M.	*He is an ill companion that has a good memory.* • Tides {9.4 9.1	*Fine*
10	Tu.	Queen Victoria married Prince Albert, 1840 • Early morning tornado, Albany, Ga., 1940 • {9.3 8.8	*and*
11	W.	☿ stat. • Opening day of first Canada Winter Games, Quebec City, 1967 • Tides {9.2 8.5	*dandy*
12	Th.	☌♄☾ • U.S. president Abraham Lincoln born, 1809 • Actor Lorne Greene born, 1915	*for*
13	Fr.	Astronomer Tycho Brahe outlined his solar system structure, 1588 • Tides {9.4 8.4	*Valentine*
14	Sa.	**Sts. Cyril & Methodius** • **Valentine's Day** • ☾ runs low • {9.7 8.6	*candy.*
15	D	**Quinquagesima** • ☌♇☾ • Canada adopted Maple Leaf flag, 1965	*Snow*
16	M.	**Washington's Birthday (observed)** • Winter's back breaks. • {10.7 9.7	*spittin';*
17	Tu.	**Shrove Tuesday** • ☌☿☾ • 9-lb. 6-oz. chain pickerel caught, Homerville, Ga., 1961	*if*
18	W.	**Ash Wednesday** • **New** ● • *Huckleberry Finn* published, 1885	*you're*
19	Th.	**Chinese New Year (Sheep or Goat)** • ☾ at perig. • ☌♆☾ • {12.0 11.4	*not*
20	Fr.	☾ on eq. • ☌♀☾ • ☌♂☾ • Abolitionist Frederick Douglass died, 1895	*mitten-*
21	Sa.	☾ at ☋ • ☌♀♂ • ☌♅☾ • Tides {11.6 11.9	*smitten,*
22	D	**1st S. in Lent** • F. W. Woolworth discount store chain started, Utica, N.Y., 1879	*you'll*
23	M.	**Pure Monday** • 97°F, San Antonio, Tex., 1996 • {11.4 10.7	*be*
24	Tu.	**St. Matthias** • ☿ gr. elong. (27° west) • Skunks mate now.	*frostbitten!*
25	W.	Ember Day • ☌♆☉ • "Battle of Los Angeles" w/ UFO, Calif., 1942 • {10.5 9.4	*By*
26	Th.	*Turn your face to the Sun and the shadows fall behind you.*	*jing-y,*
27	Fr.	Ember Day • ☾ rides high • Tides {9.7 8.6	*feels*
28	Sa.	**St. Romanus** • Ember Day • Natasha Veruschka swallowed 22.83" sword, 2009	*spring-y.*

Tradition wears a snowy beard,
Romance is always young.
–John Greenleaf Whittier

Farmer's Calendar

■ There's a basswood on our road that looks like someone has tried to make it into a cribbage board. All around its trunk, and as far up as I can see, there are rows of holes, maybe an eighth of an inch in diameter. Lots of holes: I counted 17 in one 6-inch row.

These are the work of the yellow-bellied sapsucker, which has been tapping trees for a lot longer than people have. It possesses one of the worst names in ornithology—three insults in two words, implying cowardice, stupidity, and gullibility. It's misleading, too. Granted, the bird does suck sap, but there's little yellow on its belly. The bright red patch on the male's head is what stands out. Why not "red-capped sapsucker"?

Its Latin name, *Sphyrapicus,* is more dignified. *Sphyra* means hammer, and the bird is, indeed, fond of hammering on metal surfaces such as road signs, chimney flashing, and mailboxes at dawn, a habit that does not endear it to human neighbors.

In Roman mythology, Picus was a mortal man who loved Pomona, a goddess of the orchards. He made the mistake of spurning the affections of the witch Circe, who was famous for turning men into swine, so she changed him into a woodpecker. What a sap.

The Third Month • 2015

SKY WATCH ☆ *The Moon meets Jupiter on the 2nd. Venus stands very near Uranus on the 4th, with Mars below them, in Pisces. Orange Mars has a close conjunction with green Uranus on the 11th, with dazzling Venus above; use binoculars. Saturn in Scorpius, rises after midnight in midmonth. The 20th brings the vernal equinox at 6:45* P.M. *and a total solar eclipse over the Faroe Islands, off Scotland; the path of totality then marches directly to—and stops at—the North Pole. The crescent Moon meets Mars on the 21st and passes to the left of Venus on the 22nd. Mars vanishes in the Sun's glare at month's end. Jupiter hovers near the Moon on the 29th.*

○	**Full Moon**	5th day	13th hour	5th minute
◑	**Last Quarter**	13th day	13th hour	48th minute
●	**New Moon**	20th day	5th hour	36th minute
◐	**First Quarter**	27th day	3rd hour	43rd minute

After 2:00 A.M. *on March 8, Eastern Daylight Time is given.*

Get these pages with times set to your zip code at Almanac.com/Access.

Day of Year	Day of Month	Day of Week	☼ Rises h. m.	Rise Key	☼ Sets h. m.	Set Key	Length of Day h.	m.	Sun Fast m.	Declination of Sun °	'	High Tide Times Boston		☾ Rises h. m.	Rise Key	☾ Sets h. m.	Set Key	☾ Astron. Place	☾ Age
60	1	**D**	6:19	D	**5:33**	C	11	14	4	7 s.	31	8	**8¾**	**2:03**	C	3:44	E	GEM	11
61	2	M.	6:18	D	**5:34**	C	11	16	4	7	08	9	**9½**	**2:59**	C	4:22	E	CAN	12
62	3	Tu.	6:16	D	**5:36**	C	11	20	4	6	45	9¾	**10¼**	**3:55**	C	4:57	E	CAN	13
63	4	W.	6:15	D	**5:37**	C	11	22	4	6	22	10½	**10¾**	**4:52**	D	5:28	D	LEO	14
64	5	Th.	6:13	D	**5:38**	C	11	25	4	5	59	11	**11½**	**5:49**	D	5:57	D	SEX	15
65	6	Fr.	6:11	D	**5:39**	C	11	28	5	5	36	11¾	—	**6:45**	D	6:26	D	LEO	16
66	7	Sa.	6:10	D	**5:41**	C	11	31	5	5	12	12	**12¼**	**7:43**	D	6:54	C	VIR	17
67	8	**D**	7:08	C	**6:42**	C	11	34	5	4	49	12½	**2**	**9:40**	E	8:23	C	VIR	18
68	9	M.	7:06	C	**6:43**	C	11	37	5	4	25	2¼	**2½**	**10:38**	E	8:53	C	VIR	19
69	10	Tu.	7:05	C	**6:44**	C	11	39	6	4	02	2¾	**3¼**	**11:37**	E	9:27	C	LIB	20
70	11	W.	7:03	C	**6:45**	C	11	42	6	3	38	3½	**4**	—	–	10:04	B	LIB	21
71	12	Th.	7:01	C	**6:46**	C	11	45	6	3	15	4¼	**4¾**	12:35	E	10:46	B	SCO	22
72	13	Fr.	6:59	C	**6:48**	C	11	49	6	2	51	5	**5¾**	1:33	E	11:34	B	OPH	23
73	14	Sa.	6:58	C	**6:49**	C	11	51	7	2	27	6	**6¾**	2:28	E	**12:29**	B	SAG	24
74	15	**D**	6:56	C	**6:50**	C	11	54	7	2	04	7	**7¾**	3:20	E	**1:31**	C	SAG	25
75	16	M.	6:54	C	**6:51**	C	11	57	7	1	40	8	**8¾**	4:08	E	**2:38**	C	SAG	26
76	17	Tu.	6:53	C	**6:52**	C	11	59	8	1	16	9	**9¾**	4:52	E	**3:49**	C	AQU	27
77	18	W.	6:51	C	**6:53**	C	12	02	8	0	53	10	**10½**	5:34	E	**5:03**	D	CAP	28
78	19	Th.	6:49	C	**6:55**	C	12	06	8	0	29	11	**11½**	6:12	D	**6:18**	D	AQU	29
79	20	Fr.	6:47	C	**6:56**	C	12	09	8	0 s.	05	11¾	—	6:50	D	**7:33**	E	PSC	0
80	21	Sa.	6:46	C	**6:57**	C	12	11	9	0 n.	18	12¼	**12¾**	7:28	C	**8:46**	E	PSC	1
81	22	**D**	6:44	C	**6:58**	C	12	14	9	0	41	1	**1½**	8:07	C	**9:58**	E	PSC	2
82	23	M.	6:42	C	**6:59**	C	12	17	9	1	05	2	**2½**	8:47	C	**11:06**	E	ARI	3
83	24	Tu.	6:40	C	**7:00**	C	12	20	10	1	29	2¾	**3¼**	9:31	B	—	–	TAU	4
84	25	W.	6:39	C	**7:01**	C	12	22	10	1	52	3½	**4¼**	10:19	B	12:09	E	TAU	5
85	26	Th.	6:37	C	**7:03**	C	12	26	10	2	16	4½	**5¼**	11:09	B	1:06	E	TAU	6
86	27	Fr.	6:35	C	**7:04**	C	12	29	10	2	39	5½	**6¼**	**12:02**	B	1:57	E	GEM	7
87	28	Sa.	6:34	C	**7:05**	D	12	31	11	3	03	6½	**7¼**	**12:57**	C	2:43	E	GEM	8
88	29	**D**	6:32	C	**7:06**	D	12	34	11	3	26	7½	**8¼**	**1:53**	C	3:22	E	CAN	9
89	30	M.	6:30	C	**7:07**	D	12	37	11	3	49	8½	**9¼**	**2:49**	C	3:58	E	CAN	10
90	31	Tu.	6:28	C	**7:08**	D	12	40	12	4 n.	13	9½	**10**	**3:45**	C	4:30	E	LEO	11

 To use this page, see p. 124; for Key letters, see p. 252. ☞ **Bold** = P.M. ☞ Light = A.M.

March hath 31 days • 2015

Frozen ruts and slippery walks;
Gray old crops of last year's stalks. –Christopher Pearse Cranch

Day of Month	Day of Week	Dates, Feasts, Fasts, Aspects, Tide Heights	Weather
1	**D**	2nd S. in Lent • **Sunday of Orthodoxy** • Georgetown College chartered, D.C., 1815	*Flurries—*
2	M.	St. Chad • 3.5 earthquake rattled parts of southern Quebec, 2005 • Tides { 9.7 / 9.0	*wear*
3	Tu.	☌♃☾ • National Advisory Committee for Aeronautics (NACA), NASA predecessor, founded, 1915	*your*
4	W.	☌♀♅ • *March sun lets snow stand on a stone.* • { 9.9 / 9.4	*furries.*
5	Th.	St. Piran • **Full Worm** ○ • ☾ at apo. • Tides { 10.0 / 9.6	*Shovel-*
6	Fr.	☾ on Eq. • First machine patent issued in North America, to Joseph Jenkes, Mass., 1646 • { 10.0 / —	*ready,*
7	Sa.	St. Perpetua • ☾ at ☊ • Major ice storm in much of Iowa, 1990 • Tides { 9.7 / 9.9	*then*
8	**D**	**3rd S. in Lent** • **Daylight Saving Time begins, 2:00 A.M.** • Tides { 9.8 / 9.8	*warm*
9	M.	Food additive saccharin banned in Canada, 1977 • { 9.8 / 9.5	*and*
10	Tu.	Salvation Army officially began work in the U.S. (Battery Park, N.Y.C.), 1880 • Tides { 9.8 / 9.3	*heady,*
11	W.	☌♂♅ • Architect Thomas Hastings born, 1860 • { 9.7 / 9.0	*Freddie.*
12	Th.	☌♄☾ • Singer Al Jarreau born, 1940 • Tides { 9.6 / 8.8	*Better*
13	Fr.	☾ runs low • Discovery of Pluto formally announced, 1930 • Tides { 9.6 / 8.6	*pull*
14	Sa.	♄ stat. • *Kill a flea in March and you kill a hundred in summer.* • Tides { 9.6 / 8.7	*on*
15	**D**	**4th S. in Lent** • Beware the ides of March. • ☌♇☾ • { 9.8 / 9.0	*some*
16	M.	Wabash River crested 11 feet above flood stage, Terre Haute, Ind., 1939 • Tides { 10.2 / 9.5	*waders,*
17	Tu.	**St. Patrick's Day** • ☌☿♆ • Camp Fire Girls established, 1910 • Tides { 10.7 / 10.1	*you*
18	W.	☌♆☾ • Engineer Alonzo G. Decker Jr. died, 2002	*St. Pat's*
19	Th.	St. Joseph • ☾ at perig. • ☌☿☾ • Tides { 11.6 / 11.4	*paraders!*
20	Fr.	**Vernal Equinox** • **New** ● • **Eclipse** ☉ • ☾ on Eq. • ☾ at ☋	*Equinox*
21	Sa.	☌♂☾ • ☌♅☾ • Soviet sub collided with USS *Kitty Hawk*, 1984 • Tides { 11.8 / 11.9	*day*
22	**D**	**5th S. in Lent** • ☌♀☾ • British Stamp Act passed, 1765 • { 12.0 / 11.6	*is*
23	M.	World Meteorological Organization established by UN, 1950 • Tides { 11.9 / 11.2	*bright*
24	Tu.	Harry Houdini born as Ehrich Weisz, Budapest, Hungary, 1874 • Tides { 11.6 / 10.6	*but*
25	W.	Annunciation • Chipmunks emerge from hibernation now.	*shivery.*
26	Th.	☾ rides high • *Write injuries in sand, kindnesses in marble.* • Tides { 10.4 / 9.3	*Rain*
27	Fr.	25-lb. 2-oz. burbot caught, Lake Diefenbaker, Sask., 2010 • { 9.9 / 8.9	*and*
28	Sa.	Brewer August Anheuser Busch Jr. born, 1899 • { 9.5 / 8.6	*snow*
29	**D**	**Palm Sunday** • U.S. president John Tyler born, 1790	*come*
30	M.	☌♃☾ • Tex. readmitted to the Union, 1870 • { 9.2 / 8.8	*"splashal*
31	Tu.	*30th–31st:* 20.4" snow in 24 hours, St. Louis, Mo., 1890	*delivery"!*

Farmer's Calendar

■ Gas generators start with a slow, thumping *putt-putt-puttputtputtputtputt* that speeds up until it becomes a whir—unless the generator fails to catch. Then it fades with a discouraged wheeze, and the owner has to try again. Once started during winter power outages, though, it makes a staccato sound that we hardly notice.

Then one warm spring day, while walking the dogs, we were surprised to hear what sounded like a generator starting up in the woods. The ice and snow had long since departed. Who needed a generator now?

When we got home, I went out on the screened porch to read, and the generator started up again, right behind our house: *putt-putt-puttputtputtputtputt-wheeze.* It was coming from less than 10 yards away.

Abandoning the generator theory, I took a few steps in that direction, and a brown rocket exploded out of a brush pile, making me jump. The mysterious noise was a male ruffed grouse, drumming to attract a lady friend.

The bird "drums" not by striking a log, as was once supposed, but by opening and closing his wings so rapidly that they become a blur. One authority compares the sound to "an engine starting up in the distance."

Just so.

THE FOURTH MONTH • 2015

SKY WATCH ☆ *A total lunar eclipse on the 4th is visible before dawn from the western states and provinces; elsewhere in North America, only its beginning phase can be glimpsed before the Moon sets. Mars is now too close to the Sun to be seen. Venus passes just left of the Seven Sisters star cluster between the 10th and the 13th. Jupiter stands high in the south at nightfall. Mercury begins a fine apparition in the west at dusk on the 23rd. The crescent Moon passes just left of Venus on the 21st and meets Jupiter on the 25th and 26th. Saturn rises before 11:00 P.M. in Scorpius. Mercury passes just left of the Seven Sisters on the 30th; use binoculars.*

○ **Full Moon**	4th day	8th hour	6th minute
◑ **Last Quarter**	11th day	23rd hour	44th minute
● **New Moon**	18th day	14th hour	57th minute
◐ **First Quarter**	25th day	19th hour	55th minute

All times are given in Eastern Daylight Time.

Get these pages with times set to your zip code at Almanac.com/Access.

Day of Year	Day of Month	Day of Week	☼ Rises h. m.	Rise Key	☼ Sets h. m.	Set Key	Length of Day h.	m.	Sun Fast m.	Declination of Sun °	'	High Tide Times Boston		☾ Rises h. m.	Rise Key	☾ Sets h. m.	Set Key	☾ Astron. Place	☾ Age
91	1	W.	6:27	C	**7:09**	D	12	42	12	4 N.	36	10¼	**10¾**	**4:42**	D	5:00	D	LEO	12
92	2	Th.	6:25	C	**7:10**	D	12	45	12	4	59	11	**11¼**	**5:39**	D	5:29	D	LEO	13
93	3	Fr.	6:23	C	**7:12**	D	12	49	13	5	22	11½	12	**6:36**	D	5:57	C	VIR	14
94	4	Sa.	6:21	C	**7:13**	D	12	52	13	5	45	**12¼**	—	**7:34**	E	6:26	C	VIR	15
95	5	**D**	6:20	C	**7:14**	D	12	54	13	6	08	12½	**12¾**	**8:32**	E	6:56	C	VIR	16
96	6	M.	6:18	B	**7:15**	D	12	57	13	6	30	1	**1½**	**9:31**	E	7:28	C	VIR	17
97	7	Tu.	6:16	B	**7:16**	D	13	00	14	6	53	1¾	**2¼**	**10:30**	E	8:04	B	LIB	18
98	8	W.	6:15	B	**7:17**	D	13	02	14	7	15	2¼	**2¾**	**11:27**	E	8:45	B	LIB	19
99	9	Th.	6:13	B	**7:18**	D	13	05	14	7	38	3	**3½**	—	–	9:31	B	OPH	20
100	10	Fr.	6:11	B	**7:19**	D	13	08	14	8	00	3¾	**4½**	12:23	E	10:23	B	SAG	21
101	11	Sa.	6:10	B	**7:21**	D	13	11	15	8	22	4½	**5¼**	1:15	E	11:21	B	SAG	22
102	12	**D**	6:08	B	**7:22**	D	13	14	15	8	44	5½	**6¼**	2:03	E	**12:24**	C	SAG	23
103	13	M.	6:06	B	**7:23**	D	13	17	15	9	06	6½	**7¼**	2:47	E	**1:31**	C	CAP	24
104	14	Tu.	6:05	B	**7:24**	D	13	19	15	9	27	7¾	**8¼**	3:28	E	**2:41**	D	CAP	25
105	15	W.	6:03	B	**7:25**	D	13	22	16	9	49	8¾	**9¼**	4:06	D	**3:53**	D	AQU	26
106	16	Th.	6:02	B	**7:26**	D	13	24	16	10	10	9¾	**10¼**	4:43	D	**5:06**	D	PSC	27
107	17	Fr.	6:00	B	**7:27**	D	13	27	16	10	31	10½	**11**	5:20	C	**6:19**	E	PSC	28
108	18	Sa.	5:58	B	**7:28**	D	13	30	16	10	52	11½	**11¾**	5:58	C	**7:32**	E	PSC	0
109	19	**D**	5:57	B	**7:30**	D	13	33	17	11	13	**12½**	—	6:37	C	**8:43**	E	ARI	1
110	20	M.	5:55	B	**7:31**	D	13	36	17	11	34	12¾	**1¼**	7:21	B	**9:50**	E	ARI	2
111	21	Tu.	5:54	B	**7:32**	D	13	38	17	11	54	1½	**2**	8:07	B	**10:53**	E	TAU	3
112	22	W.	5:52	B	**7:33**	D	13	41	17	12	15	2¼	**3**	8:58	B	**11:48**	E	TAU	4
113	23	Th.	5:51	B	**7:34**	D	13	43	17	12	35	3¼	**3¾**	9:51	B	—	–	ORI	5
114	24	Fr.	5:49	B	**7:35**	D	13	46	18	12	55	4	**4¾**	10:47	C	12:37	E	GEM	6
115	25	Sa.	5:48	B	**7:36**	D	13	48	18	13	14	5	**5¾**	11:44	C	1:20	E	GEM	7
116	26	**D**	5:46	B	**7:37**	D	13	51	18	13	34	6	**6¾**	**12:40**	C	1:58	E	CAN	8
117	27	M.	5:45	B	**7:39**	D	13	54	18	13	53	7	**7½**	**1:37**	C	2:31	D	LEO	9
118	28	Tu.	5:43	B	**7:40**	E	13	57	18	14	12	8	**8½**	**2:34**	D	3:02	D	LEO	10
119	29	W.	5:42	B	**7:41**	E	13	59	18	14	30	8¾	**9¼**	**3:31**	D	3:31	D	LEO	11
120	30	Th.	5:41	B	**7:42**	E	14	01	18	14 N.	49	9½	**10**	**4:28**	D	3:59	C	VIR	12

 To use this page, see p. 124; for Key letters, see p. 252. ☞ **Bold = P.M.** ☞ Light = A.M.

APRIL HATH 30 DAYS • 2015

April the Beautiful, with streaming eyes,
Weeps o'er the havoc that rude March has made. –John Askham

Day of Month	Day of Week	Dates, Feasts, Fasts, Aspects, Tide Heights	Weather
1	W.	All Fools' • ☾ at apo. • *One fool makes many.* • Tides {9.5 / 9.4}	*Showers*
2	Th.	Maundy Thursday • ☾ on eq. • 140-mph winds, Mt. Washington, N.H., 1975	*briefly,*
3	Fr.	Good Friday • ☾ at ☊ • Outlaw Jesse James died, 1882 • {9.8 / 9.9}	*then*
4	Sa.	First day of Passover • Full Pink ○ • Eclipse ☾ • Tides {9.8 / —}	*sunny*
5	D	Easter • Anne Sullivan taught blind/deaf Helen Keller her first word, "water," 1887 • {10.0 / 9.8}	*and*
6	M.	Easter Monday • ☌♅☉ • Tides {10.2 / 9.7}	*pleasant,*
7	Tu.	Booker T. Washington first African-American pictured on a U.S. postage stamp, 1940 • {10.2 / 9.6}	*chiefly.*
8	W.	☌☿♅ • ☌♄☾ • ♃ stat. • William Pigott opened first inn in N.S. (Halifax), 1751	*Drip,*
9	Th.	Army of Northern Virginia surrendered, Appomattox Court House, Va., 1865 • Tides {10.1 / 9.2}	*drap,*
10	Fr.	☾ runs low • ☿ in sup. ☌ • Safety pin patented by Walter Hunt, 1849 • {10.1 / 9.1}	*rain*
11	Sa.	☌♇☾ • 47 tornadoes hit Midwest, 1965 • Tides {10.0 / 9.1}	*on*
12	D	2nd S. of Easter • Orthodox Easter • 21" snow, Selby, S.Dak., 1995	*tap,*
13	M.	U.S. president Thomas Jefferson born, 1743 • *Transit-1B*, first navigational satellite, launched, Fla., 1960 • {10.1 / 9.5}	*all*
14	Tu.	Massive fireball, seen over several states, possibly caused by meteor that may have landed in Wis., 2010 • {10.3 / 10.0}	*over*
15	W.	☌♆☾ • U.S. president Abraham Lincoln died, 1865 • First national lottery drawing, Can., 1974	*the*
16	Th.	☾ on eq. • ☾ at perig. • Magnitude 7.0 earthquake west of Eureka, Calif., 1899 • {11.0 / 11.2}	*map.*
17	Fr.	☾ at ☋ • ☌♅☾ • ♇ stat. • U.S. statesman Ben Franklin died, 1790	*Dreamy—*
18	Sa.	New ● • Beatification ceremony for Joan of Arc, Rome, Italy, 1909 • {11.4 / 12.0}	*brilliant*
19	D	3rd S. of Easter • ☌☿☾ • ☌♂☾ • {11.4 / —}	*and*
20	M.	Tony Gemignani spun 17.6 oz. of dough for 2 minutes to form pizza base 33.2" wide, Minneapolis, Minn., 2006	*beamy,*
21	Tu.	☌♀☾ • Actor Anthony Quinn born, 1915 • Tides {11.9 / 10.8}	*almost*
22	W.	☾ rides high • *A rainbow in spring indicates fair weather for 24 hours.* • {11.5 / 10.3}	*steamy!*
23	Th.	St. George • ☌☿♂ • Playwright Shakespeare born, 1564; died, 1616 • {11.0 / 9.8}	*Watch*
24	Fr.	*Old Farmer's Almanac* founder Robert B. Thomas born, 1766	*for*
25	Sa.	St. Mark • Scrabble board game trademark registered, 1950 • Tides {9.8 / 9.0}	*a*
26	D	4th S. of Easter • ☌♃☾ • Geologist Eduard Suess died, 1914	*cooling*
27	M.	Poplars leaf out about now. • Baseball player Rogers Hornsby born, 1896 • {9.1 / 8.8}	*trend*
28	Tu.	☾ at apo. • *A Chorus Line* closed after 6,137 performances on Broadway, N.Y.C., 1990 • {9.0 / 9.0}	*at*
29	W.	*It is no disgrace to move out of the way of the elephant.*	*month's*
30	Th.	☾ on eq. • Marguerite Bourgeoys opened first school in Montreal, Que., 1658 • {9.2 / 9.5}	*end.*

Hope is the only bee that makes honey without flowers. –Robert Ingersoll

Farmer's Calendar

■ The ice on our pond melted early this year, and it wasn't long before the snapping turtles started climbing up on a half-submerged log to bask in the strengthening sun. Some days, you can see half a dozen snappers of various sizes there. The log is on the far side of the pond, maybe 60 yards from our path, and from that distance their shells have a dull-black sheen. They look like cast-iron frying pans turned upside down.

There must be a lot of snappers in the pond. We've seen their burrows with fragments of eggs in them, either where the young have hatched or where predators have dug them up and eaten them. There's evidence of the snappers' predation as well. We saw two Canada geese convoying a flock of goslings around the pond one day this month, but we haven't seen the little ones since. Perhaps they became snacks for the snappers.

Several years ago, while walking the dogs, I stumbled upon an enormous snapper lying in the middle of the path. It was probably 3 feet long from beak to tail and looked like a bonsai dinosaur. The experience reminded me of the final line of Emily Dickinson's poem "A Narrow Fellow in the Grass," about encountering a snake and feeling "zero at the bone."

SKY WATCH ☆ *Mercury has its best evening star appearance of 2015 in the first half of the month, in Taurus. It stands to the left of the Pleiades on the 1st and is brightest for the first few days of the month. Jupiter stands high in the southwest at dusk and sets after midnight. It stands above the waxing Moon on the 23rd. Venus is at its highest and sets before midnight. The month belongs to Saturn, brighter than it has appeared in over a decade. It stands at opposition on the night of the 22nd, rising at dusk and remaining out all night long. Its rings are nearly as wide "open" as possible, a glorious sight through any telescope magnification above 30×.*

○	**Full Moon**	3rd day	23rd hour	42nd minute
◑	**Last Quarter**	11th day	6th hour	36th minute
●	**New Moon**	18th day	0 hour	13th minute
◐	**First Quarter**	25th day	13th hour	19th minute

All times are given in Eastern Daylight Time.

Get these pages with times set to your zip code at Almanac.com/Access.

Day of Year	Day of Month	Day of Week	☼ Rises h. m.	Rise Key	☼ Sets h. m.	Set Key	Length of Day h. m.	Sun Fast m.	Declination of Sun ° '	High Tide Times Boston		☾ Rises h. m.	Rise Key	☾ Sets h. m.	Set Key	☾ Astron. Place	☾ Age
121	1	Fr.	5:39	B	7:43	E	14 04	19	15 N.07	10½	10¾	5:25	E	4:27	C	VIR	13
122	2	Sa.	5:38	B	7:44	E	14 06	19	15 25	11	11¼	6:24	E	4:57	C	VIR	14
123	3	**D**	5:37	B	7:45	E	14 08	19	15 43	11¾	12	7:23	E	5:29	C	VIR	15
124	4	M.	5:35	B	7:46	E	14 11	19	16 00	**12½**	—	8:23	E	6:04	C	LIB	16
125	5	Tu.	5:34	B	7:47	E	14 13	19	16 17	12½	1	9:22	E	6:43	B	LIB	17
126	6	W.	5:33	B	7:49	E	14 16	19	16 34	1¼	1¾	10:19	E	7:28	B	OPH	18
127	7	Th.	5:31	B	7:50	E	14 19	19	16 51	2	2½	11:12	E	8:19	B	OPH	19
128	8	Fr.	5:30	B	7:51	E	14 21	19	17 07	2½	3¼	—	–	9:15	B	SAG	20
129	9	Sa.	5:29	B	7:52	E	14 23	19	17 23	3½	4	12:02	E	10:16	C	SAG	21
130	10	**D**	5:28	B	7:53	E	14 25	19	17 39	4¼	5	12:47	E	11:21	C	CAP	22
131	11	M.	5:27	B	7:54	E	14 27	19	17 55	5¼	6	1:28	E	**12:29**	C	AQU	23
132	12	Tu.	5:26	B	7:55	E	14 29	19	18 10	6¼	7	2:06	D	**1:38**	D	AQU	24
133	13	W.	5:25	B	7:56	E	14 31	19	18 25	7¼	8	2:42	D	**2:49**	D	AQU	25
134	14	Th.	5:24	B	7:57	E	14 33	19	18 39	8¼	8¾	3:17	D	**4:00**	E	PSC	26
135	15	Fr.	5:22	B	7:58	E	14 36	19	18 54	9¼	9¾	3:53	C	**5:11**	E	PSC	27
136	16	Sa.	5:21	B	7:59	E	14 38	19	19 08	10¼	10¾	4:30	C	**6:21**	E	PSC	28
137	17	**D**	5:21	A	8:00	E	14 39	19	19 21	11¼	11½	5:11	B	**7:30**	E	ARI	29
138	18	M.	5:20	A	8:01	E	14 41	19	19 35	**12**	—	5:56	B	**8:35**	E	TAU	0
139	19	Tu.	5:19	A	8:02	E	14 43	19	19 48	12¼	1	6:44	B	**9:35**	E	TAU	1
140	20	W.	5:18	A	8:03	E	14 45	19	20 00	1¼	1¾	7:37	B	**10:28**	E	TAU	2
141	21	Th.	5:17	A	8:04	E	14 47	19	20 12	2	2½	8:33	B	**11:15**	E	GEM	3
142	22	Fr.	5:16	A	8:05	E	14 49	19	20 24	2¾	3½	9:30	C	**11:55**	E	GEM	4
143	23	Sa.	5:15	A	8:06	E	14 51	19	20 36	3½	4¼	10:28	C	—	–	CAN	5
144	24	**D**	5:15	A	8:07	E	14 52	19	20 47	4½	5	11:26	C	12:31	E	CAN	6
145	25	M.	5:14	A	8:08	E	14 54	19	20 58	5¼	6	**12:23**	C	1:03	D	LEO	7
146	26	Tu.	5:13	A	8:09	E	14 56	19	21 09	6¼	6¾	**1:20**	D	1:33	D	SEX	8
147	27	W.	5:12	A	8:10	E	14 58	19	21 19	7¼	7¾	**2:17**	D	2:01	D	LEO	9
148	28	Th.	5:12	A	8:11	E	14 59	18	21 29	8	8½	**3:14**	D	2:29	C	VIR	10
149	29	Fr.	5:11	A	8:11	E	15 00	18	21 38	9	9¼	**4:13**	E	2:58	C	VIR	11
150	30	Sa.	5:11	A	8:12	E	15 01	18	21 47	9¾	10	**5:12**	E	3:29	C	VIR	12
151	31	**D**	5:10	A	8:13	E	15 03	18	21 N.56	10½	10¾	**6:12**	E	4:02	B	LIB	13

May hath 31 days • 2015

Thou art winsome, light, and gay,
Smiling May. –George Burden

Day of Month	Day of Week	Dates, Feasts, Fasts, Aspects, Tide Heights	Weather
1	Fr.	Sts. Philip & James • May Day • ☾ at ☊ • Tides {9.3 / 9.8	*Sopping,*
2	Sa.	St. Athanasius • Northern Dancer first Canadian horse to win Kentucky Derby, 1964	*and*
3	**D**	**5th S. of Easter** • Vesak • **Full Flower** ○ • {9.6 / 10.3	*with*
4	M.	First general meeting of Society of the Cincinnati, Philadelphia, 1784 • Tides {9.7 / —	*no*
5	Tu.	**Cinco de Mayo** • ☌♄☾ • Rain, large hail, 70-mph winds, Tarrant County, Tex., 1995 • {10.5 / 9.7	*sign*
6	W.	Film director Orson Welles born, 1915 • Tides {10.6 / 9.6	*of*
7	Th.	☾ runs low • ☿ gr. elong. (21° east) • Tides {10.6 / 9.6	*stopping,*
8	Fr.	St. Julian of Norwich • ☌♇☾ • *Whistling parrots indicate rain.*	*either—*
9	Sa.	St. Gregory of Nazianzus • Singer Hank Snow born, 1914 • Tides {10.5 / 9.5	*then*
10	**D**	**Rogation S.** • **Mother's Day** • 14.2" snow, Marquette, Mich., 1990	*a*
11	M.	Tornado hit Newark, N.J., 1865 • **Three** • {10.3 / 9.8	*breather.*
12	Tu.	☌♆☾ • Manitoba Act passed and given royal assent, 1870 • **Chilly** • {10.2 / 10.1	*Warm*
13	W.	☾ on Eq. • Cranberries in bud now. • Psychologist Dr. Joyce Brothers died, 2013 • **Saints**	*again,*
14	Th.	**Ascension** • ☾ at ☋ • ☾ at perig. • Tides {10.4 / 10.9	*storm*
15	Fr.	☌♅☾ • Ellen Church became first airline stewardess, Boeing Air Transport, 1930	*again—*
16	Sa.	Marie Antoinette (age 14) married future French king Louis XVI (age 15), 1770 • Tides {10.7 / 11.7	*what*
17	**D**	**1st S. af. Asc.** • *A kind word is like a spring day.* • Tides {10.8 / 11.9	*is*
18	M.	**Victoria Day (Canada)** • **New** ● • ☌♂☾ • Tides {10.7 / —	*the*
19	Tu.	St. Dunstan • ☌☿☾ • ☿ stat. • "Dark Day" in New England, 1780	*norm,*
20	W.	☾ rides high • Historian Allan Nevins born, 1890 • {11.6 / 10.3	*again?*
21	Th.	Orthodox Ascension • ☌♀☾ • American Red Cross founded, 1881 • {11.2 / 10.0	*It's*
22	Fr.	♄ at ☍ • Wrestler Alastair Ralphs born, 1977 • {10.8 / 9.7	*fine,*
23	Sa.	*A pound of pluck is worth a ton of luck.* • Tides {10.2 / 9.4	*it's*
24	**D**	**Whit. S.** • **Pentecost** • Shavuot • ☌♃☾ • {9.8 / 9.1	*not,*
25	M.	St. Bede • **Memorial Day (observed)** • Brooklyn-Battery Tunnel opened, N.Y.C., 1950 • {9.3 / 9.0	*it's*
26	Tu.	☾ at apo. • Boat of Pharaoh Cheops discovered near Great Pyramid of Giza, Egypt, 1954 • {9.0 / 9.0	*suddenly*
27	W.	Ember Day • ☾ on Eq. • ☌☿♂ • Tides {8.8 / 9.1	*hot:*
28	Th.	☾ at ☊ • 100°F, Portland, Oreg., 1983 • Tides {8.8 / 9.4	*Boom,*
29	Fr.	Ember Day • R.I. became 13th U.S. state, 1790 • Tides {8.9 / 9.6	*crash,*
30	Sa.	Ember Day • ☿ in inf. ☌ • *Self-assurance is two-thirds of success.* • {9.0 / 9.9	*lightning*
31	**D**	**Trinity** • Orthodox Pentecost • Actress Brooke Shields born, 1965	*flash!*

Farmer's Calendar

■ We never got around to felling any trees for firewood last fall, so here we are in spring with a skimpy woodpile, most of it white birch, which looks pretty in a fireplace but doesn't supply much heat. When you live in the woods, it's embarrassing to buy cordwood. So we're scavenging for dead wood, which won't need to dry.

There's quite a bit of it, mostly from oaks decapitated by ice storms. We can snap off kindling-length branches with our fingers. The real prizes are snags, dead trees still standing on their stumps. When their bark sloughs off, it deprives insects of shelter and prevents rotting. The wood is as smooth and hard as ivory and burns with a clear white flame.

Summer is the best time to look for snags: They stand out from the other trees because they have no leaves. Even so, we sometimes get fooled by a stubborn survivor, dead at the ground, dead at the top, but still flying its green pennants from a branch or two.

For a while, we couldn't see the dead trees for the forest. In time, we learned how to look at them with new eyes, and now it's amazing how many we have. I counted 50 on a ¼-mile walk. In places, they outnumber the living trees. As it says in The Book of Common Prayer, "In the midst of life, we are in death."

The Sixth Month • 2015

SKY WATCH ☆ *Venus reaches its greatest elongation from the Sun on the 6th and is near maximum brightness, though lower than during the past 2 months. Getting closer to brilliant Jupiter, it meets the Beehive star cluster on the 13th and 14th. The 14th also marks Mars's passage behind the Sun in a conjunction. The crescent Moon joins Venus and Jupiter on the 19th and 20th, respectively, creating truly eye-catching conjunctions at dusk. Summer begins with the solstice on the 21st, at 12:38* P.M. *The nearly full Moon stands just above Saturn on the 28th, the same day that a 5-day conjunction between Venus and Jupiter begins.*

○	**Full Moon**	2nd day	12th hour	19th minute
◑	**Last Quarter**	9th day	11th hour	42nd minute
●	**New Moon**	16th day	10th hour	5th minute
◐	**First Quarter**	24th day	7th hour	3rd minute

All times are given in Eastern Daylight Time.

Get these pages with times set to your zip code at Almanac.com/Access.

Day of Year	Day of Month	Day of Week	☼ Rises h. m.	Rise Key	☼ Sets h. m.	Set Key	Length of Day h. m.	Sun Fast m.	Declination of Sun ° ′	High Tide Times Boston		☾ Rises h. m.	Rise Key	☾ Sets h. m.	Set Key	☾ Astron. Place	☾ Age
152	1	M.	5:10	A	**8:14**	E	15 04	18	22 N.04	11¼	**11¼**	**7:12**	E	4:40	B	LIB	14
153	2	Tu.	5:09	A	**8:15**	E	15 06	18	22 12	**12**	—	**8:11**	E	5:23	B	SCO	15
154	3	W.	5:09	A	**8:15**	E	15 06	18	22 19	12	**12¾**	**9:07**	E	6:12	B	OPH	16
155	4	Th.	5:08	A	**8:16**	E	15 08	17	22 26	12¾	**1½**	**9:59**	E	7:07	B	SAG	17
156	5	Fr.	5:08	A	**8:17**	E	15 09	17	22 33	1½	**2¼**	**10:47**	E	8:08	C	SAG	18
157	6	Sa.	5:08	A	**8:17**	E	15 09	17	22 39	2¼	**3**	**11:30**	E	9:13	C	CAP	19
158	7	**D**	5:07	A	**8:18**	E	15 11	17	22 45	3¼	**3¾**	—	–	10:21	C	AQU	20
159	8	M.	5:07	A	**8:19**	E	15 12	17	22 51	4	**4¾**	12:08	D	11:29	D	AQU	21
160	9	Tu.	5:07	A	**8:19**	E	15 12	16	22 56	5	**5½**	12:44	D	**12:39**	D	AQU	22
161	10	W.	5:07	A	**8:20**	E	15 13	16	23 01	6	**6½**	1:19	D	**1:48**	D	PSC	23
162	11	Th.	5:06	A	**8:20**	E	15 14	16	23 05	7	**7½**	1:54	C	**2:58**	E	PSC	24
163	12	Fr.	5:06	A	**8:21**	E	15 15	16	23 09	8	**8½**	2:29	C	**4:07**	E	PSC	25
164	13	Sa.	5:06	A	**8:21**	E	15 15	16	23 12	9	**9½**	3:07	C	**5:14**	E	ARI	26
165	14	**D**	5:06	A	**8:22**	E	15 16	15	23 15	10	**10¼**	3:49	C	**6:20**	E	TAU	27
166	15	M.	5:06	A	**8:22**	E	15 16	15	23 18	11	**11¼**	4:35	B	**7:21**	E	TAU	28
167	16	Tu.	5:06	A	**8:23**	E	15 17	15	23 20	11¾	—	5:25	B	**8:17**	E	TAU	0
168	17	W.	5:06	A	**8:23**	E	15 17	15	23 22	12	**12¾**	6:19	B	**9:07**	E	ORI	1
169	18	Th.	5:06	A	**8:23**	E	15 17	15	23 24	12¾	**1½**	7:16	B	**9:51**	E	GEM	2
170	19	Fr.	5:06	A	**8:24**	E	15 18	14	23 25	1½	**2¼**	8:15	C	**10:29**	E	CAN	3
171	20	Sa.	5:07	A	**8:24**	E	15 17	14	23 25	2¼	**3**	9:13	C	**11:03**	D	CAN	4
172	21	**D**	5:07	A	**8:24**	E	15 17	14	23 26	3	**3¾**	10:12	C	**11:34**	D	LEO	5
173	22	M.	5:07	A	**8:24**	E	15 17	14	23 25	3¾	**4½**	11:09	D	—	–	LEO	6
174	23	Tu.	5:07	A	**8:24**	E	15 17	13	23 25	4¾	**5¼**	**12:06**	D	12:03	D	LEO	7
175	24	W.	5:08	A	**8:25**	E	15 17	13	23 24	5½	**6**	**1:03**	D	12:31	C	VIR	8
176	25	Th.	5:08	A	**8:25**	E	15 17	13	23 22	6½	**6¾**	**2:00**	E	12:59	C	VIR	9
177	26	Fr.	5:08	A	**8:25**	E	15 17	13	23 20	7¼	**7¾**	**2:58**	E	1:29	C	VIR	10
178	27	Sa.	5:09	A	**8:25**	E	15 16	13	23 18	8¼	**8½**	**3:58**	E	2:00	C	VIR	11
179	28	**D**	5:09	A	**8:25**	E	15 16	12	23 15	9	**9¼**	**4:58**	E	2:36	B	LIB	12
180	29	M.	5:10	A	**8:25**	E	15 15	12	23 12	9¾	**10**	**5:57**	E	3:16	B	LIB	13
181	30	Tu.	5:10	A	**8:25**	E	15 15	12	23 N.09	10¾	**10¾**	**6:56**	E	4:02	B	OPH	14

 To use this page, see p. 124; for Key letters, see p. 252. ☞ **Bold = P.M.** ☞ Light = A.M.

JUNE HATH 30 DAYS • 2015

June brings tulips, lilies, roses,
Fills the children's hands with posies. –Sara Coleridge

Day of Month	Day of Week	Dates, Feasts, Fasts, Aspects, Tide Heights	Weather
1	M.	**Visit. of Mary**[T] • ☌♄☾ • Cable News Network (CNN) debuted, 1980 • {9.3 10.5	*Hotter*
2	Tu.	**Full Strawberry** ○ • *Some of the sweetest berries grow among the sharpest thorns.* • {9.5 —	*than*
3	W.	☾ RUNS LOW • Edward White first U.S. astronaut to perform spacewalk, 1965 • {10.8 9.7	*Hades,*
4	Th.	☌♇☾ • *3rd–5th:* Early hurricane wreaked havoc along Atlantic coast, 1825 • {11.0 9.8	*ladies!*
5	Fr.	**St. Boniface** • U.S. president Ronald Reagan died, 2004	*Black*
6	Sa.	D-Day, 1944 • ♀ GR. ELONG. (45° EAST) • 4.0" snow, Regent, N.Dak., 2009 • {11.1 10.0	*clouds*
7	**D**	**Corpus Christi** • **Orthodox All Saints'** • Tides {11.0 10.1	*hover*
8	M.	☌♆☾ • *Every head is a world.* • Tides {10.8 10.2	*while*
9	Tu.	British private Timothy O'Hea put out fire in gunpowder-loaded railcar, earning Victoria Cross, Danville, Que., 1866	*golfers*
10	W.	☾ ON EQ. • ☾ AT ☋ • ☾ AT PERIG. • *Phoenix* steamboat first in U.S. to sail on open sea, 1809	*run*
11	Th.	**St. Barnabas** • ☌⛢☾ • ☿ STAT. • Tides {10.1 10.8	*for*
12	Fr.	♆ STAT. • England created municipal government in New York, 1665 • Tides {10.0 11.0	*cover.*
13	Sa.	Poet William Butler Yeats born, 1865 • Tides {10.0 11.3	*It's*
14	**D**	**3rd S. af. P.** • ☌☿☾ • ☌♂☉ • Tides {10.0 11.4	*cool—*
15	M.	George Washington chosen as commander in chief of Continental Army, 1775 • 5.0" rain, Cadiz, Ohio, 1990	*no*
16	Tu.	**New** ● • ☾ RIDES HIGH • ☌♂☾ • Comedian Stan Laurel born, 1890 • {10.1 —	*more*
17	W.	*Wednesday clearing, clear till Sunday.* • Tides {11.4 10.0	*school!*
18	Th.	**First day of Ramadan** • Napoleon defeated at Waterloo (present-day Belgium), 1815 • {11.2 9.9	*Liberation*
19	Fr.	Garfield the Cat made comic strip debut, 1978 • {10.9 9.8	*calls*
20	Sa.	☌♀☾ • ☌♃☾ • Samuel Morse granted patent for telegraph, 1840 • {10.5 9.6	*for*
21	**D**	**4th S. af. P.** • **Father's Day** • **Summer Solstice** • {10.1 9.4	*youthful*
22	M.	**St. Alban** • Ashrita Furman traveled 23.11 miles by pogo stick, 1997 • {9.7 9.3	*celebration,*
23	Tu.	☾ ON EQ. • ☾ AT APO. • Olympic gold medalist Wilma Rudolph born, 1940 • {9.3 9.2	*but*
24	W.	**Nativ. John the Baptist** • **Midsummer Day** • ☾ AT ☊ • ☿ GR. ELONG. (23° WEST)	*daily*
25	Th.	Actor John Fiedler, voice of Piglet in Winnie-the-Pooh Disney cartoons, died, 2005 • {8.8 9.3	*drenchers*
26	Fr.	*It is not summer until the crickets sing.* • Tides {8.6 9.4	*forestall*
27	Sa.	100°F, Fort Yukon, Alaska, 1915 • Tides {8.6 9.7	*adventures.*
28	**D**	**5th S. af. P.** • ☌♄☾ • Football player John Elway born, 1960	*Thunderous,*
29	M.	**Sts. Peter & Paul** • Last stone placed for second lighthouse at Minot's Ledge, Mass., 1860	*then*
30	Tu.	Michigan Territory established, 1805 • Tides {9.2 10.7	*wondrous.*

Better a diamond with a flaw than a pebble without one. –Confucius

Farmer's Calendar

■ We had seen wild strawberries on the path by the pond when we moved in 36 years ago. Then, to our surprise, we found them in our yard; just a small patch at first, but it has been growing steadily. The area covered is now approximately 90 square feet. It's hard to avoid the conclusion that they're taking over.

Our immigration policy toward the yard has always been lenient; we welcome dandelions, clover, and other interlopers, and the strawberries, with their cheerful white flowers, make us look forward to summer. They lie practically flat on the ground, so mowing doesn't disturb them. The berries are so tiny—hardly larger than BBs—that it's not worth trying to gather them to sprinkle on cereal. In any case, birds usually beat us to them, and the dogs graze on them, too. When they do, their breath afterward smells like the topping on strawberry shortcake.

Could the dogs be responsible, indirectly, for our recent bounty? The patch in our yard straddles the path we take to walk them to and from the pond, and as we inadvertently tread on the berries, their rapturous aroma rises into our nostrils. Perhaps the crushed berries have been hitchhiking on our shoes? On the paws of the dogs? Or in their guts? If so, there's another argument for owning dogs.

C
A
L
E
N
D
A
R

SKY WATCH ☆ *The first few days of the month bring a spectacular conjunction of Venus and Jupiter. The pair stands 14 degrees high in the west, 1 hour after sunset. On the 6th, Earth reaches aphelion, its annual point farthest from the Sun. The Sun is now 7 percent dimmer than in January, although its near-peak elevation in Northern Hemisphere skies makes its rays more intense than in winter. On the 25th, the Moon sits to the right of Saturn, which has been retrograding into Libra since May. The 31st brings a "Blue Moon," a popular term for a second full Moon in a calendar month, which happens every 2½ years, on average.*

○	**Full Moon**	1st day	22nd hour	20th minute
☽	**Last Quarter**	8th day	16th hour	24th minute
●	**New Moon**	15th day	21st hour	24th minute
◑	**First Quarter**	24th day	0 hour	4th minute
○	**Full Moon**	31st day	6th hour	43rd minute

All times are given in Eastern Daylight Time.

Get these pages with times set to your zip code at Almanac.com/Access.

Day of Year	Day of Month	Day of Week	☼ Rises h. m.	Rise Key	☼ Sets h. m.	Set Key	Length of Day h. m.	Sun Fast m.	Declination of Sun ° ′	High Tide Times Boston		☾ Rises h. m.	Rise Key	☾ Sets h. m.	Set Key	☾ Astron. Place	☾ Age
182	1	W.	5:10	A	8:24	E	15 14	12	23 N. 05	11½	11½	7:51	E	4:55	B	SAG	15
183	2	Th.	5:11	A	8:24	E	15 13	12	23 01	12¼	—	8:42	E	5:55	B	SAG	16
184	3	Fr.	5:12	A	8:24	E	15 12	11	22 56	12½	1	9:28	E	7:00	C	SAG	17
185	4	Sa.	5:12	A	8:24	E	15 12	11	22 51	1¼	1¾	10:09	E	8:08	C	AQU	18
186	5	**D**	5:13	A	8:24	E	15 11	11	22 45	2	2¾	10:47	D	9:19	C	CAP	19
187	6	M.	5:13	A	8:23	E	15 10	11	22 39	2¾	3½	11:23	D	10:29	D	AQU	20
188	7	Tu.	5:14	A	8:23	E	15 09	11	22 33	3¾	4¼	11:57	C	11:40	D	PSC	21
189	8	W.	5:15	A	8:23	E	15 08	11	22 26	4¾	5¼	—	–	12:49	E	CET	22
190	9	Th.	5:15	A	8:22	E	15 07	11	22 19	5¾	6¼	12:32	C	1:58	E	PSC	23
191	10	Fr.	5:16	A	8:22	E	15 06	10	22 12	6¾	7¼	1:09	C	3:05	E	ARI	24
192	11	Sa.	5:17	A	8:21	E	15 04	10	22 04	7¾	8¼	1:48	B	4:10	E	ARI	25
193	12	**D**	5:18	A	8:21	E	15 03	10	21 56	8¾	9¼	2:31	B	5:12	E	TAU	26
194	13	M.	5:18	A	8:20	E	15 02	10	21 47	9¾	10	3:19	B	6:09	E	TAU	27
195	14	Tu.	5:19	A	8:20	E	15 01	10	21 38	10¾	11	4:11	B	7:01	E	ORI	28
196	15	W.	5:20	A	8:19	E	14 59	10	21 29	11½	11¾	5:06	B	7:47	E	GEM	0
197	16	Th.	5:21	A	8:18	E	14 57	10	21 19	12¼	—	6:03	C	8:27	E	GEM	1
198	17	Fr.	5:22	A	8:18	E	14 56	10	21 09	12½	1	7:02	C	9:03	D	CAN	2
199	18	Sa.	5:23	A	8:17	E	14 54	10	20 59	1¼	1¾	8:00	C	9:35	D	LEO	3
200	19	**D**	5:23	A	8:16	E	14 53	9	20 48	2	2½	8:58	C	10:05	D	LEO	4
201	20	M.	5:24	A	8:15	E	14 51	9	20 37	2½	3	9:55	D	10:34	D	LEO	5
202	21	Tu.	5:25	A	8:14	E	14 49	9	20 25	3¼	3¾	10:52	D	11:02	C	VIR	6
203	22	W.	5:26	A	8:14	E	14 48	9	20 14	4	4½	11:49	D	11:30	C	VIR	7
204	23	Th.	5:27	A	8:13	E	14 46	9	20 01	4¾	5¼	12:46	E	—	–	VIR	8
205	24	Fr.	5:28	A	8:12	E	14 44	9	19 49	5¾	6	1:44	E	12:00	C	VIR	9
206	25	Sa.	5:29	A	8:11	E	14 42	9	19 36	6½	7	2:42	E	12:33	B	LIB	10
207	26	**D**	5:30	A	8:10	E	14 40	9	19 23	7½	7¾	3:42	E	1:10	B	LIB	11
208	27	M.	5:31	B	8:09	E	14 38	9	19 10	8¼	8¾	4:40	E	1:53	B	OPH	12
209	28	Tu.	5:32	B	8:08	E	14 36	9	18 56	9¼	9½	5:37	E	2:42	B	OPH	13
210	29	W.	5:33	B	8:07	E	14 34	9	18 42	10¼	10¼	6:30	E	3:38	B	SAG	14
211	30	Th.	5:34	B	8:06	E	14 32	9	18 27	11	11¼	7:19	E	4:41	C	SAG	15
212	31	Fr.	5:35	B	8:05	E	14 30	9	18 N. 13	11¾	—	8:04	E	5:49	C	CAP	16

JULY HATH 31 DAYS • 2015

Summer is a glorious season,
Warm and bright and pleasant. –Denis Florence Macarthy

Day of Month	Day of Week	Dates, Feasts, Fasts, Aspects, Tide Heights	Weather
1	W.	Canada Day • Full Buck ○ • ☾ RUNS LOW • ☌♀♃	*Independence*
2	Th.	☌♇☾ • 89-mph wind gust, Lavon Dam, Tex., 1989	*Day*
3	Fr.	Dog Days begin. • Idaho became 43rd U.S. state, 1890 • Tides {11.3 10.1	*booming,*
4	Sa.	Independence Day • Alice Lidell received first copy of *Alice in Wonderland*, 1865	*thunderclouds*
5	D	6th S. af. P. • ☾ AT PERIG. • Tides {11.5 10.6	*looming,*
6	M.	☌♆☾ • ♇ AT ☍ • ⊕ AT APHELION • Armadillos mate now. • {11.3 10.7	*but*
7	Tu.	☾ ON EQ. • ☾ AT ☋ • *Storms burst as the tide turns.* • Tides {11.0 10.8	*after*
8	W.	☌♅☾ • Congress authorized trademark registration, 1870 • Tides {10.6 10.8	*the*
9	Th.	Aviator Walter Brookins flew higher than a mile, 1910 • Tides {10.2 10.8	*cannonade,*
10	Fr.	♀ GR. ILLUM. EXT. • 134°F, Greenland Ranch, Calif., 1913	*lovely*
11	Sa.	Cornscateous air is everywhere. • Baseball-size hail caused more than $600 million damage, Colo., 1990 • {9.6 10.8	*days*
12	D	7th S. af. P. • U.S. First Lady Dolley Madison died, 1849 • Tides {9.5 10.9	*for*
13	M.	Actor Sir Patrick Stewart born, 1940 • Tides {9.5 10.9	*hot*
14	Tu.	Bastille Day • ☾ RIDES HIGH • *Mariner 4* photographed Mars, 1965	*dogs*
15	W.	St. Swithin • New ● • ☌☿☾ • ☌♂☾ • {9.6 10.9	*and*
16	Th.	☌☿♂ • District of Columbia established, 1790	*lemonade.*
17	Fr.	*An angry man opens his mouth and shuts his eyes.* • {10.7 9.7	*Ideal*
18	Sa.	☌♃☾ • ☌♀☾ • First train ride between U.S. and Canada, 1853	*circumstances*
19	D	8th S. af. P. • Mary I declared Queen of England, 1553 • {10.3 9.6	*for*
20	M.	Connecticut state agricultural experiment station established, 1875 • Tides {10.0 9.5	*barbecues*
21	Tu.	☾ ON EQ. • ☾ AT ☊ • ☾ AT APO. • Black-eyed Susans in bloom now. • {9.7 9.4	*and*
22	W.	St. Mary Magdalene • Canadian prime minister William Lyon Mackenzie King died, 1950	*country*
23	Th.	☿ IN SUP. ☌ • ♀ STAT. • Union Act approved, uniting Upper and Lower Canada, 1840	*dances.*
24	Fr.	Steamer *Eastland* overturned, killing 844, Chicago River, Ill., 1915 • Tides {8.7 9.3	*Sticky*
25	Sa.	St. James • Adult gypsy moths emerge. • Tides {8.5 9.4	*situation:*
26	D	9th S. af. P. • ☌♄☾ • ♅ STAT. • Tides {8.5 9.6	*Cool*
27	M.	*Deliver your words not by number but by weight.* • {8.6 10.0	*off*
28	Tu.	☾ RUNS LOW • Cross-country runner Terry Fox born, 1958 • Tides {8.9 10.4	*with*
29	W.	St. Martha • ☌♇☾ • Schooner *Bluenose II* donated to Nova Scotia, 1971 • {9.3 10.9	*a*
30	Th.	Jake, a dog, swam in annual 1.25-mile race from Alcatraz to San Francisco, Calif., 2005 • {9.7 11.3	*beach*
31	Fr.	St. Ignatius of Loyola • Full Thunder ○ (blue Moon) • ☌♀♃	*vacation!*

Farmer's Calendar

■ Turkeys are a common sight here all winter. We watch them moving through our woods in ghostly battalions, and when the snow is too deep for them in the woods, their unmistakable four-toed tracks draw hieroglyphics up and down our driveway.

But when the first big tom set foot in our yard on a hot summer day, we were startled. He was followed by four females, who crisscrossed the far end of the field as if they were partners in a quadrille. They stalked deliberately to and fro, their heads and beaks dipping rhythmically to dine on bugs.

Then they sat down in the sun, like ladies at a 19th-century church picnic, spreading their voluminous skirts. Perhaps they were taking a dust bath—that end of the yard is the first to dry out. They stayed half an hour, looking contented.

Recently there was a kerfuffle in the local paper when a letter to the editor proposed that turkeys should be hunted year-round because they carry deer ticks, which in turn carry Lyme disease. The suggestion was answered by a salvo from outraged correspondents challenging the writer's knowledge of turkeys, ticks, and good sense.

Do turkeys read the papers? Maybe that's why they looked contented.

CALENDAR

SKY WATCH ☆ *All planets except Saturn now fall into the Sun's glare and become difficult or impossible to see. The close conjunction between Jupiter and Mercury, extremely low in bright twilight on the 6th, is visually challenging. The absence of the Moon on the night of the 11th makes conditions ideal for viewing the great Perseid meteor shower, which peaks after midnight. Expect a "shooting star" every minute. On the 15th, Venus slides behind the Sun in an inferior conjunction, ending its evening star apparition. It reappears as a morning star in the east at month's end. The gibbous Moon floats to the upper left of Saturn on the 22nd. Saturn remains a bright evening star throughout the month.*

◑	**Last Quarter**	6th day	22nd hour	3rd minute
●	**New Moon**	14th day	10th hour	53rd minute
◐	**First Quarter**	22nd day	15th hour	31st minute
○	**Full Moon**	29th day	14th hour	35th minute

All times are given in Eastern Daylight Time.

Get these pages with times set to your zip code at Almanac.com/Access.

Day of Year	Day of Month	Day of Week	☼ Rises h. m.	Rise Key	☼ Sets h. m.	Set Key	Length of Day h.	m.	Sun Fast m.	Declination of Sun °	'	High Tide Times Boston		☾ Rises h. m.	Rise Key	☾ Sets h. m.	Set Key	☾ Astron. Place	☾ Age
213	1	Sa.	5:36	B	**8:04**	E	14	28	9	17 N.	58	12	**12½**	**8:44**	D	7:00	C	AQU	17
214	2	**D**	5:37	B	**8:02**	E	14	25	10	17	42	12¾	**1½**	**9:22**	D	8:13	D	AQU	18
215	3	M.	5:38	B	**8:01**	E	14	23	10	17	27	1¾	**2¼**	**9:58**	D	9:26	D	AQU	19
216	4	Tu.	5:39	B	**8:00**	E	14	21	10	17	11	2½	**3**	**10:34**	C	10:38	E	PSC	20
217	5	W.	5:40	B	**7:59**	E	14	19	10	16	55	3½	**4**	**11:11**	C	11:48	E	PSC	21
218	6	Th.	5:41	B	**7:57**	E	14	16	10	16	38	4½	**5**	**11:50**	C	**12:57**	E	PSC	22
219	7	Fr.	5:42	B	**7:56**	E	14	14	10	16	22	5½	**6**	—	–	**2:03**	E	ARI	23
220	8	Sa.	5:43	B	**7:55**	E	14	12	10	16	05	6½	**7**	12:32	B	**3:06**	E	TAU	24
221	9	**D**	5:44	B	**7:54**	E	14	10	10	15	47	7½	**8**	1:17	B	**4:04**	E	TAU	25
222	10	M.	5:45	B	**7:52**	E	14	07	10	15	30	8½	**9**	2:07	B	**4:57**	E	TAU	26
223	11	Tu.	5:46	B	**7:51**	E	14	05	11	15	12	9½	**9¾**	3:00	B	**5:44**	E	GEM	27
224	12	W.	5:47	B	**7:49**	D	14	02	11	14	54	10½	**10¾**	3:56	B	**6:26**	E	GEM	28
225	13	Th.	5:48	B	**7:48**	D	14	00	11	14	36	11¼	**11½**	4:53	C	**7:03**	E	CAN	29
226	14	Fr.	5:49	B	**7:47**	D	13	58	11	14	18	**12**	—	5:51	C	**7:37**	E	CAN	0
227	15	Sa.	5:51	B	**7:45**	D	13	54	11	13	59	12¼	**12¾**	6:49	C	**8:07**	D	LEO	1
228	16	**D**	5:52	B	**7:44**	D	13	52	12	13	40	12¾	**1¼**	7:47	D	**8:36**	D	SEX	2
229	17	M.	5:53	B	**7:42**	D	13	49	12	13	21	1½	**1¾**	8:43	D	**9:04**	C	LEO	3
230	18	Tu.	5:54	B	**7:41**	D	13	47	12	13	02	2	**2½**	9:40	D	**9:33**	C	VIR	4
231	19	W.	5:55	B	**7:39**	D	13	44	12	12	42	2¾	**3¼**	10:37	E	**10:02**	C	VIR	5
232	20	Th.	5:56	B	**7:38**	D	13	42	12	12	23	3½	**3¾**	11:34	E	**10:33**	C	VIR	6
233	21	Fr.	5:57	B	**7:36**	D	13	39	13	12	03	4¼	**4½**	**12:31**	E	**11:08**	C	LIB	7
234	22	Sa.	5:58	B	**7:35**	D	13	37	13	11	43	5	**5½**	**1:28**	E	**11:47**	B	LIB	8
235	23	**D**	5:59	B	**7:33**	D	13	34	13	11	22	6	**6¼**	**2:26**	E	—	–	SCO	9
236	24	M.	6:00	B	**7:31**	D	13	31	13	11	02	6¾	**7¼**	**3:22**	E	12:32	B	OPH	10
237	25	Tu.	6:01	B	**7:30**	D	13	29	14	10	41	7¾	**8**	**4:16**	E	1:23	B	SAG	11
238	26	W.	6:02	B	**7:28**	D	13	26	14	10	20	8¾	**9**	**5:06**	E	2:21	B	SAG	12
239	27	Th.	6:03	B	**7:26**	D	13	23	14	9	59	9½	**10**	**5:53**	E	3:26	C	SAG	13
240	28	Fr.	6:04	B	**7:25**	D	13	21	15	9	38	10½	**10¾**	**6:36**	E	4:35	C	AQU	14
241	29	Sa.	6:05	B	**7:23**	D	13	18	15	9	17	11¼	**11¾**	**7:16**	D	5:48	C	CAP	15
242	30	**D**	6:06	B	**7:22**	D	13	16	15	8	56	**12¼**	—	**7:54**	D	7:03	D	AQU	16
243	31	M.	6:07	B	**7:20**	D	13	13	15	8 N.	34	12½	**1**	**8:31**	C	8:17	D	PSC	17

 To use this page, see p. 124; for Key letters, see p. 252. ☞ **Bold = P.M.** ☞ Light = A.M.

AUGUST HATH 31 DAYS • 2015

And the thin, wasted, shining summer rills
Grew joyful with the coming of the rain. –William Morris

Day of Month	Day of Week	Dates, Feasts, Fasts, Aspects, Tide Heights	Weather
1	Sa.	Lammas Day • MTV: Music Television debuted, 1981	*Broiling—*
2	D	10th S. af. P. • ☾ AT PERIG. • ☌♆☾ • ♄ STAT. • {11.8/11.0}	*skin*
3	M.	☾ ON EQ. • ☾ AT ☋ • Christopher Columbus sailed from Spain with *Niña, Pinta,* and *Santa Maria,* 1492	*needs*
4	Tu.	*Sound traveling far and wide, / A stormy day will betide.*	*oiling.*
5	W.	☌☿♀ • ☌⛢☾ • Historian Joseph Justus Scaliger born, 1540 • Tides {11.1/11.2}	*Storm*
6	Th.	Transfiguration • 4" of hail, Adair and Union counties, Iowa, 1890 • {10.6/11.0}	*clouds*
7	Fr.	☌☿♃ • Gray squirrels have second litters now.	*roiling.*
8	Sa.	St. Dominic • Canada's Hundred Days began, WWI, 1918 • Tides {9.6/10.6}	*Too*
9	D	11th S. af. P. • Donald Duck received star on Hollywood Walk of Fame, 2004 • {9.3/10.5}	*hot*
10	M.	St. Lawrence • ☾ RIDES HIGH • Rocket scientist Robert Goddard died, 1945 • {9.2/10.4}	*for*
11	Tu.	St. Clare • Dog Days end. • *11th–13th:* View the Perseids meteor shower after midnight.	*toiling!*
12	W.	Cathy Gerring won Stratton Mountain LPGA Golf Classic, Vt., 1990 • Tides {9.3/10.4}	*Rumble,*
13	Th.	☌♂☾ • Canso Causeway opened, linking Cape Breton to mainland, N.S., 1955 • {9.5/10.4}	*grumble,*
14	Fr.	New ● • ☌♀☾ • Blackout, NE and Midwest U.S. and Ontario, 2003	*temperatures*
15	Sa.	Assumption • ☌♃☾ • ♀ IN INF. ☌ • Tides {10.4/9.6}	*tumble.*
16	D	12th S. af. P. • ☌☿☾ • Tides {10.3/9.7}	*Keep*
17	M.	Cat Nights commence. • ☾ ON EQ. • ☾ AT ☊ • ☾ AT APO. • Tides {10.1/9.7}	*an*
18	Tu.	*One good head is better than a hundred strong hands.* • {9.9/9.7}	*eye*
19	W.	Jockey Willie Shoemaker born, 1931 • 103°F, Rexton, N.B., 1935 • {9.6/9.6}	*on*
20	Th.	Ragweed in bloom. • 563-lb. 8-oz. giant sea bass caught, Anacapa Island, Calif., 1968 • {9.3/9.5}	*the*
21	Fr.	Princess Margaret, younger sister of Queen Elizabeth II, born, 1930 • Tides {9.0/9.4}	*sky*
22	Sa.	☌♄☾ • William Sheppard patented a liquid soap, 1865 • Tides {8.7/9.4}	*and*
23	D	13th S. af. P. • Fannie Farmer opened cooking school, Boston, Mass., 1902	*your*
24	M.	St. Bartholomew • ☾ RUNS LOW • Tides {8.5/9.7}	*bobber,*
25	Tu.	Hummingbirds migrate south. • Hoax about Moon printed in New York *Sun,* 1835	*too,*
26	W.	☌♃☉ • ☌♇☾ • Storm blew canoe into phone lines, Lake County, Ind., 1965 • {9.1/10.5}	*or*
27	Th.	First English theatrical performance in American colonies, Va., 1665 • Tides {9.6/11.0}	*lightning*
28	Fr.	St. Augustine of Hippo • Children's writer Tasha Tudor born, 1915 • {10.2/11.5}	*just*
29	Sa.	St. John the Baptist • Full Sturgeon ○ • ☌♀♂ • ☌♆☾	*might*
30	D	14th S. af. P. • ☾ AT PERIG. • *Take hold of a good minute.* • {11.3/—}	*clobber*
31	M.	☾ ON EQ. • ☾ AT ☋ • Laurence Olivier married Vivien Leigh, 1940 • {12.0/11.6}	*you!*

Farmer's Calendar

■ It's been a year of abundant rain, which means abundant mushrooms. Walking the dogs has been like leading children through a bakery. Wiggles doesn't eat many, but Echo is voracious, and we're constantly jerking her head away from some tasty-looking fungus, or reaching into her mouth to remove one, or yelling "Drop it!" just too late. Then, a few hours later, she is temporarily sick when her innards rebel.

I can hardly blame her inability to resist temptation. I've never seen such variety of colors and shapes, and they all look like bread, rolls, and pastries. There are toasty-brown dinner rolls and toadstools with bumps on top that look like cinnamon muffins. A whole village of red cupcakes popped up at the far end of the pond trail, and over by the south shore there was a 3-day eruption of orange-and-yellow discs, looking like air-dropped pizzas.

When the mushroom feasting began, I nurtured a foolish hope that the dogs would instinctively avoid any species that would make them sick. Alas, no. Dogs not only eat poisonous varieties, but they also gobble down hallucinogenic mushrooms and then spend hours chasing and snapping at illusions. Experts advise removing mushrooms from the yard, but my yard is a thousand acres of woods. And it's still raining.

C A L E N D A R

SKY WATCH ☆ *Neptune, in its closest approach of the year, is in opposition on the 1st. Mars, Jupiter, and Venus have crossed into the morning sky, but only Venus is easily seen at dawn, as it rapidly rises higher each morning. It hovers just to the upper right of the waning crescent Moon in the wee hours of the 10th. The autumnal equinox brings the start of autumn on the 23rd at 4:21 A.M. Saturn gets lower each evening in the southwest at dusk. The year's best lunar eclipse for North American viewers unfolds on the 27th; the partial phase begins at 9:07 P.M., when the Moon enters Earth's umbral shadow. Totality begins at 10:11 P.M. and ends at 11:24 P.M.*

◗	**Last Quarter**	5th day	5th hour	54th minute
●	**New Moon**	13th day	2nd hour	41st minute
◐	**First Quarter**	21st day	4th hour	59th minute
○	**Full Moon**	27th day	22nd hour	50th minute

All times are given in Eastern Daylight Time.

Get these pages with times set to your zip code at Almanac.com/Access.

Day of Year	Day of Month	Day of Week	☼ Rises h. m.	Rise Key	☼ Sets h. m.	Set Key	Length of Day h. m.	Sun Fast m.	Declination of Sun ° '	High Tide Times Boston		☾ Rises h. m.	Rise Key	☾ Sets h. m.	Set Key	☾ Astron. Place	☾ Age
244	1	Tu.	6:09	B	7:18	D	13 09	16	8 N.12	1½	1¾	9:09	C	9:31	E	PSC	18
245	2	W.	6:10	B	7:16	D	13 06	16	7 51	2¼	2¾	9:49	C	10:43	E	PSC	19
246	3	Th.	6:11	C	7:15	D	13 04	16	7 29	3¼	3½	10:30	B	11:52	E	ARI	20
247	4	Fr.	6:12	C	7:13	D	13 01	17	7 07	4¼	4½	11:16	B	12:58	E	TAU	21
248	5	Sa.	6:13	C	7:11	D	12 58	17	6 44	5¼	5½	—	–	1:58	E	TAU	22
249	6	**D**	6:14	C	7:10	D	12 56	17	6 22	6¼	6½	12:05	B	2:53	E	TAU	23
250	7	M.	6:15	C	7:08	D	12 53	18	6 00	7¼	7½	12:57	B	3:42	E	GEM	24
251	8	Tu.	6:16	C	7:06	D	12 50	18	5 37	8¼	8½	1:52	B	4:26	E	GEM	25
252	9	W.	6:17	C	7:04	D	12 47	18	5 14	9¼	9½	2:48	C	5:04	E	CAN	26
253	10	Th.	6:18	C	7:03	D	12 45	19	4 52	10¼	10¼	3:45	C	5:38	E	CAN	27
254	11	Fr.	6:19	C	7:01	D	12 42	19	4 29	10¾	11	4:43	C	6:10	D	LEO	28
255	12	Sa.	6:20	C	6:59	C	12 39	20	4 06	11½	11¾	5:40	D	6:39	D	LEO	29
256	13	**D**	6:21	C	6:57	C	12 36	20	3 43	12¼	—	6:37	D	7:08	D	LEO	0
257	14	M.	6:22	C	6:56	C	12 34	20	3 20	12½	12¾	7:33	D	7:36	C	VIR	1
258	15	Tu.	6:23	C	6:54	C	12 31	21	2 57	1	1¼	8:30	D	8:05	C	VIR	2
259	16	W.	6:24	C	6:52	C	12 28	21	2 34	1¾	2	9:27	E	8:35	C	VIR	3
260	17	Th.	6:25	C	6:50	C	12 25	21	2 11	2¼	2½	10:24	E	9:09	B	LIB	4
261	18	Fr.	6:26	C	6:49	C	12 23	22	1 48	3	3¼	11:20	E	9:45	B	LIB	5
262	19	Sa.	6:28	C	6:47	C	12 19	22	1 24	3¾	4	12:17	E	10:27	B	LIB	6
263	20	**D**	6:29	C	6:45	C	12 16	22	1 01	4½	4¾	1:12	E	11:14	B	OPH	7
264	21	M.	6:30	C	6:43	C	12 13	23	0 38	5¼	5¾	2:05	E	—	–	SAG	8
265	22	Tu.	6:31	C	6:41	C	12 10	23	0 N.14	6¼	6½	2:56	E	12:07	B	SAG	9
266	23	W.	6:32	C	6:40	C	12 08	23	0 S.08	7¼	7½	3:43	E	1:07	C	SAG	10
267	24	Th.	6:33	C	6:38	C	12 05	24	0 31	8¼	8½	4:26	E	2:12	C	CAP	11
268	25	Fr.	6:34	C	6:36	C	12 02	24	0 55	9¼	9½	5:07	E	3:22	C	CAP	12
269	26	Sa.	6:35	C	6:34	C	11 59	24	1 18	10	10½	5:46	D	4:35	D	AQU	13
270	27	**D**	6:36	C	6:33	C	11 57	25	1 41	11	11¼	6:24	D	5:49	E	PSC	14
271	28	M.	6:37	C	6:31	C	11 54	25	2 05	11¾	—	7:02	C	7:04	E	PSC	15
272	29	Tu.	6:38	C	6:29	C	11 51	25	2 28	12¼	12½	7:41	C	8:19	E	PSC	16
273	30	W.	6:39	C	6:27	C	11 48	26	2 S.51	1	1½	8:24	C	9:32	E	ARI	17

SEPTEMBER HATH 30 DAYS • 2015

In every orchard Autumn stands,
With apples in his golden hands. –Alexander Smith

Day of Month	Day of Week	Dates, Feasts, Fasts, Aspects, Tide Heights	Weather
1	Tu.	☌♅☾ • ♆ at ☍ • French king Louis XIV died, 1715 • Tides {11.9 11.8	*Bring*
2	W.	*He that runs fastest, runs by himself.* • Tides {11.6 11.7	*umbrellas,*
3	Th.	19-inning baseball game began, Fenway Park, Boston, 1981 • Tides {11.1 11.5	*fellas.*
4	Fr.	☿ GR. ELONG. (27° EAST) • Swimmer Mark Spitz won his 7th gold medal at Summer Olympics, 1972	*Cool*
5	Sa.	♀ STAT. • First Labor Day parade, N.Y.C., 1882 • Tides {9.9 10.6	*and*
6	**D**	**15th S. af. P.** • ☾ RIDES HIGH • Tides {9.4 10.3	*dry*
7	M.	**Labor Day** • Cranberry bog harvest begins, Cape Cod, Mass. • Tides {9.2 10.1	*as*
8	Tu.	Don Pedro Menéndez de Avilés founded what became St. Augustine, Fla., 1565 • Tides {9.1 10.0	*fine*
9	W.	Artist John Singleton Copley died, 1815 • {9.2 10.0	*champagne;*
10	Th.	☌♀☾ • ☌♂☾ • American Forestry Association organized, 1875	*warming*
11	Fr.	**Patriot Day** • Writer O. Henry born, 1862 • Tides {9.5 10.1	*up,*
12	Sa.	☌♃☾ • *Courtesy on one side never lasts long.* • {9.7 10.1	*a*
13	**D**	**16th S. af. P.** • **New ●** • **Eclipse ☉** • ☾ ON EQ.	*little*
14	M.	**Holy Cross** • **Rosh Hashanah** • ☾ AT ☊ • ☾ AT APO.	*rain.*
15	Tu.	☌☿☾ • Football player Merlin Olsen born, 1940 • Tides {9.9 9.9	*Summer's*
16	W.	Ember Day • Sam Ackerman (age 101) married Eva Powers (age 95), New Rochelle, N.Y., 1990	*refrain*
17	Th.	☿ STAT. • Battle of Antietam, Md., 1862 • Tides {9.5 9.8	*may*
18	Fr.	Ember Day • ☌♄☾ • Final day of streetcar service in Winnipeg, Man., 1955	*fry*
19	Sa.	Ember Day • 92°F, Harrisburg, Pa., 1983 • Tides {9.0 9.6	*the*
20	**D**	**17th S. af. P.** • Frank Schuman patented wire safety glass, 1892 • {8.8 9.6	*brain!*
21	M.	**St. Matthew** • ☾ RUNS LOW • ♀ GR. ILLUM. EXT. • {8.7 9.6	*It's*
22	Tu.	☌♇☾ • 3.3 earthquake near Rathdrum, Idaho, 2003 • Tides {8.7 9.8	*wetter:*
23	W.	**Yom Kippur** • Harvest Home • **Autumnal Equinox** • Tides {9.0 10.1	*Better*
24	Th.	♇ STAT. • *If red the Sun begin his race, Be sure the rain will fall apace.* • Tides {9.4 10.5	*wear*
25	Fr.	*Publick Occurrences* became first newspaper in "U.S.," 1690 • Tides {10.1 11.0	*some*
26	Sa.	☌♆☾ • Woodchucks hibernate now. • Tides {10.7 11.4	*galoshes*
27	**D**	**Full Harvest ○** • **Eclipse ☾** • ☾ ON EQ. • ☾ AT ☋ • ☾ AT PERIG.	*while*
28	M.	**Sukkoth** • ☌♅☾ • 150th flight of X-15, 1965 • {11.9 —	*picking*
29	Tu.	**St. Michael** • Hurricane struck SE La., 1915 • Tides {11.8 12.1	*up*
30	W.	**St. Gregory the Illuminator** • ☿ IN INF. ☌ • {11.7 12.2	*McIntoshes!*

Lack of pep is often mistaken for patience. –Kin Hubbard

Farmer's Calendar

■ We planted a pear tree in the backyard many years ago and forgot about it. It grew up tall and skinny, with no flowers, and hence no fruit.

Two years ago, it flowered for the first time; by that September, its branches were heavy with fruit. We sampled a few from lower limbs (most were 20 to 30 feet up). Puckery, but delicious; we decided to pick up windfalls when they were more ripe. We watched the green fruit turn rosy with great anticipation.

Then one morning, there were no pears. None on the tree; none on the ground. We tried to imagine what had happened to them. Birds? Insects? The day before, there had been no sign of holes or chewing. And how many birds or insects would it have taken to denude a 60-foot-high pear tree in a single night?

It took a day or two to come up with a hypothesis. We have a bear, maybe two, in the neighborhood. We've seen one quite close to the house, once at the foot of the front steps.

The tree and its branches are far too slender to hold the weight of a hungry bear, but for the same reason, it would be easy for a hungry bruin to shake the tree hard enough to dislodge ripe fruit. It seems that we were not the only ones who had been looking for the proper moment to harvest.

THE TENTH MONTH • 2015

SKY WATCH ☆ *Saturn, the only remaining evening star, begins the month low in the southwest at dusk and vanishes by month's end. Low in the predawn eastern sky on the 1st is a worthy sight for insomniacs—a dramatic vertical lineup of (from top to bottom) Venus, Leo's bright star Regulus, Mars, and Jupiter. From the 8th to the 11th, Mercury and the Moon join the festivities. Mercury is much lower than the others. The waning crescent Moon pays each planet a call on successive mornings: Venus, with Regulus to its left, on the 8th; Mars on the 9th; Jupiter on the 10th; and Mercury on the 11th. Uranus reaches opposition on the 11th. Venus and Jupiter are very close on the 25th.*

◑ **Last Quarter**	4th day	17th hour	6th minute
● **New Moon**	12th day	20th hour	6th minute
◐ **First Quarter**	20th day	16th hour	31st minute
○ **Full Moon**	27th day	8th hour	5th minute

All times are given in Eastern Daylight Time.

Get these pages with times set to your zip code at Almanac.com/Access.

Day of Year	Day of Month	Day of Week	☼ Rises h. m.	Rise Key	☼ Sets h. m.	Set Key	Length of Day h. m.	Sun Fast m.	Declination of Sun ° '	High Tide Times Boston		☾ Rises h. m.	Rise Key	☾ Sets h. m.	Set Key	☾ Astron. Place	☾ Age
274	1	Th.	6:40	C	**6:26**	C	11 46	26	3 s. 15	2	**2¼**	**9:09**	B	10:42	E	ARI	18
275	2	Fr.	6:42	C	**6:24**	C	11 42	26	3 38	2¾	**3¼**	**9:58**	B	11:47	E	TAU	19
276	3	Sa.	6:43	C	**6:22**	C	11 39	27	4 01	3¾	**4**	**10:51**	B	**12:46**	E	TAU	20
277	4	**D**	6:44	D	**6:20**	C	11 36	27	4 24	4¾	**5**	**11:46**	B	**1:39**	E	ORI	21
278	5	M.	6:45	D	**6:19**	C	11 34	27	4 47	5¾	**6¼**	—	–	**2:25**	E	GEM	22
279	6	Tu.	6:46	D	**6:17**	C	11 31	28	5 10	7	**7¼**	12:42	C	**3:05**	E	CAN	23
280	7	W.	6:47	D	**6:15**	C	11 28	28	5 33	8	**8¼**	1:40	C	**3:40**	E	CAN	24
281	8	Th.	6:48	D	**6:14**	C	11 26	28	5 56	8¾	**9**	2:37	C	**4:13**	D	LEO	25
282	9	Fr.	6:49	D	**6:12**	C	11 23	29	6 19	9¾	**10**	3:34	C	**4:42**	D	LEO	26
283	10	Sa.	6:50	D	**6:10**	C	11 20	29	6 42	10¼	**10¾**	4:31	D	**5:11**	D	LEO	27
284	11	**D**	6:52	D	**6:09**	C	11 17	29	7 04	11	**11¼**	5:27	D	**5:39**	C	VIR	28
285	12	M.	6:53	D	**6:07**	C	11 14	29	7 27	11½	12	6:24	D	**6:08**	C	VIR	0
286	13	Tu.	6:54	D	**6:05**	C	11 11	30	7 49	**12¼**	—	7:21	E	**6:38**	C	VIR	1
287	14	W.	6:55	D	**6:04**	C	11 09	30	8 12	12½	**12¾**	8:18	E	**7:10**	B	VIR	2
288	15	Th.	6:56	D	**6:02**	B	11 06	30	8 34	1¼	**1½**	9:15	E	**7:46**	B	LIB	3
289	16	Fr.	6:57	D	**6:01**	B	11 04	30	8 56	1¾	**2**	10:12	E	**8:25**	B	LIB	4
290	17	Sa.	6:59	D	**5:59**	B	11 00	30	9 18	2½	**2¾**	11:07	E	**9:10**	B	OPH	5
291	18	**D**	7:00	D	**5:57**	B	10 57	31	9 40	3¼	**3½**	**12:00**	E	**10:01**	B	OPH	6
292	19	M.	7:01	D	**5:56**	B	10 55	31	10 02	4	**4¼**	**12:51**	E	**10:56**	B	SAG	7
293	20	Tu.	7:02	D	**5:54**	B	10 52	31	10 23	5	**5¼**	**1:37**	E	**11:58**	C	SAG	8
294	21	W.	7:03	D	**5:53**	B	10 50	31	10 45	5¾	**6**	**2:21**	E	—	–	CAP	9
295	22	Th.	7:04	D	**5:51**	B	10 47	31	11 06	6¾	**7¼**	**3:01**	E	1:03	C	AQU	10
296	23	Fr.	7:06	D	**5:50**	B	10 44	31	11 27	7¾	**8¼**	**3:39**	D	2:12	C	AQU	11
297	24	Sa.	7:07	D	**5:48**	B	10 41	32	11 48	8¾	**9¼**	**4:16**	D	3:23	D	AQU	12
298	25	**D**	7:08	D	**5:47**	B	10 39	32	12 09	9¾	**10**	**4:53**	D	4:36	D	PSC	13
299	26	M.	7:09	D	**5:46**	B	10 37	32	12 29	10½	**11**	**5:31**	C	5:51	E	PSC	14
300	27	Tu.	7:10	D	**5:44**	B	10 34	32	12 50	11¼	12	**6:12**	C	7:05	E	PSC	15
301	28	W.	7:12	D	**5:43**	B	10 31	32	13 10	**12¼**	—	**6:57**	C	8:18	E	ARI	16
302	29	Th.	7:13	D	**5:41**	B	10 28	32	13 30	12¾	**1**	**7:46**	B	9:28	E	TAU	17
303	30	Fr.	7:14	D	**5:40**	B	10 26	32	13 49	1¾	**2**	**8:38**	B	10:32	E	TAU	18
304	31	Sa.	7:15	D	**5:39**	B	10 24	32	14 s. 09	2½	**2¾**	**9:34**	B	11:29	E	ORI	19

 To use this page, see p. 124; for Key letters, see p. 252. ☞ **Bold = P.M.** ☞ Light = A.M.

OCTOBER HATH 31 DAYS • 2015

Witch-hazel shakes her gold curls out,
Mid the red maple's flying rout. –Lucy Larcom

Day of Month	Day of Week	Dates, Feasts, Fasts, Aspects, Tide Heights	Weather
1	Th.	*Much rain in October, much wind in December.* • {11.4 / 12.0}	*Autumn*
2	Fr.	Estimated 7.1 earthquake, Pleasant Valley, Nev., 1915 • {10.9 / 11.5}	*haze,*
3	Sa.	☾ RIDES HIGH • East and West Germany reunited as one nation, 1990 • {10.3 / 11.0}	*perfect*
4	D	19th S. af. P. • *4th–5th:* First nonstop trans-Pacific flight, Japan to Wash., 1931	*days.*
5	M.	Laurie Skreslet first Canadian to summit Mt. Everest, 1982 • Tides {9.3 / 9.9}	*Drizzle*
6	Tu.	Benjamin Hanks applied for patent for self-winding clock, 1783 • Tides {9.1 / 9.7}	*leaves*
7	W.	Physicist Niels Bohr born, 1885 • Tides {9.1 / 9.6}	*the*
8	Th.	☌♀☾ • ☿ STAT. • Cardinal Eugenio Pacelli (later Pope Pius XII) began tour of U.S., 1936	*foliage*
9	Fr.	☌♂☾ • ☌♃☾ • Musician John Lennon born, 1940 • {9.4 / 9.6}	*pearly—*
10	Sa.	London Bridge dedicated, Lake Havasu City, Ariz., 1971	*snow*
11	D	☾ ON EQ. • ☾ AT ☊ • ☾ AT APO. • ☌☿☾ • ♅ AT ☍ • {9.8 / 9.8}	*comes*
12	M.	**Columbus Day (observed)** • **Thanksgiving Day (Canada)** • **New ●** • {10.0 / 9.8}	*early!*
13	Tu.	*Good to begin well, better to end well.* • Tides {10.1 / —}	*Blue*
14	W.	Hail in southern Okla. caused major crop and property damage, 1925 • Tides {9.7 / 10.2}	*skies,*
15	Th.	**Islamic New Year** • ☿ GR. ELONG. (18° WEST) • 15.88" rain, Ft. Lauderdale, Fla., 1965	*blue*
16	Fr.	☌♄☾ • Texas governor Francis Lubbock born, 1815 • Tides {9.4 / 10.1}	*lips;*
17	Sa.	St. Ignatius of Antioch • ☌♂♃ • Tides {9.3 / 10.0}	*rain*
18	D	21st S. af. P. • ☾ RUNS LOW • Tides {9.1 / 9.9}	*up*
19	M.	St. Luke[T] • ☌♇☾ • First wedding in a balloon Cincinnati, Ohio, 1874 • {8.9 / 9.8}	*to*
20	Tu.	Explorer Sir Richard Burton died, 1890 • Tides {8.9 / 9.8}	*our*
21	W.	Native American saint Kateri Tekakwitha canonized, 2012 • Tides {9.0 / 9.9}	*hips.*
22	Th.	*Honor and ease are seldom bedfellows.* • Tides {9.4 / 10.1}	*Lovely!*
23	Fr.	St. James of Jerusalem • ☌♆☾ • Tides {9.9 / 10.4}	*Leafers*
24	Sa.	Little brown bats hibernate now. • Nylon stockings on sale for first time, Wilmington, Del., 1939	*by*
25	D	22nd S. af. P. • ☾ ON EQ. • ☾ AT ☋ • {11.2 / 11.1}	*the*
26	M.	☾ AT PERIG. • ☌♀♃ • ☌♅☾ • ♀ GR. ELONG. (46° WEST) • {11.7 / 11.4}	*busloads*
27	Tu.	**Full Hunter's ○** • Harvard expedition observed solar eclipse in British-occupied Penobscot Bay, Maine, 1780	*jam*
28	W.	Sts. Simon & Jude • Timber rattlesnakes move to winter dens. • {12.3 / —}	*highways*
29	Th.	Biographer James Boswell born, 1740 • Tides {11.3 / 12.2}	*and*
30	Fr.	*Foolish fear doubleth danger.* • Comedian Steve Allen died, 2000 • {11.0 / 11.9}	*back*
31	Sa.	**All Hallows' Eve** • **Reformation Day** • ☾ RIDES HIGH • {10.6 / 11.4}	*roads.*

Farmer's Calendar

■ We speak of foliage season as if it were only one season. Actually, it is at least four.

Call the first "Scarlet Fever," flaring up in the swamps and along the highways in distressed trees by mid-August. The color comes so early that you feel disoriented; Columbus Day weekend is still 2 months away!

The second season, when the reds are joined by fiery oranges and yellows, might be called "Conflagration": The colors are intense, almost glaring. At full Conflagration, the sun passing through the maple outside our bedroom sends a shaft of pink light through the window.

A little later, after rains and wind, we enter the "Empire of Yellow." Walking the dogs on a gloomy day in late October, I kept looking up, thinking that the Sun had come out. But it was only flashes of the golden canopy as I passed under darker trees.

November brings "Tannery," a leathery collection of browns in many shades. The oaks are the last to shed their leaves, covering the fading Oriental carpet rolled out by the previous residents.

Even then, however, come occasional surprises. Last week on a secluded woods road, we were surprised to encounter a single, brilliant, sugar maple torch, the last survivor of Scarlet Fever.

NOVEMBER

THE ELEVENTH MONTH • 2015

SKY WATCH ☆ *Venus stands very near Mars from the 1st to the 3rd, just before dawn in the east, with Jupiter closely above them. The crescent Moon passes to the right of Jupiter on the 6th and to the right of Venus on the 7th, with nearby Mars just above them both. This planet group forms a nice little triangle, although the Martian "point," at magnitude 1.7, is so dim that it might easily be overlooked; Venus is 200 times brighter! Look at the crescent Moon to see earthshine—a faint glow on its dark portion caused by reflection of sunlight from Earth. Saturn passes behind the Sun in a conjunction on the 29th, ending its evening star role.*

◑	**Last Quarter**	3rd day	7th hour	24th minute
●	**New Moon**	11th day	12th hour	47th minute
◐	**First Quarter**	19th day	1st hour	27th minute
○	**Full Moon**	25th day	17th hour	44th minute

After 2:00 A.M. on November 1, Eastern Standard Time is given.

Get these pages with times set to your zip code at Almanac.com/Access.

Day of Year	Day of Month	Day of Week	☼ Rises h. m.	Rise Key	☼ Sets h. m.	Set Key	Length of Day h. m.	Sun Fast m.	Declination of Sun ° '	High Tide Times Boston		☾ Rises h. m.	Rise Key	☾ Sets h. m.	Set Key	☾ Astron. Place	☾ Age
305	1	**D**	6:17	D	**4:37**	B	10 20	32	14 s. 28	2½	**2¾**	**9:32**	B	11:20	E	GEM	20
306	2	M.	6:18	D	**4:36**	B	10 18	32	14 47	3½	**3½**	**10:31**	C	**12:03**	E	GEM	21
307	3	Tu.	6:19	D	**4:35**	B	10 16	32	15 06	4¼	**4½**	**11:29**	C	**12:41**	E	CAN	22
308	4	W.	6:20	D	**4:34**	B	10 14	32	15 25	5¼	**5½**	—	–	**1:15**	E	LEO	23
309	5	Th.	6:22	E	**4:32**	B	10 10	32	15 43	6¼	**6½**	12:27	C	**1:45**	D	LEO	24
310	6	Fr.	6:23	E	**4:31**	B	10 08	32	16 01	7¼	**7½**	1:24	D	**2:14**	D	LEO	25
311	7	Sa.	6:24	E	**4:30**	B	10 06	32	16 19	8	**8¼**	2:20	D	**2:42**	C	VIR	26
312	8	**D**	6:25	E	**4:29**	B	10 04	32	16 36	8¾	**9¼**	3:17	D	**3:10**	C	VIR	27
313	9	M.	6:27	E	**4:28**	B	10 01	32	16 54	9½	**9¾**	4:14	E	**3:40**	C	VIR	28
314	10	Tu.	6:28	E	**4:27**	B	9 59	32	17 10	10	**10½**	5:11	E	**4:11**	C	VIR	29
315	11	W.	6:29	E	**4:26**	B	9 57	32	17 27	10¾	**11¼**	6:09	E	**4:46**	B	LIB	0
316	12	Th.	6:30	E	**4:25**	B	9 55	32	17 43	11¼	**11¾**	7:06	E	**5:24**	B	LIB	1
317	13	Fr.	6:32	E	**4:24**	B	9 52	32	18 00	**12**	—	8:03	E	**6:08**	B	OPH	2
318	14	Sa.	6:33	E	**4:23**	B	9 50	31	18 15	12½	**12½**	8:58	E	**6:57**	B	OPH	3
319	15	**D**	6:34	E	**4:22**	B	9 48	31	18 31	1¼	**1¼**	9:49	E	**7:51**	B	SAG	4
320	16	M.	6:35	E	**4:21**	B	9 46	31	18 46	2	**2**	10:37	E	**8:50**	C	SAG	5
321	17	Tu.	6:37	E	**4:20**	B	9 43	31	19 01	2¾	**2¾**	11:20	E	**9:53**	C	SAG	6
322	18	W.	6:38	E	**4:19**	B	9 41	31	19 15	3½	**3¾**	**12:01**	E	**10:59**	C	AQU	7
323	19	Th.	6:39	E	**4:19**	B	9 40	30	19 29	4½	**4¾**	**12:38**	D	—	–	CAP	8
324	20	Fr.	6:40	E	**4:18**	B	9 38	30	19 43	5½	**5¾**	**1:14**	D	12:07	D	AQU	9
325	21	Sa.	6:41	E	**4:17**	B	9 36	30	19 56	6¼	**6¾**	**1:49**	D	1:16	D	PSC	10
326	22	**D**	6:43	E	**4:17**	B	9 34	30	20 09	7¼	**7¾**	**2:25**	C	2:28	E	CET	11
327	23	M.	6:44	E	**4:16**	B	9 32	29	20 22	8¼	**8¾**	**3:03**	C	3:40	E	PSC	12
328	24	Tu.	6:45	E	**4:15**	A	9 30	29	20 34	9¼	**9¾**	**3:45**	C	4:52	E	ARI	13
329	25	W.	6:46	E	**4:15**	A	9 29	29	20 46	10	**10¾**	**4:31**	B	6:04	E	TAU	14
330	26	Th.	6:47	E	**4:14**	A	9 27	29	20 57	10¾	**11½**	**5:22**	B	7:11	E	TAU	15
331	27	Fr.	6:48	E	**4:14**	A	9 26	28	21 08	11¾	—	**6:17**	B	8:13	E	TAU	16
332	28	Sa.	6:50	E	**4:13**	A	9 23	28	21 19	12¼	**12½**	**7:16**	B	9:09	E	GEM	17
333	29	**D**	6:51	E	**4:13**	A	9 22	27	21 29	1¼	**1¼**	**8:16**	C	9:57	E	GEM	18
334	30	M.	6:52	E	**4:13**	A	9 21	27	21 s. 39	2	**2¼**	**9:16**	C	10:38	E	CAN	19

 To use this page, see p. 124; for Key letters, see p. 252. ☞ **Bold = P.M.** ☞ Light = A.M.

NOVEMBER HATH 30 DAYS • 2015

The winds are out with loud increasing shout,
Where late before them walked the biting frost. –Jones Very

Day of Month	Day of Week	Dates, Feasts, Fasts, Aspects, Tide Heights	Weather
1	**D**	All Saints' • **Daylight Saving Time ends, 2:00 A.M.** • Tides {10.1 10.8	*Clear,*
2	M.	All Souls' • *Thunder in November, a fertile year to come.* • Tides {9.6 10.2	*brittle:*
3	Tu.	**Election Day** • ☌♀♂ • Actress Mary Martin died, 1990 • {9.2 9.6	*Rains*
4	W.	Computational wizard Shakuntala Devi born, 1929 • {9.0 9.3	*a*
5	Th.	Cartoonist Al Capp died, 1979 • 2" snow, Salisbury, Mo., 1995 • Tides {9.0 9.1	*little,*
6	Fr.	☌♃☾ • Talking headlight installed on locomotive, Schenectady, N.Y., 1934 • {9.1 9.1	*but*
7	Sa.	☾ ON EQ. • ☾ AT ☊ • ☾ AT APO. • ☌♀☾ • ☌♂☾	*warmish.*
8	**D**	**24th S. af. P.** • Black bears head to winter dens now. • {9.6 9.3	*Stormish!*
9	M.	Peak of multiday storm that caused 12 major shipwrecks on Great Lakes, U.S./Ont., 1913 • {9.9 9.4	*Snow*
10	Tu.	*Luna 17* spacecraft launched, 1970 • Tides {10.1 9.4	*north,*
11	W.	St. Martin of Tours • **Veterans Day** • **New** ● • ☌☿☾ • {10.2 9.5	*rain*
12	Th.	Indian Summer • ☌♄☾ • Social reformer Elizabeth Cady Stanton born, 1815 • {10.4 9.4	*south.*
13	Fr.	Lobsters move to offshore waters now. • Tides {10.4 —	*Wetter*
14	Sa.	☾ RUNS LOW • Artist Claude Monet born, 1840 • Tides {9.4 10.4	*and*
15	**D**	**25th S. af. P.** • ☌♇☾ • Tennis pro Helen Mersi Kelesi born, 1969	*milder,*
16	M.	Walt Disney announced plans to build Epcot Center, 1965 • Tides {9.3 10.2	*now*
17	Tu.	St. Hugh of Lincoln • ☿ IN SUP. ☌ • Crab apples are ripe now. • {9.2 10.1	*colder*
18	W.	♆ STAT. • Twain's *The Celebrated Jumping Frog of Calaveras County* published, 1865 • {9.3 10.0	*and*
19	Th.	☌♆☾ • Frederick Blaisdell granted patent for paper-wrapped pencil, 1895 • {9.5 10.0	*wilder.*
20	Fr.	*Be slow of giving advice, ready to do a service.* • {9.8 10.0	*Murky—*
21	Sa.	☾ ON EQ. • ☾ AT ☋ • William C. Bullitt became first U.S. ambassador to U.S.S.R., 1933	*turkeys*
22	**D**	26th S. af. P. • ☌♅☾ • Ferris wheel inventor George W. G. Ferris Jr., died, 1896	*won't*
23	M.	St. Clement • ☾ AT PERIG. • –38°F, Chinook, Mont., 1985 • {11.3 10.5	*be*
24	Tu.	Justus Falckner first Lutheran pastor ordained in America (Philadelphia), 1703 • Tides {11.7 10.7	*hard*
25	W.	**Full Beaver** ○ • ☌☿♄ • Albert Einstein submitted paper on theory of relativity, 1915	*to*
26	Th.	**Thanksgiving Day** • *You may believe any thing that is good of a grateful man.* • {12.1 10.7	*track*
27	Fr.	☾ RIDES HIGH • Basketball player Wilt Chamberlain scored 18 baskets in a row, 1963 • Tides {12.0 —	*over*
28	Sa.	Ferdinand Magellan first entered Pacific Ocean from Atlantic, through what is now Strait of Magellan, 1520	*the*
29	**D**	**1st S. of Advent** • ☌♄☉ • Tides {10.2 11.1	*snow-*
30	M.	St. Andrew • Comedienne Lucille Ball married Desi Arnaz, 1940 • Tides {9.9 10.6	*pack!*

At table, it becomes no one to be bashful. –Plautus

Farmer's Calendar

■ Until she died at the age of 100, my mother-in-law, Betty, was a Thanksgiving magnet. She drew dozens of interesting guests, such as two former Lost Boys of the Sudan, to her table. I should say "tables"—every flat surface in the house had to be set up to entertain the crowd.

Everyone shared the cooking and cleaning while Betty sat in the front parlor, interrogating the guests. She wasn't much interested in talking about herself. The kids made place cards for everyone, or learned to play mah-jongg, or just raced around the 1813 colonial that had a spinning wheel and a cavalry saber in the attic. A favorite tradition was to teach the younger children how to hang spoons off their noses.

Another was to give prospective sons-in-law an antique chair that was guaranteed to collapse under them and then observe their reactions. I got one of these chairs in 1970, my first Thanksgiving there. My son-in-law got one almost three decades later. It was probably the same chair.

When Betty passed away, so did the farmhouse Thanksgivings. It was a natural transition from the crowds and card tables and chaos to less complicated gatherings. The food is just as good, the company equally diverse and stimulating. But I miss Betty, and the spoons, and the collapsing chairs.

C
A
L
E
N
D
A
R

SKY WATCH ☆ *It's still a postmidnight party for all of the bright planets. Dawn now finds Jupiter at its highest, in the southeast, with Venus lowest, floating left of Virgo's blue main star Spica. Still faint but brightening Mars hovers in between. The Moon passes just below Jupiter on the 4th and eye-catchingly close to Venus during the wee hours of the 7th, for a major don't-miss conjunction. This year brings a rare second fabulous meteor shower under ideal moonless skies, when the Geminids blaze on the 13th starting at around 8:00 P.M. These "shooting stars" are strangely slow, at half the speed of summer's Perseids. Winter begins with the solstice on the 21st, at 11:48 P.M.*

◐	**Last Quarter**	3rd day	2nd hour	40th minute
●	**New Moon**	11th day	5th hour	29th minute
◑	**First Quarter**	18th day	10th hour	14th minute
○	**Full Moon**	25th day	6th hour	11th minute

All times are given in Eastern Standard Time.

Get these pages with times set to your zip code at Almanac.com/Access.

Day of Year	Day of Month	Day of Week	☼ Rises h. m.	Rise Key	☼ Sets h. m.	Set Key	Length of Day h. m.	Sun Fast m.	Declination of Sun ° '	High Tide Times Boston		☾ Rises h. m.	Rise Key	☾ Sets h. m.	Set Key	☾ Astron. Place	☾ Age
335	1	Tu.	6:53	E	**4:12**	A	9 19	27	21 s. 49	3	3	**10:15**	C	11:15	E	CAN	20
336	2	W.	6:54	E	**4:12**	A	9 18	26	21 58	3¾	4	**11:13**	C	11:47	D	LEO	21
337	3	Th.	6:55	E	**4:12**	A	9 17	26	22 06	4¾	5	—	–	**12:17**	D	LEO	22
338	4	Fr.	6:56	E	**4:11**	A	9 15	26	22 15	5½	5¾	12:11	D	**12:45**	D	LEO	23
339	5	Sa.	6:57	E	**4:11**	A	9 14	25	22 22	6½	6¾	1:07	D	**1:13**	C	VIR	24
340	6	**D**	6:58	E	**4:11**	A	9 13	25	22 30	7¼	7¾	2:04	D	**1:42**	C	VIR	25
341	7	M.	6:59	E	**4:11**	A	9 12	24	22 37	8	8½	3:01	E	**2:12**	C	VIR	26
342	8	Tu.	7:00	E	**4:11**	A	9 11	24	22 43	8¾	9¼	3:59	E	**2:45**	C	LIB	27
343	9	W.	7:01	E	**4:11**	A	9 10	23	22 49	9½	10	4:57	E	**3:22**	B	LIB	28
344	10	Th.	7:02	E	**4:11**	A	9 09	23	22 55	10¼	10¾	5:55	E	**4:04**	B	SCO	29
345	11	Fr.	7:03	E	**4:11**	A	9 08	23	23 00	10¾	11½	6:51	E	**4:51**	B	OPH	0
346	12	Sa.	7:03	E	**4:11**	A	9 08	22	23 04	11½	—	7:45	E	**5:44**	B	SAG	1
347	13	**D**	7:04	E	**4:11**	A	9 07	22	23 09	12	12¼	8:35	E	**6:43**	C	SAG	2
348	14	M.	7:05	E	**4:12**	A	9 07	21	23 12	12¾	1	9:21	E	**7:46**	C	SAG	3
349	15	Tu.	7:06	E	**4:12**	A	9 06	21	23 16	1½	1¾	10:03	E	**8:51**	C	AQU	4
350	16	W.	7:06	E	**4:12**	A	9 06	20	23 18	2¼	2½	10:41	D	**9:58**	C	CAP	5
351	17	Th.	7:07	E	**4:12**	A	9 05	20	23 21	3¼	3½	11:17	D	**11:06**	D	AQU	6
352	18	Fr.	7:08	E	**4:13**	A	9 05	19	23 23	4	4½	11:51	D	—	–	AQU	7
353	19	Sa.	7:08	E	**4:13**	A	9 05	19	23 24	5	5½	**12:25**	C	12:15	D	PSC	8
354	20	**D**	7:09	E	**4:14**	A	9 05	18	23 25	6	6½	**1:01**	C	1:25	E	PSC	9
355	21	M.	7:09	E	**4:14**	A	9 05	18	23 26	7	7½	**1:39**	C	2:35	E	CET	10
356	22	Tu.	7:10	E	**4:15**	A	9 05	17	23 26	8	8½	**2:22**	C	3:44	E	ARI	11
357	23	W.	7:10	E	**4:15**	A	9 05	17	23 25	8¾	9½	**3:09**	B	4:52	E	TAU	12
358	24	Th.	7:11	E	**4:16**	A	9 05	16	23 24	9¾	10½	**4:01**	B	5:56	E	TAU	13
359	25	Fr.	7:11	E	**4:16**	A	9 05	16	23 23	10½	11¼	**4:58**	B	6:55	E	ORI	14
360	26	Sa.	7:12	E	**4:17**	A	9 05	15	23 21	11½	—	**5:58**	C	7:47	E	GEM	15
361	27	**D**	7:12	E	**4:18**	A	9 06	15	23 18	12	12¼	**6:59**	C	8:32	E	GEM	16
362	28	M.	7:12	E	**4:18**	A	9 06	14	23 16	12¾	1	**8:00**	C	9:12	E	CAN	17
363	29	Tu.	7:12	E	**4:19**	A	9 07	14	23 12	1½	1¾	**9:00**	C	9:46	D	LEO	18
364	30	W.	7:13	E	**4:20**	A	9 07	13	23 09	2¼	2½	**9:58**	D	10:18	D	LEO	19
365	31	Th.	7:13	E	**4:21**	A	9 08	13	23 s. 04	3	3¼	**10:56**	D	10:47	D	LEO	20

Now see stern Winter nearer draw,
Sol's feeble rays refuse to thaw. –William Cole

Day of Month	Day of Week	Dates, Feasts, Fasts, Aspects, Tide Heights	Weather
1	Tu.	Dupree Gardens opened, Land O' Lakes, Fla., 1940	*A million*
2	W.	St. Viviana • Statesman Jean-Charles Chapais born, 1811 • Tides { 9.2 / 9.4	*snowflakes*
3	Th.	*Daylight will peep through a small hole.* • Tides { 9.0 / 9.0	*fall to*
4	Fr.	☾ ON EQ. • ☾ AT ☍ • ♂♃☾ First television appearance of mime Marcel Marceau, 1955	*earth,*
5	Sa.	☾ AT APO. • ♂♂☾ Electric eels lit Christmas tree, Living Planet Aquarium, Sandy, Utah, 2012	*as*
6	**D**	2nd **S.** of **Advent** • St. Nicholas • Tides { 9.2 / 8.6	*from*
7	M.	St. Ambrose • First day of Chanukah • Nat'l Pearl Harbor Remembrance Day • ♂♀☾	*a great*
8	Tu.	John McCrae's *In Flanders Fields* poem published, 1915 • Tides { 9.7 / 8.9	*saltshaker.*
9	W.	Winterberry fruit especially showy now. • Tides { 10.0 / 9.1	*A billion*
10	Th.	St. Eulalia • ♂♄☾ Businessman Armand Hammer died, 1990 • Tides { 10.3 / 9.2	*more*
11	Fr.	New ● Bijou Theater opened, first in U.S. lit by electricity, Boston, 1882 • Tides { 10.5 / 9.3	*arrive*
12	Sa.	Our Lady of Guadalupe • ☾ RUNS LOW • ♂♂☾ • Tides { 10.6 / 9.3	*a day*
13	**D**	3rd **S.** of **Advent** • St. Lucia • ♂♃☾ • { 9.5 / 10.7	*or two*
14	M.	Halcyon Days begin. • Capt. Sue Dauser, Navy Nurse Corps, received Distinguished Service Medal, 1945	*later.*
15	Tu.	Sioux chief Sitting Bull died, 1890 • *Echo 1* commemorative stamp issued, D.C., 1960 • { 9.6 / 10.7	*A trillion*
16	W.	Ember Day • *December cold with snow, good for rye.* • { 9.7 / 10.5	*now*
17	Th.	♂♆☾ • France formally recognized American independence, 1777 • Tides { 9.8 / 10.2	*descend*
18	Fr.	Ember Day • ☾ ON EQ. • ☾ AT ☍ • Tides { 10.0 / 10.0	*en masse,*
19	Sa.	Ember Day • ♂♀♇ • ♂☽☾ • Tides { 10.2 / 9.8	*rising*
20	**D**	4th **S.** of **Advent** • Name "Canadian National Railways" authorized, 1918	*by the*
21	M.	St. Thomas • Winter Solstice • ☾ AT PERIG. • Tides { 10.7 / 9.7	*meter;*
22	Tu.	Composer Giacomo Puccini born, 1858 • Tides { 11.1 / 9.9	*let's*
23	W.	Home economist Marjorie Child Husted died, 1986 • 9.6" snow, Wilmington, N.C., 1989 • { 11.4 / 10.0	*hope,*
24	Th.	*A happy heart is better than a full purse.* • Tides { 11.5 / 10.1	*whatever*
25	Fr.	**Christmas** • Full Cold ○ • ☾ RIDES HIGH • Tides { 11.6 / 10.2	*comes*
26	Sa.	St. Stephen • Boxing Day (Canada) • First day of Kwanzaa • ☉ STAT.	*to pass,*
27	**D**	1st **S.** af. **Ch.** • Beware the Pogonip. • { 10.1 / 11.2	*that*
28	M.	Holy Innocents • ☿ GR. ELONG. (20° EAST) • Westminster Abbey consecrated, London, 1065	*'16*
29	Tu.	St. John† • Morning "silvered by the icicles everywhere shining," New London, Conn., 1747	*will*
30	W.	Writer Rudyard Kipling born, 1865 • Tides { 9.5 / 9.8	*be*
31	Th.	St. Sylvester • ☾ AT ☍ • ♂♃☾ • Tides { 9.3 / 9.3	*sweeter!*

Farmer's Calendar

■ *Dec. 1:* Every year, we watch the pond with conflicting hopes. We like snow, but we love black ice, which happens only when the pond freezes before the first snow.

Black ice is perfectly smooth and perfectly transparent. Many years ago, we lived on a pond farther north, where one winter we had a full week of black ice. While we were skating, we could occasionally see beaver swimming beneath our blades.

One night, a powdery snow fell and we went out for a final skate. Even as the inches piled up, we glided along as if we were flying above the clouds. The next morning, the snow had frozen and the skating was done.

Dec. 5: It's been in the 20s every night for the past week, and we had some light snow overnight. There's a little bit of open water at the northwest end of the pond, where a brook tumbles in, but otherwise it's a white sheet, so there'll be no black ice this year.

Dec. 9: Spoke too soon. When we walked past the pond this morning, there was not a shard of ice on it, as if we had been transported back in time to September. Two days of rain and two more of mild temperatures and southern breezes had restored our little pond to a liquid state.

Temporarily.

Holidays and Observances

Federal holidays are listed in bold. For Movable Religious Observances, see page 127.

Jan. 1	New Year's Day
Jan. 19	**Martin Luther King Jr.'s Birthday** *(observed)* Robert E. Lee Day *(Fla., Ky.)*
Feb. 2	Groundhog Day
Feb. 12	Abraham Lincoln's Birthday
Feb. 14	Valentine's Day
Feb. 15	Susan B. Anthony's Birthday, traditional *(Fla.)*
Feb. 16	**Washington's Birthday** *(observed)*
Feb. 17	Mardi Gras *(Baldwin & Mobile counties, Ala.; La.)*
Mar. 2	Texas Independence Day
Mar. 3	Town Meeting Day *(Vt.)*
Mar. 15	Andrew Jackson Day *(Tenn.)*
Mar. 17	St. Patrick's Day Evacuation Day *(Suffolk Co., Mass.)*
Mar. 30	Seward's Day *(Alaska)*
Apr. 2	Pascua Florida Day
Apr. 20	Patriots Day *(Maine, Mass.)*
Apr. 21	San Jacinto Day *(Tex.)*
Apr. 22	Earth Day
Apr. 24	National Arbor Day
May 5	Cinco de Mayo
May 8	Truman Day *(Mo.)*
May 10	Mother's Day
May 16	Armed Forces Day
May 18	Victoria Day *(Canada)*
May 22	National Maritime Day
May 25	**Memorial Day** *(observed)*
June 5	World Environment Day
June 11	King Kamehameha I Day *(Hawaii)*
June 14	Flag Day
June 17	Bunker Hill Day *(Suffolk Co., Mass.)*
June 19	Emancipation Day *(Tex.)*
June 20	West Virginia Day, traditional
June 21	Father's Day
July 1	Canada Day

July 4	**Independence Day**
July 24	Pioneer Day *(Utah)*
Aug. 1	Colorado Day
Aug. 3	Civic Holiday *(parts of Canada)*
Aug. 16	Bennington Battle Day, traditional *(Vt.)*
Aug. 19	National Aviation Day
Aug. 26	Women's Equality Day
Sept. 7	**Labor Day**
Sept. 9	Admission Day *(Calif.)*
Sept. 11	Patriot Day
Sept. 13	Grandparents Day
Sept. 17	Constitution Day
Sept. 21	International Day of Peace
Oct. 5	Child Health Day
Oct. 9	Leif Eriksson Day
Oct. 12	**Columbus Day** *(observed)* Native Americans' Day *(S.Dak.)* Thanksgiving Day *(Canada)*
Oct. 18	Alaska Day, traditional
Oct. 24	United Nations Day
Oct. 30	Nevada Day
Oct. 31	Halloween
Nov. 3	Election Day
Nov. 4	Will Rogers Day *(Okla.)*
Nov. 11	**Veterans Day** Remembrance Day *(Canada)*
Nov. 19	Discovery Day *(Puerto Rico)*
Nov. 26	**Thanksgiving Day**
Nov. 27	Acadian Day *(La.)*
Dec. 7	National Pearl Harbor Remembrance Day
Dec. 15	Bill of Rights Day
Dec. 17	Wright Brothers Day
Dec. 25	**Christmas Day**
Dec. 26	Boxing Day *(Canada)* First day of Kwanzaa

Love calendar lore? Find more at Almanac.com/Calendar.

Tidal Glossary

Apogean Tide: A monthly tide of decreased range that occurs when the Moon is at apogee (farthest from Earth).

Diurnal Tide: A tide with one high water and one low water in a tidal day of approximately 24 hours.

Mean Lower Low Water: The arithmetic mean of the lesser of a daily pair of low waters, observed over a specific 19-year cycle called the National Tidal Datum Epoch.

Neap Tide: A tide of decreased range that occurs twice a month, when the Moon is in quadrature (during its first and last quarters, when the Sun and the Moon are at right angles to each other relative to Earth).

Perigean Tide: A monthly tide of increased range that occurs when the Moon is at perigee (closest to Earth).

Semidiurnal Tide: A tide with one high water and one low water every half day. East Coast tides, for example, are semidiurnal, with two highs and two lows during a tidal day of approximately 24 hours.

Spring Tide: A tide of increased range that occurs at times of syzygy each month. Named not for the season of spring but from the German *springen* ("to leap up"), a spring tide also brings a lower low water.

Syzygy: The nearly straight-line configuration that occurs twice a month, when the Sun and the Moon are in conjunction (on the same side of Earth, at the new Moon) and when they are in opposition (on opposite sides of Earth, at the full Moon). In both cases, the gravitational effects of the Sun and the Moon reinforce each other, and tidal range is increased.

Vanishing Tide: A mixed tide of considerable inequality in the two highs and two lows, so that the lower high (or higher low) may appear to vanish. ∎

Glossary of Almanac Oddities

■ Many readers have expressed puzzlement over the rather obscure entries that appear on our **Right-Hand Calendar Pages, 129–155.** These "oddities" have long been fixtures in the Almanac, and we are pleased to provide some definitions. (Once explained, they may not seem so odd after all!)

–Beth Krommes

Ember Days: The four periods observed by some Christian denominations for prayer, fasting, and the ordination of clergy are called Ember Days. Specifically, these are the Wednesdays, Fridays, and Saturdays that occur in succession following (1) the First Sunday in Lent; (2) Whitsunday–Pentecost; (3) the Feast of the Holy Cross, September 14; and (4) the Feast of St. Lucia, December 13. The word *ember* is perhaps a corruption of the Latin *quatuor tempora,* "four times."

Folklore has it that the weather on each of the 3 days foretells the weather for the next 3 months; that is, in September, the first Ember Day, Wednesday, forecasts the weather for October; Friday predicts November; and Saturday foretells December.

Distaff Day (January 7): This was the first day after Epiphany (January 6), when women were expected to return to their spinning following the Christmas holiday. A distaff is the staff that women used for holding the flax or wool in spinning.

(Hence the term "distaff" refers to women's work or the maternal side of the family.)

Plough Monday (January): Traditionally, the first Monday after Epiphany was called Plough Monday because it was the day when men returned to their plough, or daily work, following the Christmas holiday. (Every few years, Plough Monday and Distaff Day fall on the same day.) It was customary at this time for farm laborers to draw a plough through the village, soliciting money for a "plough light," which was kept burning in the parish church all year. This traditional verse captures the spirit of it:

> *"Yule is come and Yule is gone,*
> *and we have feasted well;*
> *so Jack must to his flail again*
> *and Jenny to her wheel."*

Three Chilly Saints (May): Mamertus, Pancras, and Gervais were three early Christian saints. Because their feast days, on May 11, 12, and 13, respectively, are traditionally cold, they have come to be known as the Three Chilly Saints. An old French saying translates to: "St. Mamertus, St. Pancras, and St. Gervais do not pass without a frost."

Midsummer Day (June 24): To the farmer, this day is the midpoint of the growing season, halfway between planting and harvest. (Midsummer Eve is an occasion for festivity and celebrates fertility.) The Anglican church considered it a "Quarter Day," one of the four major divisions of the liturgical year. It also marks the feast day of St. John the Baptist.

Cornscateous Air (July): First used by early almanac makers, this term signifies warm, damp air. Though it signals ideal climatic conditions for growing corn, it poses a danger to those affected by asthma and other respiratory problems.

Dog Days (July 3–August 11): These 40 days are traditionally the year's hottest and unhealthiest. They once coincided with the year's heliacal (at sunrise) rising of the Dog Star, Sirius. Ancient folks thought that the "combined heat" of Sirius and the Sun caused summer's swelter.

Lammas Day (August 1): Derived from the Old English *hlaf maesse,* meaning "loaf mass," Lammas Day marked the beginning of the harvest. Traditionally, loaves of bread were baked from the first-ripened grain and brought to the churches to be consecrated. Eventually, "loaf mass" became "Lammas." In Scotland, Lammastide fairs became famous as the time when trial marriages could be made. These marriages could end after a year with no strings attached.

Cat Nights Begin (August 17): This term harks back to the days when people believed in witches. An Irish legend says that a witch could turn into a cat and regain herself eight times, but on the ninth time (August 17), she couldn't change back, hence the saying: "A cat has nine lives." Because August is a "yowly" time for cats, this may have initially prompted the speculation about witches on the prowl.

Harvest Home (September): In Europe and Britain, the conclusion of the harvest each autumn was marked by festivals of fun, feasting, and thanksgiving known as "Harvest Home." It was also a time to hold elections, pay workers, and collect rents. These festivals usually took place around the autumnal equinox.

Certain groups in the United States, particularly the Pennsylvania Dutch, have kept the tradition alive.

St. Luke's Little Summer (October): This is a spell of warm weather that occurs on or near St. Luke's feast day (October 18) and is sometimes called Indian summer.

Indian Summer (November): A period of warm weather following a cold spell or a hard frost, Indian summer can occur between St. Martin's Day (November 11) and November 20. Although there are differing dates for its occurrence, for more than 200 years the Almanac has adhered to the saying "If All Saints' (November 1) brings out winter, St. Martin's brings out Indian summer." The term may have come from early Native Americans, some of whom believed that the condition was caused by a warm wind sent from the court of their southwestern god, Cautantowwit.

Halcyon Days (December): This refers to about 2 weeks of calm weather that often follow the blustery winds of autumn's end. Ancient Greeks and Romans experienced this weather around the time of the winter solstice, when the halcyon, or kingfisher, was brooding in a nest floating on the sea. The bird was said to have charmed the wind and waves so that the waters were especially calm during this period.

Beware the Pogonip (December): The word *pogonip* refers to an uncommon occurrence—frozen fog. The word was coined by Native Americans to describe the frozen fogs of fine ice needles that occur in the mountain valleys of the western United States and Canada. According to their tradition, breathing the fog is injurious to the lungs. ■

Where
Does the

For disappearing
acts, it's hard to
beat what happens
to the 8 hours
supposedly left
after 8 of sleep and
8 of work.
—Doug Larson,
columnist (b. 1926)

Time

Go?

Contributor
Andrea Curry
has a few answers—
and four ideas for
getting it back.

A lot of time goes to
JUST LIVING

WE SLEEP

As any good mattress salesperson will tell you, you're going to spend a third of your lifetime sleeping: On average, Americans sleep for 26 years; Canadians, 27 years.

WE WORK

If you work a 40-hour week from age 22 to age 65 (with a 2-week vacation each year), you'll have spent 9 years, 10 months on the job. Surprised that this number is so low? Weekends make a big difference. A 40-hour workweek is less than a quarter of the 168 hours in the week.

WE COMMUTE

Americans and Canadians are now likely to spend a little over a year of their lives commuting to and from work, at the current average of 52 minutes per day.

In the United States, New Yorkers and Marylanders spend the most time commuting; North Dakotans, the least.

WE COOK AND CLEAN

We give over about 2 hours of every day to housework.

The average American woman will spend 6 years of her life doing house-work; the average American man, 3 years, 8 months.

The average Canadian woman will devote 6 years, 9 months to the task; the average Canadian man, almost exactly 4 years.

WE WATCH TV

Over a lifetime, Americans will spend 9 years, 2 months watching TV, at the current average of 2.8 hours a day.

Canadians will spend 7 years, 6 months watching TV, an average of 2.2 hours a day.

Time passes . . . and we underestimate
HOW QUICKLY.

Think supply and demand: Our demand for time is unlimited, so the supply often seems to come up short—even over short intervals. Most people underestimate time intervals by an average of 7 minutes per hour.

Our estimate of how much time has passed might be off by more than 7 minutes, depending on what we're doing. Compare the 1-hour back massage and the 1-hour root canal.

According to research from Laval University in Quebec, time passes most quickly when we're absorbed in an

Living on a schedule that doesn't fit your chronotype can

HOW MUCH TIME DO YOU HAVE?

The current average life expectancy for Americans is **78.62** years; for Canadians, it's **81.57** years. Specifically:

American men
76.19 years
American women
81.17 years
Canadian men
78.98 years
Canadian women
84.31 years

Of course, no one knows for certain how much time he or she has.

–2013 estimates, *CIA World Factbook*

activity; time passes most slowly when we're thinking specifically about how long something is taking—perhaps most often when we're waiting. That's why "the watched pot never boils," even though the watched pot actually takes 9½ minutes to boil, just the same as that pot that boiled (and then boiled dry!) while you were on the phone with your sister.

Time lags when it doesn't
MATCH OUR TYPE.

Research has shown that individuals vary widely in their personal chronotype, the daily rhythm that is most natural for their bodies to follow.

Time management advice often emphasizes early rising, and most cultures have an "early bird" saying like this one from Russia: "The early riser gathers mushrooms, the sleepy and lazy one goes later for the nettles."

German biologist Till Roenneberg, who studies body clocks, argues that in our 24/7, industrialized world, early bird proverbs no longer hold true and that an early schedule can do more harm than good for some people. Living on a schedule that doesn't fit your chronotype can leave you tired all the time, even if you're getting enough sleep. Roenneberg calls this phenomenon "social jet lag."

Time tries to
KEEP PACE.

For many modern Americans and Canadians, especially city-dwellers, living

leave you tired all the time, even if you're getting enough sleep.

with a long to-do list makes time seem to pass more quickly. Social psychologist Robert Levine, a specialist in this topic, has quantified "pace of life" through research in cities and other areas all over the world, noting, for example, how quickly people walk and how long it takes to buy a postage stamp. The results contain some surprises:

- Boston is the fastest-paced American city, followed by Buffalo, New York City, and Salt Lake City.
- As a nation, due to a much slower pace in small towns and rural areas, the United States comes in 16th in pace-of-life when compared with other nations. Canada comes in 17th.
- Switzerland, Ireland, Germany, and Japan, in that order, were fastest.
- The slowest-paced nations were Brazil, Mexico, and Indonesia.

Time is
ELIMINATED.

In 1582, most of Europe went straight from Thursday, October 4, to Friday, October 15, eliminating the 10 days in between. Pope Gregory XIII and his team of mathematicians had devised this plan to bring the calendar back in step with the Sun.

Since Julius Caesar's reign, the Julian calendar year had been longer than the Sun's year by 10 minutes, 45 seconds, which added up. Gregory's 10 deleted days and some tinkering with the rule for leap years solved the problem. Our Gre-

United States comes in 16th in pace-of-life when compared with other nations. Canada comes in 17th.

To outsiders, the American, Canadian, Japanese, and northern European disposition to cram as much activity as possible into the day doesn't make sense. Levine writes that in many parts of the world, "periods of nonactivity are understood to be necessary precursors to any meaningful action." Consider the Mexican proverb *Darle tiempo a tiempo:* "Give time to time." In the fastest-paced cities and nations of the world, people give time to time only grudgingly.

gorian calendar year is now only 27 seconds longer than the Sun's year.

Sixteenth-century people weren't happy about losing 10 days, especially when their landlords came looking for a full month of October rent—there was widespread confusion, outrage, and even riots. The British Empire, soon to include much of eastern North America, simply ignored the Pope and kept going, out of step with the Sun and all.

Some 170 years later, the British

admitted that the Pope's "new" calendar was a good idea. By that time, they had to skip 11 days to put the calendar right, so in 1752, the British Empire went directly from September 2 to September 14.

To make the most of
YOUR TIME:

EAT, EXERCISE, AND SNOOZE

Lately, the buzz in business is less about "time management" and more about "energy management." The idea is that when we feel refreshed and energetic, we can use our time to greater effect. To increase energy, snack wisely (eat nuts, fish, and whole grains, which contain magnesium), take exercise breaks periodically, and get more sleep.

STOP STOPPING

A growing body of research shows that often what looks like "multitasking" is actually "rapid task-switching," especially when technology is involved.

One study of computer programmers showed that as they attempted to work, they interrupted themselves or were interrupted about every 3 minutes, usually to check email.

Other studies have shown that it's now common for office workers to interrupt what they're doing to check email 30 to 40 times an hour and that the more a worker self-interrupts, the more stress

A TIME-ALTERING EXPERIENCE

In 1938, 43-year-old researcher Nathaniel Kleitman (pictured) and his student, 25-year-old Bruce Richardson, descended into the belly of Kentucky's Mammoth Cave in a serious quest for more hours in the week. They theorized that hidden away from the Sun and its inexorable 24-hour day, they might be able to cheat their need for sleep—just a little—and come out with more waking hours in the day.

For almost 5 weeks, they lived a reinvented 28-hour day in which they were awake for 19 hours and then slept for nine. The result? Richardson adapted to the 28-hour-day without symptoms of sleep deprivation, but Kleitman did not.

The data they gathered made an enormous contribution to our understanding of human circadian rhythms. Kleitman went on to become the father of modern sleep research, codiscover REM (rapid eye movement) sleep, and live to be 104 years old.

he or she experiences.

Studies of college students show that while trying to study, they lose focus every 3 minutes on average, for example, to check Facebook or text a friend. The more often they interrupt themselves to "multitask," the worse they do on tests.

Multitasking with technology is no way to make the most of your time—those emails can wait!

SHARPEN UP!

When you concentrate on the present moment, you can enjoy it fully and remember it once it's over. Have you ever wondered why certain memories stick and others don't or why some memories are clear while others are fuzzy? There are many factors, but the evolving neuroscience of memory points to concentration as the most important factor: Studies show that "the sharper the attention, the sharper the memory," summarizes writer and historian Nicholas Carr.

DO IMPORTANT THINGS FIRST

Think about how you want to spend your lifetime and then, as you can, spend your days accordingly.

Many writers on time management advise using the morning for things that are important (meaningful) but not urgent (demanding of your attention right then). President Dwight D. Eisenhower was the first person to point out that "urgent" and "important" are not the same and that urgent things can take up all of your time, if you let them.

Your schedule may not allow you to use the mornings this way or your chro-

NIGHT OWL OR EARLY BIRD?

When nothing interferes with your sleep, at what times do you go to bed and get up? The point halfway through your sleep phase is your "midsleep." If you go to sleep at 10:00 P.M. and get up at 7:00 A.M., your midsleep is 2:30 A.M. The average midsleep among German biologist Till Roenneberg's study population of 100,000 participants (mostly Europeans) was 4:30 A.M., with 60 percent having midsleep between 3:30 and 5:30 A.M.

• 4% were extreme night owls, with midsleep between 7:00 and 7:30 A.M.

• 0.5% were extreme "larks" (early birds), with midsleep between 1:30 and 2:00 A.M.

notype may not favor the early hours. But if you can set aside any time daily to do things that are important but not urgent, you will be fighting against "the tyranny of the urgent," which otherwise can consume all waking hours.

Now, when you hear the question "Where does the time go?," you have a few answers. ■

Andrea Curry lives in North Carolina and fights warring impulses to "get stuff done" and "give time to time." Developing this article made her want to do more of the latter.

Talk Show Doctor Reveals Digestion Remedy That Works Instantly!

Television host and best selling author explains how a new aloe-vera extract can make bouts of **heartburn**, **acid-reflux**, **constipation**, **gas**, **bloating**, **diarrhea**, and other **stomach nightmares** disappear!

By Damian Wexler, Freelance Health Reporter

Recently, alternative medicine expert Bryce Wylde, a frequent guest on the Dr. Oz show, revealed a simple secret that amazed millions who suffer with digestion nightmares. And people haven't stopped talking about it since.

"I'D GIVE ANYTHING TO MAKE IT STOP!"

That's what most people will tell you when asked about their digestive problems. "It's just horrible says Ralph Burns, a former digestion victim. I was tortured for years by my Acid-Reflux. Sometimes I'd almost pass out from the pain. My wife suffers with digestion problems too. If she eats one wrong thing, she spends hours stuck in the bathroom dealing with severe bouts of constipation or diarrhea."

FDA WARNS ABOUT POPULAR ANTACIDS

A recent FDA warning explained that excessive use of antacids could lead to an increased risk of hip, wrist, and spine fractures. Especially in people over the age of 50. So when alternative medicine expert Bryce Wylde discussed an alternative on National TV, you can imagine how thrilled people were to find out they could finally get relief without having to rely on *Prevacid®*, *Nexium®*, *Prilosec®* and other dangerous antacids. But now, according to Wylde, your stomach problems could be over by simply drinking a small amount of a tasty Aloe Vera extract. It's as simple as that!

FINALLY THERE'S HOPE...

This delicious "digestion cocktail" is doing amazing things for people who suffer with stomach problems --- even if they've had them for years. Here's how it works...

STOP STOMACH AGONY

Your stomach naturally produces acid so strong, it can dissolve an aluminum spoon in just 30 minutes! And when excess acid escapes into your esophagus, throat and stomach lining, it unleashes the scorching pain of Acid-Reflux, heartburn, ulcers and more misery. Add the problems of stress, and "all hell breaks loose."

Dr. Liza Leal, a well known expert on chronic pain management explains... "The *AloeCure* can work genuine miracles. It buffers high acid levels with amazing speed. So your stomach feels completely at ease just moments after drinking it." In fact, it could wipe out stomach pain, discomfort, and frantic runs to the bathroom.

Doctor recommended AloeCure® may be the most important application ever discovered for digestive health!

UNTIL NOW, LITTLE COULD BE DONE...

But "*AloeCure®* can help virtually anyone. Even people with chronic stomach pain can feel better right away," says Dr. Leal. And what's really exciting is *AloeCure®* aids in keeping your digestive tract healthy, so intestinal distress stops coming back.

Digestion Defender #1: Balances Stomach Acid - Your first line of defense is calcium malate. This natural acid buffer instantly sends stomach acid levels plunging. And holds acid levels down so they don't return!

Digestion Defender #2: Instant, Soothing Relief - *AloeCure®* is brimming with polysaccharides, a "wonder" compound that gently coats the throat, esophagus and stomach, carrying instant relief to cells scorched by excess acid.

HERE'S WHAT DOCTORS ARE SAYING!

AloeCure® is backed by important scientific studies that confirm... aloe calms stomach acid and allows your body to heal itself.

Dr. Liza Leal, M.D & Chief Medical Officer at Meridian Medical, says, "That's why I recommend it to patients who suffer from bouts of heartburn, Acid-Reflux, ulcers, and irritable bowel syndrome..."

Dr. Santiago Rodriguez agrees. "Just two ounces of *AloeCure®* reduces the acids in your stomach by ten times."

Francisco DeWeever, a Certified Nutritional Microscopist, "My patients report their IBS, Crohn's, Colitis, Constipation, Acid-Reflux and a host of other digestive problems have all but disappeared."

SAFE AND EASY TO USE

AloeCure® is safe, all-natural and has absolutely no side effects. It's simple to use so you can just start enjoying immediate life-changing relief!

The makers of *AloeCure®* have agreed to send you up to 6 FREE bottles PLUS 2 free bonus gifts with your order— they're yours to keep no matter what. That's enough *AloeCure®* for 30 days of powerful digestive relief, absolutely free!

CALL NOW, TOLL-FREE!
1-855-689-1061

THESE STATEMENTS HAVE NOT BEEN EVALUATED BY THE FDA. THESE PRODUCTS ARE NOT INTENDED TO DIAGNOSE, TREAT, CURE OR PREVENT ANY DISEASE.

Best Fishing Days and Times

The best times to fish are when the fish are naturally most active. The Sun, Moon, tides, and weather all influence fish activity. For example, fish tend to feed more at sunrise and sunset, and also during a full Moon (when tides are higher than average). However, most of us go fishing when we can get the time off, not because it is the best time. But there *are* best times, according to fishing lore:

The Best Fishing Days for 2015, when the Moon is between new and full:

January 1–4

January 20–February 3

February 18–March 5

March 20–April 4

April 18–May 3

May 18–June 2

June 16–July 1

July 15–31

August 14–29

September 13–27

October 12–27

November 11–25

December 11–25

■ One hour before and one hour after high tides, and one hour before and one hour after low tides. (The times of high tides for Boston are given on pages 128–154; also see pages 250–251. Inland, the times for high tides correspond with the times when the Moon is due south. Low tides are halfway between high tides.)

■ During the "morning rise" (after sunup for a spell) and the "evening rise" (just before sundown and the hour or so after).

■ During the rise and set of the Moon.

■ When the barometer is steady or on the rise. (But even during stormy periods, the fish aren't going to give up feeding. The smart fisherman will find just the right bait.)

■ When there is a hatch of flies—caddis flies or mayflies, commonly.

■ When the breeze is from a westerly quarter, rather than from the north or east.

■ When the water is still or slightly rippled, rather than during a wind.

How to Estimate the Weight of a Fish

Measure the fish from the tip of its nose to the tip of its tail. Then measure its girth at the thickest portion of its midsection.

The weight of a fat-bodied fish (bass, salmon) = (length x girth x girth)/800

The weight of a slender fish (trout, northern pike) = (length x girth x girth)/900

Example: If a fish is 20 inches long and has a 12-inch girth, its estimated weight is (20 x 12 x 12)/900 = 2,880/900 = 3.2 pounds

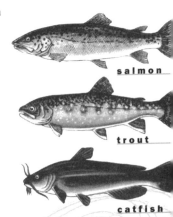

salmon

trout

catfish

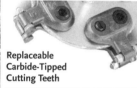

Try Getting Bumped in the Night

By Bob Scammell • Illustrations by Tim Robinson

*From ghoulies and
ghosties and
long-leggedy beasties
and things that go
bump in the night:
Good Lord, deliver us!*

–old Scottish prayer

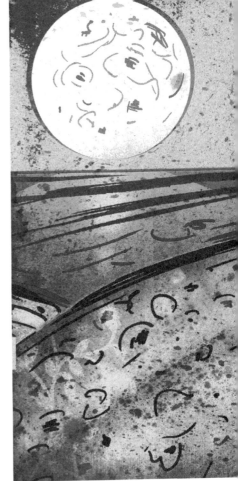

W ell, some fishermen prefer taking their bumps in the night to receiving divine deliverance any day.

Your last frontier for fantastic fishing may be nearer than fabled places such as Kamchatka, Patagonia, Cuba, and the like; it may be as close as your favorite home fishing hole. The transforming trick is to fish this familiar water at night.

Both the allure and the article of faith of night fishing is that if a river, lake, or stream routinely produces bigger-than-average fish in daylight, the fish caught at night will be much larger, especially if the species are scotopic, or have good vision under low light, such as walleyes and bass. Perhaps the best night fishing of all is for old brown trout whoppers, which tend totally to nocturnal feeding, being both scotopic, and, seemingly, photophobic, or afraid of the light.

In addition to their acute night vision, brown trout and walleyes have super-sensitive lateral lines plus sharp hearing, which enable them to locate prey species from their vibrations and sounds. Brook and rainbow trout are also good potential catches by night fishermen. The best night fishing species may be adept at finding their prey in the dark, but they seem to have trouble locating their predators and will often feed right under the tip of the angler's rod.

For night angler success and safety, the water must be familiar because it has been fished often by daylight; a 100-yard stretch of a river or stream is more than enough. A good way to ease into night fishing is to stay until well after dark at a favorite spot once in a while and observe what goes on. From 50 years of night fishing, I now realize that many of my favorite places are just one pool in a river or stream. In fact, one pool on my home brown trout stream is known as The Night Hole.

Occasionally, nymph emergences or adult egg-laying flights of the giant salmon fly occur at night on the home stream water I know best, but I have never enjoyed the epic night fishing that a fabled "super hatch" produces because fast, rocky, stone fly water is too danger-

Perhaps the best night fishing of all is for old brown trout whoppers, which tend totally to nocturnal feeding...

ous in the dark. Falling, hitting the head on a boulder, and drowning is a common cause of angler deaths, even in broad daylight. Fortunately, much of the best night fishing takes place in environments with fewer boulders and slower flows.

Some of the best night fishing for trout is during major night hatches of our largest mayflies, the western green drake, the brown drake, and, in particular, the Hex *(Hexagenia limbata)*—arguably North America's largest mayfly. The latter two species in-

habit soft-bottom lakes and quick-silty streams that can be hazardous, boot-sucking traps for wading anglers.

Nonwading night fishing for big walleyes from shore or boats in lakes and rivers can be excellent. After sundown, big walleyes start herding baitfish into the shallows, particularly where smaller streams flow into a lake or river. This is when huge, depths-loving walleyes can be taken in scant inches of water, often on floating plugs.

Another upside of night fishing is that the crowds are gone; the downside is that there is no one to fish you out when you fall in or make some self-injurious bump in the night of your own. So, take along your own deliverer, a fishing buddy. Strong insect repellent helps with the gazillions of buzzing, biting beasties. A quality headlamp is mandatory, preferably one with a red lens mode to preserve your night vision, help in avoiding hazards, and use in changing flies and lures, untangling leaders, landing and unhooking monsters, and so forth. Just avoid shining the light on the water.

Sounds, the bumps in the night of huge feeding fish, are often the only means of locating and casting to them in the dark. You notice more sounds than on the same water in daylight: coyotes, singing from the bank just behind you; owls hooting; and, hopefully, the swish of the millions of wings of a Hex hatch that will inspire "glops" of brown trout to feast on them like hogs slopping in a trough. Then there's the occasional cougar, which, during a good brown drake hatch one night, was continuously screaming from the ridge just behind us; my buddy and I retreated to the nearest bar.

Ghoulies, ghosties, and long-leggedy beasties, among other things that go bump in the night? You learn to release weird catches at night: bats on the back cast; skunks, even; and sometimes yourself from lurking coils of barbed wire that strike like rattlesnakes. One night, my buddy hooked a beaver, which was merely interesting until he insisted on landing it. We returned in the wee hours, beslimed, brush-torn, and babbling weird truths.

Myths are perpetuated by writers who may not have fished much at night: that a full Moon ruins night fishing and that only very large wet flies or lures that "move lots of water" will work at night. In The Night Hole one full Moon night, I felt through my waders the movements of a big brown trout feeding on tiny caddis flies. I choked up on the rod so that I could dap a tiny (#18) Elk Hair Caddis on the trout's neb and was rewarded by the hooked brute repeatedly bucking into the air across the pool, leaving a phosphorescent bubble contrail. I took my

"Fairies," flotillas of huge Hex duns, came sailboating down, and the air was a-swish with the wings of mating Hex spinners.

lifetime largest brown trout and largest rainbow trout at night on small dry flies: the 30-inch brown trout on a #14 caddis imitation and the 28-inch rainbow on a minuscule #20 Griffith's Gnat.

My longtime night fishing buddy was recently fishing the Hex hatch with a young friend at 2:00 A.M. on a dream of an almost Shakespearean midsummer night: "Fairies," flotillas of huge Hex duns, came sailboating down, and the air was a-swish with the wings of mating Hex spinners. Young friend, waist deep, was gently moving a 26-inch brown trout back and forth in the water to revive it prior to release when the big brown yawned and gulped yet one more of the big Hex duns floating down. Startled, young friend shuffled one step to the side and dropped into a hole so deep that his hat was floating. This says a lot about fishing in the dark.

Night fishing is not for everyone, but every angler should try it to see whether he gets hooked by the adventure, what he catches, the sounds, the sights in his headlamp, or the annual miracle of those giant mayfly hatches. ∎

Bob Scammell is an outdoors sportswriter from Alberta. A member of the Alberta Sports Hall of Fame and Museum, he is the author of *Good Old Guys, Alibis, and Outright Lies* (Johnson Gorman Publishers, 1996). Last year, he received one of Canada's Recreational Fisheries Awards.

Gestation and Mating Tables

		Proper Age or Weight for First Mating	Period of Fertility (yrs.)	Number of Females for One Male	Period of Gestation (days) AVERAGE	RANGE
CATTLE:	Cow	15–18 mos.[1]	10–14		283	279–290[2] 262–300[3]
	Bull	1 yr., well matured	10–12	50[4] / thousands[5]		
GOAT:	Doe	10 mos. or 85–90 lbs.	6		150	145–155
	Buck	well matured	5	30		
HORSE:	Mare	3 yrs.	10–12		336	310–370
	Stallion	3 yrs.	12–15	40–45[4] / record 252[5]		
PIG:	Sow	5–6 mos. or 250 lbs.	6		115	110–120
	Boar	250–300 lbs.	6	50[6] / 35–40[7]		
RABBIT:	Doe	6 mos.	5–6		31	30–32
	Buck	6 mos.	5–6	30		
SHEEP:	Ewe	1 yr. or 90 lbs.	6		147 / 151[8]	142–154
	Ram	12–14 mos., well matured	7	50–75[6] / 35–40[7]		
CAT:	Queen	12 mos.	6		63	60–68
	Tom	12 mos.	6	6–8		
DOG:	Bitch	16–18 mos.	8		63	58–67
	Male	12–16 mos.	8	8–10		

[1]Holstein and beef: 750 lbs.; Jersey: 500 lbs. [2]Beef; 8–10 days shorter for Angus. [3]Dairy. [4]Natural. [5]Artificial. [6]Hand-mated. [7]Pasture. [8]For fine wool breeds.

Incubation Period of Poultry (days)

Chicken..................................21
Duck 26–32
Goose 30–34
Guinea..................................26–28
Turkey..................................28

Average Life Span of Animals in Captivity (years)

Cat (domestic) 14	Goose (domestic) 20
Chicken (domestic) 8	Horse................. 22
Dog (domestic).......... 13	Pig................... 12
Duck (domestic).......... 10	Rabbit 6
Goat (domestic) 14	Turkey (domestic).......10

	Estral/Estrous Cycle (including heat period) AVERAGE	RANGE	Length of Estrus (heat) AVERAGE	RANGE	Usual Time of Ovulation	When Cycle Recurs If Not Bred
Cow	21 days	18–24 days	18 hours	10–24 hours	10–12 hours after end of estrus	21 days
Doe goat	21 days	18–24 days	2–3 days	1–4 days	Near end of estrus	21 days
Mare	21 days	10–37 days	5–6 days	2–11 days	24–48 hours before end of estrus	21 days
Sow	21 days	18–24 days	2–3 days	1–5 days	30–36 hours after start of estrus	21 days
Ewe	16½ days	14–19 days	30 hours	24–32 hours	12–24 hours before end of estrus	16½ days
Queen cat		15–21 days	3–4 days, if mated	9–10 days, in absence of male	24–56 hours after coitus	Pseudo-pregnancy
Bitch	24 days	16–30 days	7 days	5–9 days	1–3 days after first acceptance	Pseudo-pregnancy

Clear Overgrown Property Fast!

Take control with a DR® FIELD and BRUSH MOWER.

CUT A 44"-WIDE PATH
Attaches easily to your ATV or riding mower.

MOW WEEDS, BRUSH, even 2"-thick saplings — with up to 20 HP of V-Twin power!

REMOTE CONTROL lets you manage all blade, clutch, and engine functions from your towing vehicle!

OUTRIGGER™ TOW BAR
enables cutting 100% outside the path of towing vehicle to mow along fences, under trees.

Powerful Self-Propelled Brush Mowers also available!

84039X © 2014

DRfieldbrush.com

Till While You Ride!

DR® ROTO-HOG™ POWER TILLER

FAR FASTER & EASIER to use than hard-to-handle, walk-behind tillers.

TILLS A 3-FOOT SWATH with each pass — twice the width of most walk-behind tillers!

24 STEEL BOLO TINES turn at 230 rpm to create perfect seedbeds for planting.

For Smaller Jobs...

The DR® ROTO-HOG™ Mini Tiller is perfect for cultivating.

84040X © 2014

TOWS BEHIND RIDING MOWERS, ATVS, OR LAWN TRACTORS.

DRrototiller.com

Try a DR® at Home for 6 Months!
Call for details.

Call for a FREE DVD and Catalog!
Includes product specifications and factory-direct offers.

TOLL FREE **800-731-0493**

Almonds

Pine Nuts

Honey

Oysters

HUNGRY

FOR

LOVE?

ROMANCE MAY BE ONLY A
SPRINKLE, SIP, OR SPOONFUL AWAY.

BY ANN THURLOW

SAY THAT YOU'VE CAST YOUR PEEPERS ON A gorgeous gal, but she won't give you the time of day. Or maybe you've got your heart set on a hunk who doesn't seem to care two figs for you.

Join the club! Since ancient times, the lonely and the lovelorn have sought out potions to excite feelings of love (or, let's face it, lust) in the objects of their affection. Many of these potions involve food that can be found in the market, in the garden, or even in the wild.

In the 15th century, Sheikh Nefzawi suggested, in his book *The Perfumed Garden of Sensual Delight,* that those looking for love should eat 20 almonds and 100 grains of pulverized pine tree heavily covered with honey just before going to bed. This would allegedly make a person more attractive.

No appetite for pulverized pine? The Roman scholar Galen suggested 100 pine nuts before bed—a suggestion that actually has some merit. Pine nuts contain lots of zinc, which some believe may turn the tame into tigers. Oysters are also rich in zinc. And they have been credited—even by romantic ancient Romans—with being the mollusk of choice for those looking for love.

LOTS OF HERBS HAVE REPUTATIONS FOR helping love along. If you rub your skin with a little thyme, it's said that you're certain to attract a sweetheart. Once you've got that sweetheart, keep him or her devoted forever with a liberal sprinkling of lovage (on you, not him or her).

Trying to get that guy to pop the question? Sneak a little borage into his drink to give him the courage to ask. And if your sweetheart isn't giving you enough attention, sprinkle a little chervil on his or her food to put a little pep into the proceedings.

If you're trying to heat up a potential sweetheart, give him or her a cup of ginger tea. Ginger has long been touted for its aphrodisiac properties. It is warming and calming and stimulates the circulation—the perfect recipe for romance. Want more? Add a little honey to that tea. The Greek physician Hippocrates recognized honey for its ability to stimulate desire. Ever since, in cultures all around the world, honey has been both a symbol of, and a prescription for, love. In ancient Persia, newlyweds drank honey wine every day for the first month after they were married because it was believed to be an aphrodisiac. (This is a popular theory about the origin of the term "honeymoon.")

THEN THERE'S THE HUMBLE CARROT. IN THE Middle Ages, the most powerful tool in a witch's love potion arsenal was this simple root vegetable,

Thyme

Lovage

Borage

Chervil

Ginger

Ginger Tea

Carrots

which makes carrot ginger soup (see page 42) a doubly ideal meal for seduction.

IN FACT, HOT FOOD—IN EVERY SENSE OF the word—has long been known for its capacity to captivate. Thanks to their ability to stimulate "feel good" endorphins and to set the heart racing, chiles have long been associated with desire. The Aztec ruler Montezuma was reputed to have mixed chiles with a chocolate drink before visiting his concubines.

Or you could just skip the chiles and go right for the chocolate. If you're thinking that a box of chocolates is the way to your intended's heart, you may be on the

THINGS GO BETTER WITH BASIL

Of all the herbs associated with love, basil is among the most popular. Put a pot of basil on your doorstep to let the world know that you're looking for love. Ladies, tuck a little basil in your undergarments; the scent is said to drive men wild. Or add a little basil to some lightly warmed cooking oil and rub it on your skin.

Better yet, serve it for dinner. In matters of love, it seems that the Italians have basil right. Basil, garlic, and pine nuts, when made into pesto, are a delicious food for attracting that special someone. A simple recipe: ¼ cup of pine nuts, 2 cloves of garlic, 2 cups of basil leaves, ⅓ cup of olive oil, ½ cup of Parmesan cheese (Italians have also long considered cheese an aphrodisiac). In a food processor, chop the first two ingredients, then add the basil until lightly chopped. With the processor running, slowly stream in the olive oil, then stir in the cheese. Serve on pasta or crackers.

FLIRT WITH FRAGRANCE

Scent is well recognized as playing a big part in the alchemy of attraction, and each gender reacts differently to different scents. The scent of roses can make a woman flirtatious. Meanwhile, a man's amorous side can be stimulated by the smell of vanilla.

It's easy to make your own perfume to stimulate the attentions of a reluctant Romeo. Gently warm an essential oil such as rosewood or clary sage oil. Add a few drops of botanical extracts. Some popular stimulants include jasmine, cedarwood, and ylang ylang. Place a small amount on pulse points like wrists and temples.

Chile

Chocolates

right track. Dark chocolate contains chemicals like serotonin that make us feel good. And when we feel good, we might be more receptive to romantic suggestion.

Here's another great reason to give thanks when the harvest holiday rolls around. Pumpkin has long been lauded for its ability to increase ardor. The scent of pumpkin pie spice is reputed to drive men wild. (Is it just a coincidence that more babies are born in the United States in August than in any other month?)

FINALLY, WE'VE ALL POPPED A BREATH MINT after a nice, garlicky dinner. But this may be a mistake. Tibetan monks of yesteryear were not allowed to enter the monastery after eating garlic because it incited feelings of passion.

As in all matters, moderation is the key. Even if the object of your affection fails to fall for you, at the very least you're going to have a good supper. ■

Pumpkin

Ann Thurlow is a writer from Charlottetown, PEI, who believes that kindness is always the best way to a person's heart.

Garlic

What ARE THE Odds?

By Danielle S. Hammelef

Hardly a day goes by when we do not consider the likelihood, or chance, of an event happening. Here are 70 real odds in a variety of categories. Some may surprise you, some will tickle your funny bone, others may make you scratch your head. Some may make you say, "I've beaten those odds!"

Illustrations by Tim Robinson

How to Calculate Odds

Let's say that you want to be a farmer in the United States. The Environmental Protection Agency's agricultural report confirms that there are approximately 2 million U.S. farms. About 500,000 of these farms make sufficient income to meet farm family living expenses.

What are the odds that your farm will make enough money to take care of you and your family? The calculation is a ratio of prosperous farms to the total number of farms: 500,000/2,000,000. This works out to ¼, so this means that your farm has a 1-in-4 chance of being able to support you.

As the difference, or spread, between the numbers in an odds ratio increases, the likelihood of an event happening decreases.

And Now, the Odds . . .

FEARS

■ of being acrophobic (afraid of falling):
1 in 3

■ of being arachnophobic (afraid of spiders):
1 in 4

■ of being ariophobic (afraid of flying):
1 in 5

■ of being claustrophobic (afraid of small spaces):
1 in 3

■ of being cynophobic (afraid of dogs):
1 in 9

- of being entomophobic (afraid of insects):
1 in 4

- of being glossophobic (afraid of public speaking):
2 in 5

- of being herpetophobic (afraid of snakes):
1 in 2

- of being iatrophobic (afraid of doctors):
1 in 11

- of being lygophobic (afraid of the dark):
1 in 20

- of being musophobic (afraid of mice):
1 in 5

- of being mysophobic (afraid of germs):
1 in 4

- of being trypanophobic (afraid of needles and injections):
1 in 5

NATURAL DISASTERS

- of a tsunami impacting the East Coast of North America:
1 in 1,000

- of a tsunami impacting the West Coast of North America:
about 1 in 2

- of an asteroid hitting Earth:
1 in 100,000,000

- of being struck by lightning during any 12-month span:
1 in 700,000

- of a major earthquake occurring in the eastern United States in the next 50 years:
1 in 67

- of a major earthquake occurring in the central United States in the next 50 years:
1 in 10

- of a major earthquake occurring in the north-western United States in the next 50 years:
1 in 3

- that if a tornado develops, it occurs in the United States:
3 in 4

BIRTH

- of being double-jointed:
3 in 100

- of being left-handed:
1 in 10

(continued)

183

■ of being born a quadruplet:
1 in 700,000

■ of being born an identical twin:
1 in 285

INJURY

■ of a surgeon leaving an instrument inside a patient:
1 in 7,000

■ of contracting food poisoning:
1 in 6

■ of injury while handling fireworks:
3 in 100,000

■ of a person injured while launching fireworks in the month surrounding July 4 being an amateur:
2 in 3

■ of requiring hospital care after slipping on a wet bathroom floor:
1 in 1,000

■ of hospitalization for an injury incurred on an amusement park ride:
1 in 7,000,000

AMERICAN HISTORY & POLITICS

■ of an American being a descendant of a *Mayflower* pilgrim:
1 in 10

■ of an American not being able to name a single justice of the U.S. Supreme Court:
1 in 3

■ of an American adult not being able to name the U.S. vice president:
1 in 3

■ of an American not knowing the title of the U.S. national anthem:
2 in 5

■ of a bill introduced in Congress being signed into law:
1 in 25

FOOD

■ of being a vegetarian in Canada or the United States:
1 in 20

■ of being a vegan in Canada or the United States:
1 in 50

■ of being a person who can eat all that he or she wants, thanks to "skinny genes":
1 in 2,000

■ of getting "brain freeze" after eating ice cream too quickly:
1 in 3

PERSONAL HABITS/ BEHAVIORS

■ of an adult biting his or her fingernails:
1 in 6

■ of a child biting his or her fingernails:
3 in 10

■ of having a tattoo:
1 in 5

■ of being a compulsive shopper:
1 in 16

■ of being a chronic procrastinator:
1 in 5

■ of someone pretending to talk on a cell phone to avoid interacting with others:
1 in 8

(continued)

EDUCATION & INTELLIGENCE

■ of having an IQ above 135:
1 in 100

■ of an American young adult not being able to locate the United States on a map:
6 in 100

■ of an American young adult not being able to locate the state of New York on a map:
1 in 2

■ of an American not knowing that Earth revolves around the Sun:
1 in 4

SPORTS

■ of surviving being buried by an avalanche for 45 minutes:
3 in 10

■ of being injured while alpine skiing:
1 in 500

■ of winning an Olympic gold medal:
1 in 660,000

■ of a mountain climber who begins ascending Mt. Everest reaching the peak:
3 in 10

■ of becoming a professional athlete:
1 in 22,000

■ of an average golfer making a hole-in-one:
1 in 12,000

■ of a professional golfer making a hole-in-one:
1 in 3,000

■ of bowling a perfect 300 game:
1 in 11,500

■ of a Major League Baseball player being caught stealing a base:
3 in 10

■ of a Major League Baseball fan catching a ball hit into the stands:
1 in 563

MISCELLANY

■ of a person believing in ghosts:
1 in 2

■ of a person always dreaming in color:
4 in 5

■ of a person claiming blue as his or her favorite color:
2 in 5

■ of an American worker not using all of his or her available vacation days:
4 in 7

■ of a Canadian worker not using all of his or her available vacation days:
4 in 10

■ of a person turning his or her head to the right when kissing:
2 in 3

■ of finding a four-leaf clover:
1 in 10,000

■ of a lottery winner keeping his or her job:
2 in 3 ■

Danielle S. Hammelef is the author of *This Book Beats the Odds* (Capstone Press, 2012).

Mind~Manglers

By Heidi Stonehill

Color Curiosities

Pair each description with its true color

DESCRIPTION	COLOR
A? **1.** clear, early American "pattern glass" containing manganese that has been exposed to sunlight for too long	**a.** red
	b. orange
D **2.** a ripe banana under a black light	
3. a rare (1 in 2 million) variant of the normally olive-brown American lobster	**c.** yellow
B **4.** a traditional Chinese wedding gown	**d.** green
C **5.** the protective enamel on a beaver's four continuously growing front teeth	**e.** blue
C **6.** a penalty card used by soccer referees to caution a player about unsportsmanlike conduct	**f.** indigo
7. the sheath of a ground wire, according to U.S. and Canadian electrical codes	**g.** purple

ANSWERS ON PAGE 262

Heidi Stonehill, an editor at *The Old Farmer's Almanac,* was tickled pink when, out of the blue, she got the green light to develop a game. Now that it is in black and white, she hopes that it passes with flying colors and is widely "red" by all.

> *The best things in life are often within arm's reach.*
> *The good is always beautiful, the beautiful is good!*
> –John Greenleaf Whittier, American poet (1807–92)

BEAUTY
on a Budget

BY MARTIE MAJOROS

Throughout history, people have relied on techniques and special formulas to enhance their attractiveness. Some were based on ingredients that were found in the home or, in some cases, the barnyard (think boiled calves' feet as an ingredient in facial cream). Here's an assortment of safe beauty treatments that you can make easily from items available in natural food stores or that perhaps you already have in your pantry.

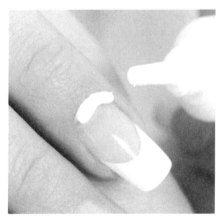

FOR FINGERTIPS

Cuticle Massage

5 red seedless grapes
1 tablespoon sugar

Wash the grapes, then slice them in half widthwise. Dip the cut side into the sugar. Using half a grape for each finger, massage the skin around each fingernail for about 30 seconds each. Wipe off the excess sugar with a soft towel, then rub hand cream onto hands and cuticles.

Photo: Valua Vitaly/Media Bakery

FOR HAIR

To restore luster to your tresses and make them more manageable.

Aromatic Conditioner

6 drops lavender essential oil
6 drops bay essential oil
6 drops sandalwood essential oil
6 ounces warm sesame oil

Mix the oils together in a bowl until blended. Part your hair in sections, put a few drops of the blended oil on your fingertips, and massage into your scalp. Cover your head with a towel for 15 minutes, then shampoo. (You may need to shampoo twice.)

Herbal Conditioner

1 teaspoon burdock root
1 teaspoon calendula flowers
1 teaspoon chamomile flowers
1 teaspoon lavender flowers
1 teaspoon rosemary leaves
1 tablespoon vinegar

Pour 1 pint of boiling water over the herbs in a bowl and let them steep for 30 minutes. Strain the liquid into a second bowl and add the vinegar. Shampoo, rinse, then pour the conditioner on your hair. Comb the conditioner through evenly. Do not rinse. *(continued)*

FOR THE FACE

Regular cleansing removes surface dirt and oils, but facial masks clean out the toxins that are found deep in pores.

Fruit Facial

This nutrient-rich cleansing facial mask contains many of the same age-defying ingredients—such as alpha hydroxy acid (in grapes), vitamin B (in cranberries), and vitamin C (in grapefruit)—that are found in store-bought products. Gelatin, which is often used in commercial facial peels, dries and stiffens. When it is peeled off, it helps to remove dead skin and unclog pores.

1 cup crushed seedless red grapes
1 cup crushed fresh cranberries
2 teaspoons grapefruit juice
1 envelope unflavored gelatin

Mix the ingredients together in a bowl until they form a paste. Cover and refrigerate for 45 minutes to let the mixture thicken. Remove from the refrigerator and let warm to room temperature. Spread the mixture on washed, dry skin. Avoid the area around the eyes. Sit or lie down for 15 minutes, then rinse off with warm water.

Chickpea Facial

Use Kasturi turmeric *(Curcuma aromatica)* because regular turmeric can temporarily stain the skin.

¼ cup chickpea flour
¼ cup Kasturi turmeric powder
yogurt, as needed

In a small bowl, mix the chickpea flour and turmeric. Store the mixture in an airtight bottle. When ready to use, place a teaspoon of the mixture in a small bowl and add enough yogurt to make a paste. Apply the paste evenly to the face and leave on until it dries, about 10 to 15 minutes. Wash off with warm water.

Wrinkle Relaxer

6 to 8 green seedless grapes

Wash the grapes, then cut them in half. Gently massage each half onto the face and neck. Let dry for 20 minutes, then rinse off and pat dry. Repeat every day, or as needed.

(continued)

Martie Majoros, a frequent contributor to Almanac publications, writes from the shores of Lake Champlain in Burlington, Vermont.

FOR SKIN

Walnut Scrub

Get rid of rough patches on your hands, feet, and elbows! The oil in the walnuts provides gentle exfoliation and the olive oil adds extra moisture. The honey helps to seal the moisture into the skin.

¼ cup shelled walnuts
½ cup olive oil
1 tablespoon honey

Combine all of the ingredients in a food processor and pulse until the mixture is reduced to fine particles. Gently rub on hands, feet, or elbows for several minutes. Rinse with warm water.

Coffee Scrub

Coffee grounds work to help diminish cellulite and varicose veins, in addition to improving circulation and smoothing the skin's texture.

2 cups used coffee grounds
½ cup sugar or sea salt
⅔ tablespoon unscented massage oil

Mix all of the ingredients in a large bowl. Massage gently on the skin, then rinse with warm water.

Citrus Splash Toner

For oily skin

1 cup water
⅔ cup witch hazel
½ cup lemon juice

Mix all of the ingredients in a bowl and apply to the face, using a cotton ball. Store the remaining mixture in a jar. Shake before using again.

Herbal Splash Toner

For normal or dry skin

1 cup boiling water
½ cup parsley

Chop the parsley and place in a small bowl. Pour the water over the parsley and let it cool. Strain the liquid into a jar. Apply to the face, using a cotton ball.

EXTREME MAKEOVERS

• Women in ancient Rome rubbed the ashes of ground snails on their skin to get rid of dark spots, mixed soot with water and applied it to their eyebrows to darken them, and "shaved" off body hair by rubbing their skin with a pumice stone.

• Women of the 17th century cut small star or Moon shapes from velvet or silk fabric and pasted them on their faces to cover facial scars, which were often the result of smallpox.

• Women in the 18th and 19th centuries pasted strips of mouse fur on top of their eyebrows to enhance their allure, covered blemishes with mercury, dabbed white lead on their faces to attain a pale complexion, and ate small amounts of arsenic to brighten their skin and eyes. ■

How We Predict the Weather

W e derive our weather forecasts from a secret formula that was devised by the founder of this Almanac, Robert B. Thomas, in 1792. Thomas believed that weather on Earth was influenced by sunspots, which are magnetic storms on the surface of the Sun.

Over the years, we have refined and enhanced that formula with state-of-the-art technology and modern scientific calculations. We employ three scientific disciplines to make our long-range predictions: solar science, the study of sunspots and other solar activity; climatology, the study of prevailing weather patterns; and meteorology, the study of the atmosphere. We predict weather trends and events by comparing solar patterns and historical weather conditions with current solar activity.

Our forecasts emphasize temperature and precipitation deviations from averages, or normals. These are based on 30-year statistical averages prepared by government meteorological agencies and updated every 10 years. The most-recent tabulations span the period 1981 through 2010.

We believe that nothing in the universe happens haphazardly, that there is a cause-and-effect pattern to all phenomena. However, although neither we nor any other forecasters have as yet gained sufficient insight into the mysteries of the universe to predict the weather with total accuracy, our results are almost always very close to our traditional claim of 80%.

How Accurate Was Our Forecast Last Winter?

Our prediction for winter 2013–14—"we expect much of the nation to have below-normal winter temperatures and above-normal snowfall"—was correct, although conditions were even colder and snowier than we had forecast in the eastern two-thirds of the nation. Our forecast of above-normal precipitation for the Pacific coast was incorrect, as California instead had one of its driest winters on record. In retrospect, perhaps we should have forecast this drought, as the highly amplified pattern that would lead to a cold and snowy winter in the East also suggests a mild and dry winter in the Southwest. We apologize for not giving this factor more weight.

We were correct in our forecast for temperature change from the previous winter in 15 of the 18 regions, an 83% accuracy rate, missing only the Pacific Southwest and the Desert Southwest. Our prediction for the change in precipitation from the previous winter was 78% accurate, missing in the Pacific and Intermountain states and the Appalachians. Overall, our accuracy rate for the winter season was 80.6%.

The accuracy of our winter season temperature forecasts is shown below, using a city selected from each region. On average, our forecasts differed from actual conditions by 1.78 degrees F.

Region/ City	Nov.–Mar. Temp. Variations From Normal (degrees F) PREDICTED	ACTUAL	Region/ City	Nov.–Mar. Temp. Variations From Normal (degrees F) PREDICTED	ACTUAL
1/Caribou, ME	−0.0	−2.9	10/Omaha, NE	−0.9	−3.5
2/Richmond, VA	−0.9	−1.5	11/San Antonio, TX	+0.3	−0.1
3/Asheville, NC	−1.4	−2.0	12/Denver, CO	−0.1	−0.5
4/Raleigh, NC	−2.4	−2.4	13/Boise, ID	−0.3	−0.8
5/Jacksonville, FL	−1.4	−0.1	14/Albuquerque, NM	−1.6	+1.4
6/Rochester, NY	+0.5	−4.2	15/Seattle, WA	0.0	+0.8
7/Charleston, WV	−1.0	−3.3	16/San Francisco, CA	−0.9	+2.3
8/Montgomery, AL	−1.0	−1.3	17/Anchorage, AK	+0.2	+1.3
9/Green Bay, WI	+0.2	−7.0	18/Lihue, HI	−0.4	−0.6

Weather Regions

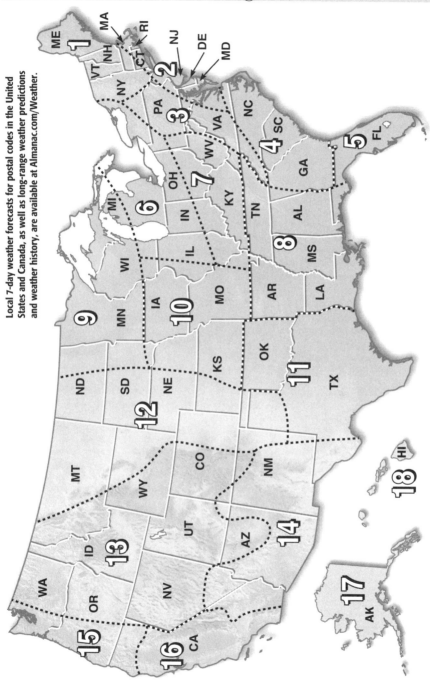

Local 7-day weather forecasts for postal codes in the United States and Canada, as well as long-range weather predictions and weather history, are available at Almanac.com/Weather.

WEATHER

2015   The Old Farmer's Almanac   195

Northeast

SUMMARY: Winter will be much colder than normal, with near-normal precipitation and below-normal snowfall. The coldest periods will be in mid- and late December, early and mid-January, and mid- to late February. The snowiest periods will be in mid- to late November, mid- and late December, and early to mid-March.

April and May will be warmer and wetter than normal in the north and much warmer and drier than normal in the south.

Summer will be hotter than normal, with below-normal rainfall. The hottest periods will occur in early June, early July, mid- to late July, and early August.

September and October will be warmer and slightly wetter than normal.

NOV. 2014: Temp. 37° (1° above avg. north, 3° below south); precip. 3.5" (avg.). 1–8 Rainy periods, mild. 9–10 Flurries and sprinkles. 11–13 Rain to snow, turning cold. 14–21 Snow showers, cold. 22–24 Rain to snow. 25–30 Snow showers, cold.

DEC. 2014: Temp. 24° (4° below avg.); precip. 5" (2" above avg.). 1–5 Rainy periods, mild. 6–11 Snow showers, cold. 12–18 Snowstorm, then sunny, bitter cold. 19–23 Heavy rain and snow, then sunny, cold. 24–31 Snow, then sunny, very cold.

JAN. 2015: Temp. 18° (5° below avg.); precip. 2" (1" below avg.). 1–9 Snow showers, very cold. 10–17 Snow, then flurries, cold. 18–22 Snow, then rain, turning mild. 23–27 Sunny, then rainy, quite mild. 28–31 Snow, then sunny, mild.

FEB. 2015: Temp. 20° (3° below avg.); precip. 1.5" (1" below avg.). 1–2 Sunny, mild. 3–8 Rain, then snowy periods, very cold. 9–15 Sunny, seasonable. 16–20 Snow showers, very cold. 21–24 Flurries, cold. 25–28 Showers, mild.

MAR. 2015: Temp. 33° (1° below avg.); precip. 3" (1" above avg. north, 1" below south). 1–4 Snow showers, cold. 5–12 Snow, then sunny, turning warmer. 13–20 Periods of rain and snow, mild. 21–25 Sunny, cold. 26–31 Heavy rain to snow, then sunny, cool.

APR. 2015: Temp. 49° (3° above avg.); precip. 3" (1" above avg. north, 1" below south). 1–9 Showers, then sunny, turning warm. 10–17 Rainy periods, cool. 18–23 Sunny, becoming very warm. 24–30 A few showers, turning cool.

MAY 2015: Temp. 57.5° (1° below avg. north, 4° above south); precip. 3.5" (1" above avg. north, 1" below south). 1 Rainy, cool. 2–7 Showers; cool north, warm south. 8–13 Showers, then sunny, seasonable. 14–19 Showers, cool. 20–23 Sunny, cool. 24–31 Scattered t-storms; very warm, then cool.

JUNE 2015: Temp. 65° (avg.); precip. 3" (0.5" below avg.). 1–4 Sunny, hot. 5–7 T-storms, then sunny, cool. 8–12 Scattered t-storms, warm. 13–22 A few showers, cool. 23–26 Daily showers, turning warm. 27–30 T-storms, then sunny, seasonable.

JULY 2015: Temp. 72° (2° above avg.); precip. 2.5" (1.5" below avg.). 1–3 Sunny, very warm. 4–8 Scattered showers, cool. 9–15 T-storms, then sunny, nice. 16–20 Sunny, hot. 21–26 A few t-storms, hot and humid. 27–31 Sunny, cool.

AUG. 2015: Temp. 67° (1° above avg.); precip. 4" (avg.). 1–4 Sunny, hot. 5–9 T-storms, then sunny, hot. 10–18 Scattered t-storms, cool. 19–21 T-storms, warm. 22–31 Scattered t-storms, cool.

SEPT. 2015: Temp. 61° (2° above avg.); precip. 6" (2" above avg.). 1–6 Showers, then sunny, cool. 7–14 Scattered showers, turning warm. 15–19 Showers, mild north; sunny, hot south. 20–26 Rainy periods, turning cool. 27–30 Sunny, turning warm.

OCT. 2015: Temp. 52° (4° above avg.); precip. 2.5" (1" below avg.). 1–4 Sunny, warm. 5–8 Showers, mild. 9–13 Rain to snow, then sunny, cold. 14–19 Rainy periods, mild. 20–26 Sunny; seasonable, then warm. 27–31 Sprinkles, seasonable.

Map labels: Caribou, Augusta, Burlington, Concord, Albany

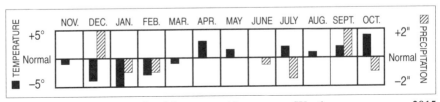

Atlantic Corridor

SUMMARY: Winter will be colder and slightly wetter than normal, with above-normal snowfall. The coldest periods will be in late December and early and mid-January. The snowiest periods will be in mid- and late December, mid-January, and early to mid-February.

April and May will be warmer and generally drier than normal.

Summer will be hotter and drier than normal, despite a tropical storm threat in early to mid-August. The hottest periods will occur in early June, mid- to late July, and early to mid-August.

September and October will be warmer than normal, with near-normal rainfall.

NOV. 2014: Temp. 44° (3° below avg.); precip. 3.5" (avg.). 1–2 Rainy; mild north, cool south. 3–7 Rainy north, showers south; mild. 8–11 Sunny, cold nights. 12–15 Rain, then sunny, cold. 16–22 Scattered showers, cool. 23–30 Showers and flurries, then sunny, cold.

DEC. 2014: Temp. 37° (2° below avg.); precip. 6" (3" above avg.). 1–2 Heavy rain, then sunny, mild. 3–5 Heavy rain, then sunny, mild. 6–13 Rain to snow, then flurries, cold. 14–17 Heavy rain, then flurries, cold. 18–21 Stormy, rain and snow; then sunny, cold. 22–29 Rain and snow, then sunny, cold. 30–31 Snowy, cold.

JAN. 2015: Temp. 31° (4° below avg.); precip. 2" (1.5" below avg.). 1–3 Sunny, very cold. 4–9 Flurries, cold. 10–17 Rain to snow, then sunny, very cold. 18–21 Snow, then sunny, mild. 22–24 Rain, then sunny, cold. 25–31 Rain to snow, then sunny, cold.

FEB. 2015: Temp. 33° (1° below avg.); precip. 2.5" (0.5" below avg.). 1–4 Sunny, then rainy, mild. 5–8 Sunny, then snowstorm. 9–14 Rain to snow, then sunny, seasonable. 15–22 A few rain and snow showers, turning cold. 23–28 Snow north, rain south; then sunny, cold.

MAR. 2015: Temp. 41° (3° below avg.); precip. 5" (1" above avg.). 1–4 Sunny, cool. 5–10 Rain to snow, then sunny, cold. 11–16 Rainy, cool. 17–21 Showers, mild. 22–26 Stormy, rain coast; wet snow interior. 27–31 Showers, cool.

APR. 2015: Temp. 53° (1° above avg.); precip. 2.5" (1" below avg.). 1–5 Showers, then sunny, cool. 6–8 Sunny north, heavy rain south. 9–11 Sunny, warm. 12–17 Rainy periods, cool north; showers, warm south. 18–25 Sunny north, scattered

t-storms south; warm. 26–30 Scattered showers, cool.

MAY 2015: Temp. 65° (3° above avg.); precip. 3" (2" above avg. north, 2" below south). 1–4 Scattered showers, turning hot. 5–9 Showers, turning cool. 10–19 Scattered t-storms, warm. 20–26 Sunny, turning hot. 27–31 Rain and mist north, scattered t-storms south; turning cool.

JUNE 2015: Temp. 71.5° (1° below avg. north, 2° above south); precip. 2.5" (1" below avg.). 1–4 Sunny, hot. 5–9 T-storms, cool. 10–15 Showers, cool north; t-storms, hot south. 16–17 Sunny. 18–22 T-storms, then showers, cool. 23–26 Drizzly, cool north; t-storms, hot south. 27–30 T-storms, then sunny, nice.

JULY 2015: Temp. 77° (1° above avg.); precip. 3" (1" below avg.). 1–4 Scattered t-storms, warm. 5–10 Scattered t-storms; cool north, hot south. 11–16 A few showers, turning cool. 17–21 T-storms, then sunny, hot. 22–26 Scattered t-storms, hot. 27–31 Sunny, cool.

AUG. 2015: Temp. 76° (2° above avg.); precip. 3" (1" below avg.). 1–9 Scattered t-storms, turning hot. 10–11 Tropical storm threat, mainly southeast. 12–15 T-storms, then sunny, cooler. 16–19 Rain, then sunny, cool. 20–24 Scattered t-storms, hot. 25–27 Sunny, cool. 28–31 T-storms, then sunny, cool.

SEPT. 2015: Temp. 70° (3° above avg.); precip. 2" (1.5" below avg.). 1–3 A few showers, turning warm. 4–10 Rainy periods, cool north; sunny, hot south. 11–19 T-storms, then sunny, hot. 20–25 T-storms, then sunny, cool. 26–30 Showers, then sunny, cool.

OCT. 2015: Temp. 59° (3° above avg.): precip. 5" (1.5" above avg.). 1–7 Sunny, warm. 8–13 Rain, then sunny, cool. 14–19 Rainy periods, mild. 20–25 Sunny, cool north; showers, warm south. 26–31 Rainy periods, turning cooler.

Boston
Hartford
Providence
New York
Philadelphia
Baltimore
Atlantic City
Washington
Richmond

W
E
A
T
H
E
R

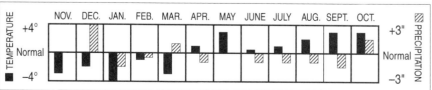

Appalachians

SUMMARY: Winter will be much colder than normal, with slightly below-normal precipitation and snowfall. The coldest periods will occur in early to mid-December, from late December into early January, and in mid- and late January. The snowiest periods will occur in mid-December and early February.

April and May will be warmer and drier than normal.

Summer rainfall and temperatures will be close to normal, on average, with the hottest periods in mid- to late June, mid- to late July, and mid-September.

September and October will be warmer than normal. Rainfall will be below normal in the north and above normal in the south.

NOV. 2014: Temp. 40° (4° below avg.); precip. 2.5" (1" below avg.). 1–6 Showers, then sunny, cool. 7–11 Rain and snow showers, then sunny, cool. 12–19 Rain to snow, then sunny, chilly. 20–30 Snow showers, cool.

DEC. 2014: Temp. 32° (4° below avg.); precip. 4" (1" above avg.). 1–5 Showers, mild. 6–14 Snow, then flurries, cold. 15–17 Snowstorm, then sunny, very cold. 18–21 Heavy snow, then flurries, cold. 22–31 Snow showers, cold.

JAN. 2015: Temp. 26° (4° below avg.); precip. 2" (1" below avg.). 1–3 Sunny, very cold. 4–8 Snow showers, cold. 9–11 Sunny, mild. 12–17 Snow showers, very cold. 18–22 Rain and snow showers, turning quite mild. 23–25 Sunny, mild. 26–31 Rain, then flurries, cold.

FEB. 2015: Temp. 29° (1° below avg.); precip. 1.5" (1" below avg.). 1–4 Periods of rain and snow, mild. 5–8 Snowstorm south, flurries north; cold. 9–10 Sunny north, rain south. 11–17 Sunny, cold, then mild. 18–20 Snow showers, cold. 21–28 Snow showers north, showers south; seasonable.

MAR. 2015: Temp. 35° (5° below avg.); precip. 4.5" (1.5" above avg.). 1–4 Sunny, cool. 5–10 Snow north, rain south; then sunny, cold. 11–16 Rain and snow showers, cool. 17–21 Sunny, cool. 22–31 Snowstorm north, rain south; then sunny, cool.

APR. 2015: Temp. 52° (2° above avg.); precip. 2" (0.5" below avg.). 1–5 Sunny, cool. 6–11 Showers, then sunny, mild. 12–16 A few show-

ers, cool. 17–24 Sunny, warm. 25–30 Rain, then sunny, cool.

MAY 2015: Temp. 63° (3° above avg.); precip. 2.5" (1.5" below avg.). 1–5 Sunny, warm. 6–11 Showers, cool. 12–15 Sunny, warm. 16–23 T-storms, then sunny, cool. 24–27 Scattered t-storms, warm. 28–31 Showers, cool.

JUNE 2015: Temp. 68° (avg.); precip. 4" (avg.). 1–4 Showers, then sunny, warm. 5–9 T-storms, then sunny, cool. 10–17 T-storms, then sunny; cool north, warm south. 18–22 T-storms, then sunny, cool. 23–27 A couple of t-storms, hot. 28–30 Sunny, nice.

JULY 2015: Temp. 72° (1° below avg.); precip. 3.5" (avg.). 1–4 Scattered t-storms, cool. 5–11 Sunny, warm. 12–16 Rainy periods, cool. 17–25 Scattered t-storms, hot and humid. 26–31 Sunny, cool.

AUG. 2015: Temp. 71° (avg.); precip. 4" (1" below avg. north, 2" above south). 1–3 Sunny north; rainy, cool south. 4–6 Sunny, warm. 7–13 Scattered t-storms, warm. 14–19 T-storms, then sunny, cool. 20–22 Sunny, warm. 23–26 T-storms, then sunny, cool. 27–31 Showers, warm, then cool.

SEPT. 2015: Temp. 67° (3° above avg.); precip. 3" (0.5" below avg.). 1–6 Rain, then sunny, nice. 7–13 Showers, then sunny, cooler north; sunny, hot south. 14–19 Sunny, hot. 20–25 Showers, then sunny, cool. 26–30 Rain, then sunny, cool.

OCT. 2015: Temp. 55° (2° above avg.); precip. 4" (1" below avg. north, 3" above south). 1–6 Sunny, warm. 7–12 Rain, then sunny, cool. 13–21 Rain, then sunny, cool. 22–28 Showers, mild north; heavy rains, cool south. 29–31 Sunny, nice.

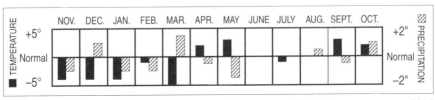

Southeast

SUMMARY: Winter will be colder and drier than normal, with near- to above-normal snowfall. The coldest periods will be in early to mid-December, from late December through early January, and in mid- and late January. The snowiest periods will be in early and mid-January.

April and May will be a warmer than normal. Rainfall will be below normal in the north and slightly above in the south. Watch for an early tropical storm threat in mid- to late May.

Summer will bring near-normal temperatures, on average, with the hottest periods in early to mid-June, mid- to late July, and mid- to late August. Rainfall will be below normal in the north and above in the south. Watch for a tropical storm threat in mid-July.

September and October will be warmer and drier than normal.

NOV. 2014: Temp. 50° (5° below avg.); precip. 1.5" (1.5" below avg.). 1–4 Sunny, cool. 5–10 Rain, then sunny, cold. 11–16 Rain, then sunny, cool. 17–28 Showers, then sunny, cold. 29–30 Rainy, cool.

DEC. 2014: Temp. 43° (4° below avg.); precip. 4" (0.5" above avg.). 1–6 Rain, then sunny, cold. 7–13 Showers, then sunny, cold. 14–19 Rainy periods, chilly. 20–24 Sunny, turning warm. 25–28 Rain, then sunny, cold. 29–31 Rain coast, rain to snow inland, then sunny, cold.

JAN. 2015: Temp. 38° (5° below avg.); precip. 3" (1.5" below avg.). 1–3 Sunny, very cold. 4–7 Rain to snow north, rain south, then sunny, cold. 8–11 Rainy periods, milder. 12–17 Rain to snow, then sunny, cold. 18–23 Rainy periods, mild. 24–31 Rain, then sunny, cold.

FEB. 2015: Temp. 46° (avg.); precip. 3" (1" below avg.). 1–7 Rain to snow, then sunny, cold. 8–14 Rainy, mild, then sunny, cold. 15–18 Rain arriving, milder. 19–22 Sunny, cold, then mild. 23–28 Rainy periods, mild.

MAR. 2015: Temp. 53° (2° below avg.); precip. 6.5" (2" above avg.). 1–4 Sunny, cool north; rainy, mild south. 5–10 Rain, then sunny, cold. 11–16 Rainy, cool. 17–22 Showers, turning warm. 23–31 Rainy periods, cool.

APR. 2015: Temp. 66° (3° above avg.); precip. 2.5" (0.5" below avg.). 1–4 Sunny, nice. 5–9 Rain, then sunny, nice. 10–21 A few t-storms, warm. 22–25 Sunny, warm. 26–30 Rain, then sunny, cool.

MAY 2015: Temp. 72° (1° above avg.); precip. 3.5" (1" below avg. north, 1" above south). 1–3 Sunny, warm. 4–10 Scattered t-storms; warm, then cool. 11–17 Sunny, warm. 18–20 Tropical storm threat. 21–31 A few showers, cool north; t-storms, warm south.

JUNE 2015: Temp. 78° (avg.); precip. 2" (2.5" below avg.). 1–5 Sunny, cool. 6–13 T-storms, then sunny, hot. 14–20 A few t-storms; cool north, hot south. 21–23 Sunny, cool. 24–27 Isolated t-storms, hot. 28–30 Sunny, cool.

JULY 2015: Temp. 81° (1° below avg.); precip. 4" (0.5" below avg.). 1–9 A few t-storms; cool north, hot south. 10–15 A few t-storms; cool north, warm south. 16–18 Tropical storm threat. 19–25 Scattered PM t-storms, hot. 26–31 Isolated t-storms, cool.

AUG. 2015: Temp. 81° (1° above avg.); precip. 7" (avg. north, 4" above south). 1–6 A few t-storms, cool. 7–17 Isolated t-storms, warm and humid. 18–24 Scattered t-storms, turning hot. 25–31 Scattered t-storms, very warm.

SEPT. 2015: Temp. 76° (2° above avg.); precip. 1.5" (3" below avg.). 1–3 Sunny, nice. 4–12 T-storms, then sunny, hot. 13–19 T-storms, then sunny, very warm. 20–30 T-storms, then sunny, cool.

OCT. 2015: Temp. 66° (2° above avg.); precip. 5.5" (1.5" above avg.). 1–8 A few showers, warm. 9–12 Sunny, cool. 13–16 T-storms, then sunny, warm. 17–21 Sunny, nice. 22–26 Heavy rain, then showers, warm. 27–31 Sunny, cool.

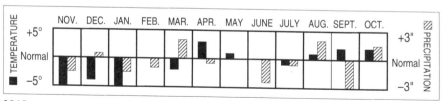

Florida

SUMMARY: Winter will be colder and rainier than normal. The coldest temperatures will occur in early January, with other cool periods in mid- and late January.

April and May will be hotter than normal, with below-normal rainfall in the north and above in the south. Watch for an early tropical storm in mid-May.

Summer will be hotter than normal, with the hottest periods in late June, early to mid-July, late July, and late August. Rainfall will be above normal in the north, but a bit below normal in the south. Watch for a tropical storm threat in mid-July.

September and October will be warmer than normal. Rainfall will be below normal in the north and above in the south. Watch for a hurricane threat in mid- to late September.

NOV. 2014: Temp. 66° (3° below avg.); precip. 1" (1.5" below avg.). 1–4 Sunny, cool. 5–9 T-storms, then sunny, quite cool. 10–15 Showers, then sunny, cool. 16–21 Showers, warm. 22–28 Sunny, cool. 29–30 Rainy, mild.

DEC. 2014: Temp. 60° (3° below avg.); precip. 3.5" (3" above avg. north, 1" below south). 1–13 Heavy rain, then sunny, cool. 14–19 Showers, cool. 20–22 Sunny, nice. 23–31 Rainy periods, turning cool.

JAN. 2015: Temp. 56° (4° below avg.); precip. 5.5" (3" above avg.). 1–4 Sunny, cold. 5–11 Rainy periods, warm. 12–18 Sunny, cool. 19–22 Showers, warm. 23–31 Rainy periods, cool.

FEB. 2015: Temp. 60° (1° below avg.); precip. 2.5" (avg.). 1–6 Rain, then sunny, cool. 7–16 T-storms, then sunny, cool. 17–21 T-storms, then sunny, cool. 22–28 Showers, warm.

MAR. 2015: Temp. 68° (1° above avg.); precip. 4" (1" above avg.). 1–5 Rainy periods, warm. 6–9 Sunny, cool. 10–14 Rain, then sunny, warm. 15–20 Scattered showers, cool. 21–31 A few t-storms, warm.

APR. 2015: Temp. 75° (4° above avg.); precip. 0.5" (2" below avg.). 1–3 Sunny, warm. 4–8 T-storms, then sunny, warm. 9–13 Scattered t-storms, warm. 14–23 Sunny, very warm. 24–30 Isolated t-storms; warm, then cool.

MAY 2015: Temp. 79° (2° above avg.); precip. 5.5" (1" above avg. north, 4" above south). 1–9 Sunny, warm. 10–16 Isolated t-storms, warm. 17–19 Tropical storm threat. 20–31 Scattered t-storms, seasonable.

JUNE 2015: Temp. 83° (1° above avg.); precip. 4.5" (2" below avg.). 1–9 Scattered t-storms, cool. 10–16 Sunny, hot north; a few t-storms south. 17–20 Scattered t-storms, seasonable. 21–24 Sunny, cool north; scattered t-storms south. 25–30 A few t-storms; hot north, seasonable south.

JULY 2015: Temp. 84° (1° above avg.); precip. 8.5" (2" above avg.). 1–5 Daily t-storms, seasonable. 6–8 Sunny, hot. 9–14 Scattered t-storms, warm. 15–17 Tropical storm threat. 18–22 A few t-storms, seasonable. 23–31 Isolated t-storms; hot north, seasonable south.

AUG. 2015: Temp. 83° (1° above avg.); precip. 8.5" (3" above avg. north, 1" below south). 1–8 Daily t-storms, cool north; scattered t-storms south. 9–11 Sunny, hot north; isolated t-storms south. 12–21 A few t-storms, seasonable. 22–25 Sunny, hot north; scattered t-storms south. 26–31 A few t-storms north, sunny south; hot.

SEPT. 2015: Temp. 82° (2° above avg.); precip. 5" (3" below avg. north, 2" above south). 1–3 Sunny, hot. 4–20 T-storms, very warm and humid. 21–22 Hurricane threat, mainly south. 23–25 Sunny, cool. 26–30 Scattered t-storms, warm.

OCT. 2015: Temp. 76° (1° above avg.); precip. 3" (1" below avg.). 1–4 Scattered t-storms, very warm. 5–9 Sunny, very warm north and central; a few t-storms south. 10–11 Sunny, cool. 12–23 Scattered t-storms, warm. 24–31 Sunny, cool.

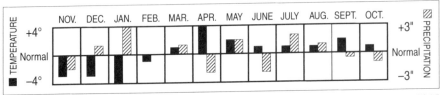

Lower Lakes

SUMMARY: Winter will be colder than normal, with the coldest periods in late December, throughout January, and in early February. Precipitation will be below normal in the east and near normal in the west. Snowfall will be above normal in most of the region, with the snowiest periods in mid-December, early and mid-January, and early February.

April and May will be warmer than normal, with near-normal rainfall.

Summer will be hotter than normal, with near-normal rainfall. The hottest periods will be in early June, mid- to late July, and mid- to late August.

September and October will be warmer and slightly rainier than normal.

NOV. 2014: Temp. 38° (3° below avg.); precip. 3.5" (avg. east, 2" above west). 1–5 Showers, mild. 6–9 Snow showers, cold. 10–14 Rain, then snow showers, cold. 15–20 Sunny, mild. 21–30 Snowy periods, cold.

DEC. 2014: Temp. 28° (4° below avg.); precip. 2.5" (0.5" below avg.). 1–7 Rain and snow showers, mild. 8–15 Snow showers, cold. 16–19 Lake snows, cold. 20–26 Snow showers; cold east, seasonable west. 27–31 Lake snows, very cold.

JAN. 2015: Temp. 23° (4° below avg.); precip. 1.5" (1" below avg.). 1–7 Lake snows, very cold. 8–17 Snowstorm, then lake snows, bitter cold. 18–25 Occasional rain and snow, mild. 26–28 Snow, then flurries, very cold. 29–31 Sunny, mild.

FEB. 2015: Temp. 28° (1° above avg.); precip. 2.5" (0.5" above avg.). 1–9 Snow, then snow showers, cold. 10–14 Sunny, mild, then flurries, cold. 15–17 Sunny, mild. 18–22 Snow showers, cold. 23–28 Showers, mild.

MAR. 2015: Temp. 33° (5° below avg.); precip. 2" (1" below avg.). 1–10 Snow showers, cold. 11–14 Showers, mild. 15–24 Snow, then flurries, cold. 25–31 Snow, then a few showers, cool.

APR. 2015: Temp. 53° (5° above avg.); precip. 3.5" (1" below avg. east, 1" above west). 1–5 Sunny; warm, then cool. 6–10 Sunny, turning warm. 11–17 Scattered t-storms, warm. 18–23 Sunny, turning hot. 24–30 T-storms,

then sunny, cool.

MAY 2015: Temp. 63° (5° above avg.); precip. 3.5" (avg.). 1–9 A few t-storms, warm. 10–15 Sunny, nice. 16–21 T-storms, then sunny, cool. 22–26 T-storms, warm. 27–31 Sunny, cool.

JUNE 2015: Temp. 68° (2° above avg.); precip. 3.5" (avg.). 1–4 Sunny, hot. 5–10 A few t-storms, very warm. 11–15 T-storms, then sunny, cool. 16–21 Scattered t-storms, cool. 22–25 T-storms, warm east; sunny, hot west. 26–30 T-storms, then sunny, cool.

JULY 2015: Temp. 72° (1° above avg.); precip. 4.5" (1" above avg.). 1–3 T-storms, cool. 4–8 Scattered t-storms, very warm. 9–16 T-storms, then sunny, cool. 17–20 Sunny, turning hot. 21–25 T-storms, hot and humid. 26–31 Sunny, cool.

AUG. 2015: Temp. 71° (2° above avg.); precip. 3" (1" below avg.). 1–4 Sunny, warm. 5–9 Scattered t-storms, warm. 10–17 A couple of t-storms, cool. 18–26 Sunny; very warm, then cool. 27–31 Showers, turning cool.

SEPT. 2015: Temp. 64° (2° above avg.); precip. 3.5" (avg.). 1–3 Scattered t-storms, warm. 4–12 Showers, cool. 13–19 T-storms, warm. 20–28 Showers east, sunny west; cool. 29–30 Sunny, warm.

OCT. 2015: Temp. 55° (3° above avg.); precip. 3.5" (1" above avg.). 1–4 Rainy periods, turning cool. 5–7 T-storms, warm. 8–12 Sunny, cool. 13–20 Rain, then sunny, nice. 21–27 Rainy periods, turning cool. 28–31 Sunny, cool.

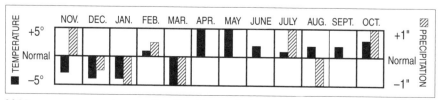

Ohio Valley

SUMMARY: Winter will be much colder than normal, with the coldest periods in mid-December, from late December through early January, and in mid- and late January. Precipitation will be slightly below normal, but snowfall will be above normal, with the snowiest periods in early to mid-November, mid- and late December, late January, early February, and early to mid-March.

April and May will be warmer and slightly drier than normal.

Summer will be hotter and drier than normal, with the hottest periods in mid- to late June, mid- to late July, and early to mid-August.

September and October will be warmer than normal, with rainfall above normal in the east, below in the west.

NOV. 2014: Temp. 41° (5° below avg.); precip. 3" (0.5" below avg.). 1–4 Sunny, mild. 5–9 Snow, then sunny, cold. 10–14 Rain to snow, then sunny, cold. 15–22 Showers, then sunny, cold. 23–30 Snow showers, cold.

DEC. 2014: Temp. 32° (5° below avg.); precip. 3" (avg.). 1–2 Sunny. 3–13 Rain to snow, then snow showers, cold. 14–21 Snow, then snow showers, cold. 22–23 Rainy, mild. 24–31 Rain to snow, then snow showers, cold.

JAN. 2015: Temp. 29° (4° below avg.); precip. 2" (1" below avg.). 1–5 Snow showers, very cold. 6–10 Sunny, turning mild. 11–17 Rain to snow, then snow showers, very cold. 18–25 Showers, mild. 26–31 Rain to snow, then snow showers, cold.

FEB. 2015: Temp. 35° (1° above avg.); precip. 3" (avg.). 1–4 Periods of rain and snow, turning cold. 5–7 Snow showers, cold. 8–12 Rain, then sunny, mild. 13–17 Sunny; cold, then mild. 18–22 Snow, then sunny, mild. 23–28 Showers, then sunny, cool.

MAR. 2015: Temp. 39° (6° below avg.); precip. 4.5" (0.5" above avg.). 1–4 Sunny, cool. 5–11 Snowy periods, cold. 12–18 Rain and snow showers, cool. 19–21 Sunny, nice. 22–26 Snow, then showers, cool. 27–31 Sunny, cool.

APR. 2015: Temp. 60° (5° above avg.); precip. 2.5" (1" below avg.). 1–4 Sunny; warm, then cool. 5–10 A few showers, turning warm. 11–16 Scattered showers, warm. 17–24 T-storms, then

sunny, hot. 25–30 Showers, then sunny, cool.

MAY 2015: Temp. 69° (6° above avg.); precip. 4.5" (avg.). 1–2 Sunny, warm. 3–8 Scattered t-storms, warm. 9–15 Sunny; cool, then warm. 16–24 T-storms, then sunny, nice. 25–31 A few t-storms, turning cool.

JUNE 2015: Temp. 73° (2° above avg.); precip. 3" (1" below avg.). 1–5 Sunny, warm. 6–11 Scattered t-storms, turning hot. 12–16 Sunny, cool. 17–22 Scattered t-storms, cool. 23–26 Sunny, hot. 27–30 T-storms, then sunny, cool.

JULY 2015: Temp. 75° (avg.); precip. 3.5" (0.5" below avg.). 1–7 T-storms, then sunny, nice. 8–12 Scattered t-storms, warm. 13–16 Sunny, cool. 17–25 Scattered t-storms, very warm. 26–31 Sunny, cool.

AUG. 2015: Temp. 75° (2° above avg.); precip. 4" (avg.). 1–5 Isolated t-storms, warm. 6–10 Sunny, hot. 11–18 T-storms, then sunny, nice. 19–22 Sunny, hot. 23–31 A few t-storms, warm.

SEPT. 2015: Temp. 71° (4° above avg.); precip. 2.5" (0.5" below avg.). 1–5 T-storms, then sunny, cool. 6–10 Sunny, hot. 11–17 Scattered t-storms, turning hot. 18–23 Scattered showers, cool. 24–27 T-storms, then sunny, cool. 28–30 Sunny, warm.

OCT. 2015: Temp. 60° (3° above avg.); precip. 3" (2" above avg. east, 1" below west). 1–7 Sunny, then scattered t-storms, warm. 8–12 Sunny, chilly. 13–21 Rain, then sunny, nice. 22–26 Rainy periods, mild. 27–31 Sunny, cool.

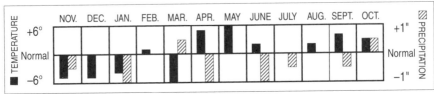

Deep South

SUMMARY: Winter will be much colder than normal, with below-normal precipitation. Snowfall will be near or slightly above normal in the north, but significant snowfall is unlikely in central or southern areas. The coldest periods will occur in late December and January, with the snowiest periods across the north in mid- and late December and early January.

April and May will be warmer than normal, with rainfall above normal in all but easternmost areas.

Summer will be hotter than normal, with near-normal rainfall despite hurricane threats in mid- and late July. The hottest periods will occur in early to mid-June, mid- to late June, mid- to late July, and late August.

September and October will be warmer than normal, with a hurricane threat in mid-September.

NOV. 2014: Temp. 52° (3° below avg.); precip. 4" (1" below avg.). 1–3 Sunny, cool. 4–9 Rain, then sunny, cold. 10–14 Rain, then sunny, cold. 15–18 Showers, mild. 19–27 Sunny, cool. 28–30 Heavy rain.

DEC. 2014: Temp. 44° (4° below avg.); precip. 5.5" (2" above avg. north, 1" below south). 1–6 Rain, then sunny, cool. 7–13 Snow north, then sunny, cold. 14–18 Periods of rain and snow, cold north; showers, mild south. 19–20 Sunny, cold. 21–28 Heavy rain north, t-storms south, then sunny, cold. 29–31 Rain and snow, then bitter cold.

JAN. 2015: Temp. 41° (4° below avg.); precip. 3.5" (1.5" below avg.). 1–3 Sunny, bitter cold. 4–10 Snow, then sunny, turning mild. 11–16 Snow showers north, sunny south; cold. 17–21 Sunny, turning warm. 22–26 Showers, turning cool. 27–28 Snow showers, cold. 29–31 Showers, turning mild.

FEB. 2015: Temp. 46° (1° below avg.); precip. 4" (1" below avg.). 1–6 Rain to snow, then sunny, cold. 7–14 Rain, then sunny, cold. 15–19 Showers, then sunny, cold. 20–25 Rainy periods, mild. 26–28 Sunny, seasonable.

MAR. 2015: Temp. 53° (3° below avg.); precip. 5" (1" below avg.). 1–3 Sunny, mild. 4–9 Rain, then sunny, cool. 10–14 Rainy, cool. 15–23 Showers, cool. 24–31 T-storms, then sunny, cool.

APR. 2015: Temp. 66° (3° above avg.); precip. 4.5" (2" above avg. north, 2" below south). 1–4 Sunny, nice. 5–14 Scattered t-storms, turning warm. 15–23 A few t-storms north, sunny south; very

warm. 24–27 T-storms, then sunny, cool. 28–30 Sunny, warm.

MAY 2015: Temp. 73° (2° above avg.); precip. 6" (1" above avg.). 1–13 Isolated t-storms, warm. 14–19 Sunny, very warm. 20–26 A few t-storms, warm and humid. 27–31 T-storms north, sunny south; cool.

JUNE 2015: Temp. 79° (1° above avg.); precip. 4" (1" below avg.). 1–5 Sunny, nice. 6–12 Scattered t-storms, hot and humid. 13–16 T-storms, cool north; sunny, hot south. 17–21 T-storms, then sunny, nice. 22–26 Scattered t-storms, hot. 27–30 Sunny; cool north, hot south.

JULY 2015: Temp. 81° (avg.); precip. 4.5" (avg.). 1–12 A few t-storms, warm. 13–17 Hurricane threat east. 18–27 A few t-storms; hot. 28–31 T-storms east, hurricane threat west.

AUG. 2015: Temp. 81° (1° above avg.); precip. 5.5" (1" below avg. north, 3" above south). 1–2 T-storms, seasonable. 3–9 Sunny north, a few t-storms south, seasonable. 10–16 Scattered t-storms, seasonable. 17–26 Sunny north, several t-storms south; cool, then hot. 27–31 T-storms, then sunny, hot.

SEPT. 2015: Temp.79° (3° above avg.); precip. 3.5" (1" below avg.). 1–4 Scattered t-storms; cool north, hot south. 5–16 A few t-storms, hot and humid. 17–18 Hurricane threat. 19–28 Sunny, turning cooler. 29–30 T-storms, warm.

OCT. 2015: Temp. 64° (1° below avg.); precip. 4" (1" above avg.). 1–4 T-storms, then sunny, cool. 5–10 T-storms, then sunny, cool. 11–15 T-storms, then sunny, cool. 16–22 Scattered t-storms, warm. 23–31 Sunny, cool.

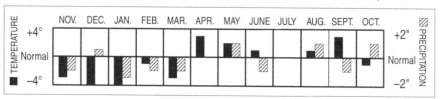

Upper Midwest

SUMMARY: Winter temperatures, precipitation, and snowfall all will be below normal. The coldest periods will be in late December, early to mid-January, late January, and early to mid-February. The snowiest periods will occur in late November, mid- to late December, early to mid-January, and mid- to late February.

April and May will be warmer than normal in the east, with near-normal precipitation, while the west will be cooler and wetter than normal.

Summer will be hotter and drier than normal. The hottest periods will occur in mid- to late June, early and mid-July, and early August.

September and October will be warmer and rainier than normal.

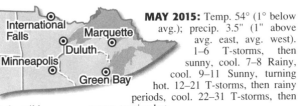

NOV. 2014: Temp. 32° (3° above avg.); precip. 1.5" (0.5" below avg.). 1–4 Sunny, mild. 5–8 Rain and snow showers, cold. 9–13 Rain, then snow showers, cold. 14–18 Sunny, mild. 19–20 Flurries, cold. 21–25 Sunny, mild. 26–30 Snowy periods, mild.

DEC. 2014: Temp. 16° (avg.); precip. 1.5" (0.5" above avg.). 1–10 Snow showers, mild. 11–19 Sunny, then snowy periods, seasonable. 20–27 Snowstorm, then flurries, cold. 28–31 Snow showers, very cold.

JAN. 2015: Temp. 10° (3° below avg.); precip. 0.5" (0.5" below avg.). 1–8 Snow showers, turning milder. 9–14 Snowstorm, then lake snows east, sunny west; very cold. 15–25 Snowy periods, turning mild. 26–28 Flurries, very cold. 29–31 Sunny, mild.

FEB. 2015: Temp. 10° (2° below avg.); precip. 1.5" (0.5" above avg.). 1–2 Sunny, mild. 3–8 Snow, then sunny, very cold. 9–16 Snow, then sunny, mild. 17–21 Snowstorm, then flurries, cold. 22–28 Snowstorm, then sunny, cold.

MAR. 2015: Temp. 23° (5° below avg.); precip. 0.5" (1" below avg.). 1–5 Sunny, cold. 6–9 Snow, then sunny, cold. 10–15 Snowy periods; mild east, cold west. 16–18 Sunny, mild. 19–27 Snow, then flurries, cold. 28–31 Sunny, turning warm.

APR. 2015: Temp. 42.5° (4° above avg. east, 3° below west); precip. 2" (1" below avg. east, 1" above west). 1–4 Sunny, cool. 5–10 Showers; cool east, turning warm west. 11–15 Rain to snow, then sunny, cool. 16–20 Sunny, warm. 21–25 Rain, then sunny, cool. 26–30 Showers, turning warm.

MAY 2015: Temp. 54° (1° below avg.); precip. 3.5" (1" above avg. east, avg. west). 1–6 T-storms, then sunny, cool. 7–8 Rainy, cool. 9–11 Sunny, turning hot. 12–21 T-storms, then rainy periods, cool. 22–31 T-storms, then sunny, turning hot.

JUNE 2015: Temp. 65° (2° above avg.); precip. 3" (1" below avg.). 1–2 Sunny, very warm. 3–10 A few t-storms, warm and humid. 11–18 Isolated t-storms, cool. 19–23 Sunny, hot. 24–28 T-storms, then sunny, hot. 29–30 T-storms, hot.

JULY 2015: Temp. 70° (2° above avg.); precip. 3" (1" above avg. east, 2" below west). 1–4 Sunny, hot. 5–15 T-storms, then sunny, cooler. 16–18 Sunny, hot. 19–24 T-storms, warm. 25–31 Sunny, cool.

AUG. 2015: Temp. 69° (3° above avg.); precip. 2.5" (1" below avg.). 1–6 Sunny, hot. 7–11 T-storms, then sunny, nice. 12–15 Scattered t-storms, cool. 16–20 Sunny; cool east, hot west. 21–24 T-storms, then sunny, cool. 25–31 A few t-storms, warm.

SEPT. 2015: Temp. 58° (avg.); precip. 4" (1" above avg.). 1–6 T-storms, the sunny, cool. 7–10 Rainy periods, cool. 11–15 Scattered t-storms, warm. 16–21 Rain, then sunny, cool. 22–28 Showers, cool east; sunny, warm west. 29–30 Sunny, warm.

OCT. 2015: Temp. 49° (2° above avg.); precip. 3" (0.5" above avg.). 1–8 Rain, then sunny, cool. 9–14 Sunny, warm days. 15–20 Rainy periods, mild. 21–27 Showers, cool. 28–31 Sunny, nice.

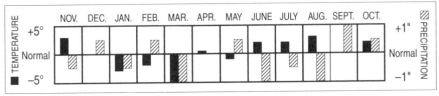

Heartland

SUMMARY: Winter temperatures, precipitation, and snowfall all will be below normal. The coldest periods will occur in early and mid- to late December and early and mid-January. The snowiest periods will be in mid-December, early February, and early and mid- to late March.

April and May will be warmer than normal, while rainfall will be a bit below normal in the north and a bit above in the south.

Summer will be hotter and slightly drier than normal, with the hottest periods in mid- to late June, mid- to late July, and early to mid- and mid- to late August.

September and October will be slightly cooler than normal, with above-normal rainfall.

NOV. 2014: Temp. 44° (1° above avg.); precip. 4" (1.5" above avg.). 1–4 Sunny, mild. 5–13 Rain to snow, then sunny, cold. 14–19 Sunny, mild. 20–26 Showers, then sunny, turning mild. 27–30 Rain to snow.

DEC. 2014: Temp. 30° (2° below avg.); precip. 0.5" (1" below avg.). 1–5 Rain and snow showers, then sunny, cold. 6–12 Sunny, seasonable. 13–19 Snowy periods, then sunny, cold. 20–27 Snowy periods, cold. 28–31 Sunny, very cold.

JAN. 2015: Temp. 29° (avg.); precip. 0.5" (0.5" below avg.). 1–2 Sunny, very cold. 3–9 Snow showers, then sunny, mild. 10–15 Snow showers, very cold. 16–25 Sunny, turning quite mild. 26–27 Snow showers, cold. 28–31 Sunny, mild.

FEB. 2015: Temp. 34° (3° above avg.); precip. 0.5" (1" below avg.). 1–5 Rain and snow, then sunny, seasonable. 6–9 Snow, then sunny, cold. 10–17 Sunny, turning mild. 18–23 Rain and snow, then showers, warm. 24–28 Sunny, mild.

MAR. 2015: Temp. 37° (7° below avg.); precip. 1.5" (1" below avg.). 1–8 Rain to snow, then sunny, cold. 9–16 Snow, then sunny, cold. 17–23 Rain and snow showers, chilly. 24–31 Snow, then sunny, turning warm.

APR. 2015: Temp. 59° (5° above avg.); precip. 3.5" (1" below avg. north, 1" above south). 1–4 Sunny, warm. 5–9 Rainy periods, cool. 10–14 Showers north, heavy rain south; cool. 15–21 Rain, then sunny, warm. 22–25 Heavy t-storms, then sunny, cool. 26–30 Isolated showers, turning warm.

MAY 2015: Temp. 68° (4° above avg.); precip. 4.5" (avg.). 1–7 A few t-storms, warm. 8–14 Sunny; cool, then warm. 15–21 T-storms, then sunny, warm. 22–29 Rainy periods, cool. 30–31 Sunny, nice.

JUNE 2015: Temp. 74° (2° above avg.); precip. 3.5" (1" below avg.). 1–3 Sunny, warm. 4–11 Scattered t-storms, then sunny, cool. 12–16 Showers, cool. 17–20 T-storms, then sunny, cool. 21–25 Sunny, hot. 26–30 T-storms, then sunny, cool.

JULY 2015: Temp. 78° (1° above avg.); precip. 4" (1" above avg. north, 1" below south). 1–5 Sunny, warm. 6–11 Scattered t-storms, warm. 12–16 Sunny, cool. 17–26 Scattered t-storms, hot. 27–31 Heavy t-storms; cool north, hot south.

AUG. 2015: Temp. 77° (2° above avg.); precip. 3.5" (1" below avg. north, 1" above south). 1–6 T-storms, then sunny, cool. 7–12 Scattered t-storms, turning hot. 13–15 T-storms, cool. 16–25 Sunny, hot. 26–31 Heavy t-storms, warm.

SEPT. 2015: Temp. 68° (1° above avg.); precip. 5.5" (2" above avg.). 1–4 T-storms, then sunny, cool. 5–10 Rain and t-storms; cool north, warm south. 11–13 Sunny, warm. 14–21 T-storms, then sunny, cool. 22–28 Sunny, warm. 29–30 T-storms, warm.

OCT. 2015: Temp. 54° (2° below avg.); precip. 3" (avg.). 1–4 Heavy rain north, showers south; then sunny, cool. 5–11 Showers, then sunny, cool. 12–20 Rainy periods, mild. 21–28 Showers and flurries, chilly. 29–31 Sunny, mild.

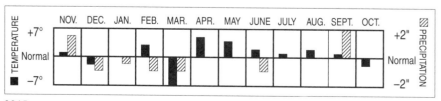

Texas–Oklahoma

SUMMARY: Winter temperatures, precipitation, and snowfall all will be below normal. The coldest periods will be in mid- and late December, early January, and mid- to late January, while the snowiest periods across the north will occur in mid- to late December and early to mid-January.

April and May will be warmer and rainier than normal, on average.

Summer will be hotter and drier than normal, despite a hurricane threat in late July. The hottest periods will be in late June, early July, and early and late August.

September and October will be cooler and rainier than normal, with three hurricane threats in September.

W E A T H E R

NOV. 2014: Temp. 57° (avg.); precip. 3" (1" below avg. north, 1" above south). 1–5 Sunny, warm. 6–8 Sunny, cool. 9–14 Rain, then sunny, cool. 15–20 Showers, warm. 21–23 Sunny north, rainy south; cool. 24–26 Sunny, nice. 27–30 Rainy, cool.

DEC. 2014: Temp. 53° (1° below avg. north, 1° above south); precip. 2" (0.5" below avg.). 1–10 Rain, then sunny, turning warm. 11–20 Showers, then sunny, mild. 21–25 Snow north, rain south, then sunny, cold. 26–31 Sunny north, rainy periods south; cold.

JAN. 2015: Temp. 48° (1° below avg.); precip. 1.5" (0.5" below avg.). 1–7 Sunny north, rainy periods south; cold. 8–13 Snow showers north, rain south, then sunny, cold. 14–21 Flurries north, rain south, then sunny, warm. 22–27 Rainy periods, then sunny, cold. 28–31 Sunny north, rainy south; turning warm.

FEB. 2015: Temp. 52° (2° above avg.); precip. 2" (avg.). 1–3 Showers, cool. 4–6 Sunny, mild. 7–11 Rain, then sunny, warm. 12–14 Showers, cool. 15–19 Rain, then sunny, cool. 20–28 Rainy periods, mild.

MAR. 2015: Temp. 54° (5° below avg.); precip. 1.5" (1" below avg.). 1–2 Sunny, warm. 3–8 Flurries north, rain south, then sunny, cold. 9–14 Rain and snow north, rainy periods south; chilly. 15–20 Sunny, cool. 21–28 Rainy, cool north; showers, warm south. 29–31 Sunny, nice.

APR. 2015: Temp. 69° (3° above avg.); precip. 4" (1" above avg.). 1–8 Sunny north, a few t-storms south; warm. 9–11 T-storms, warm. 12–21

Isolated t-storms; cool, then warm. 22–30 Heavy t-storms, then sunny, cool.

MAY 2015: Temp. 72° (1° below avg.); precip. 7" (2" above avg.). 1–6 Sunny, warm. 7–11 T-storms, then sunny, cool. 12–20 Sunny north, scattered t-storms south; seasonable. 21–31 Heavy t-storms, then sunny, cool.

JUNE 2015: Temp. 81° (2° above avg.); precip. 2" (2" below avg.). 1–4 Scattered t-storms, warm. 5–11 Sunny, hot. 12–18 A couple of t-storms, warm. 19–25 Sunny, very warm. 26–30 T-storms, then sunny, hot.

JULY 2015: Temp. 81° (avg.); precip. 3" (1" below avg. north, 1" above south). 1–12 Sunny, hot, Gulf t-storms. 13–19 Sunny north, a couple t-storms south; cool. 20–28 Isolated t-storms; hot north, seasonable south. 29–31 Hurricane threat.

AUG. 2015: Temp. 83° (2° above avg.); precip. 1.5" (1" below avg.). 1–12 Scattered t-storms, hot. 13–20 T-storms, then sunny, cooler north; scattered t-storms, hot south. 21–26 A few t-storms, seasonable. 27–31 Sunny, hot.

SEPT. 2015: Temp. 77° (1° above avg.); precip. 6.5" (3" above avg.). 1–5 Isolated t-storms, warm. 6–8 Hurricane threat. 9–15 Scattered t-storms, warm. 16–17 Hurricane threat. 18–26 T-storms, then sunny, cooler. 27–30 Hurricane threat.

OCT. 2015: Temp. 63° (4° below avg.); precip. 3" (1" below avg.). 1–7 T-storms, then sunny, cool. 8–13 Showers, chilly. 14–19 Scattered showers, turning warm. 20–29 T-storms, then sunny, cold. 30–31 Sunny, mild.

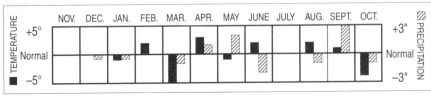

High Plains

SUMMARY: Winter will be colder and slightly drier than normal in the north and milder than normal with near-normal precipitation in the south. The coldest periods will be in late December, early to mid-January, mid- to late February, and early March. Snowfall will be below normal in the east and near normal in the west, with the snowiest periods in early to mid-November, mid- to late December, mid-January, and early and mid- to late March.

April and May will be cooler than normal, with precipitation above normal in the north and below normal in the south.

Summer will be hotter and drier than normal, with the hottest periods in early and late July and early and mid-August.

September and October will be cooler than normal, with near-normal precipitation.

NOV. 2014: Temp. 41° (4° above avg.); precip. 0.5" (0.5" below avg.). 1–4 Sunny, mild. 5–8 Rain to snow, then sunny. 9–11 Rain and snow, then sunny, cold. 12–18 Sunny, mild. 19–20 Rain and snow showers. 21–26 Sunny, mild. 27–30 Snow showers, cold.

DEC. 2014: Temp. 27° (1° below avg.); precip. 0.5" (avg.). 1–3 Snow showers, cold. 4–10 Sunny, mild. 11–17 Rain and snow showers, mild. 18–28 Snowy periods, cold. 29–31 Sunny, very cold.

JAN. 2015: Temp. 28.5° (2° below avg. north, 3° above south); precip. 0.5" (avg.). 1–7 Sunny, turning mild. 8–13 Snowy periods, very cold north; sunny, cold, then mild south. 14–21 Rain and snow showers north, sunny south; quite mild. 22–27 Snow showers, cold. 28–31 Sunny, mild.

FEB. 2015: Temp. 29.5° (1° below avg. north, 4° above south); precip. 0.5" (avg.). 1–3 Sunny, mild. 4–6 Snow showers, cold. 7–9 Sunny, mild. 10–19 Snow, then sunny, mild. 20–28 Snowy periods, very cold north; sunny, mild south.

MAR. 2015: Temp. 34° (5° below avg.); precip. 1" (0.5" below avg. north, 0.5" above south). 1–6 Snow, then sunny, cold. 7–12 Snow showers, cold. 13–16 Sunny, mild. 17–27 Snowy periods, cold. 28–31 Sunny, turning warm.

APR. 2015: Temp. 45° (3° below avg.); precip. 2.5" (2" above avg. north, 1" below south). 1–2 Sunny. 3–8 Snowy periods, cold north; sunny, turning cool south. 9–15 Snowy periods, cold north; rain, then sunny, nice south. 16–17

Sunny, cool. 18–22 Snow, cold north; sunny, warm south. 23–28 Showers, then sunny, turning warm. 29–30 Showers north, sunny south; warm.

MAY 2015: Temp. 58.5° (1° below avg. north, 2° above south); precip. 2.5" (1" above avg. north, 1" below south). 1–7 Rainy periods, cool north; sunny, hot south. 8–15 Showers north; sunny, warm south. 16–24 Showers, seasonable. 25–31 Snow north; showers, cool south.

JUNE 2015: Temp. 69° (2° above avg.); precip. 2.5" (avg.). 1–7 T-storms, turning cool north; sunny south. 8–12 Showers north; sunny, hot south. 13–21 Isolated t-storms, very warm. 22–23 T-storms, cool. 24–30 Scattered t-storms, turning hot.

JULY 2015: Temp. 73° (1° above avg.); precip. 1.5" (0.5" below avg.) 1–5 Sunny, hot. 6–11 Isolated t-storms; cool, then hot. 12–17 T-storms, then sunny, cool. 18–31 Scattered t-storms, hot.

AUG. 2015: Temp. 75° (4° above avg.); precip. 1" (1" below avg.). 1–5 Sunny, hot periods. 6–11 Scattered t-storms, turning hot. 12–19 T-storms, then sunny, turning hot. 20–23 A couple of t-storms. 24–31 Scattered t-storms; hot, then cooler.

SEPT. 2015: Temp. 59° (2° below avg.); precip. 1.5" (avg.). 1–3 T-storms, then sunny. 4–6 Snow north, sunny south. 7–8 Showers, cool. 9–12 Sunny, warm. 13–19 Showers, then sunny, cool. 20–27 Sunny, warm. 28–30 Rain and snow.

OCT. 2015: Temp. 46° (3° below avg.); precip. 1" (avg.). 1–4 Sunny, cold. 5–17 Rain and snow, then sunny, turning mild. 18–27 Rain and snow showers, cold. 28–31 Sunny, mild.

W E A T H E R

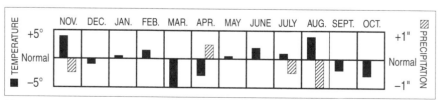

Intermountain

SUMMARY: Winter temperatures will be above normal, with below-normal snowfall and with precipitation above normal north, below south. The coldest periods will be late December and mid- to late February north, and mid-December south. The snowiest period in northern and central sections will be in early December; mid-February and early to mid-March in the south.

April and May will be slightly drier than normal, with near-normal temperatures.

Summer will be hotter than normal, with above-normal rainfall. The hottest periods will be in mid- and late June, early July, and mid- to late July.

September and October will be cooler than normal, with precipitation slightly above normal in the north and below in the south.

NOV. 2014: Temp. 38° (2° below avg.); precip. 0.5" (1" below avg.). 1–7 Sunny; mild north, cold south. 8–14 Rain and snow showers, then sunny, cold. 15–23 Snow showers, cold. 24–30 Snow showers, cold north; sunny, mild south.

DEC. 2014: Temp. 35° (2° above avg.); precip. 1.5" (0.5" above avg. north, 0.5" below south). 1–3 Snow showers, cold north; sunny, mild south. 4–7 Rainy north, sunny south; mild. 8–10 Sunny. 11–15 Rainy, mild north; sunny, cold south. 16–21 Rain, then snow showers north; sunny, cold south. 22–31 Snow showers; cold north, mild south.

JAN. 2015: Temp. 39° (7° above avg.); precip. 2" (2" above avg. north, 1" below south). 1–10 Periods of rain and snow north and central; sunny, mild south. 11–16 Rainy periods, mild north; sunny south. 17–21 Periods of rain and snow north, sunny south; mild. 22–31 Rain and snow showers, mild.

FEB. 2015: Temp. 39° (5° above avg.); precip. 2.5" (1" above avg.). 1–3 Sunny, mild. 4–10 Rain and snow showers, mild. 11–20 Sunny, mild north; snowstorm, then sunny, seasonable south. 21–26 Snow, then sunny, cold. 27–28 Showers, mild.

MAR. 2015: Temp. 41° (2° below avg.); precip. 1" (0.5" below avg.). 1–9 A few showers, mild. 10–14 Sunny, cool north; snowstorm south. 15–19 Sunny; mild north, cool south. 20–26 Rain and snow showers north; sunny, mild south. 27–31 Sunny, mild.

APR. 2015: Temp. 46° (3° below avg.); precip. 0.5" (0.5" below avg.). 1–5 Periods of rain and snow, cool. 6–9 Rain and snow showers, cool. 10–16 Rain and snow showers north and central; snow, then sunny south; cool. 17–23 Rain and snow showers north; snow central; sunny, mild south. 24–30 Sunny, warm.

MAY 2015: Temp. 60° (3° above avg.); precip. 0.5" (0.5" below avg.). 1–7 Showers, cool north; sunny, warm south. 8–18 Sunny, then showers, warm. 19–24 Showers, then sunny, cool. 25–31 Scattered showers, warm north; sunny, cool south.

JUNE 2015: Temp. 67° (1° above avg.); precip. 1" (0.5" above avg.). 1–9 Showers, cool north; sunny, hot south. 10–15 Sunny, hot. 16–23 A couple of t-storms, turning cool. 24–30 Sunny, warm.

JULY 2015: Temp. 75° (2° above avg.); precip. 0.5" (avg.). 1–4 Sunny north, t-storms south; hot. 5–20 Isolated t-storms, warm. 21–31 Scattered t-storms; cool, then hot.

AUG. 2015: Temp. 73° (1° above avg.); precip. 1.5" (0.5" above avg.). 1–6 Sunny, turning hot north; a few t-storms south. 7–12 Sunny, warm. 13–19 Sunny, hot north; scattered t-storms south. 20–31 Scattered t-storms; hot, then cool.

SEPT. 2015: Temp. 58° (4° below avg.); precip. 0.8" (0.5" above avg. north, 1" below south). 1–11 Sunny, chilly. 12–19 Scattered showers, cool. 20–26 Sunny, warm. 27–30 Showers, cool.

OCT. 2015: Temp. 48° (3° below avg.); precip. 1" (avg.). 1–10 Showers, then sunny, cool. 11–16 Showers, cool. 17–25 Sunny north, rain and snow showers south; cool. 26–31 Showers north, sunny south; mild.

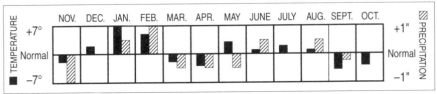

Desert Southwest

SUMMARY: Winter temperatures, precipitation, and snowfall will be above normal in the east and below in the west. The coldest periods will occur in late December, mid- to late January, and mid-February, with the snowiest periods in mid-November in the east and mid- to late December in the north.

April and May will be cooler than normal, with near-normal rainfall.

Summer will be slightly rainier than normal, with near-normal temperatures. The hottest periods will be in mid- and late June, early July, and mid- to late July.

September and October will be much cooler and slightly drier than normal.

NOV. 2014: Temp. 55° (1° below avg.); precip. 1.2" (0.2" above avg.). 1–6 Showers, then sunny, warm. 7–17 Showers, then sunny, cool. 18–21 Snow east; sunny, mild west. 22–27 Scattered showers, seasonable. 28–30 Sunny west, rain and snow showers east; cool.

DEC. 2014: Temp. 47° (1° above avg. east, 3° below west); precip. 0.1" (0.4" below avg.). 1–5 Sunny, cool. 6–19 Sunny; mild east, seasonable west. 20–26 Snow showers east, sunny west; cold. 27–31 Sunny, cold.

JAN. 2015: Temp. 50° (4° above avg. east, avg. west); precip. 0.2" (0.3" below avg.). 1–8 Isolated showers; cool, then mild. 9–20 Sunny, mild. 21–24 Sunny, cold. 25–31 Showers and flurries, then sunny, turning mild.

FEB. 2015: Temp. 53° (2° above avg.); precip. 1" (0.5" above avg.). 1–7 Scattered showers, mild. 8–12 Sunny, turning cool. 13–20 A few showers east, sunny west; seasonable. 21–26 Rainy periods, chilly west; a shower, mild east. 27–28 Sunny, cool.

MAR. 2015: Temp. 55° (3° below avg.); precip. 0.5" (0.4" above avg. east, 0.4" below west). 1–2 Sunny; warm east, cool west. 3–10 Sunny, cool. 11–18 Showers, then sunny, nice. 19–29 Showers, then sunny, cool. 30–31 Sunny, warm.

APR. 2015: Temp. 62° (3° below avg.); precip. 0.5" (avg.). 1–8 Sunny; warm east; warm, then cool west. 9–17 Showers, then sunny; season-able east, cool west. 18–25 Showers, then sunny, cool. 26–30 Sunny, warm.

MAY 2015: Temp. 76° (2° above avg.); precip. 0.5" (avg.). 1–13 Sunny, turning warm. 14–20 Scattered t-storms, warm. 21–27 Sunny; turning cool east, hot west. 28–31 Scattered t-storms, cool.

JUNE 2015: Temp. 82° (1° below avg.); precip. 0.5" (avg.). 1–11 Sunny, cool west; isolated t-storms, turning hot east. 12–17 Scattered t-storms east; sunny, hot west. 18–24 Isolated t-storms, turning cooler. 25–30 Scattered t-storms, hot.

JULY 2015: Temp. 88° (1° above avg.); precip. 2" (0.5" above avg.). 1–12 Isolated t-storms, hot. 13–21 Scattered t-storms, not as hot. 22–25 Sunny, hot. 26–31 A couple of t-storms.

AUG. 2015: Temp. 85° (avg.); precip. 2" (0.5" above avg.). 1–11 Scattered t-storms, very warm and humid. 12–16 Scattered t-storms, hot and humid. 17–21 Sunny, hot. 22–27 Isolated t-storms, hot. 28–31 T-storms, then sunny, cool.

SEPT. 2015: Temp. 76° (3° below avg.); precip. 0.7" (0.3" below avg.). 1–2 Sunny, warm. 3–11 Scattered t-storms, turning cool. 12–19 T-storms, then sunny, cool. 20–30 A couple of t-storms, cool.

OCT. 2015: Temp. 64° (4° below avg.); precip. 0.5" (0.5" below avg.). 1–7 Sunny, cool. 8–13 Showers, then sunny, cool. 14–28 Showers, then sunny, cool. 29–31 Sunny, mild.

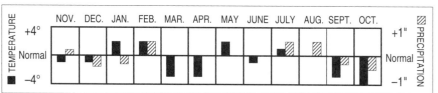

THE OLD FARMER'S ALMANAC

Pacific Northwest

SUMMARY: Winter temperatures will be higher than normal, with below-normal snowfall. Precipitation will be below normal in Washington and Oregon and near normal in northern California. The coldest periods will be in late December, mid- to late January, and late February, with the snowiest periods in late December and mid- to late January.

April and May will be slightly drier than normal, with near-normal temperatures.

Summer will be drier than normal, with temperatures near normal in the north and above elsewhere. The hottest periods will occur in mid- and late June and early to mid-July.

September and October will be cooler and drier than normal.

W E A T H E R

NOV. 2014: Temp. 47° (0.5° above avg. north, 1° below south); precip. 1.5" (5" below avg.). 1–6 Showers, mild. 7–16 Rainy periods, seasonable. 17–25 Sunny, cool. 26–30 Showers, cool.

DEC. 2014: Temp. 46° (3° above); precip. 8" (avg. north, 3" above south). 1–3 Rainy, mild. 4–6 Heavy rain, windy, mild. 7–19 Rainy periods, mild. 20–26 Sunny, cool. 27–31 Snow, then sunny, cold.

JAN. 2015: Temp. 46° (3° above avg.); precip. 11" (5" above avg.). 1–4 Rainy, cool. 5–7 Heavy rain, mild. 8–13 Rainy periods, mild. 14–19 Heavy rain, mild. 20–22 Rain and snow showers, cold. 23–31 Occasional rain, mild.

FEB. 2015: Temp. 47° (3° above avg.); precip. 4" (1" below avg.). 1–4 Sunny, mild. 5–10 Rainy, mild. 11–14 Sunny, mild. 15–20 A few showers, seasonable. 21–28 Showers, cool.

MAR. 2015: Temp. 47° (avg.); precip. 2" (2" below avg.). 1–2 Sunny, cool. 3–9 Rainy periods, mild. 10–12 Sunny, cool. 13–18 Sprinkles, cool. 19–22 Showers, mild. 23–31 Sunny, then showers, cool.

APR. 2015: Temp. 48° (2° below avg.); precip. 3" (avg.). 1–4 Rainy periods, cool. 5–10 Sunny, nice. 11–22 Occasional rain, cool. 23–27 Sunny, warm. 28–30 Showers, cool.

Seattle
Portland
Eugene
Eureka

MAY 2015: Temp. 57° (2° above avg.); precip. 1" (1" below avg.). 1–5 Rainy periods, cool. 6–9 Sunny, warm. 10–15 A few showers, cool. 16–18 Sunny, very warm. 19–22 Rainy periods, cool. 23–26 Sunny, turning hot. 27–31 Showers, then sunny, very warm.

JUNE 2015: Temp. 63° (1° above avg. north, 5° above south); precip. 1" (0.5° below avg.). 1–8 A few showers, cool. 9–19 Sunny, turning hot. 20–24 Showers, cool. 25–30 Sunny, hot.

JULY 2015: Temp. 64° (1° below avg.); precip. 0.2" (0.3" below avg.). 1–6 Sunny, turning cool. 7–8 Sunny, hot. 9–16 T-storms, then sunny, turning cool. 17–24 Showers, then sunny, cool. 25–31 Scattered showers, cool.

AUG. 2015: Temp. 66° (avg.); precip. 1" (avg.). 1–4 Sunny, hot. 5–15 Showers, then sunny, nice. 16–25 Scattered showers, seasonable. 26–31 Rainy periods, cool.

SEPT. 2015: Temp. 60° (1° below avg.); precip. 1" (0.5° below avg.). 1–8 Sunny, cool. 9–14 Rainy periods, cool. 15–18 Showers, then sunny, cool. 19–26 Sunny, warm. 27–30 Rainy periods, cool.

OCT. 2015: Temp. 54.5° (0.5° above avg.); precip. 3" (avg.). 1–4 Showers, mild. 5–9 Sunny, cool. 10–17 Rainy, cool. 18–27 Sunny, turning warm. 28–31 Rainy, mild.

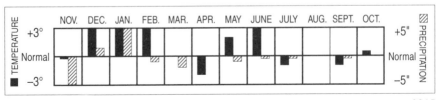

Pacific Southwest

SUMMARY: Winter will be warmer than normal, with the coldest periods in late December and early to mid- and late February. Rainfall will be above normal in the north and below in the south. Mountain snows will be below normal, with the snowiest periods in early to mid-January and mid- to late February.

April and May will be drier than normal, with temperatures near normal in the north and below in the south. Summer will be cooler than normal, with near-normal rainfall. The hottest periods will be in mid- and late June in the central valley; in mid- to late June, early August, and mid-September near the northern coast; and in late June, early August, and mid- to late September near the southern coast.

September and October will bring near-normal temperatures, with rainfall above normal in the north and below in the south.

NOV. 2014: Temp. 61° (3° above avg.); precip. 0.5" (1" below avg.). 1–7 Sunny north, showers south; warm. 8–15 Showers, then sunny, cool. 16–23 Sunny, mild. 24–30 Isolated showers; cool inland, mild coast.

DEC. 2014: Temp. 55° (3° above avg. north, 0.5° below south); precip. 2" (1" above avg. north, 1" below south). 1–9 Rain, then sunny; mild north, cool south. 10–12 Rainy north, sunny south; mild. 13–19 Rainy periods, mild. 20–31 Sunny, cool.

JAN. 2015: Temp. 56° (4° above avg. north, avg. south); precip. 4" (3" above avg. north, 1.5" below south). 1–4 Rainy; mild north, cool south. 5–6 Showers, mild. 7–9 Rain, heavy north; mild. 10–11 Sunny. 12–17 Rainy, mild north; sprinkles, seasonable south. 18–24 Showers north, sunny south; seasonable. 25–31 Sunny; mild north, cool south.

FEB. 2015: Temp. 56° (1° above avg.); precip. 3" (0.5" below avg. north, 1" above south). 1–4 Rainy periods, mild. 5–9 Rainy periods, mild north; sunny, seasonable south. 10–19 Sunny; cool, then warm. 20–25 Rain, some heavy; turning cool. 26–28 Showers, cool.

MAR. 2015: Temp. 59° (2° above avg.); precip. 0.5" (2" below avg.). 1–7 Showers, turning mild. 8–18 Sunny, nice. 19–24 Sunny, mild north; sprinkles, cool south. 25–31 Sunny, warm.

APR. 2015: Temp. 58° (2° below avg.); precip. 0.6" (0.4" below avg.). 1–5 Sunny, nice. 6–11 Showers, then sunny, cool. 12–20 Scattered showers, cool. 21–26 Sunny, turning very warm. 27–30 Sunny, cool.

MAY 2015: Temp. 64° (2° above avg. north, 1° below south); precip. 0.3" (0.2" below avg.). 1–6 Sunny inland, sprinkles, P.M. sun coast; cool. 7–10 Sunny, hot. 11–20 Sunny, warm inland; A.M. clouds and sprinkles, P.M. sun coast. 21–24 Sunny; turning hot north, warm south. 25–31 Sunny, hot inland; A.M. clouds and sprinkles, P.M. sun coast.

JUNE 2015: Temp. 68° (avg.); precip. 0.2" (0.2" above avg. north, avg. south). 1–2 Showers, cool. 3–18 Sunny, turning hot inland; A.M. clouds and sprinkles, P.M. sun coast. 19–22 Showers, then sunny, cool. 23–26 Sunny, hot. 27–30 Sunny, hot inland; A.M. clouds, P.M. sun coast.

JULY 2015: Temp. 70° (1° below avg.); precip. 0" (avg.). 1–13 Sunny, hot inland; A.M. clouds, P.M. sun, cool coast. 14–26 Sunny, nice. 27–31 Sunny inland; A.M. clouds and sprinkles, P.M. sun coast.

AUG. 2015: Temp. 70° (1° below avg.); precip. 0.1" (avg.). 1–3 Sunny, hot. 4–11 Sunny; cool north, warm south. 12–16 Scattered showers north, sunny south; cool. 17–27 Sunny, cool. 28–31 Sunny; hot north, cool south.

SEPT. 2015: Temp. 71° (1° above avg.); precip. 0.1" (0.1" below avg.). 1–5 Sunny, hot inland; A.M. clouds, P.M. sun, cool coast. 6–12 Sunny, cool. 13–24 Sunny, turning very warm. 25–30 Scattered showers, then sunny, cool.

OCT. 2015: Temp. 64° (1° below avg.); precip. 1" (1" above avg. north, 0.5" below south). 1–10 Sunny, cool. 11–16 Showers, mainly north; cool. 17–22 Sunny, cool. 23–26 Showers north, sunny south. 27–31 Rainy north, showers south; mild.

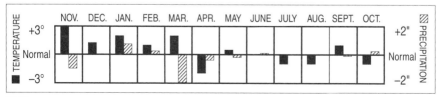

Alaska

SUMMARY: Winter temperatures will be above normal, with January the coldest period. Precipitation and snowfall will be below normal, with the snowiest periods in mid- to late December N (see Key below), mid-February and mid-March EC and WC, mid- and late January SC, late January A, and early to mid-November, late December, late January, and late March P.

April and May will be warmer than normal, with near-normal precipitation and less snowfall than normal.

Summer temperatures will be below normal, on average, with the warmest periods in mid-July and other warm periods in early July N and mid- to late June S and C.

September and October temperatures will be colder than normal, with below-normal precipitation and near-normal snowfall.

KEY: Panhandle (**P**), Aleutians (**A**), North (**N**), Central (**C**), South (**S**), East-Central (**EC**), West-Central (**WC**), South-Central (**SC**), Elsewhere (**EW**)

NOV. 2014: Temp. 2° N, 42° S (avg. N, 6° above S); precip. 0.1" N, 8" S (3" above avg. P, 0.3" below EW). 1–3 Flurries, cold N+C; showers, mild S. 4–14 Frequent snow P; clear, very cold EW. 15–30 Flurries, turning quite mild N+C; Rainy periods, mild S.

DEC. 2014: Temp. 0° N, 38° S (7° above avg.); precip. 0.2" N, 3" S (avg. N, 2" below S). 1–6 Flurries, turning cold N+C; rain and wet snow S. 7–15 Snow, then clear, turning mild. 16–26 Snow showers N+C, rainy periods S; mild. 27–31 Snowy periods P, clear EW; cold.

JAN. 2015: Temp. –13° N, 28° S (1° below avg.); precip. 0.2" N, 4.5" S (avg. N, 0.5" below S). 1–8 Freezing mist, mild N; clear, cold EW. 9–19 Flurries, cold, then milder. 20–31 Snow showers, cold N+C; periods of rain and snow S.

FEB. 2015: Temp. –14° N, 41° S (4° above avg. N, 12° above avg. S); precip. 0.2" N, 3.5" S (avg. N, 0.5" below S). 1–10 Flurries N, showers S; mild. 11–21 Flurries N; snow C; rain, some heavy S; mild. 22–28 Snow showers, turning cold.

MAR. 2015: Temp. –11° N, 42° S (2° above avg. N, 8° above S); precip. 0.5" N, 6" S (avg. N, 1" above N). 1–4 Clear, turning mild. 5–17 Flurries, cold N; snow showers, mild C; rainy periods, mild S. 18–24 Snow showers N+C, rainy periods S; mild. 25–31 Clear N, snowy periods C+S; cold.

APR. 2015: Temp. 2° N, 41° S (avg.); precip. 0.7" N, 3" S (avg.). 1–4 Snow showers, cold. 5–15 Snow showers, mild N+C; showers, cool S. 16–22 Flurries, cold N; showers, mild C+S. 23–30 Flurries N, showers S; cool.

MAY 2015: Temp. 22° N, 48° EW (1° above avg.); precip. 0.6" N, 3" S (avg.). 1–8 Showers, cool P+A; sunny, mild EW. 9–19 Flurries and freezing drizzle N, a few showers C+S; seasonable. 20–31 A few showers; cool WC+P, seasonable EW.

JUNE 2015: Temp. 34° N, 54° EW (1° below avg.); precip. 0.2" N, 2.5" S (1" above avg. C, 0.5" below EW). 1–6 Flurries N, scattered showers EW; cool. 7–12 Showers P+A, sunny EW; cool. 13–22 A few showers; cool N, warm EW. 23–30 Sunny N, showers C+S; cool.

JULY 2015: Temp. 40° N, 55° EW (2° below avg.); precip. 1.7" N, 4.5" S (0.5" above avg.). 1–7 Sunny, warm N; showers, cool C+S. 8–15 Sunny N, rainy periods C+S; cool. 16–20 Sunny, turning very warm. 21–31 Showers, cool.

AUG. 2015: Temp. 38° N, 54° EW (2° below avg.); precip. 0.7" N, 4.5" S (0.5" below avg.). 1–15 Showers C, cool. 16–20 Showers N+C, sunny S; cool. 21–31 Freezing mist, cold N; sunny, cool WC; rainy, cool P+A; showers, mild EW.

SEPT. 2015: Temp. 29° N, 51° EW (3° below avg.); precip. 0.6" N, 6.5" S (0.5" below avg.). 1–5 Sprinkles, mild N; rain arriving, cool, then mild C; rain, then sunny, cool S. 6–13 Freezing mist and flurries N, showers EW; cool. 14–24 Flurries, cold N+C; rainy periods, turning mild S. 25–30 Snow showers N, snowy periods C, rainy periods S; cold.

OCT. 2015: Temp. 8° N, 45° S (4° below avg. N, 2° above S); precip. 0.1" N, 6.6" S (0.4" below avg.). 1–7 Flurries, very cold N; snowy periods, some heavy C; rainy periods, mild S. 8–19 Snow showers, very cold N+C; rain, then rain and snow showers S. 20–24 Snow showers N+WC; snow, then showers C; rainy periods S; turning mild. 25–31 Snow showers, mild N+C; rain, then clear, cold A; rainy periods, mild SC+P.

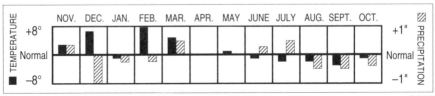

Hawaii

SUMMARY: Winter temperatures will be near or slightly above normal, with the coolest periods in late December, early and mid-January, and early and mid-February. Rainfall will be greater than normal on Oahu, Lanai, and Molokai, but below normal elsewhere.

April and May will be rainier than normal, especially on the Big Island. Temperatures will be near or slightly above normal.

Summer temperatures will be near normal, with the hottest periods in mid- and late July. Rainfall will be above normal, with a tropical storm threat in mid- to late August.

September and October temperatures will be slightly cooler than normal, with above-normal rainfall.

KEY: East (E), Central (C), West (W)

NOV. 2014: Temp. 77° (0.5° below avg.); precip. 4.5" (2" above avg.). 1–4 Sunny, nice E; t-storms W. 5–8 Heavy t-storms E+C, sunny W; seasonable. 9–18 Scattered showers, warm C+W; rainy periods, cool E. 19–22 Sunny, nice C+W; a few t-storms E. 23–27 Sunny E, a few showers C+W; warm. 28–30 Showers E, sunny C+W; warm.

DEC. 2014: Temp. 75.5° (0.5° above avg.); precip. 2.3" (1" below avg.). 1–7 A few showers; cool E, warm C+W. 8–16 Scattered t-storms E, sunny C+W; cool. 17–22 A few t-storms, some heavy; warm. 23–26 T-storms E+W, sunny C; warm. 27–31 Showers and heavy t-storms, cool.

JAN. 2015: Temp. 74° (1° above avg.); precip. 1.5" (1" below avg.). 1–3 Sunny, cool. 4–14 Sunny, warm E+C; a few t-storms, cool, then warm W. 15–16 T-storms, cool. 17–19 Sunny E+C, showers W; warm. 20–25 Showers E+C, sunny W; warm. 26–31 Sunny, seasonable.

FEB. 2015: Temp. 72° (1° below avg.); precip. 0.7" (3" below avg. E+W, 2" above C). 1–8 Widely separated showers, cool. 9–13 T-storms, then sunny, nice. 14–19 Showers and heavy t-storms E+C, scattered showers W; cool. 20–28 Daily showers, warm, then cool E+C; isolated showers, seasonable W.

MAR. 2015: Temp. 74.5° (0.5° above avg.); precip. 0.7" (4" below avg. E+W, 4" above C). 1–6 Scattered showers, cool. 7–15 Showers and heavier t-storms, seasonable E+C; scattered showers, warm W. 16–24 Scattered showers, warm E+W; showers and t-storms, cool C. 25–31 Showers and heavier t-storms, warm.

APR. 2015: Temp. 76° (0.5° above avg.); precip. 7.7" (11" above avg. E, 3" above W). 1–9 Rain and heavy t-storms E+C, showers W; warm. 10–14 Showers and t-storms E+W, heavy rain C. 15–18 Rainy periods, cool. 19–25 Showers, warm E+W; heavy rain and t-storms, cool C. 26–30 Showers, seasonable.

MAY 2015: Temp. 77° (avg.); precip. 4.7" (8" above avg. E, avg. W). 1–8 Rainy periods, cool. 9–15 Showers, seasonable. 16–21 Scattered showers, warm E+W; showers and heavy t-storms, cool C. 22–31 Scattered showers, seasonable.

JUNE 2015: Temp. 80° (0.5° above avg.); precip. 2.4" (2" above avg.). 1–10 Daily showers, cool. 11–17 Scattered showers E+W, daily light showers C; warm. 18–30 Frequent showers E, scattered showers and heavy t-storms C+W; cool, then warm.

JULY 2015: Temp. 81.5 (0.5° above avg.); precip. 1.5" (1" above avg.). 1–11 Daily showers, scattered t-storms; cool, then warm. 12–19 Scattered showers; very warm E, seasonable W. 20–31 Daily showers, seasonable E+C; scattered showers, very warm W.

AUG. 2015: Temp. 80.5° (1° below avg.); precip. 3.6" (3" above avg.). 1–11 Showers; warm, then cool. 12–17 Daily showers; cool E, warm W. 18–23 Scattered showers, warm E; tropical storm threat C+W, heavy rains and t-storms. 24–31 Daily showers; warm E+W, cool C.

SEPT. 2015: Temp. 81° (0.5° below avg.); precip. 1.8" (1" above avg.). 1–6 Scattered showers; cool E, warm W. 7–19 Showers; warm E+W, cool C. 20–26 Scattered showers, cool E+W; sunny, very warm C. 27–30 Daily showers E+C, scattered showers W; seasonable.

OCT. 2015: Temp. 79.5° (0.5° below avg.); precip. 4" (2" above avg.). 1–7 Showers, then sunny; cool. 8–10 Sunny, cool. 11–20 Scattered showers, warm E+W; daily showers and scattered heavy t-storms, cool C. 21–31 Showers, cool.

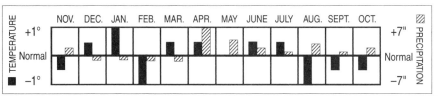

Frosts and Growing Seasons

■ Dates given are normal averages for a light freeze; local weather and topography may cause considerable variations. The possibility of frost occurring after the spring dates and before the fall dates is 50 percent. The classification of freeze temperatures is usually based on their effect on plants. **Light freeze:** 29° to 32°F—tender plants killed. **Moderate freeze:** 25° to 28°F—widely destructive to most vegetation. **Severe freeze:** 24°F and colder—heavy damage to most plants. *–courtesy of National Climatic Data Center*

State	City	Growing Season (days)	Last Spring Frost	First Fall Frost	State	City	Growing Season (days)	Last Spring Frost	First Fall Frost
AK	Juneau	148	May 8	Oct. 4	ND	Bismarck	129	May 14	Sept. 21
AL	Mobile	273	Feb. 28	Nov. 29	NE	Blair	167	Apr. 25	Oct. 10
AR	Pine Bluff	240	Mar. 16	Nov. 12	NE	North Platte	137	May 9	Sept. 24
AZ	Phoenix	*	*	*	NH	Concord	123	May 20	Sept. 21
AZ	Tucson	332	Jan. 19	Dec. 18	NJ	Newark	217	Apr. 3	Nov. 7
CA	Eureka	322	Jan. 27	Dec. 16	NM	Carlsbad	215	Mar. 31	Nov. 2
CA	Sacramento	296	Feb. 10	Dec. 4	NM	Los Alamos	149	May 11	Oct. 8
CA	San Francisco	*	*	*	NV	Las Vegas	283	Feb. 16	Nov. 27
CO	Denver	156	Apr. 30	Oct. 4	NY	Albany	153	May 2	Oct. 3
CT	Hartford	165	Apr. 26	Oct. 9	NY	Syracuse	167	Apr. 28	Oct. 13
DE	Wilmington	202	Apr. 10	Oct. 30	OH	Akron	192	Apr. 18	Oct. 28
FL	Miami	*	*	*	OH	Cincinnati	192	Apr. 13	Oct. 23
FL	Tallahassee	239	Mar. 22	Nov. 17	OK	Lawton	222	Mar. 29	Nov. 7
GA	Athens	227	Mar. 24	Nov. 7	OK	Tulsa	224	Mar. 27	Nov. 7
GA	Savannah	268	Mar. 1	Nov. 25	OR	Pendleton	187	Apr. 13	Oct. 18
IA	Atlantic	148	May 2	Sept. 28	OR	Portland	236	Mar. 23	Nov. 15
IA	Cedar Rapids	163	Apr. 25	Oct. 6	PA	Franklin	163	May 6	Oct. 17
ID	Boise	148	May 10	Oct. 6	PA	Williamsport	167	Apr. 30	Oct. 15
IL	Chicago	186	Apr. 20	Oct. 24	RI	Kingston	147	May 8	Oct. 3
IL	Springfield	182	Apr. 13	Oct. 13	SC	Charleston	260	Mar. 9	Nov. 25
IN	Indianapolis	181	Apr. 17	Oct. 16	SC	Columbia	213	Apr. 1	Nov. 1
IN	South Bend	175	Apr. 26	Oct. 19	SD	Rapid City	140	May 9	Sept. 27
KS	Topeka	174	Apr. 19	Oct. 11	TN	Memphis	235	Mar. 22	Nov. 13
KY	Lexington	192	Apr. 15	Oct. 25	TN	Nashville	204	Apr. 6	Oct. 28
LA	Monroe	256	Mar. 3	Nov. 15	TX	Amarillo	184	Apr. 18	Oct. 20
LA	New Orleans	301	Feb. 12	Dec. 11	TX	Denton	242	Mar. 18	Nov. 16
MA	Worcester	170	Apr. 26	Oct. 14	TX	San Antonio	269	Feb. 28	Nov. 25
MD	Baltimore	200	Apr. 11	Oct. 29	UT	Cedar City	132	May 21	Oct. 1
ME	Portland	156	May 2	Oct. 6	UT	Spanish Fork	167	May 1	Oct. 16
MI	Lansing	145	May 10	Oct. 3	VA	Norfolk	247	Mar. 20	Nov. 23
MI	Marquette	154	May 11	Oct. 13	VA	Richmond	206	Apr. 6	Oct. 30
MN	Duluth	124	May 21	Sept. 23	VT	Burlington	147	May 8	Oct. 3
MN	Willmar	153	Apr. 30	Oct. 1	WA	Seattle	251	Mar. 10	Nov. 17
MO	Jefferson City	187	Apr. 13	Oct. 18	WA	Spokane	153	May 2	Oct. 3
MS	Columbia	247	Mar. 13	Nov. 16	WI	Green Bay	150	May 6	Oct. 4
MS	Vicksburg	240	Mar. 20	Nov. 16	WI	Sparta	133	May 13	Sept. 24
MT	Fort Peck	140	May 8	Sept. 26	WV	Parkersburg	183	Apr. 21	Oct. 22
MT	Helena	121	May 19	Sept. 18	WY	Casper	119	May 22	Sept. 19
NC	Fayetteville	221	Mar. 28	Nov. 5					

Frosts do not occur every year.

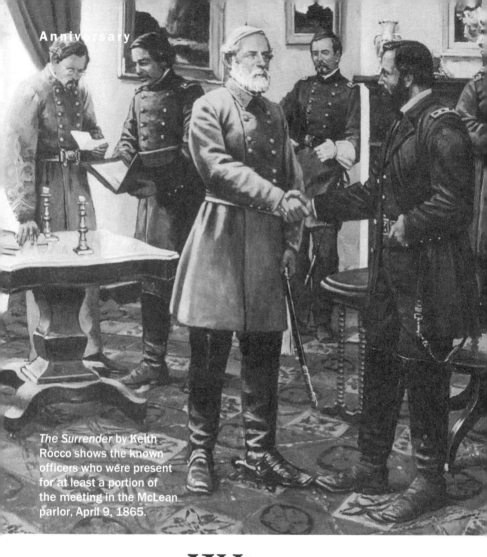

The Surrender by Keith Rocco shows the known officers who were present for at least a portion of the meeting in the McLean parlor, April 9, 1865.

✒ Witnesses to

What became of the men present at the

✦→ BY TIM CLARK ✦→

When Robert E. Lee surrendered his army to Ulysses S. Grant in Appomattox Court House, Virginia, on April 9, 1865, effectively ending the Civil War, only 16 men witnessed the event in Wilmer

McLean's parlor. Although some faded into obscurity over the next six decades, these 10 continued to make history.

Lieutenant General Grant became the 18th president of the United States.

Painting: Appomattox Court House National Historical Park

the Surrender

conclusion of the Civil War 150 years ago?

Some historians regard him as a failure in that office, but in his own time, he was enormously popular. First elected in 1868, he was returned to office by a landslide in 1872.

Grant wrote his memoirs, which were published by Mark Twain, while in a race with throat cancer. In spite of his illness, he wrote 275,000 words in less than a year and completed the book shortly before his death in 1885. It was a best-seller and remains one of the greatest military memoirs ever put to paper. Both Union and Confederate veterans marched in his funeral procession.

General in Chief Lee, who might have been tried for treason had it not been for the personal intervention of Grant, became president of Virginia's Washington College (now Washington and Lee University). To avoid any suggestion that he might return to the fight, he refused to even march in step with his college's cadets. He died in 1870, revered by millions.

pocket when he was killed in a railroad accident 11 months after Appomattox.

Brig. Gen. Orville E. Babcock became President Grant's private secretary. In this position, he wielded enormous influence and power and faced many temptations.

In 1875, he was indicted by a St. Louis grand jury in a scandal known as the Whiskey Ring. With the help of a deposition filed in his defense by President Grant—a type of White House intervention not occurring before or since—he was acquitted in the following year.

Ulysses S. Grant

Robert E. Lee

Theodore S. Bowers

One of the first surrender witnesses to die was former Illinois newspaperman **Lt. Col. Theodore S. Bowers,** known to his friends as "Joe." He came into the army as a private, was assigned to headquarters as a clerk, won Grant's liking, and was commissioned a staff officer.

Early in the war, Bowers grew angry about traders who were buying cotton from secessionist farmers. In Grant's presence, he once burst out, "Well, I think I'll resign and go into cotton. At least I would if I had the money." Grant tossed him a silver half-dollar and said, "Here, Joe, take this for a stake." Bowers had those words engraved on the coin, which he kept as a good luck charm. It was in his

After being indicted, tried, and acquitted in a second corruption case, Babcock was able to escape Washington politics thanks to an appointment by Grant as chief engineer of two lighthouse districts. He drowned when his small boat overturned in the Mosquito Inlet, Florida, in 1884.

Maj. Gen. Philip H. Sheridan commanded the Union cavalry at the end of the war. Grant said, "I believe General Sheridan has no superior as a general, either living or dead, and perhaps not an equal." He backed up his high opinion of Sheridan by relying on him for the toughest assignments during and after the war.

After Lee's surrender, Grant immediately sent Sheridan to the Southwest to restore Texas and Louisiana to Union control and help the Mexican leader Benito Juárez get rid of a French occupying army.

Sheridan's next assignment was to pacify the Plains Indians, which he achieved using the same scorched-earth tactics that he had employed against the Confederates. Although he was reputed to have said "the only good Indian is a dead Indian" (he denied it all his life), in 1878 he spoke up for his former foes: "We took away their country and their

a train platform, only to be pulled to safety by the famous actor Edwin Booth. Badeau, who knew both Edwin and his younger brother, John Wilkes Booth, from his days writing theater reviews in New York, wrote to Edwin to thank him for saving the president's son.

Badeau aided Grant in the preparation of the president's memoirs, but there was a dispute about payment and credit. Badeau subsequently settled with Grant's heirs for $10,000. He died in 1895, having written several books about his Civil War experiences.

Orville E. Babcock

Philip H. Sheridan

Adam Badeau

means of support, broke up their mode of living, their habits of life, introduced disease and decay among them, and it was for this and against this they made war. Could anyone expect less?"

Even in peacetime, Sheridan moved swiftly and decisively. He mobilized troops to fight the Great Chicago Fire of 1871, and, in the 1880s, he was instrumental in preserving the Yellowstone wilderness from commercial development. Sheridan died in 1888.

Lt. Col. Adam Badeau served as one of Grant's aides. Capt. Robert Todd Lincoln, who was also on Grant's staff, told Badeau how he had once fallen off

Lt. Col. Ely S. Parker, a full-blooded chief of the Seneca nation, wrote out the final copy of the terms of Lee's surrender. When he was introduced to Parker, Lee said, "I am glad to see one real American here." Parker later stated, "I shook his hand and said, 'We are all Americans.'"

In 1869, President Grant appointed Parker as the first Native American Commissioner of the Bureau of Indian Affairs. Parker did his best to promote Grant's policy of peaceful relations with the western tribes but was undercut by white bureaucrats and criticized by his own people for marrying a white woman. He left the government, made a fortune on Wall Street, lost it, and ended his days as a clerk in the New York City Police Department. He died in 1895. In 1897, his body was reinterred in Buffalo, New York, next to the famous Seneca chief Red Jacket, one of his ancestors.

As assistant provost marshal, **Brig. Gen. George H. Sharpe** paroled 28,000 Confederate Army soldiers—including General Lee—after the surrender. In 1867, he went to Europe looking for Americans who might have been involved in the assassination of President Lincoln. He managed to bring back John Surratt, son of one of the convicted conspirators, whose eventual trial ended in a hung jury. Sharpe lived until 1900.

Lt. Col. Horace Porter, who had been awarded the Congressional Medal of Honor for his conduct at the Battle of Chickamauga, was U.S. ambassador to France from 1897 to 1905. He spent 6 years of his tenure and a great deal of his own money searching Paris for the long-lost grave of Revolutionary War hero John Paul Jones. Porter found the leaden coffin in a long-abandoned Protestant cemetery and hired experts to identify the body.

Ely S. Parker
⋗⇒ ● ⇐⋖

George H. Sharpe
⋗⇒ ● ⇐⋖

Horace Porter
⋗⇒ ● ⇐⋖

Robert T. Lincoln
⋗⇒ ● ⇐⋖

Satisfied that it was Jones, Porter notified President Theodore Roosevelt, who sent four Navy warships to accompany the body home, where it was reinterred at the Naval Academy in Annapolis, Maryland. Porter received the unanimous thanks of both houses of Congress. He died in 1921.

Capt. Robert T. Lincoln, the youngest and lowest-ranking officer present at the surrender, was the president's oldest son. A strange series of coincidences put Lincoln at or near the sites of three Presidential assassinations. He had turned down an invitation to accompany his parents to Ford's Theatre. Sixteen years later, he witnessed the shooting of President James Garfield at a train station in Washington, D.C. And he was in Buffalo, New York, at President McKinley's invitation, when that president was assassinated in 1901.

Later, he refused another presidential invitation, saying, "There is a certain fatality about presidential functions when I am present."

Lincoln died in 1926, the last surviving witness to Lee's surrender. ∎

Tim Clark has been a Civil War buff since he was 10 years old.

Table of Measures

APOTHECARIES'
1 scruple = 20 grains
1 dram = 3 scruples
1 ounce = 8 drams
1 pound = 12 ounces

AVOIRDUPOIS
1 ounce = 16 drams
1 pound = 16 ounces
1 hundredweight = 100 pounds
1 ton = 2,000 pounds
1 long ton = 2,240 pounds

LIQUID
4 gills = 1 pint
63 gallons = 1 hogshead
2 hogsheads = 1 pipe or butt
2 pipes = 1 tun

DRY
2 pints = 1 quart
4 quarts = 1 gallon
2 gallons = 1 peck
4 pecks = 1 bushel

LINEAR
1 hand = 4 inches
1 link = 7.92 inches

1 span = 9 inches
1 foot = 12 inches
1 yard = 3 feet
1 rod = 5½ yards
1 mile = 320 rods = 1,760 yards = 5,280 feet
1 international nautical mile = 6,076.1155 feet
1 knot = 1 nautical mile per hour
1 fathom = 2 yards = 6 feet
1 furlong = ⅛ mile = 660 feet = 220 yards
1 league = 3 miles = 24 furlongs
1 chain = 100 links = 22 yards

SQUARE
1 square foot = 144 square inches
1 square yard = 9 square feet
1 square rod = 30¼ square yards = 272¼ square feet
1 acre = 160 square rods = 43,560 square feet
1 square mile = 640 acres = 102,400 square rods
1 square rod = 625 square links

1 square chain = 16 square rods
1 acre = 10 square chains

CUBIC
1 cubic foot = 1,728 cubic inches
1 cubic yard = 27 cubic feet
1 cord = 128 cubic feet
1 U.S. liquid gallon = 4 quarts = 231 cubic inches
1 imperial gallon = 1.20 U.S. gallons = 0.16 cubic foot
1 board foot = 144 cubic inches

KITCHEN
3 teaspoons = 1 tablespoon
16 tablespoons = 1 cup
1 cup = 8 ounces
2 cups = 1 pint
2 pints = 1 quart
4 quarts = 1 gallon

TO CONVERT CELSIUS AND FAHRENHEIT :
$°C = (°F − 32)/1.8$
$°F = (°C × 1.8) + 32$

Metric Conversions

LINEAR
1 inch = 2.54 centimeters
1 centimeter = 0.39 inch
1 meter = 39.37 inches
1 yard = 0.914 meter
1 mile = 1.61 kilometers
1 kilometer = 0.62 mile

SQUARE
1 square inch = 6.45 square centimeters
1 square yard = 0.84 square meter

1 square mile = 2.59 square kilometers
1 square kilometer = 0.386 square mile
1 acre = 0.40 hectare
1 hectare = 2.47 acres

CUBIC
1 cubic yard = 0.76 cubic meter
1 cubic meter = 1.31 cubic yards

HOUSEHOLD
½ teaspoon = 2 mL
1 teaspoon = 5 mL
1 tablespoon = 15 mL

¼ cup = 60 mL
⅓ cup = 75 mL
½ cup = 125 mL
⅔ cup = 150 mL
¾ cup = 175 mL
1 cup = 250 mL
1 liter = 1.057 U.S. liquid quarts
1 U.S. liquid quart = 0.946 liter
1 U.S. liquid gallon = 3.78 liters
1 gram = 0.035 ounce
1 ounce = 28.349 grams
1 kilogram = 2.2 pounds
1 pound = 0.45 kilogram

Winners in the 2014
Essay Contest

My Most Unusual Coincidence

First Prize: $250

I was 7 years old and my mom bought a trinket for me to give to the pretty girl next door. It was a heart in two pieces that snapped together. She told me to give the girl half since we were moving.

About 10 years later, I was sitting beside a beautiful woman on a flight. We figured out that we both went to UNC Chapel Hill and were born in the same town, but with no more time to talk, we went our separate ways.

I am now 47, living in Atlanta. I sit down for dinner at a restaurant and a woman sits near me. Finally, she says, "I know why you are staring at me. We were on a flight about 20 years ago, you are from Greenville, we both went to UNC, and I never forgot you."

It did not take long to figure out that we were those kids from 40 years ago, so I pulled my good luck charm from my pocket. With that she started crying, telling me that she still had the other half. We are now married.

–Carl White, Atlanta, Georgia

Second Prize: $150

In 1984, on a turbulent flight into my hometown, I comforted the flyer next to me who was in tears until the wheels touched down. She thanked me, and we shared a laugh.

In 1985, I found myself in dire straits and really needed a job. On my way to an interview, I spotted a woman whose car had broken down. She looked frantic. Hoping that I wouldn't be late, I offered her a ride. It was the woman from the plane! We recognized each other, shared another laugh, and determined that we were headed to the same block.

We parted ways in a garage and I headed for my interview. When my name was called and I was ushered into an office, I saw behind the desk . . . *the lady!* We burst out laughing, and she said, "You're hired!" She's the best boss I've ever had.

–Nancy Pullen, Mt. Juliet, Tennessee

Third Prize: $100

My boyfriend and I were fishing for largemouth. He liked trying out different lures and rubber worms, so he tied on a distinctive silver and black rubber worm. One bass swallowed it, hook and all, so he cut the line and set him free.

A couple of weeks later, we went back with my brother. We usually catch and release, but my brother's friend had asked him to keep a few for him. As he was cleaning the fish for his buddy, my brother cut open one of the bass—and there inside it was that distinctive black and silver worm.

–Amy Jo Wilson, Paris, Ohio

Honorable Mentions

When my son was 18 years old, he and several friends went to our summer home on a lake in Maine.

On the first day, they went waterskiing and, as the boat left the dock, my son felt his class ring fly off his finger. The boys searched for the ring but never found it.

When friends visited 27 years later, one of the children called out that he had found a ring. It was my son's class ring! When it was lost, my husband was 45 years old. When it was found, my son was 45 years old, and it was my husband's birthday. He had passed away several years earlier.

–Janice Daring, Shapleigh, Maine

My grandfather's family was from Three Rivers, Massachusetts. In 1917, my grandfather moved to Cohoes, New York, where I was born and raised. In 2001, I relocated to Enfield, Connecticut. In May 2006, in an antique shop in Somers, Connecticut, I noticed some vintage postcards. I picked up one that had a picture of mountains and a lake, turned it over, and let out a yell: The postcard was addressed to my great aunt in Three Rivers and postmarked May 2, 1906—100 years to the day that I had it in my hand! I purchased the card and keep it on my bulletin board.

–Kim Hebert, Enfield, Connecticut

Announcing the 2015 Essay Contest Topic: My Best Car Story

ESSAY AND RECIPE CONTEST RULES

Cash prizes (first, $250; second, $150; third, $100) will be awarded for the best essay (in 200 words or less) on the subject "My Best Car Story" and the best recipe in the category "Dips & Spreads." (The recipe must be yours, original, and unpublished. Amateur cooks only, please. One recipe per person.) All entries become the property of Yankee Publishing, which reserves all rights to the material. The deadline for entries is Friday, January 30, 2015. Label "Essay Contest" or "Recipe Contest" and mail to The Old Farmer's Almanac, P.O. Box 520, Dublin, NH 03444. You can also enter at Almanac.com/EssayContest or Almanac.com/RecipeContest. Include your name, mailing address, and email address. Winners will appear in *The 2016 Old Farmer's Almanac* and on our Web site, Almanac.com.

3

UNPARALLELED PIONEERS

BY KEVIN CHONG

75 YEARS AGO:
In Memoriam, a Memorable Song

Pianist Ruth Lowe spent the summer of 1939 hiding in her mother's Toronto apartment, heartbroken.

Ruth was a grocer's daughter with dreams of adventure and stardom as a musician and composer—until her father died. Then, she put off those aspirations to help to support her family. She took a job at the Song Shop on Yonge Street playing piano sheet music for customers. While there, she learned that Ina Ray Hutton's All-Girl Band needed a piano player. Following an audition, the band took her on and she toured with them for 4 years. On the road, she fell in love with a music publicist named Harold Cohen, and they married in 1938. Less than a year later, he suddenly died after a kidney ailment.

This was how the 24-year-old widow came to be in her mother's third-floor apartment. One night, she was inspired to compose a ballad for Harold. A melancholy tune poured out of her and onto the keyboard. Within 10 minutes, she had written the lyrics and melody of "I'll Never Smile Again." Soon it was played and recorded on CBC Radio.

Ruth slipped an acetate of the CBC performance to a saxophonist friend who was playing with bandleader Tommy Dorsey, who happened to be in Toronto for the Canadian National Exhibition. In 1940, Dorsey, with his vocalist, Frank

224

RUTH LOWE WITH
TOMMY DORSEY

Sinatra, recorded an arrangement of Ruth's work. It was Sinatra's first recording. "Everybody suddenly was very quiet," Sinatra later recalled. "There was a feeling of a kind of eeriness . . . , as though we all knew that this would be a big, big hit, and that it was a lovely song."

"I'll Never Smile Again" was indeed a hit: It launched Frank Sinatra's recording career, was number one for 12 weeks, won a Grammy, and became a World War II anthem.

Ruth eventually relocated to New York City, where her early career dreams came to life. For Sinatra, she also wrote "Put Your Dreams Away (for Another Day)," which became his signature concert tune until he replaced it with Paul Anka's "My Way." Ruth's "Too Beautiful to Last" appeared in *Ziegfeld Girl,* a 1941 film.

> "There was a feeling of a kind of eeriness . . . , as though we all knew that this would be a big, big hit."

In the 1950s, a movie producer offered to make a film of Ruth's life, starring Judy Garland. Ruth declined. By then, she had remarried and was raising two sons in Toronto. She continued to compose and encourage musicians (she opened one of Toronto's first night clubs, Club One Two) until her death in 1981.

"I'll Never Smile Again" has been recorded over 100 times, by artists such as Fats Waller, Billie Holiday, and Barry Manilow. Ruth was inducted into the American Music Hall of Fame in 1982 and the Canadian Songwriters Hall of Fame in 2003.

95 YEARS AGO:
A Career Bloomed and Flowered

Shortly after World War II, an admiral in the Japanese Navy who loved lilies arrived in the United States as part of a friendship exchange. When asked what he would like to see, the Admiral said, "I would really like to travel to Canada to meet Miss Isabella Preston."

Born in 1881 in Lancaster, England, with, she later remarked, "green fingers," Isabella Preston emigrated to Canada with her sister, in 1912, and soon after enrolled in horticulture classes at the Ontario Agricultural College (OAC) in Guelph. Before long, she quit to work in plant breeding with professor J. W. Crow.

She had found her calling.

In 1916, Isabella caught the attention of hybridists across North America with the 'George C. Creelman' lily. Named after the OAC's president, this lily cross was late-blooming, strong-growing, fragrant, and 5 feet tall at maturity. It helped to make lilies accessible for home gardeners and today is used as a parent in contemporary hybrids.

In 1920, Isabella relocated to Ottawa to join the government's Central Experimental Farm as a day laborer. Researchers there were attempting to breed ornamental flowers that could withstand the extreme cold of Prairie winters.

Isabella did not stay in her position long. That same year, William T. Macoun, head of the Horticultural Division, hired her as a "specialist in ornamental horticulture." (Her director later made it known that the department had "failed to locate promising men" for the job and therefore hired Isabella.)

Isabella worked at the Farm for more than 20 years. During this time, she produced numerous hybrids, including lilacs, roses, and columbines. She created 23 hybrids of Siberian irises, which she named after Canadian rivers; two, 'Ottawa' and 'Gatineau', won Awards of Merit from the Royal Horticultural Society. Between 1928 and 1940, she originated 33 hybrids that she named after Canadian lakes; of these, 'Athabasca' and 'Simcoe' won awards. She named a series of lilacs after Shakespearean heroines (e.g., 'Adriana', 'Portia') and World War II fighter aircraft (e.g., 'Hurricane', 'Mosquito'). In all, she originated 200 hybrids in her lifetime. In 1929, she authored *Garden Lilies,* the first book about lily cultivation in Canada. All of this earned her a reputation as the "dean of hybridists" and the "Grand Lady of Canadian Horticulture," as well as attention from the press and fans, yet she never shed her shyness. At a Philadelphia Flower Show, she advised her niece: "Don't say a word to anyone who I am or they'll flock around me."

Isabella retired in 1946. Slightly stooped from bending to look at lilies, she continued experimenting with lily and iris hybrids until her death in Georgetown, Ontario, in 1965.

Today, her legacy lives on in the Isabella Preston Trophy, established by the North American Lily Society for best stalks in its shows, and the 'Preston Lilacs', a collection of winter-hardy, late-blooming lilacs that are still available at most nurseries.

Remarkably, Isabella's achievements came despite almost no formal education in horticulture. She taught herself, adding to her on-the-job experience by "reading all the books in the library."

(continued)

ISABELLA PRESTON

"Don't say a word to anyone who I am or they'll flock around me."

Photo: Center for Canadian Historical Horticulture Studies, Royal Botanical Gardens

100 YEARS AGO:
Love Forged a Life on the Frontier

"I love to meet a cougar if I have a gun," Ada Annie Rae-Arthur was fond of saying. Born in 1888, the tomboy daughter of a Sacramento, California, veterinarian, Annie moved herself, her three young children, and her husband Willie from Vancouver to an isolated piece of forested land, accessible only by boat, in Clayoquot Sound in 1915. She did it to save Willie from opium addiction.

Faced with cold winters and a charming but unhelpful spouse, Annie was de-

COUGAR ANNIE

"Widower preferred. Object matrimony."

termined to survive. She cleared 5 acres, built a business selling flower bulbs by mail order across western Canada, and ran a post office and general store on her property, where she also kept chickens and goats. Before Willie died in 1936, she gave birth to eight more children.

In need of help on the homestead, she placed a personal ad in the *Western Producer,* a Prairie newspaper: "BC Widow

with Nursery and orchard wishes partner. Widower preferred. Object matrimony."

The ad, or a version of it, led Annie to three husbands. Some believe that the self-inflicted accidental gunshot that killed the first of these was fired by her. Despite this, and perhaps due in part to her blue eyes and fondness for hats, Annie had many male admirers. Some would buy postage stamps from her to keep her and her post office afloat. (Although frugal, Annie was always cash-strapped; she even sold eggs that had gone bad rather than throw them away.)

Annie was renowned for her marksmanship. To protect her livestock, she killed cougars, luring them to an iron trap with a goat as bait. She would wait for a cougar to become ensnared, then shoot it with her 20-gauge shotgun. By 1957, Annie claimed to have killed 62 cougars and "about 80" black bears. Long before this, she had earned the nickname "Cougar Annie."

Annie outlived all of her husbands and died in 1985, at age 97. Her legacy lives on through her garden. The beautiful, wild property and heritage English garden are stewarded by two federally registered charities, the Boat Basin Foundation and Ecotrust Canada. Six cabins and a retreat center are opened occasionally to private groups by prearrangement. ■

Kevin Chong is the author of five books, most recently *Northern Dancer* (Viking Canada, 2014). His writing has appeared in the *Globe and Mail, The Walrus, Maclean's,* and *Vancouver Magazine.* He teaches creative writing at the University of British Columbia.

Photo: image C-04904 by John Manning, Royal BC Museum, BC Archives

Hydrogen Peroxide for Aches, Pains and Clogged Arteries?

the Greatest Deals in history!

By Alice Cary

Historic **Proportions**

On September 21, 1915, an Englishman named Cecil Chubb (1876–1934) happened upon an auction in Salisbury, England. On a whim and, some say, as a gift for his wife, he bid 6,600 pounds on Lot 15, 30 acres of land and a prehistoric monument that had been in private hands since the Middle Ages. Chubb's bid won.

Eventually, Chubb decided that the property should remain in local hands, so 3 years later he turned it over to the English government, on condition that the entrance fee never be more than a shilling. An arrangement with the Parish Council ensured that an adjacent road would be moved and area residents would be granted free access to the site—Stonehenge.

A Meager **Harvest**

Ephraim Wales Bull (1806–95) worked in Boston, Massachusetts, as a gold beater, producing gold leaf. The constant

Stonehenge

dust of his trade irritated his lungs, and his passion was growing grapes. So, in 1836, he moved to nearby Concord, to pursue this love.

By chance, one of Bull's grape strains cross-pollinated with a wild grape growing on his hillside. The result was a robust variety, and he spent 6 years cultivating the seedlings. In 1853, he presented his new "Concord grape" to the Massachusetts Horticultural Society, which

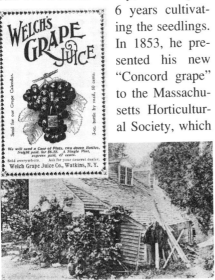

The Bull house, home of the Concord grape

proclaimed it bigger and better than any grown before. The next year, Bull began to sell Concord grape seedlings and cuttings for $5 each, earning $3,200.

Nurseries that had purchased Bull's plants cultivated and freely sold the seedlings. People loved the fruit. In 1869, Thomas Bramwell Welch, a communion steward at a Methodist church in Vineland, New Jersey, with his son Charles, began experimenting on grape juice–making processes so that they could use the juice, instead of wine, at church services. By some 28 years later, Charles had perfected pasteurization of Concord grape juice, built a factory, and changed the name of the beverage to Welch's Grape Juice.

Forgotten through it all was Ephraim Bull. When Bull was selling his original seedlings, plants had no patent protection. In 1891, he fell from a ladder while pruning a grapevine. Four years later, he died a poor, embittered man. His tombstone reads: "He Sowed; Others Reaped."

A Net **Profit**

In 1974, brothers Daniel and Ozzie Silna were owners of a successful New Jersey knitting company. Daniel's passion was basketball, yet he knew that the only position he could ever hold on a team would be "owner." So, with Ozzie, he bought the Carolina Cougars, an American Basketball Association (ABA) team, for $1 million. Hoping to profit in the largest U.S. television market without a professional basketball team, the brothers moved the

Maurice Lucas of the Spirits of St. Louis chats with coach Bob MacKinnon.

231

team to St. Louis and changed the name to the Spirits of St. Louis.

Two years later, the National Basketball Association (NBA) merged with some teams in the fledgling ABA, but the Spirits were left out of the deal. The brothers turned down $3 million in compensation, choosing instead an ongoing share of the television revenue from all of the ABA teams included in the merger. As a business deal, this was a slam dunk. In the years since, the Silnas (and their lawyer) have earned an estimated $300 million in TV profits, causing some to call theirs the "greatest sports deal of all time."

The deal got even sweeter in January 2014, when the NBA agreed to pay the Silnas $500 million to end the arrangement for good. The brothers have collected $800 million from their initial $1 million investment.

Tag Sale
Triumph

In Summer 2007, a family in New York bought a small white bowl for $3 at a yard sale. They liked it well enough to display it in their living room for several years and eventually decided to have it appraised. The resulting report brought shocking news: The bowl was a rare, 1,000-year-old specimen of Chinese Northern Song Dynasty pottery, estimated to be worth between $200,000 and $300,000.

At an auction in 2013, a London dealer purchased the bowl for $2.2 million.

A Truly
Bad Call

In 1876, William Orton, president of the Western Union Telegraph Company, declined an offer from Gardiner Hubbard to buy, for $100,000, the patent for an invention by Hubbard's son-in-law. Orton called the contraption an "interesting novelty [with] no commercial possibilities."

Hubbard's son-in-law was Alexander Graham Bell, and the patent was for telephone.

Orton soon realized his error and hired Thomas Edison and Elisha Gray

to create a rival phone system. Before long, they had one up and running, prompting the Bell Company to sue for patent infringement. Ultimately, the fight was abandoned by Western Union. In

Alexander Graham Bell

1879, it agreed to get out of the telephone business. The price of Bell Telephone stock immediately shot through the roof.

A Fine
Catch

One Sunday in 1799, 12-year-old Conrad Reed went fishing in Meadow Creek in Mecklenburg County, North Carolina, instead of going to church. In the

Nothing astonishes men so much as common sense and plain dealing.

-Ralph Waldo Emerson, American writer (1803-82)

1850 map of North Carolina showing the gold region discovered by Conrad Reed

creek, he spotted a yellow rock, which he promptly lugged home.

Conrad's father, John, used the 17-pound stone as a doorstop. Eventually, the elder Reed asked a local silversmith to identify the mass, but the man could not. In 1802, another jeweler informed Reed that the rock was gold and that he would like to buy it. They agreed on what Reed felt was a "big" price: $3.50.

In fact, it was worth about $3,600.

Reed soon smartened up, and, legend has it, returned to the jeweler and got about $1,000 more. Then he and his family returned to Meadow Creek, where John partnered with a wealthy landowner, a minister, and his brother-in-law. Before long, one of the landowner's slaves found a 28-pound specimen worth more than $6,600.

Conrad Reed's Sunday diversion, the first documented gold strike in the United States, made his family wealthy over the years. North Carolina led the nation in gold production until the California gold rush began in 1848. The Reed Gold Mine remains open for tours.

C'est la Vie

In 1965, French lawyer André-François Raffray agreed to purchase an apartment in Arles, France, from a 90-year-old woman. Under the arrangement, he would pay her 2,500 francs (about $500) a month until she died. Upon her death, the apartment would become his. (Such arrangements are common in France.)

Thirty years later, Raffray died at age 77, having paid about $184,000 for an apartment that he had never used. His widow continued to pay the apartment's owner, Jeanne Calment, until August 4, 1997, when Calment died at age 122, setting a world record for longevity. ∎

Jeanne Calment

Alice Cary, a longtime contributor, grew up watching *Let's Make a Deal.*

Why We Need WEEDS

**What is a weed?
A plant whose
virtues have not yet
been discovered.**

*–Ralph Waldo Emerson,
American writer (1803–82)*

Tired of weeding your garden? Then don't! Change the way you think about weeds. Some weeds can help you to determine where to plant perennial flowers that don't require rich soil or find the most fertile ground for vegetables. They also encourage beneficial bugs to visit your garden.

BY KRIS WETHERBEE

WEEDS Tell a Lot About Your Soil

Weeds help you to assess current soil conditions.
This is a long-held principle best explained by American botanist Frederic E. Clements (1874–1945), who wrote, "Each plant is an indicator . . . the product of the conditions under which it grows, and is thereby a measure of these conditions."

As you survey your soil, remember that you can learn a lot more from a variety of weeds growing together in one area than from a single species. For example . . .

If you have . . .	Your soil is . . .
mugwort and common mullein	not very fertile
dead nettle, pigweed, lamb's-quarter, or purslane	high in nutrients
quack grass, crabgrass, plantain, or field bindweed	hardpan or compacted
Joe Pye weed, marsh mallow, horsetail, cattail, or rushes	wet or poorly drained
dock, horsetail, bracken fern, nettle, daisies, or Virginia creeper	acidic
lamb's-quarter and wild mustard	alkaline

Above left: Mullein
Above right: Pigweed
Right: Lamb's-quarter

WEEDS Act Like Fertilizer

Many "weeds," such as comfrey, wild mustard, and most clover, have deep roots that penetrate the subsoil, where they harvest valuable nutrients and trace minerals far beyond the reach of other garden plants. As the weeds gradually decompose, the nutrients are recycled back into the soil. For example . . .

If you have . . .	Your soil has . . .
dandelions	iron, potassium, and phosphate
nettle	iron and nitrogen
yarrow	iron and phosphate
comfrey	nitrogen, potassium, and phosphorus (especially beneficial to tomatoes)
legume-type weeds, such as vetch, wild lupine, and clover; also buckwheat, Canadian thistle, comfrey, dandelion, horsetail, wild mustard, nettle, and yarrow	nitrogen; these plants are "nitrogen fixers" (Bacteria living in the plants' roots collect nitrogen from the air and convert it into a plant-friendly fertilizer.)

That's not all: As the annual weeds chickweed, common mallow, lamb's-quarter, mayweed, and purslane die back, their decaying tissues contribute additional organic matter that, in turn, helps to aerate the soil and make it looser.

You can take advantage of this free fertilizer by growing these weeds as part of your rotation. Simply broadcast seeds onto the soil (an average of 1½ cups to a 100-square-foot area should do just fine), work them in with a rake, and then cover with additional soil to a depth three times the diameter of a seed.

Remember, too, that weeds are "nature's meadow"—a blanket of living mulch that helps to conserve water and protect bare ground against heavy rains and wind that can cause soil compaction and erosion. Even shallow-rooted weeds, such as ground ivy, purslane, and oxalis, can help to prevent erosion.

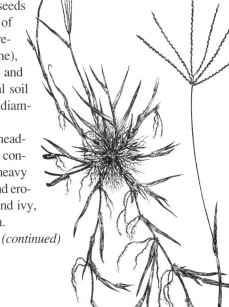

(continued)

Above: Quack grass
Right: Crabgrass

WEEDS Bring Beneficial Bugs

Weed species of *Solanum*, *Amaranthus*, and *Solidago* are the favored housing for a variety of beneficial ground beetles, and their flowers provide excellent sources of pollen and nectar for beneficial insects. Having a food source not only encourages beneficial insects to stay around, but it also makes them healthier and increases their effectiveness: They lay more eggs and so are better able to control the bad bugs.

In general, small flowers attract small bugs and large flowers attract large bugs.

Small-flowered weeds such as . . .	Attract . . .
clover, fennel, goldenrod, lamb's-quarter, mint, Queen Anne's lace, *Solanum*, and wild mustard	tiny parasitic wasps; lacewings; hover flies that feast on caterpillars, aphids, and leafhoppers; and tachinid flies—voracious destroyers of pests such as Japanese beetles, Mexican bean beetles, cutworms, and grasshoppers
Large-flowered weeds such as . . .	**Attract . . .**
amaranth, calendula, cosmos (considered a weed by many because it self-sows), and daisies	large predatory insects, such as ground beetles, that gorge on cucumber beetles, caterpillars, and grasshoppers

So, the next time you're thinking about pulling those weeds, remember that they may actually be of benefit—and can help you to grow your best garden ever!

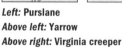

Left: Purslane
Above left: Yarrow
Above right: Virginia creeper

Weeds of Wisdom

In general, weed 2 to 3 weeks before you plant flowers. The new plants will benefit from the mined nutrients left behind.

■

Keep deep-rooted Canadian thistle in check by thinning to a few plants and cutting the flowers before they set seed.

■

Avoid tilling comfrey and other aggressive weeds that spread by underground roots. Tilling just causes them to reproduce more vigorously.

■

To control comfrey and maximize benefits, grow it as a separate patch and use the leaves to make a nutrient-rich garden tea. To make the tea, loosely fill a trash can or large bucket two-thirds full with bruised or torn comfrey leaves, then add water to cover. Stir daily and allow to steep in the sun for several days or until the brew is a rich brown color. Strain the tea and use it as a fertilizing spray on foliage and vegetables.

■

Organic gardener **Kris Wetherbee** hosts an 8,000-square-foot garden, an orchard, and a very drought-resistant Mediterranean courtyard garden in Oregon.

THE MOST UNWELCOME WEEDS

To learn how to get rid of bindweed and poison ivy safely, go to **Almanac.com/Gardening.**

Above left: Queen Anne's lace
Above center: Goldenrod
Above right: Dock
Right: Bindweed

"Being Diabetic, I never had pain-free feet - UNTIL NOW!"

Pain Doctor Discovers Blood Flow-Busting Material Into 'Miracle Socks' for Diabetics and Foot Pain Sufferers!

Breakthrough circulation-boosting fibers improve blood flow, relieve swelling, boost oxygen flow, and eliminate foot fatigue - naturally in as little as 5 minutes!

If you suffer from poor circulation, injury, swelling or any condition that leaves your feet fatigued and sore, then read on to discover the breakthrough that can change your life.

Good news comes in the form of a 'pain-busting microfiber' that is used to weave a circulation-boosting sock, called Bambusa™.

Better Blood Flow

The 'miracle sock' is made from a new, patented anion-technology that is weaved into every strand of thread used to make a Bambusa™ sock. This special micro-fiber thread is made from revolutionary bamboo charcoal to stimulate blood flow and revitalize feet. When this material comes in contact with body-heat it is proven to release circulation-boosting ions.

The 3D-weave technology used in the material has been compared to infrared light therapy to help revitalize stiff and sore muscles. The manufacturer, who also makes a back and wrist sleeve, says the material provides almost instant relief to any part of the body it touches, making it ideal for diabetics, athletes, inflammation, stiffness and swelling.

Doctor Recommended

Pain specialist of 30 years, Dr. Ronald Jahner comments on the 3D-weave technology, "Infrared therapy has been used for years at medical clinics to treat vascular

3 Degrees Warmer in 5 Minutes!

Without Bambusa™ socks — Max Temp with no Bambusa™ 22.3°C

After wearing Bambusa™ socks — Max Temp with Bambusa™ 25.6°C

and circulatory conditions. Physical therapists use infrared therapy to speed up recovery. Better blood flow equals less pain. This microfiber works much the same way."

Relief for Tired, Swollen Feet

Bambusa™ socks are not a medical device or compression sock because they don't restrict blood flow. Utilizing the special negative-anion technology, they comfortably increase blood flow and oxygen to tissues.

They are ideal for diabetics and those suffering from neuropathy, or injury from repetitive use. Bambusa™ socks can also bring comfort to tired legs within minutes of putting them on, energizing individuals who spend long hours on their feet.

BENEFITS:
• Increased blood flow and oxygen
• Reduced swelling and pain
• Anti-microbial
• Wicks away moisture
• Increased range of motion

Goodbye to Pain and Numbness

"I went out on the golf course for 18 holes, and when I got home my feet weren't swollen, they weren't sweating and my feet didn't hurt!" Lou B., NY.

"While recovering from a broken ankle I wore my Bambusa™ socks, and my doctor was amazed at how quickly the swelling went down!" Cathy K., PA.

Tom from NJ reports, "I suffer from chronic foot cramps. My feet were sore for days after the cramping. My wife gave me the Bambusa™ socks, I wore them, and the foot cramps stopped. I replaced all my socks with Bambusa™. My feet feel great now."

Try Bambusa Risk Free!

Order Bambusa™ at no risk and receive two bonus pairs of socks absolutely free! The technology used in Bambusa™ socks is independently tested to boost circulation, blood flow, and oxygen. These circulation-boosting socks allow you to wrap yourself in relief.

Bambusa™ is backed by a satisfaction guarantee so you can experience the short and long term results risk free.

Receive 2 Free Pairs of Socks!
1-800-398-7136

This product has not been approved by the Food and Drug Administration. It is not intended to cure, treat or prevent any disease or illness. Individual results will vary. Dr. Ronald Jahner is compensated for his opinions.

*A wise man should consider that health is the
greatest of human blessings and learn how by his own thought
to derive benefit from his illnesses.*

–Hippocrates, Greek physician (c. 460–c. 377 B.C.)

SIGNS OF GOOD HEALTH

BY CELESTE LONGACRE

N O MATTER OUR AGE, occupation, or avocation, we all want to feel good, to be healthy. The ancients understood that every person, based on his sign of the zodiac, has a weakness, a potential vulnerability that needs to be considered when looking at his health profile. Even Hippocrates, the "Father of Medicine," insisted that all of his students learn astrology. Of course, this meant that they looked at the person's entire astrological chart, not just the Sun sign. Nonetheless, the Sun sign is a good place to start.

The Sun travels through the entire zodiac in one year. It spends about a month in each sign. These "months" do not align exactly with calendar months, so the calendar dates for each sign are given at the beginning of each profile here.

The part can never be well unless the whole is well.
–Plato, Greek philosopher (c. 428–c. 348 B.C.)

MARCH 21–APRIL 20

Aries is ruled by the head. Have you ever noticed how these individuals tuck their chins and move forward like their totem, the ram? Once they decide on a course of action, get out of their way. They are always in a hurry, moving in a straight line much like a runaway train, and when they bump into people or things, the head often takes the brunt of it. Therefore, headaches are common. Arians can benefit greatly by slowing down and taking a few deep breaths on a regular basis.

APRIL 21–MAY 20

Taurus is ruled by the throat. Many individuals born under this sign have beautiful voices. Scarves and necklaces often adorn their neck. They are the earthiest of the earth signs: Should germs appear around these individuals, they are likely to attack the throat first. Gargling with warm salt water at the first hint of a problem can do much to keep the nasties at bay. Taureans are fond of comfort; keeping the house warm in the winter and cool in the summer is also helpful.

MAY 21–JUNE 20

Gemini is ruled by the lungs. These individuals love to talk, and witty repartee flows from their mouth like lava slides down a volcano. Great gulps of air are sometimes necessary to keep the stream going, resulting in infectious agents often getting sucked right into their lungs. Maintaining a somewhat slower pace is useful, as well as donning a mask when working amid dust. Taking the time to vacuum the mattress and pillows between bedsheet changes and keeping the nightstand dust-free can make a difference.

JUNE 21–JULY 22

Cancer is ruled by the stomach. Most Cancerians love to cook and eat, and their families are extremely important to them. However, not just food fills them up; they often stuff their feelings inside. This aversion to direct communication can cause misunderstandings—and stomach discomfort. Emotions are not bad; they are real and need to be expressed. Get a beautiful blank book and spend time writing down your thoughts and feelings.

(continued)

Natural forces within us are the true healers of disease.
−Hippocrates, Greek physician (c. 460−c. 377 B.C.)

JULY 23–AUGUST 22

Leo is ruled by the heart. Fun-loving, generous, and cheerful, Leos play to an audience and thrive on response. They are loyal and devoted friends and ask only for a bit of attention in return. Leos put their heart into relationships and activities, often forgetting that the heart is one of the biggest muscles in the body. Getting adequate exercise—in fact, keeping all of the muscles in tone—is important.

AUGUST 23–SEPTEMBER 22

Virgo is ruled by the intestines. This sign enjoys analytical processes: Details matter, and Virgos strive for perfection. (Perhaps this is why more billionaires are Virgos than they are any other sign.) Aiding digestion through the consumption of proper nutrients is important. Virgos would do well to eat fresh vegetables and properly raised and fed meats, instead of food that has been treated with pesticides and/or herbicides or been overly processed or packaged for a long shelf life.

SEPTEMBER 23–OCTOBER 22

Libra is ruled by the kidneys. These individuals are relationship-oriented; a strong social life is important. Tactful and diplomatic, Libras weigh and balance pertinent information before coming to conclusions or making decisions. They are usually physically attractive (more models are Libras than they are any other sign) and enjoy working with items of beauty as well as color and design. High consumption of pure water on a constant basis is important to flush the kidneys and avoid problems.

OCTOBER 23–NOVEMBER 22

Scorpio is ruled by the reproductive organs. This strongest sign of the Zodiac is intelligent, passionate, willful, worldly, and ready for anything: Scorpios have a plan, a backup plan, and a contingency plan. Because it is important for these individuals to maintain a vital core, concern should be given to eating nutritionally dense foods. Sweet potatoes, beets, Swiss chard, and kale, as well as pastured meats, should be consumed regularly.

NOVEMBER 23–DECEMBER 21

Sagittarius is ruled by the legs. Dedicated to finding Truth (with a capital T), these individuals need a philosophy to follow as they meander through life; their main goal is to discover the Meaning of Life. Freedom is important: They love to visit exotic places, yet are attracted to both the city and the country. The practice of yoga can be invaluable, especially postures in which the feet are raised.

DECEMBER 22–JANUARY 19

Capricorn is ruled by the bones. These individuals understand at an early age the framework of society and its levels; they do not want to be at the bottom. Most are serious students focused on career and achievement. They resemble their totem, the goat, which places one sure, steady foot in front of the other until they reach the mountain's summit. Because this sign rules the skeleton, nutritious beef-, chicken-, turkey-, or lamb-bone broth soups should be eaten regularly.

JANUARY 20–FEBRUARY 19

Aquarius is ruled by the ankles. These individuals are intuitive humanitarians, tolerant of everything but intolerance, incapable of taking advantage of others. Freedom is important; they will not stay at a job where they can not do things their way. They have the capacity to see things from new perspectives—the "different drummer" point of view. Aquarius can benefit from rolling the ankles (making circles with the toes) several times a day, especially before rising.

FEBRUARY 20–MARCH 20

Pisces is ruled by the feet. Many Pisceans wear colorful and intricate socks. This sign does not possess its own energy. Rather, it is a combination of all of the signs. Sensitive and compassionate, Pisceans have a built-in radar about people and can be counted on to listen to their friends' troubles and offer soothing advice. Therefore, relaxation is important; regularly scheduled "alone time" is a must.

AS WE ARE ALL COMBINATIONS of many of the signs, practicing several (or all) of these suggestions can be helpful. Exercise, nutrient-dense foods, expression of emotions, and rest are all ingredients essential to a healthy lifestyle. ■

Celeste Longacre, the Almanac's astrologer, is an Arian. She forges ahead with her chin down—and occasionally bumps into things.

Best Days for 2015

This chart is based on the Moon's sign and shows the best days each month for certain activities.

—Celeste Longacre

	JAN.	FEB.	MAR.	APR.	MAY	JUNE	JULY	AUG.	SEPT.	OCT.	NOV.	DEC.
Quit smoking	10, 15	6, 11	10, 19	6, 15	13, 17	9, 13	6, 10	2, 6	3, 7, 30	5, 9	6, 10	3, 8
Begin diet to lose weight	10, 15	6, 11	10, 19	6, 15	13, 17	9, 13	6, 10	2, 6	3, 7, 30	5, 9	6, 10	3, 8
Begin diet to gain weight	23, 27	19, 23	22, 23	1, 19	26, 31	23, 27	19, 25	16, 21	17, 26	14, 23	20, 24	17, 21
Cut hair to encourage growth	23, 27	2, 23, 24	22, 23	3, 19, 20	1, 2, 28, 29	24, 25	21, 22, 23	18, 19	14, 15	23, 24	19, 20, 24	17, 18
Cut hair to discourage growth	11, 12	7, 8, 9	7, 8	15, 16	16, 17	12, 13	10, 11	6, 7	2, 3, 30	11	8, 9	5, 6
Have dental care	9, 10	5, 6	4, 5, 6	1, 2, 28, 29	25, 26	21, 22, 23	19, 20	15, 16, 17	11, 12, 13	9, 10	5, 6	2, 3, 4, 30, 31
Start projects	21, 22	19, 20	21, 22	20, 21	19, 20	17, 18	17, 18	15, 16	14, 15	14, 15	12, 13	12, 13
End projects	18, 19	16, 17	18, 19	17, 18	16, 17	14, 15	14, 15	12, 13	11, 12	11, 12	9, 10	9, 10
Go camping	16, 17	12, 13, 14	12, 13	8, 9	5, 6	2, 3, 30	26, 27, 28	23, 24	19, 20	16, 17, 18	12, 13, 14	10, 11
Plant aboveground crops	4, 22, 23	1, 19, 20	1, 27, 28	23, 24	3, 30, 31	27, 28	24, 25	20, 21, 22	16, 17, 18	14, 15	19, 20	17, 18
Plant belowground crops	14, 15	10, 11	9, 10, 18, 19	6, 7, 15, 16	12, 13	8, 9	14	2, 3	7, 8	4, 5	1, 28, 29	7, 8, 9, 26
Destroy pests and weeds	24, 25	21, 22	20, 21	17, 18	14, 15	10, 11	7, 8, 9	4, 5, 31	1, 28, 29	25, 26	21, 22	19, 20
Graft or pollinate	4, 5	1, 27, 28	1, 27, 28	23, 24	20, 21, 22	17, 18	14, 15	10, 11, 12	7, 8	4, 5, 31	1, 28, 29	25, 26
Prune to encourage growth	24, 25	2, 21, 22	2, 3, 29, 30, 31	25, 26, 27	23, 24	1, 29, 30	17, 18	23, 24	19, 20	16, 17, 18	13, 14	19, 20
Prune to discourage growth	7, 8, 16, 17	12, 13, 14	12, 13	8, 9	5, 6	10, 11	7, 8, 9	4, 5	9, 10	6, 7	3, 4, 30	1, 27, 28
Harvest above-ground crops	26, 27, 28	23, 24	22, 23	1, 2, 28, 29	25, 26	21, 22, 23	19, 20	15, 16, 17	21, 22, 23	19, 20	15, 24	21, 22
Harvest below-ground crops	9, 10	5, 6	6	11, 12	16, 17	12, 13, 14	10, 11	6, 7	2, 3, 30	9, 10	5, 6	2, 3, 30, 31
Can, pickle, or make sauerkraut	14, 15	10, 11	9, 10, 11	6, 7	12, 13	8, 9	5, 6	2, 3	7, 8	4, 5	1, 28, 29	26
Cut hay	24, 25	21, 22	20, 21	17, 18	14, 15	10, 11	7, 8, 9	4, 5, 31	1, 28, 29	25, 26	21, 22	19, 20
Begin logging	18, 19	15, 16	14, 15	10, 11, 12	8, 9	4, 5	1, 2, 29, 30	25, 26	21, 22, 23	19, 20	15, 16	12, 13
Set posts or pour concrete	18, 19	15, 16	14, 15	10, 11, 12	8, 9	4, 5	1, 2, 29, 30	25, 26	21, 22, 23	19, 20	15, 16	12, 13
Breed animals	14, 15	10, 11	10, 11	6, 7	3, 4, 30, 31	27, 28	24, 25	20, 21, 22	16, 17, 18	14, 15	10, 11	7, 8, 9
Wean animals or children	10, 15	6, 11	10, 19	6, 15	13, 17	9, 13	6, 10	2, 6	3, 7, 30	5, 9	6, 10	3, 8
Castrate animals	20, 21	17, 18	16, 17	13, 14	10, 11	6, 7	3, 4, 31	1, 27, 28	24, 25	21, 22	17, 18	14, 15
Slaughter livestock	14, 15	10, 11	10, 11	6, 7	3, 4, 30, 31	27, 28	24, 25	20, 21, 22	16, 17, 18	14, 15	10, 11	7, 8, 9

See what to do when at Almanac.com/BestDays.

5 things you should never buy at the dollar store!

5 documents you should always destroy!

"WHAT You Should NEVER Put in Your Will"

(By Frank K. Wood)

If you want to enjoy a carefree retirement, get all the senior discounts you're entitled to, make the most of Social Security, reduce your medical costs, and slash your taxes, you need *Retiring Well on a Poor Man's Budget,* an informative new book just released to the public by FC&A Publishing® in Peachtree City, Georgia.

You'll be amazed at how you can trim your grocery bill without buying less food, grow your savings like crazy, prevent identity theft, and much more!

The authors provide many helpful tips with full explanations.

▶ Upgrade your monthly Social Security check to a higher amount.

▶ Would you like to have the power company pay you? Who wouldn't!

▶ Get free medical testing — MRI, x-ray, blood work!

▶ If you'd like to speak to a real person, press "1." How to get the human touch!

▶ How a simple trust can take 50% of your estate out of the government's hands.

▶ Stolen identity can destroy your life! The #1 way to put the freeze on ID thieves!

▶ How to avoid paying taxes on Social Security benefits.

▶ Prescription eyeglasses for just 8 bucks? You bet! No matter where you live.

▶ Could you really cut your grocery bill in half? Yes ... if you know these sneaky secrets.

▶ The simple tip that will keep most cars on the road for 200,000 miles!

▶ By law, you're entitled to a "benefits checkup." It's free (you've already paid for it)!

▶ When you should never write checks with a pen! Find out why it could cost you your life savings — it's no joke!

▶ A nickel-and-dime approach to successful retirement! Where to go for senior discounts, bargains, and money-saving services.

▶ Never pay full price for a hotel room. Know who to call and what to ask, and you'll get up to 50% off.

▶ Want your bank to pay you more? The 7 questions they hope you never ask!

▶ Medicare will pay — 100%. Don't bypass these free services!

▶ Cut your car insurance costs by as much as 50%! Become an insurance insider.

Secrets of the Zodiac

The Man of the Signs

Ancient astrologers believed that each astrological sign influenced a specific part of the body. The first sign of the zodiac—Aries—was attributed to the head, with the rest of the signs moving down the body, ending with Pisces at the feet.

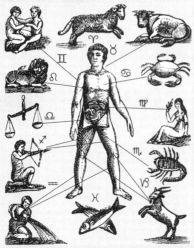

♈	Aries, head	**ARI**	*Mar. 21–Apr. 20*
♉	Taurus, neck	**TAU**	*Apr. 21–May 20*
♊	Gemini, arms	**GEM**	*May 21–June 20*
♋	Cancer, breast	**CAN**	*June 21–July 22*
♌	Leo, heart	**LEO**	*July 23–Aug. 22*
♍	Virgo, belly	**VIR**	*Aug. 23–Sept. 22*
♎	Libra, reins	**LIB**	*Sept. 23–Oct. 22*
♏	Scorpio, secrets	**SCO**	*Oct. 23–Nov. 22*
♐	Sagittarius, thighs	**SAG**	*Nov. 23–Dec. 21*
♑	Capricorn, knees	**CAP**	*Dec. 22–Jan. 19*
♒	Aquarius, legs	**AQU**	*Jan. 20–Feb. 19*
♓	Pisces, feet	**PSC**	*Feb. 20–Mar. 20*

Astrology vs. Astronomy

■ **Astrology** is a tool we use to plan events according to the placements of the Sun, the Moon, and the planets in the 12 signs of the zodiac. In astrology, the planetary movements do not cause events; rather, they explain the path, or "flow," that events tend to follow. **Astronomy** is the study of the actual placement of the known planets and constellations. *(The placement of the planets in the signs of the zodiac is not the same astrologically and astronomically.)* The Moon's astrological place is given on **page 247;** its astronomical place is given in the **Left-Hand Calendar Pages, 128–154.**

The dates in the **Best Days** table, **page 244,** are based on the astrological passage of the Moon. However, consider all indicators before making any major decisions.

When Mercury Is Retrograde

■ Sometimes the other planets appear to be traveling backward through the zodiac; this is an illusion. We call this illusion *retrograde motion.*

Mercury's retrograde periods can cause our plans to go awry. However, this is an excellent time to reflect on the past. Intuition is high during these periods, and coincidences can be extraordinary.

When Mercury is retrograde, remain flexible, allow extra time for travel, and avoid signing contracts. Review projects and plans at these times, but wait until Mercury is direct again to make any final decisions.

In 2015, Mercury will be retrograde during January 21–February 11, May 19–June 11, and September 17–October 9.

–Celeste Longacre

Gardening by the Moon's Sign

Use the chart on the next page to find the best dates for the following garden tasks:

■ **Plant, transplant, and graft:** Cancer, Scorpio, or Pisces.

■ **Harvest:** Aries, Leo, Sagittarius, Gemini, or Aquarius.

■ **Build/fix fences or garden beds:** Capricorn.

■ **Control insect pests, plow, and weed:** Aries, Gemini, Leo, Sagittarius, or Aquarius.

■ **Prune:** Aries, Leo, or Sagittarius. During a waxing Moon, pruning encourages growth; during a waning Moon, it discourages growth.

Setting Eggs by the Moon's Sign

■ Chicks take about 21 days to hatch. Those born under a waxing Moon, in the fruitful signs of Cancer, Scorpio, and Pisces, are healthier and mature faster. To ensure that chicks are born during these times, determine the best days to "set eggs" (to place eggs in an incubator or under a hen). To calculate, find the three fruitful birth signs on the chart below. Use the **Left-Hand Calendar Pages, 128–154,** to find the dates of the new and full Moons.

Using only the fruitful dates between the new and full Moons, count back 21 days to find the best days to set eggs.

E X A M P L E :

The Moon is new on May 18 and full on June 2. Between these dates, on May 20–22, the Moon is in the sign of Cancer. To have chicks born on May 20, count back 21 days; set eggs on April 29.

The Moon's Astrological Place, 2014–15

	Nov.	Dec.	Jan.	Feb.	Mar.	Apr.	May	June	July	Aug.	Sept.	Oct.	Nov.	Dec.
1	PSC	ARI	GEM	CAN	CAN	VIR	LIB	SCO	CAP	AQU	ARI	TAU	CAN	LEO
2	PSC	ARI	GEM	LEO	LEO	VIR	LIB	SAG	CAP	PSC	TAU	GEM	LEO	VIR
3	PSC	TAU	GEM	LEO	LEO	LIB	SCO	SAG	AQU	PSC	TAU	GEM	LEO	VIR
4	ARI	TAU	CAN	LEO	VIR	LIB	SCO	CAP	AQU	ARI	GEM	CAN	LEO	VIR
5	ARI	GEM	CAN	VIR	VIR	LIB	SAG	CAP	PSC	ARI	GEM	CAN	VIR	LIB
6	TAU	GEM	LEO	VIR	VIR	SCO	SAG	AQU	PSC	TAU	GEM	LEO	VIR	LIB
7	TAU	CAN	LEO	VIR	LIB	SCO	SAG	AQU	ARI	TAU	CAN	LEO	LIB	SCO
8	GEM	CAN	LEO	LIB	LIB	SAG	CAP	PSC	ARI	GEM	CAN	LEO	LIB	SCO
9	GEM	CAN	VIR	LIB	SCO	SAG	CAP	PSC	ARI	GEM	LEO	VIR	LIB	SCO
10	CAN	LEO	VIR	SCO	SCO	CAP	AQU	ARI	TAU	CAN	LEO	VIR	SCO	SAG
11	CAN	LEO	LIB	SCO	SCO	CAP	AQU	ARI	TAU	CAN	VIR	LIB	SCO	SAG
12	CAN	VIR	LIB	SAG	SAG	CAP	PSC	TAU	GEM	CAN	VIR	LIB	SAG	CAP
13	LEO	VIR	LIB	SAG	SAG	AQU	PSC	TAU	GEM	LEO	VIR	LIB	SAG	CAP
14	LEO	VIR	SCO	SAG	CAP	AQU	ARI	TAU	CAN	LEO	LIB	SCO	SAG	AQU
15	VIR	LIB	SCO	CAP	CAP	PSC	ARI	GEM	CAN	VIR	LIB	SCO	CAP	AQU
16	VIR	LIB	SAG	CAP	AQU	PSC	TAU	GEM	LEO	VIR	SCO	SAG	CAP	AQU
17	VIR	SCO	SAG	AQU	AQU	ARI	TAU	CAN	LEO	VIR	SCO	SAG	AQU	PSC
18	LIB	SCO	CAP	AQU	PSC	ARI	GEM	CAN	LEO	LIB	SCO	SAG	AQU	PSC
19	LIB	SCO	CAP	PSC	PSC	TAU	GEM	LEO	VIR	LIB	SAG	CAP	PSC	ARI
20	SCO	SAG	AQU	PSC	ARI	TAU	CAN	LEO	VIR	SCO	SAG	CAP	PSC	ARI
21	SCO	SAG	AQU	ARI	ARI	GEM	CAN	VIR	LIB	SCO	CAP	AQU	ARI	TAU
22	SAG	CAP	PSC	ARI	TAU	GEM	CAN	VIR	LIB	SCO	CAP	AQU	ARI	TAU
23	SAG	CAP	PSC	TAU	TAU	CAN	LEO	VIR	LIB	SAG	CAP	PSC	TAU	GEM
24	CAP	AQU	ARI	TAU	GEM	CAN	LEO	LIB	SCO	SAG	AQU	PSC	TAU	GEM
25	CAP	AQU	ARI	GEM	GEM	LEO	VIR	LIB	SCO	CAP	AQU	ARI	TAU	CAN
26	CAP	PSC	TAU	GEM	GEM	LEO	VIR	LIB	SAG	CAP	PSC	ARI	GEM	CAN
27	AQU	PSC	TAU	CAN	CAN	LEO	VIR	SCO	SAG	AQU	PSC	TAU	GEM	LEO
28	AQU	ARI	TAU	CAN	CAN	VIR	LIB	SCO	SAG	AQU	ARI	TAU	CAN	LEO
29	PSC	ARI	GEM	—	LEO	VIR	LIB	SAG	CAP	PSC	ARI	GEM	CAN	LEO
30	PSC	TAU	GEM	—	LEO	LIB	SCO	SAG	CAP	PSC	TAU	GEM	LEO	VIR
31	—	TAU	CAN	—	LEO	—	SCO	—	AQU	ARI	—	CAN	—	VIR

Planting by the Moon's Phase

According to this age-old practice, cycles of the Moon affect plant growth.

■ Plant flowers and vegetables that bear crops above ground during the light, or waxing, of the Moon: from the day the Moon is new to the day it is full.

■ Plant flowering bulbs and vegetables that bear crops below ground during the dark, or waning, of the Moon: from the day after it is full to the day before it is new again.

The Moon Favorable columns give the best planting days based on the Moon's phases for 2015. (See the **Left-Hand Calendar Pages, 128–154,** for the exact days of the new and full Moons.) The Planting Dates columns give the safe periods for planting in areas that receive frost. See **Frosts and Growing Seasons, page 214,** for first/last frost dates and the average length of the growing season in your area.

Get local seed-sowing dates at Almanac.com/PlantingTable.

■ Aboveground crops are marked *.
■ (E) means early; (L) means late.
■ Map shades correspond to shades of date columns.

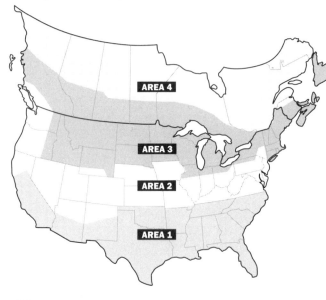

* Barley	
* Beans	(E
	(L
Beets	(E
	(L
* Broccoli plants	(E
	(L
* Brussels sprouts	
* Cabbage plants	
Carrots	(E
	(L
* Cauliflower plants	(E
	(L
* Celery plants	(E
	(L
* Collards	(E
	(L
* Corn, sweet	(E
	(L
* Cucumbers	
* Eggplant plants	
* Endive	(E
	(L
* Kale	(E
	(L
Leek plants	
* Lettuce	
* Muskmelons	
* Okra	
Onion sets	
* Parsley	
Parsnips	
* Peas	(E
	(L
* Pepper plants	
Potatoes	
* Pumpkins	
Radishes	(E
	(L
* Spinach	(E
	(L
* Squashes	
Sweet potatoes	
* Swiss chard	
* Tomato plants	
Turnips	(E
	(L
* Watermelons	
* Wheat, spring	
* Wheat, winter	

AREA 1		AREA 2		AREA 3		AREA 4	
Planting Dates	Moon Favorable	Planting Dates	Moon Favorable	Planting Dates	Moon Favorable	Planting Dates	Moon Favorable
…5–3/7	2/18–3/5	3/15–4/7	3/20–4/4	5/15–6/21	5/18–6/2, 6/16–21	6/1–30	6/1–2, 6/16–30
…5–4/7	3/20–4/4	4/15–30	4/18–30	5/7–6/21	5/18–6/2, 6/16–21	5/30–6/15	5/30–6/2
…7–31	8/14–29	7/1–21	7/1, 7/15–21	6/15–7/15	6/16–7/1, 7/15	—	—
…7–28	2/7–17	3/15–4/3	3/15–19	5/1–15	5/4–15	5/25–6/10	6/3–10
…4–30	9/1–12, 9/28–30	8/15–31	8/30–31	7/15–8/15	8/1–13	6/15–7/8	6/15, 7/2–8
…5–3/15	2/18–3/5	3/7–31	3/20–31	5/15–31	5/18–31	6/1–25	6/1–2, 6/16–25
…7–30	9/13–27	8/1–20	8/14–20	6/15–7/7	6/16–7/1	—	—
…1–3/20	2/18–3/5, 3/20	3/7–4/15	3/20–4/4	5/15–31	5/18–31	6/1–25	6/1–2, 6/16–25
…1–3/20	2/18–3/5, 3/20	3/7–4/15	3/20–4/4	5/15–31	5/18–31	6/1–25	6/1–2, 6/16–25
…5–3/7	2/15–17, 3/6–7	3/7–31	3/7–19	5/15–31	5/15–17	5/25–6/10	6/3–10
…4–9/7	8/1–13, 8/30–9/7	7/7–31	7/7–14	6/15–7/21	6/15, 7/2–14	6/15–7/8	6/15, 7/2–8
…5–3/7	2/18–3/5	3/15–4/7	3/20–4/4	5/15–31	5/18–31	6/1–25	6/1–2, 6/16–25
…7–31	8/14–29	7/1–8/7	7/1, 7/15–31	6/15–7/21	6/16–7/1, 7/15–21	—	—
…5–28	2/18–28	3/7–31	3/20–31	5/15–6/30	5/18–6/2, 6/16–30	6/1–30	6/1–2, 6/16–30
…5–30	9/15–27	8/15–9/7	8/15–29	7/15–8/15	7/15–31, 8/14–15	—	—
…1–3/20	2/18–3/5, 3/20	3/7–4/7	3/20–4/4	5/15–31	5/18–31	6/1–25	6/1–2, 6/16–25
…7–30	9/13–27	8/15–31	8/15–29	7/1–8/7	7/1, 7/15–31	—	—
…5–31	3/20–31	4/1–17	4/1–4	5/10–6/15	5/18–6/2	5/30–6/20	5/30–6/2, 6/16–20
…7–31	8/14–29	7/7–21	7/15–21	6/15–30	6/16–30	—	—
…7–4/15	3/20–4/4	4/7–5/15	4/18–5/3	5/7–6/20	5/18–6/2, 6/16–20	5/30–6/15	5/30–6/2
…7–4/15	3/20–4/4	4/7–5/15	4/18–5/3	6/1–30	6/1–2, 6/16–30	6/15–30	6/16–30
…5–3/20	2/18–3/5, 3/20	4/7–5/15	4/18–5/3	5/15–31	5/18–31	6/1–25	6/1–2, 6/16–25
…5–9/7	8/15–29	7/15–8/15	7/15–31, 8/14–15	6/7–30	6/16–30	—	—
…1–3/20	2/18–3/5, 3/20	3/7–4/7	3/20–4/4	5/15–31	5/18–31	6/1–15	6/1–2
…7–30	9/13–27	8/15–31	8/15–29	7/1–8/7	7/1, 7/15–31	6/25–7/15	6/25–7/1, 7/15
…5–4/15	2/15–17, 3/6–19, 4/5–15	3/7–4/7	3/7–19, 4/5–7	5/15–31	5/15–17	6/1–25	6/3–15
…5–3/7	2/18–3/5	3/1–31	3/1–5, 3/20–31	5/15–6/30	5/18–6/2, 6/16–30	6/1–30	6/1–2, 6/16–30
…5–4/7	3/20–4/4	4/15–5/7	4/18–5/3	5/15–6/30	5/18–6/2, 6/16–30	6/1–30	6/1–2, 6/16–30
…5–6/1	4/18–5/3, 5/18–6/1	5/25–6/15	5/25–6/2	6/15–7/10	6/16–7/1	6/25–7/7	6/25–7/1
…4–28	2/4–17	3/1–31	3/6–19	5/15–6/7	5/15–17, 6/3–7	6/1–25	6/3–15
…20–3/15	2/20–3/5	3/1–31	3/1–5, 3/20–31	5/15–31	5/18–31	6/1–15	6/1–2
…5–2/4	1/15–19, 2/4	3/7–31	3/7–19	4/1–30	4/5–17	5/10–31	5/10–17
…5–2/7	1/20–2/3	3/7–31	3/20–31	4/15–5/7	4/18–5/3	5/15–31	5/18–31
…5–30	9/15–27	8/7–31	8/14–29	7/15–31	7/15–31	7/10–25	7/15–25
…–20	3/1–5, 3/20	4/1–30	4/1–4, 4/18–30	5/15–6/30	5/18–6/2, 6/16–30	6/1–30	6/1–2, 6/16–30
…0–28	2/10–17	4/1–30	4/5–17	5/1–31	5/4–17	6/1–25	6/3–15
…7–20	3/20	4/23–5/15	4/23–5/3	5/15–31	5/18–31	6/1–30	6/1–2, 6/16–30
…1–3/1	2/4–17	3/7–31	3/7–19	4/15–30	4/15–17	5/15–6/5	5/15–17, 6/3–5
…7–21	10/1–11	9/7–30	9/7–12, 9/28–30	8/15–31	8/30–31	7/10–31	7/10–14
…–3/15	2/18–3/5	3/15–4/20	3/20–4/4, 4/18–20	5/15–31	5/18–31	6/1–25	6/1–2, 6/16–25
…7–21	10/12–21	8/1–9/15	8/14–29, 9/13–15	7/17–9/7	7/17–31, 8/14–29	7/20–8/5	7/20–31
…5–4/15	3/20–4/4	4/15–30	4/18–30	5/15–6/15	5/18–6/2	6/1–30	6/1–2, 6/16–30
…3–4/6	4/5–6	4/21–5/9	5/4–9	5/15–6/15	5/15–17, 6/3–15	6/1–30	6/3–15
…–3/15	2/18–3/5	3/15–4/15	3/20–4/4	5/1–31	5/1–3, 5/18–31	5/15–31	5/18–31
…7–20	3/20	4/7–30	4/18–30	5/15–31	5/18–31	6/1–15	6/1–2
…20–2/15	2/4–15	3/15–31	3/15–19	4/7–30	4/7–17	5/10–31	5/10–17
…–10/15	9/1–12, 9/28–10/11	8/1–20	8/1–13	7/1–8/15	7/2–14, 8/1–13	—	—
…5–4/7	3/20–4/4	4/15–5/7	4/18–5/3	5/15–6/30	5/18–6/2, 6/16–30	6/1–30	6/1–2, 6/16–30
…5–28	2/18–28	3/1–20	3/1–5, 3/20	4/7–30	4/18–30	5/15–6/10	5/18–6/2
…15–12/7	10/15–27, 11/11–25	9/15–10/20	9/15–27, 10/12–20	8/11–9/15	8/14–29, 9/13–15	8/5–30	8/14–29

Tide Corrections

■ Many factors affect the times and heights of the tides: the shoreline, the time of the Moon's southing (crossing the meridian), and the Moon's phase. The High Tide column on the **Left-Hand Calendar Pages, 128–154,** lists the times of high tide at Commonwealth Pier in Boston Harbor. The heights of some of these tides, reckoned from Mean Lower Low Water, are given on the **Right-Hand Calendar Pages, 129–155.** Use the table below to calculate the approximate times and heights of high tide at the places shown. Apply the time difference to the times of high tide at Boston and the height difference to the heights at Boston. A tide calculator can be found at **Almanac.com/Tides.**

EXAMPLE:

The conversion of the times and heights of the tides at Boston to those at Cape Fear, North Carolina, is given below:

High tide at Boston	11:45 A.M.
Correction for Cape Fear	– 3 55
High tide at Cape Fear	7:50 A.M.
Tide height at Boston	11.6 ft.
Correction for Cape Fear	– 5.0 ft.
Tide height at Cape Fear	6.6 ft.

Estimations derived from this table are *not* meant to be used for navigation. *The Old Farmer's Almanac* accepts no responsibility for errors or any consequences ensuing from the use of this table.

Tidal Site	Difference: Time (h. m.)	Height (ft.)
Canada		
Alberton, PE	*–5 45	–7.5
Charlottetown, PE......	*–0 45	–3.5
Halifax, NS	–3 23	–4.5
North Sydney, NS	–3 15	–6.5
Saint John, NB	+0 30	+15.0
St. John's, NL	–4 00	–6.5
Yarmouth, NS	–0 40	+3.0
Maine		
Bar Harbor	–0 34	+0.9
Belfast..............	–0 20	+0.4
Boothbay Harbor.......	–0 18	–0.8
Chebeague Island	–0 16	–0.6
Eastport.............	–0 28	+8.4
Kennebunkport	+0 04	–1.0
Machias.............	–0 28	+2.8
Monhegan Island.......	–0 25	–0.8
Old Orchard	0 00	–0.8
Portland.............	–0 12	–0.6
Rockland.............	–0 28	+0.1
Stonington...........	–0 30	+0.1
York	–0 09	–1.0
New Hampshire		
Hampton	+0 02	–1.3
Portsmouth	+0 11	–1.5
Rye Beach...........	–0 09	–0.9
Massachusetts		
Annisquam	–0 02	–1.1
Beverly Farms........	0 00	–0.5

Tidal Site	Difference: Time (h. m.)	Height (ft.)
Cape Cod Canal		
East Entrance	–0 01	–0.8
West Entrance.......	–2 16	–5.9
Chatham Outer Coast ..	+0 30	–2.8
Inside	+1 54	**0.4
Cohasset	+0 02	–0.07
Cotuit Highlands	+1 15	**0.3
Dennis Port	+1 01	**0.4
Duxbury–Gurnet Point. . .	+0 02	–0.3
Fall River............	–3 03	–5.0
Gloucester...........	–0 03	–0.8
Hingham	+0 07	0.0
Hull	+0 03	–0.2
Hyannis Port	+1 01	**0.3
Magnolia–Manchester ..	–0 02	–0.7
Marblehead	–0 02	–0.4
Marion..............	–3 22	–5.4
Monument Beach	–3 08	–5.4
Nahant..............	–0 01	–0.5
Nantasket...........	+0 04	–0.1
Nantucket	+0 56	**0.3
Nauset Beach........	+0 30	**0.6
New Bedford........	–3 24	–5.7
Newburyport	+0 19	–1.8
Oak Bluffs..........	+0 30	**0.2
Onset–R.R. Bridge	–2 16	–5.9
Plymouth............	+0 05	0.0
Provincetown.........	+0 14	–0.4
Revere Beach	–0 01	–0.3
Rockport	–0 08	–1.0
Salem..............	0 00	–0.5
Scituate	–0 05	–0.7

Tidal Site	Difference: Time (h. m.)	Height (ft.)
Wareham	−3 09	−5.3
Wellfleet	+0 12	+0.5
West Falmouth.	−3 10	−5.4
Westport Harbor	−3 22	−6.4
Woods Hole		
Little Harbor	−2 50	**0.2
Oceanographic		
Institute	−3 07	**0.2
Rhode Island		
Bristol	−3 24	−5.3
Narragansett Pier	−3 42	−6.2
Newport.	−3 34	−5.9
Point Judith	−3 41	−6.3
Providence.	−3 20	−4.8
Sakonnet	−3 44	−5.6
Watch Hill	−2 50	−6.8
Connecticut		
Bridgeport	+0 01	−2.6
Madison.	−0 22	−2.3
New Haven	−0 11	−3.2
New London	−1 54	−6.7
Norwalk.	+0 01	−2.2
Old Lyme		
Highway Bridge	−0 30	−6.2
Stamford	+0 01	−2.2
Stonington	−2 27	−6.6
New York		
Coney Island	−3 33	−4.9
Fire Island Light	−2 43	**0.1
Long Beach	−3 11	−5.7
Montauk Harbor	−2 19	−7.4
New York City–Battery . .	−2 43	−5.0
Oyster Bay.	+0 04	−1.8
Port Chester.	−0 09	−2.2
Port Washington	−0 01	−2.1
Sag Harbor.	−0 55	−6.8
Southampton		
Shinnecock Inlet	−4 20	**0.2
Willets Point	0 00	−2.3
New Jersey		
Asbury Park.	−4 04	−5.3
Atlantic City	−3 56	−5.5
Bay Head–Sea Girt	−4 04	−5.3
Beach Haven	−1 43	**0.24
Cape May	−3 28	−5.3
Ocean City.	−3 06	−5.9
Sandy Hook.	−3 30	−5.0
Seaside Park	−4 03	−5.4
Pennsylvania		
Philadelphia.	+2 40	−3.5
Delaware		
Cape Henlopen	−2 48	−5.3

Tidal Site	Difference: Time (h. m.)	Height (ft.)
Rehoboth Beach.	−3 37	−5.7
Wilmington	+1 56	−3.8
Maryland		
Annapolis	+6 23	−8.5
Baltimore.	+7 59	−8.3
Cambridge.	+5 05	−7.8
Havre de Grace	+11 21	−7.7
Point No Point	+2 28	−8.1
Prince Frederick		
Plum Point	+4 25	−8.5
Virginia		
Cape Charles	−2 20	−7.0
Hampton Roads	−2 02	−6.9
Norfolk	−2 06	−6.6
Virginia Beach.	−4 00	−6.0
Yorktown.	−2 13	−7.0
North Carolina		
Cape Fear.	−3 55	−5.0
Cape Lookout	−4 28	−5.7
Currituck	−4 10	−5.8
Hatteras		
Inlet.	−4 03	−7.4
Kitty Hawk	−4 14	−6.2
Ocean	−4 26	−6.0
South Carolina		
Charleston	−3 22	−4.3
Georgetown	−1 48	**0.36
Hilton Head	−3 22	−2.9
Myrtle Beach	−3 49	−4.4
St. Helena		
Harbor Entrance	−3 15	−3.4
Georgia		
Jekyll Island.	−3 46	−2.9
St. Simon's Island	−2 50	−2.9
Savannah Beach		
River Entrance	−3 14	−5.5
Tybee Light.	−3 22	−2.7
Florida		
Cape Canaveral	−3 59	−6.0
Daytona Beach.	−3 28	−5.3
Fort Lauderdale	−2 50	−7.2
Fort Pierce Inlet.	−3 32	−6.9
Jacksonville		
Railroad Bridge.	−6 55	**0.1
Miami Harbor Entrance . .	−3 18	−7.0
St. Augustine	−2 55	−4.9

Varies widely; accurate only to within 1½ hours. Consult local tide tables for precise times and heights.

**Where the difference in the Height column is so marked, the height at Boston should be multiplied by this ratio.*

Time Corrections

■ Astronomical data for Boston is given on **pages 104, 108–109,** and **128–154.** Use the Key letter shown to the right of each time on those pages with this table to find the number of minutes that you must add to or subtract from Boston time to get the correct time for your city. (Because of complex calculations for different locales, times are approximate.) For more information on the use of Key letters and this table, **see How to Use This Almanac, page 124.**

Get times simply and specifically: Download astronomical times calculated for your zip code and presented like a Left-Hand Calendar Page at **Almanac.com/Access.**

TIME ZONES: Codes represent *standard time.* Atlantic is −1, Eastern is 0, Central is 1, Mountain is 2, Pacific is 3, Alaska is 4, and Hawaii-Aleutian is 5.

State	City	North Latitude °	′	West Longitude °	′	Time Zone Code	A (min.)	B (min.)	C (min.)	D (min.)	E (min.)
AK	Anchorage	61	10	149	59	4	−46	+27	+71	+122	+171
AK	Cordova	60	33	145	45	4	−55	+13	+55	+103	+149
AK	Fairbanks	64	48	147	51	4	−127	+2	+61	+131	+205
AK	Juneau	58	18	134	25	4	−76	−23	+10	+49	+86
AK	Ketchikan	55	21	131	39	4	−62	−25	0	+29	+56
AK	Kodiak	57	47	152	24	4	0	+49	+82	+120	+154
AL	Birmingham	33	31	86	49	1	+30	+15	+3	−10	−20
AL	Decatur	34	36	86	59	1	+27	+14	+4	−7	−17
AL	Mobile	30	42	88	3	1	+42	+23	+8	−8	−22
AL	Montgomery	32	23	86	19	1	+31	+14	+1	−13	−25
AR	Fort Smith	35	23	94	25	1	+55	+43	+33	+22	+14
AR	Little Rock	34	45	92	17	1	+48	+35	+25	+13	+4
AR	Texarkana	33	26	94	3	1	+59	+44	+32	+18	+8
AZ	Flagstaff	35	12	111	39	2	+64	+52	+42	+31	+22
AZ	Phoenix	33	27	112	4	2	+71	+56	+44	+30	+20
AZ	Tucson	32	13	110	58	2	+70	+53	+40	+24	+12
AZ	Yuma	32	43	114	37	2	+83	+67	+54	+40	+28
CA	Bakersfield	35	23	119	1	3	+33	+21	+12	+1	−7
CA	Barstow	34	54	117	1	3	+27	+14	+4	−7	−16
CA	Fresno	36	44	119	47	3	+32	+22	+15	+6	0
CA	Los Angeles–Pasadena– Santa Monica	34	3	118	14	3	+34	+20	+9	−3	−13
CA	Palm Springs	33	49	116	32	3	+28	+13	+1	−12	−22
CA	Redding	40	35	122	24	3	+31	+27	+25	+22	+19
CA	Sacramento	38	35	121	30	3	+34	+27	+21	+15	+10
CA	San Diego	32	43	117	9	3	+33	+17	+4	−9	−21
CA	San Francisco–Oakland– San Jose	37	47	122	25	3	+40	+31	+25	+18	+12
CO	Craig	40	31	107	33	2	+32	+28	+25	+22	+20
CO	Denver–Boulder	39	44	104	59	2	+24	+19	+15	+11	+7
CO	Grand Junction	39	4	108	33	2	+40	+34	+29	+24	+20
CO	Pueblo	38	16	104	37	2	+27	+20	+14	+7	+2
CO	Trinidad	37	10	104	31	2	+30	+21	+13	+5	0
CT	Bridgeport	41	11	73	11	0	+12	+10	+8	+6	+4
CT	Hartford–New Britain	41	46	72	41	0	+8	+7	+6	+5	+4
CT	New Haven	41	18	72	56	0	+11	+8	+7	+5	+4
CT	New London	41	22	72	6	0	+7	+5	+4	+2	+1
CT	Norwalk–Stamford	41	7	73	22	0	+13	+10	+9	+7	+5
CT	Waterbury–Meriden	41	33	73	3	0	+10	+9	+7	+6	+5
DC	Washington	38	54	77	1	0	+35	+28	+23	+18	+13
DE	Wilmington	39	45	75	33	0	+26	+21	+18	+13	+10

State	City	North Latitude °	'	West Longitude °	'	Time Zone Code	A (min.)	B (min.)	C (min.)	D (min.)	E (min.)
FL	Fort Myers	26	38	81	52	0	+87	+63	+44	+21	+4
FL	Jacksonville	30	20	81	40	0	+77	+58	+43	+25	+11
FL	Miami	25	47	80	12	0	+88	+57	+37	+14	−3
FL	Orlando	28	32	81	22	0	+80	+59	+42	+22	+6
FL	Pensacola	30	25	87	13	1	+39	+20	+5	−12	−26
FL	St. Petersburg	27	46	82	39	0	+87	+65	+47	+26	+10
FL	Tallahassee	30	27	84	17	0	+87	+68	+53	+35	+22
FL	Tampa	27	57	82	27	0	+86	+64	+46	+25	+9
FL	West Palm Beach	26	43	80	3	0	+79	+55	+36	+14	−2
GA	Atlanta	33	45	84	24	0	+79	+65	+53	+40	+30
GA	Augusta	33	28	81	58	0	+70	+55	+44	+30	+19
GA	Macon	32	50	83	38	0	+79	+63	+50	+36	+24
GA	Savannah	32	5	81	6	0	+70	+54	+40	+25	+13
HI	Hilo	19	44	155	5	5	+94	+62	+37	+7	−15
HI	Honolulu	21	18	157	52	5	+102	+72	+48	+19	−1
HI	Lanai City	20	50	156	55	5	+99	+69	+44	+15	−6
HI	Lihue	21	59	159	23	5	+107	+77	+54	+26	+5
IA	Davenport	41	32	90	35	1	+20	+19	+17	+16	+15
IA	Des Moines	41	35	93	37	1	+32	+31	+30	+28	+27
IA	Dubuque	42	30	90	41	1	+17	+18	+18	+18	+18
IA	Waterloo	42	30	92	20	1	+24	+24	+24	+25	+25
ID	Boise	43	37	116	12	2	+55	+58	+60	+62	+64
ID	Lewiston	46	25	117	1	3	−12	−3	+2	+10	+17
ID	Pocatello	42	52	112	27	2	+43	+44	+45	+46	+46
IL	Cairo	37	0	89	11	1	+29	+20	+12	+4	−2
IL	Chicago–Oak Park	41	52	87	38	1	+7	+6	+6	+5	+4
IL	Danville	40	8	87	37	1	+13	+9	+6	+2	0
IL	Decatur	39	51	88	57	1	+19	+15	+11	+7	+4
IL	Peoria	40	42	89	36	1	+19	+16	+14	+11	+9
IL	Springfield	39	48	89	39	1	+22	+18	+14	+10	+6
IN	Fort Wayne	41	4	85	9	0	+60	+58	+56	+54	+52
IN	Gary	41	36	87	20	1	+7	+6	+4	+3	+2
IN	Indianapolis	39	46	86	10	0	+69	+64	+60	+56	+52
IN	Muncie	40	12	85	23	0	+64	+60	+57	+53	+50
IN	South Bend	41	41	86	15	0	+62	+61	+60	+59	+58
IN	Terre Haute	39	28	87	24	0	+74	+69	+65	+60	+56
KS	Fort Scott	37	50	94	42	1	+49	+41	+34	+27	+21
KS	Liberal	37	3	100	55	1	+76	+66	+59	+51	+44
KS	Oakley	39	8	100	51	1	+69	+63	+59	+53	+49
KS	Salina	38	50	97	37	1	+57	+51	+46	+40	+35
KS	Topeka	39	3	95	40	1	+49	+43	+38	+32	+28
KS	Wichita	37	42	97	20	1	+60	+51	+45	+37	+31
KY	Lexington–Frankfort	38	3	84	30	0	+67	+59	+53	+46	+41
KY	Louisville	38	15	85	46	0	+72	+64	+58	+52	+46
LA	Alexandria	31	18	92	27	1	+58	+40	+26	+9	−3
LA	Baton Rouge	30	27	91	11	1	+55	+36	+21	+3	−10
LA	Lake Charles	30	14	93	13	1	+64	+44	+29	+11	−2
LA	Monroe	32	30	92	7	1	+53	+37	+24	+9	−1
LA	New Orleans	29	57	90	4	1	+52	+32	+16	−1	−15
LA	Shreveport	32	31	93	45	1	+60	+44	+31	+16	+4
MA	Brockton	42	5	71	1	0	0	0	0	0	−1
MA	Fall River–New Bedford	41	42	71	9	0	+2	+1	0	0	−1
MA	Lawrence–Lowell	42	42	71	10	0	0	0	0	0	+1
MA	Pittsfield	42	27	73	15	0	+8	+8	+8	+8	+8
MA	Springfield–Holyoke	42	6	72	36	0	+6	+6	+6	+5	+5
MA	Worcester	42	16	71	48	0	+3	+2	+2	+2	+2

(continued)

State	City	North Latitude °	′	West Longitude °	′	Time Zone Code	A (min.)	B (min.)	C (min.)	D (min.)	E (min.)
MD	Baltimore	39	17	76	37	0	+32	+26	+22	+17	+13
MD	Hagerstown	39	39	77	43	0	+35	+30	+26	+22	+18
MD	Salisbury	38	22	75	36	0	+31	+23	+18	+11	+6
ME	Augusta	44	19	69	46	0	−12	−8	−5	−1	0
ME	Bangor	44	48	68	46	0	−18	−13	−9	−5	−1
ME	Eastport	44	54	67	0	0	−26	−20	−16	−11	−8
ME	Ellsworth	44	33	68	25	0	−18	−14	−10	−6	−3
ME	Portland	43	40	70	15	0	−8	−5	−3	−1	0
ME	Presque Isle	46	41	68	1	0	−29	−19	−12	−4	+2
MI	Cheboygan	45	39	84	29	0	+40	+47	+53	+59	+64
MI	Detroit–Dearborn	42	20	83	3	0	+47	+47	+47	+47	+47
MI	Flint	43	1	83	41	0	+47	+49	+50	+51	+52
MI	Ironwood	46	27	90	9	1	0	+9	+15	+23	+29
MI	Jackson	42	15	84	24	0	+53	+53	+53	+52	+52
MI	Kalamazoo	42	17	85	35	0	+58	+57	+57	+57	+57
MI	Lansing	42	44	84	33	0	+52	+53	+53	+54	+54
MI	St. Joseph	42	5	86	26	0	+61	+61	+60	+60	+59
MI	Traverse City	44	46	85	38	0	+49	+54	+57	+62	+65
MN	Albert Lea	43	39	93	22	1	+24	+26	+28	+31	+33
MN	Bemidji	47	28	94	53	1	+14	+26	+34	+44	+52
MN	Duluth	46	47	92	6	1	+6	+16	+23	+31	+38
MN	Minneapolis–St. Paul	44	59	93	16	1	+18	+24	+28	+33	+37
MN	Ortonville	45	19	96	27	1	+30	+36	+40	+46	+51
MO	Jefferson City	38	34	92	10	1	+36	+29	+24	+18	+13
MO	Joplin	37	6	94	30	1	+50	+41	+33	+25	+18
MO	Kansas City	39	1	94	20	1	+44	+37	+33	+27	+23
MO	Poplar Bluff	36	46	90	24	1	+35	+25	+17	+8	+1
MO	St. Joseph	39	46	94	50	1	+43	+38	+35	+30	+27
MO	St. Louis	38	37	90	12	1	+28	+21	+16	+10	+5
MO	Springfield	37	13	93	18	1	+45	+36	+29	+20	+14
MS	Biloxi	30	24	88	53	1	+46	+27	+11	−5	−19
MS	Jackson	32	18	90	11	1	+46	+30	+17	+1	−10
MS	Meridian	32	22	88	42	1	+40	+24	+11	−4	−15
MS	Tupelo	34	16	88	34	1	+35	+21	+10	−2	−11
MT	Billings	45	47	108	30	2	+16	+23	+29	+35	+40
MT	Butte	46	1	112	32	2	+31	+39	+45	+52	+57
MT	Glasgow	48	12	106	38	2	−1	+11	+21	+32	+42
MT	Great Falls	47	30	111	17	2	+20	+31	+39	+49	+58
MT	Helena	46	36	112	2	2	+27	+36	+43	+51	+57
MT	Miles City	46	25	105	51	2	+3	+11	+18	+26	+32
NC	Asheville	35	36	82	33	0	+67	+55	+46	+35	+27
NC	Charlotte	35	14	80	51	0	+61	+49	+39	+28	+19
NC	Durham	36	0	78	55	0	+51	+40	+31	+21	+13
NC	Greensboro	36	4	79	47	0	+54	+43	+35	+25	+17
NC	Raleigh	35	47	78	38	0	+51	+39	+30	+20	+12
NC	Wilmington	34	14	77	55	0	+52	+38	+27	+15	+5
ND	Bismarck	46	48	100	47	1	+41	+50	+58	+66	+73
ND	Fargo	46	53	96	47	1	+24	+34	+42	+50	+57
ND	Grand Forks	47	55	97	3	1	+21	+33	+43	+53	+62
ND	Minot	48	14	101	18	1	+36	+50	+59	+71	+81
ND	Williston	48	9	103	37	1	+46	+59	+69	+80	+90
NE	Grand Island	40	55	98	21	1	+53	+51	+49	+46	+44
NE	Lincoln	40	49	96	41	1	+47	+44	+42	+39	+37
NE	North Platte	41	8	100	46	1	+62	+60	+58	+56	+54
NE	Omaha	41	16	95	56	1	+43	+40	+39	+37	+36
NH	Berlin	44	28	71	11	0	−7	−3	0	+3	+7
NH	Keene	42	56	72	17	0	+2	+3	+4	+5	+6

State	City	North Latitude °	'	West Longitude °	'	Time Zone Code	A (min.)	B (min.)	C (min.)	D (min.)	E (min.)
NH	Manchester–Concord	42	59	71	28	0	0	0	+1	+2	+3
NH	Portsmouth	43	5	70	45	0	−4	−2	−1	0	0
NJ	Atlantic City	39	22	74	26	0	+23	+17	+13	+8	+4
NJ	Camden	39	57	75	7	0	+24	+19	+16	+12	+9
NJ	Cape May	38	56	74	56	0	+26	+20	+15	+9	+5
NJ	Newark–East Orange	40	44	74	10	0	+17	+14	+12	+9	+7
NJ	Paterson	40	55	74	10	0	+17	+14	+12	+9	+7
NJ	Trenton	40	13	74	46	0	+21	+17	+14	+11	+8
NM	Albuquerque	35	5	106	39	2	+45	+32	+22	+11	+2
NM	Gallup	35	32	108	45	2	+52	+40	+31	+20	+11
NM	Las Cruces	32	19	106	47	2	+53	+36	+23	+8	−3
NM	Roswell	33	24	104	32	2	+41	+26	+14	0	−10
NM	Santa Fe	35	41	105	56	2	+40	+28	+19	+9	0
NV	Carson City–Reno	39	10	119	46	3	+25	+19	+14	+9	+5
NV	Elko	40	50	115	46	3	+3	0	−1	−3	−5
NV	Las Vegas	36	10	115	9	3	+16	+4	−3	−13	−20
NY	Albany	42	39	73	45	0	+9	+10	+10	+11	+11
NY	Binghamton	42	6	75	55	0	+20	+19	+19	+18	+18
NY	Buffalo	42	53	78	52	0	+29	+30	+30	+31	+32
NY	New York	40	45	74	0	0	+17	+14	+11	+9	+6
NY	Ogdensburg	44	42	75	30	0	+8	+13	+17	+21	+25
NY	Syracuse	43	3	76	9	0	+17	+19	+20	+21	+22
OH	Akron	41	5	81	31	0	+46	+43	+41	+39	+37
OH	Canton	40	48	81	23	0	+46	+43	+41	+38	+36
OH	Cincinnati–Hamilton	39	6	84	31	0	+64	+58	+53	+48	+44
OH	Cleveland–Lakewood	41	30	81	42	0	+45	+43	+42	+40	+39
OH	Columbus	39	57	83	1	0	+55	+51	+47	+43	+40
OH	Dayton	39	45	84	10	0	+61	+56	+52	+48	+44
OH	Toledo	41	39	83	33	0	+52	+50	+49	+48	+47
OH	Youngstown	41	6	80	39	0	+42	+40	+38	+36	+34
OK	Oklahoma City	35	28	97	31	1	+67	+55	+46	+35	+26
OK	Tulsa	36	9	95	60	1	+59	+48	+40	+30	+22
OR	Eugene	44	3	123	6	3	+21	+24	+27	+30	+33
OR	Pendleton	45	40	118	47	3	−1	+4	+10	+16	+21
OR	Portland	45	31	122	41	3	+14	+20	+25	+31	+36
OR	Salem	44	57	123	1	3	+17	+23	+27	+31	+35
PA	Allentown–Bethlehem	40	36	75	28	0	+23	+20	+17	+14	+12
PA	Erie	42	7	80	5	0	+36	+36	+35	+35	+35
PA	Harrisburg	40	16	76	53	0	+30	+26	+23	+19	+16
PA	Lancaster	40	2	76	18	0	+28	+24	+20	+17	+13
PA	Philadelphia–Chester	39	57	75	9	0	+24	+19	+16	+12	+9
PA	Pittsburgh–McKeesport	40	26	80	0	0	+42	+38	+35	+32	+29
PA	Reading	40	20	75	56	0	+26	+22	+19	+16	+13
PA	Scranton–Wilkes-Barre	41	25	75	40	0	+21	+19	+18	+16	+15
PA	York	39	58	76	43	0	+30	+26	+22	+18	+15
RI	Providence	41	50	71	25	0	+3	+2	+1	0	0
SC	Charleston	32	47	79	56	0	+64	+48	+36	+21	+10
SC	Columbia	34	0	81	2	0	+65	+51	+40	+27	+17
SC	Spartanburg	34	56	81	57	0	+66	+53	+43	+32	+23
SD	Aberdeen	45	28	98	29	1	+37	+44	+49	+54	+59
SD	Pierre	44	22	100	21	1	+49	+53	+56	+60	+63
SD	Rapid City	44	5	103	14	2	+2	+5	+8	+11	+13
SD	Sioux Falls	43	33	96	44	1	+38	+40	+42	+44	+46
TN	Chattanooga	35	3	85	19	0	+79	+67	+57	+45	+36
TN	Knoxville	35	58	83	55	0	+71	+60	+51	+41	+33
TN	Memphis	35	9	90	3	1	+38	+26	+16	+5	−3
TN	Nashville	36	10	86	47	1	+22	+11	+3	−6	−14

(continued)

Time Corrections

State/Province	City	North Latitude °	'	West Longitude °	'	Time Zone Code	A (min.)	B (min.)	C (min.)	D (min.)	E (min.)
TX	Amarillo	35	12	101	50	1	+85	+73	+63	+52	+43
TX	Austin	30	16	97	45	1	+82	+62	+47	+29	+15
TX	Beaumont	30	5	94	6	1	+67	+48	+32	+14	0
TX	Brownsville	25	54	97	30	1	+91	+66	+46	+23	+5
TX	Corpus Christi	27	48	97	24	1	+86	+64	+46	+25	+9
TX	Dallas–Fort Worth	32	47	96	48	1	+71	+55	+43	+28	+17
TX	El Paso	31	45	106	29	2	+53	+35	+22	+6	−6
TX	Galveston	29	18	94	48	1	+72	+52	+35	+16	+1
TX	Houston	29	45	95	22	1	+73	+53	+37	+19	+5
TX	McAllen	26	12	98	14	1	+93	+69	+49	+26	+9
TX	San Antonio	29	25	98	30	1	+87	+66	+50	+31	+16
UT	Kanab	37	3	112	32	2	+62	+53	+46	+37	+30
UT	Moab	38	35	109	33	2	+46	+39	+33	+27	+22
UT	Ogden	41	13	111	58	2	+47	+45	+43	+41	+40
UT	Salt Lake City	40	45	111	53	2	+48	+45	+43	+40	+38
UT	Vernal	40	27	109	32	2	+40	+36	+33	+30	+28
VA	Charlottesville	38	2	78	30	0	+43	+35	+29	+22	+17
VA	Danville	36	36	79	23	0	+51	+41	+33	+24	+17
VA	Norfolk	36	51	76	17	0	+38	+28	+21	+12	+5
VA	Richmond	37	32	77	26	0	+41	+32	+25	+17	+11
VA	Roanoke	37	16	79	57	0	+51	+42	+35	+27	+21
VA	Winchester	39	11	78	10	0	+38	+33	+28	+23	+19
VT	Brattleboro	42	51	72	34	0	+4	+5	+5	+6	+7
VT	Burlington	44	29	73	13	0	0	+4	+8	+12	+15
VT	Rutland	43	37	72	58	0	+2	+5	+7	+9	+11
VT	St. Johnsbury	44	25	72	1	0	−4	0	+3	+7	+10
WA	Bellingham	48	45	122	29	3	0	+13	+24	+37	+47
WA	Seattle–Tacoma–Olympia	47	37	122	20	3	+3	+15	+24	+34	+42
WA	Spokane	47	40	117	24	3	−16	−4	+4	+14	+23
WA	Walla Walla	46	4	118	20	3	−5	+2	+8	+15	+21
WI	Eau Claire	44	49	91	30	1	+12	+17	+21	+25	+29
WI	Green Bay	44	31	88	0	1	0	+3	+7	+11	+14
WI	La Crosse	43	48	91	15	1	+15	+18	+20	+22	+25
WI	Madison	43	4	89	23	1	+10	+11	+12	+14	+15
WI	Milwaukee	43	2	87	54	1	+4	+6	+7	+8	+9
WI	Oshkosh	44	1	88	33	1	+3	+6	+9	+12	+15
WI	Wausau	44	58	89	38	1	+4	+9	+13	+18	+22
WV	Charleston	38	21	81	38	0	+55	+48	+42	+35	+30
WV	Parkersburg	39	16	81	34	0	+52	+46	+42	+36	+32
WY	Casper	42	51	106	19	2	+19	+19	+20	+21	+22
WY	Cheyenne	41	8	104	49	2	+19	+16	+14	+12	+11
WY	Sheridan	44	48	106	58	2	+14	+19	+23	+27	+31
CANADA											
AB	Calgary	51	5	114	5	2	+13	+35	+50	+68	+84
AB	Edmonton	53	34	113	25	2	−3	+26	+47	+72	+93
BC	Vancouver	49	13	123	6	3	0	+15	+26	+40	+52
MB	Winnipeg	49	53	97	10	1	+12	+30	+43	+58	+71
NB	Saint John	45	16	66	3	−1	+28	+34	+39	+44	+49
NS	Halifax	44	38	63	35	−1	+21	+26	+29	+33	+37
NS	Sydney	46	10	60	10	−1	+1	+9	+15	+23	+28
ON	Ottawa	45	25	75	43	0	+6	+13	+18	+23	+28
ON	Peterborough	44	18	78	19	0	+21	+25	+28	+32	+35
ON	Thunder Bay	48	27	89	12	0	+47	+61	+71	+83	+93
ON	Toronto	43	39	79	23	0	+28	+30	+32	+35	+37
QC	Montreal	45	28	73	39	0	−1	+4	+9	+15	+20
SK	Saskatoon	52	10	106	40	1	+37	+63	+80	+101	+119

A special section featuring unique mail-order products for all our readers who shop by mail.

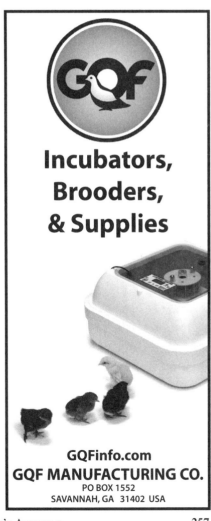

Index to Advertisers

Amusement

ANSWERS TO MIND-MANGLERS (FROM PAGE 187)

1. g. Manganese, used in some glass produced from the 1860s to about 1915, oxidizes when exposed to ultraviolet rays, turning the glass **purple**. Some collectors find the color attractive and thus create this "sun-purple" glass using sunlight or black light. Others consider sun-purple glass to be damaged, placing less value on it than its original, clear form.

2. f. As chlorophyll in banana skin decomposes, it fluoresces in the ultraviolet range. This makes it easier for insects and animals that can see ultraviolet light, such as fruit bats, to find ripe fruit, which appears **indigo** to them.

3. e. The **blue** coloring on a lobster is the result of a genetic variation. (The odds of finding another rare form, the yellow lobster, are 1 in 30 million.)

4. a. In China, **red** is traditionally the dominant color in a wedding dress. It is a symbol of good luck, love, and prosperity.

5. b. Beavers have hard **orange** enamel on the front of their four front teeth. The inner side of each tooth is soft dentin, which wears down faster, keeping the ever-growing teeth sharp.

6. c. Yellow cards indicate unsportsmanlike conduct to soccer players—but only two times per player per game. A second yellow card is immediately followed by a red card, which ejects the player from the match.

7. d. A **green** ground wire is a safety feature to protect against electrical shock; it provides a path for electricity, if a neutral wire fails. ■

General Store Classifieds

For advertising information, contact Bernie Gallagher, 203-263-7171.

ALTERNATIVE ENERGY

FREE HOT WATER FROM YOUR WOOD STOVE
Stainless steel coil mounts in stove, plumbs into existing plumbing.
Wood Stove Hot Water Coil Company, LLC
www.coilheatexchanger.com

ASTROLOGY

SOPHIA GREEN: Don't tell me, I'll tell you. Help with all problems. Help reuniting lovers. You will be satisfied with results. 956-878-7053.

GIFTED HEALER
Solves all problems, troubles, unusual sickness, bad luck, love, life. Removes evil influences, nature problems, brings back lovers to stay, good luck, money. Sister Grace, Hwy. 48, 7905 Bluff Rd., Gadsden SC 29052
803-353-0659

REV. MICHAEL removes evil spirits. Brings back the one you love. Helps in all problems. Phone: 1-888-980-6316.

AALIYAH PASHA, astrology adviser and psychic healer. Can help you with all matters in life. Phone: 772-672-1644.

MILLERS REXALL
Since 1965, Doc Miller is the number man. Send self-addressed, stamped envelope with birthdate. I'll send free numbers that hit. 87 Broad St., Atlanta GA 30303. Readings by phone—
Doc Miller 404-523-8481 w/credit card
medicinesandcurios.com

ASTROLOGY SPIRITUAL READINGS by Ann Brooks. 30 years' experience. One free question by phone. 708-991-7212.

MISS LISA. A gifted astrology reader and advisor with positive results. Will help you with all problems. Waycross, GA. 912-283-3206.

REV. BROWN removes bad luck, ritual work, sickness. Brings back loved ones. 252-823-7178.

ANNE CLARK, spiritual adviser and healer. Can help you with all matters in life. 754-234-8045.

ASTROLOGY SPIRITUAL READING by April. One call. That's all it takes! Guaranteed. One free reading. 312-898-0345.

ONE FREE "WISHES COME TRUE" RITUAL. Tell me your special wish. ElizabethZenor@gmail .com. Elizabeth, Box 9315b, San Bernardino CA 92427-9315. Call 909-473-7470.

FREE SPIRITUAL CATALOG
Luck, money, love can be yours.
Over 8,000 items.
Church Goods Co., Dept. OFA,
PO Box 718, Glenview IL 60025
www.LuckShop.com

WWW.AZUREGREEN.NET
Jewelry, amulets, incense, oils, statuary, gift items, herbs, candles, gemstones.
8,000 items.
413-623-2155

ASTROLOGY & SPIRITUAL ADVISER Lena. Free sample reading. Helps with all matters in life. 954-549-9305.

ASK NOW, PSYCHIC READINGS. Shed light on love struggles, relationship problems, and job dilemmas. 1-888-351-7811.

LOVE LIFE SPECIALIST
Do you want to know what the future holds?
Is your lover thinking about you?
I'll give you the answers you need
to restore your relationship.
Jackie: 561-400-9636 or 561-923-5654

GOD-GIFTED PSYCHIC BEVERLY DAWSAN
Love Specialist ~ Reunites Lovers
Solves impossible problems. Miracles on demand!
Never fails! 100% Successful. Guaranteed results! Call now! 972-464-9739
www.GiftedPsychicReading.com

SISTER WHITE EAGLE CHEROKEE INDIAN HEALER
Returns lovers. Removes negativity, hexes, and roots. Guaranteed to succeed where others failed!
Mt. Airy, NC. 336-719-1540
www.TarotCardLovePsychic.com

Classifieds

GOD'S MESSENGER, SISTER ANN
Religious holy worker. Reunites lovers forever.
Clears stumbling blocks. Stops rootwork!
Solves problems. Never fails!
47 years same location. Fayetteville, NC
910-864-3981

MONICA, GOD-GIFTED PSYCHIC
Reunites lovers permanently. Guaranteed!
Helps business, marriage, and health.
Removes negative energy.
Restores peace of mind. Don't wait! Call now!
Free question!
214-778-9332

REUNITES LOVERS IN 2 DAYS
Famous love psychic Katherine,
over 40 years, solves all problems,
has never failed.
Immediate results. Guaranteed.
928-221-6062

SARAH DAVIS
Helps in all problems. Removes curses, evil,
voodoo, bad luck. Returns loved ones.
Marriage, business, health, money.
Call for lucky numbers:
512-586-3696

ABIGAIL
Solves all problems. Reunites lovers,
removes bad luck and evil influence.
Restores nature. Calls enemies by name.
214-646-4865

MIRACLE LOVE SPECIALIST
Makes lover crazy for you.
Brings back lost love. Pay after results.
818-925-0854 or 713-443-0091
www.lovepsychic4u.com

GOD'S MESSENGER Alexis Morgan. Brings lovers home forever! Never fails! 10-minute free reading! 415-691-5218.

MRS. STARR, LOVE SPECIALIST. Free mini reading, tells soulmate, reunites lovers today. Guarantees results. 919-904-0289.

DO YOU WANT LUCK, LOVE, MONEY?
With spiritual cleansing, you can achieve
your goals in life. Call for your free
Tarot card reading today!
811 Saluda St., Rockhill SC 29730
803-371-7711

MASTER PSYCHIC LOUISE
Helps all problems of life.
Returns lovers, removes negativity,
succeeds where others failed.
2 free questions answered for a better tomorrow.
713-777-1729

MASTER SPIRITUALIST BROTHER DANIEL
I will end your confusion and problems for good!
Get 100% results in all life matters of love,
money, success, health, employment, court cases.
50 years' experience.
772-971-2830

CONFUSED, DEPRESSED?
Need answers?
Call Psychic Jennifer.
Reunites lover. Free readings.
386-438-8868
www.psychicjenn.com

MISS SHEILA, spiritual reader and adviser, will read your entire life without asking any questions. Gives advice on all affairs of life. Killen, AL. 256-272-8766.

PSYCHIC SPIRITUAL HEALER LAURA. Helps in all matters of life, family, business. My powerful methods provide amazingly quick results! Reuniting loved ones. Restores positive energy and luck. 925-399-6573.

LOVE SPELLS HELPING in all problems. Guaranteed. Call for a free reading. 330-678-TRUE (8783).

MISS LEEA, SPIRITUALIST. Tells past, present, and future. Solves all problems. One free question. 219-775-4246.

5TH-GENERATION CELEBRITY PSYCHIC Jennifer Green. Master astrologer reunites lovers, heals broken hearts. One free question. Call or text: 615-944-9707.

NEED HELP FAST? Spiritualist Leza cures all evil spells. Reunites lovers; potions; luck. Opelika, AL. 229-630-5386 or 334-745-0866.

Classifieds

Anecdotes & Pleasantries

A sampling from the hundreds of letters, clippings, articles, and emails sent to us by Almanac readers from all over the United States and Canada during the past year.

What Moles Mean

Does anybody believe this?
–courtesy of P.B.M., Dublin, New Hampshire

- A mole on the right side of the forehead foretells sudden wealth or honor.
- A mole on the nose indicates good luck.
- A mole on a lip is a sign that the person will be successful in affairs of the heart.
- A mole on a leg indicates indolence.
- A mole on an arm is a sign of courage.
- A mole on the right knee signifies good fortune in the choice of a partner.
- A mole on the left knee suggests an honest character.
- A hairy mole portends misfortune.
- A mole with few hairs denotes prosperity.

The Most Difficult Tongue Twister

Experts agree.
–courtesy of F. J., St. Louis, Missouri

Theophilus Thistle, the thistle-sifter, sifted a sieve of unsifted thistles. If Theophilus Thistle, the thistle-sifter, sifted a sieve of unsifted thistles, where is the sieve of unsifted thistles Theophilus Thistle, the thistle sifter, sifted?

A Little Something That You May Not Know About Cows

. . . and maybe it's best that you don't know.
–courtesy of C.J.B., Montreal, Quebec

Some months ago, methane gas from 90 flatulent cows exploded at a farm in Rasdorf, Germany, damaging the roof of the barn and injuring one of the cows (that, apparently, was particularly flatulent). High levels of gas had built up, and then a static electric charge caused the gas to explode. The lesson learned is that it's probably best to keep a few windows open in your cow barn.

(continued)

Solar Strokes

Yet another reason to worry.

–courtesy of P. R., Charlottetown,
Prince Edward Island, who credits Reuters

In a review of more than 11,000 people who suffered a stroke between 1981 and 2004, researchers in New Zealand found that strokes are 19 percent more likely to occur on days with a geomagnetic storm. (These are disruptions to Earth's magnetic field caused by solar winds and coronal mass ejections—effects of the sunspot cycle.) The storms had more effect on people under the age of 65. The good news is that solar activity is generally the lowest that it has been in more than 100 years.

Artist's depiction of solar wind particles interacting with Earth's magnetosphere

Check Your Change

U.S. paper money is printed in sheets of 32 notes. Sometimes, the sheets are misfed into the high-speed presses, resulting in misplaced or upside-down serial numbers. In 1976, a shopper in a Dallas supermarket checkout line was handed a note mistakenly printed with $20 on one side, $10 on the other. At least three currency sheets with the error were printed in 1974, so there may be as many as 96 double-denomination notes in existence. About 20 have been found. Depending on its condition, one of these bills could be worth much more than either face value.

Ten Odd Questions to Contemplate

If man evolved from monkeys and apes, why do we still have monkeys and apes?

Is there another word for synonym?

If a turtle doesn't have a shell, is it homeless or naked?

Who thinks this stuff up?

–courtesy of P. N., Davenport, Florida

Would a fly without wings be called a walk?

What was the best thing before sliced bread?

What if there were no hypothetical questions?

How do they get deer to cross only at those yellow signs?

If you try to fail and succeed, which have you done?

Can vegetarians eat animal crackers?

Artist's depiction: NASA

Proof That Teamwork Gets the Job Done

Even if it's a team of one.

–courtesy of J. B., Safford, Arizona

During the worst blizzard of the century, Mike the mailman was making his deliveries. Unfortunately, his mail truck skidded off the road into a snow bank. After struggling out of it, he walked to the nearest farmhouse seeking help.

The farmer agreed to help Mike and led him into the barn where he introduced him to Tiny, a huge draft horse that he harnessed up. As the farmer grabbed a heavy towrope, the trio set out.

At the scene of the accident, the farmer hooked the rope to both Tiny and the mail truck, and then yelled, "Pull, Sam! Pull, Blaze! Pull, Jack! Pull, Tiny!"

To the mailman's great relief, the truck was back on the road and un-damaged. He thanked the farmer and then asked, "Did you forget your horse's name? You said, 'Pull, Sam! Pull, Blaze! Pull, Jack!' before you said, 'Pull, Tiny!'"

"No, I didn't forget his name," said the farmer. "Tiny is blind, and if he thought he was the only one pulling, he wouldn't have done a darned thing!"

And Finally . . .

–courtesy of F. P., West Caldwell, New Jersey

An old tombstone in a Thurmont, Maryland, cemetery reads: "Here lies an atheist, all dressed up and no place to go." ∎

Send your contribution for *The 2016 Old Farmer's Almanac* by January 30, 2015, to "A & P," The Old Farmer's Almanac, P.O. Box 520, Dublin, NH 03444, or email it to almanac@ypi.com (subject: A & P).

Vinegar Can Be Used For WHAT?

CANTON (Special) - Research from the U.S. to Asia reports that VINEGAR-- *Mother Nature's Liquid Gold*-- is one of the most powerful aids for a healthier, longer life.

Each golden drop is a natural storehouse of vitamins and minerals to help fight ailments and extend life. In fact:

- Studies show it helps boost the immune system to help prevent cancer, ease arthritic pain, and fight cholesterol build-up in arteries.

And that's not all!

Want to control Your weight?

Since ancient times a teaspoon of apple cider vinegar in water at meals has been the answer. Try it.

Worried about age spots? Troubled by headaches? Aches and pain?

You'll find a vinegar home remedy for your problem among the 308 researched and available for the first time in the exclusive *"The Vinegar Book,"* by natural health author Emily Thacker.

As *The Wall Street Journal* wrote in a vinegar article: "Have a Problem?

Chances are Vinegar can help solve it."

This fascinating book shows you step by step how to mix *inexpensive* vinegar with kitchen staples to help:

- Lower blood pressure
- Speed up your metabolism
- Fight pesky coughs, colds
- Relieve painful leg cramps
- Soothe aching muscles
- Fade away headaches
- Gain soft, radiant skin
- Help lower cholesterol
- Boost immune system in its prevention of cancer
- Fight liver spots
- Natural arthritis reliever
- Use for eye and ear problems
- Destroy bacteria in foods
- Relieve itches, insect bites
- Skin rashes, athlete's foot
- Heart and circulatory care, and so much more

You'll learn it's easy to combine vinegar and herbs to create tenderizers, mild laxatives, tension relievers.

Enjoy bottling your own original and delicious vinegars. And tasty pickles and pickling treats that win raves!

You'll discover vinegar's amazing history through the ages *PLUS easy-to-make cleaning formulas that save you hundreds of dollars every year.*

"The Vinegar Book" is so amazing that you're invited to use and enjoy its wisdom on a **90 day No-Risk Trial basis. If not delighted simply tear off and return** *the cover only* **for a prompt refund.** To order right from the publisher at the introductory low price of $12.95 plus $3.98 postage & handling (total of $16.93, OH residents please add 6.5% sales tax) do this now:

Write "Vinegar Preview" on a piece of paper and mail it along with your check or money order payable to: James Direct Inc., Dept. V1299, 500 S. Prospect Ave., Box 980, Hartville, Ohio 44632.

You can charge to your VISA, MasterCard, Discover or American Express by mail. Be sure to include your card number, expiration date and signature.

Want to save even more? Do a favor for a relative or friend and order 2 books for only $20 postpaid. It's such a thoughtful gift.

Remember: It's not available in book stores at this time. And you're protected by the publisher's 90-Day Money Back Guarantee.

SPECIAL BONUS - Act promptly and you'll also receive Brain & Health Power Foods booklet absolutely FREE. It's yours to keep just for previewing *"The Vinegar Book."* Supplies are limited. Order today.

©2014 JDI V0124S02

http://www.jamesdirect.com

A Reference Compendium

R E F E R E N C E

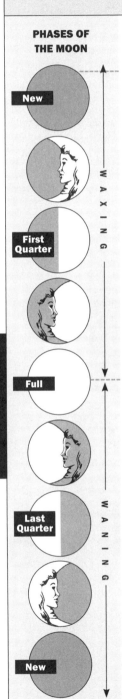

**PHASES OF
THE MOON**

New

First
Quarter

Full

Last
Quarter

New

W A X I N G

W A N I N G

When Will the Moon Rise Today?

A lunar puzzle involves the timing of moonrise. If you enjoy the out-of-doors and the wonders of nature, you may wish to commit to memory the following gem:

The new Moon always rises near sunrise;

The first quarter near noon;

The full Moon always rises near sunset;

The last quarter near midnight.

Moonrise occurs about 50 minutes later each day.

Full Moon Names

NAME	MONTH	VARIATIONS
Full Wolf Moon	**January**	Full Old Moon
Full Snow Moon	**February**	Full Hunger Moon
Full Worm Moon	**March**	Full Crow Moon Full Crust Moon Full Sugar Moon Full Sap Moon
Full Pink Moon	**April**	Full Sprouting Grass Moon Full Egg Moon Full Fish Moon
Full Flower Moon	**May**	Full Corn Planting Moon Full Milk Moon
Full Strawberry Moon	**June**	Full Rose Moon Full Hot Moon
Full Buck Moon	**July**	Full Thunder Moon Full Hay Moon
Full Sturgeon Moon	**August**	Full Red Moon Full Green Corn Moon
Full Harvest Moon*	**September**	Full Corn Moon Full Barley Moon
Full Hunter's Moon	**October**	Full Travel Moon Full Dying Grass Moon
Full Beaver Moon	**November**	Full Frost Moon
Full Cold Moon	**December**	Full Long Nights Moon

The Harvest Moon is always the full Moon closest to the autumnal equinox. If the Harvest Moon occurs in October, the September full Moon is usually called the Corn Moon.

The Origin of Full Moon Names

Historically, the Native Americans who lived in the area that is now the northern and eastern United States kept track of the seasons by giving a distinctive name to each recurring full Moon. This name was applied to the entire month in which it occurred. These names, and some variations, were used by the Algonquin tribes from New England to Lake Superior.

Meanings of Full Moon Names

January's full Moon was called the **Wolf Moon** because it appeared when wolves howled in hunger outside the villages.

February's full Moon was called the **Snow Moon** because it was a time of heavy snow. It was also called the **Hunger Moon** because hunting was difficult and hunger often resulted.

March's full Moon was called the **Worm Moon** because, as the Sun increasingly warmed the soil, earthworms became active and their castings (excrement) began to appear.

April's full Moon was called the **Pink Moon** because it heralded the appearance of the moss pink, or wild ground phlox—one of the first spring flowers.

May's full Moon was called the **Flower Moon** because blossoms were abundant everywhere at this time.

June's full Moon was called the **Strawberry Moon** because it appeared when the strawberry harvest took place.

July's full Moon was called the **Buck Moon** because it arrived when male deer started growing new antlers.

August's full Moon was called the **Sturgeon Moon** because this large fish, which is found in the Great Lakes and Lake Champlain, was caught easily at this time.

September's full Moon was called the **Corn Moon** because this was the time to harvest corn.

The **Harvest Moon** is the full Moon that occurs closest to the autumnal equinox. It can occur in either September or October. At this time, crops such as corn, pumpkins, squash, and wild rice are ready for gathering.

October's full Moon was called the **Hunter's Moon** because this was the time to hunt in preparation for winter.

November's full Moon was called the **Beaver Moon** because it was the time to set beaver traps, before the waters froze over.

December's full Moon was called the **Cold Moon.** It was also called the **Long Nights Moon** because nights at this time of year were the longest.

REFERENCE

The Origin of Month Names

January. For the Roman god Janus, protector of gates and doorways. Janus is depicted with two faces, one looking into the past, the other into the future.

February. From the Latin *februa,* "to cleanse." The Roman Februalia was a month of purification and atonement.

March. For the Roman god of war, Mars. This was the time of year to resume military campaigns that had been interrupted by winter.

April. From the Latin *aperio,* "to open (bud)," because plants begin to grow now.

May. For the Roman goddess Maia, who oversaw the growth of plants. Also from the Latin *maiores,* "elders," who were celebrated now.

June. For the Roman goddess Juno, patroness of marriage and the well-being of women. Also from the Latin *juvenis,* "young people."

July. To honor Roman dictator Julius Caesar (100 B.C.–44 B.C.). In 46 B.C., with the help of Sosigenes, he developed the Julian calendar, the precursor to the Gregorian calendar we use today.

August. To honor the first Roman emperor (and grandnephew of Julius Caesar), Augustus Caesar (63 B.C.–A.D. 14).

September. From the Latin *septem,* "seven," because this was the seventh month of the early Roman calendar.

October. From the Latin *octo,* "eight," because this was the eighth month of the early Roman calendar.

November. From the Latin *novem,* "nine," because this was the ninth month of the early Roman calendar.

December. From the Latin *decem,* "ten," because this was the tenth month of the early Roman calendar.

Easter Dates (2015–18)

Christian churches that follow the Gregorian calendar celebrate Easter on the first Sunday after the paschal full Moon on or just after the vernal equinox.

YEAR	EASTER
2015	April 5
2016	March 27
2017	April 16
2018	April 1

The Julian calendar is used by some churches, including many Eastern Orthodox. The dates below are Julian calendar dates for Easter converted to Gregorian dates.

YEAR	EASTER
2015	April 12
2016	May 1
2017	April 16
2018	April 8

Friggatriskaidekaphobia Trivia

Here are a few facts about Friday the 13th:

- In the 14 possible configurations for the annual calendar (see any perpetual calendar), the occurrence of Friday the 13th is this:

  6 of 14 years have one Friday the 13th.
  6 of 14 years have two Fridays the 13th.
  2 of 14 years have three Fridays the 13th.

- No year is without one Friday the 13th, and no year has more than three.

- 2015 has a Friday the 13th in February, March, and November.

- Months that have a Friday the 13th begin on a Sunday.

R
E
F
E
R
E
N
C
E

The Origin of Day Names

The days of the week were named by ancient Romans with the Latin words for the Sun, the Moon, and the five known planets. These names have survived in European languages, but English names also reflect Anglo-Saxon and Norse influences.

English	Latin	French	Italian	Spanish	Anglo-Saxon and Norse
Sunday	dies Solis (Sol's day)	dimanche	domenica	domingo	Sunnandaeg (Sun's day)
		from the Latin for "Lord's day"			
Monday	dies Lunae (Luna's day)	lundi	lunedì	lunes	Monandaeg (Moon's day)
Tuesday	dies Martis (Mars's day)	mardi	martedì	martes	Tiwesdaeg (Tiw's day)
Wednesday	dies Mercurii (Mercury's day)	mercredi	mercoledì	miércoles	Wodnesdaeg (Woden's day)
Thursday	dies Jovis (Jupiter's day)	jeudi	giovedì	jueves	Thursdaeg (Thor's day)
Friday	dies Veneris (Venus's day)	vendredi	venerdì	viernes	Frigedaeg (Frigga's day)
Saturday	dies Saturni (Saturn's day)	samedi	sabato	sábado	Saeterndaeg (Saturn's day)
		from the Latin for "Sabbath"			

How to Find the Day of the Week for Any Given Date

To compute the day of the week for any given date as far back as the mid–18th century, proceed as follows:

Add the last two digits of the year to one-quarter of the last two digits (discard any remainder), the day of the month, and the month key from the key box below. Divide the sum by 7; the remainder is the day of the week (1 is Sunday, 2 is Monday, and so on). If there is no remainder, the day is Saturday. If you're searching for a weekday prior to 1900, add 2 to the sum before dividing; prior to 1800, add 4. The formula doesn't work for days prior to 1753. From 2000 through 2099, subtract 1 from the sum before dividing.

Example:

The Dayton Flood was on March 25, 1913.

Last two digits of year:	13
One-quarter of these two digits:	3
Given day of month:	25
Key number for March:	4
Sum:	45

45 ÷ 7 = 6, with a remainder of 3. The flood took place on Tuesday, the third day of the week.

KEY

January	1
leap year	0
February	4
leap year	3
March	4
April	0
May	2
June	5
July	0
August	3
September	6
October	1
November	4
December	6

R E F E R E N C E

Animal Signs of the Chinese Zodiac

The animal designations of the Chinese zodiac follow a 12-year cycle and are always used in the same sequence. The Chinese year of 354 days begins 3 to 7 weeks into the western 365-day year, so the animal designation changes at that time, rather than on January 1. **See page 127** for the exact date of the start of the Chinese New Year.

RAT

Ambitious and sincere, you can be generous with your money. Compatible with the dragon and the monkey. Your opposite is the horse.

1924	1936	1948
1960	1972	1984
1996	2008	2020

DRAGON

Robust and passionate, your life is filled with complexity. Compatible with the monkey and the rat. Your opposite is the dog.

1928	1940	1952
1964	1976	1988
2000	2012	2024

MONKEY

Persuasive, skillful, and intelligent, you strive to excel. Compatible with the dragon and the rat. Your opposite is the tiger.

1932	1944	1956
1968	1980	1992
2004	2016	2028

OX OR BUFFALO

A leader, you are bright, patient, and cheerful. Compatible with the snake and the rooster. Your opposite is the sheep.

1925	1937	1949
1961	1973	1985
1997	2009	2021

SNAKE

Strong-willed and intense, you display great wisdom. Compatible with the rooster and the ox. Your opposite is the pig.

1929	1941	1953
1965	1977	1989
2001	2013	2025

ROOSTER OR COCK

Seeking wisdom and truth, you have a pioneering spirit. Compatible with the snake and the ox. Your opposite is the rabbit.

1933	1945	1957
1969	1981	1993
2005	2017	2029

TIGER

Forthright and sensitive, you possess great courage. Compatible with the horse and the dog. Your opposite is the monkey.

1926	1938	1950
1962	1974	1986
1998	2010	2022

HORSE

Physically attractive and popular, you like the company of others. Compatible with the tiger and the dog. Your opposite is the rat.

1930	1942	1954
1966	1978	1990
2002	2014	2026

DOG

Generous and loyal, you have the ability to work well with others. Compatible with the horse and the tiger. Your opposite is the dragon.

1934	1946	1958
1970	1982	1994
2006	2018	2030

RABBIT OR HARE

Talented and affectionate, you are a seeker of tranquility. Compatible with the sheep and the pig. Your opposite is the rooster.

1927	1939	1951
1963	1975	1987
1999	2011	2023

SHEEP OR GOAT

Aesthetic and stylish, you enjoy being a private person. Compatible with the pig and the rabbit. Your opposite is the ox.

1931	1943	1955
1967	1979	1991
2003	2015	2027

PIG OR BOAR

Gallant and noble, your friends will remain at your side. Compatible with the rabbit and the sheep. Your opposite is the snake.

1935	1947	1959
1971	1983	1995
2007	2019	2031

R
E
F
E
R
E
N
C
E

A Table Foretelling the Weather Through All the Lunations of Each Year, or Forever

This table is the result of many years of actual observation and shows what sort of weather will probably follow the Moon's entrance into any of its quarters. For example, the table shows that the week following January 26, 2015, will be fair and frosty, because the Moon enters the first quarter that day at 11:48 P.M. EST. (See the **Left-Hand Calendar Pages, 128–154,** for Moon phases.)

EDITOR'S NOTE: Although the data in this table is taken into consideration in the yearlong process of compiling the annual long-range weather forecasts for *The Old Farmer's Almanac,* we rely far more on our projections of solar activity.

TIME OF CHANGE	SUMMER	WINTER
Midnight to 2 A.M.	Fair	Hard frost, unless wind is south or west
2 A.M. to 4 A.M.	Cold, with frequent showers	Snow and stormy
4 A.M. to 6 A.M.	Rain	Rain
6 A.M. to 8 A.M.	Wind and rain	Stormy
8 A.M. to 10 A.M.	Changeable	Cold rain if wind is west; snow, if east
10 A.M. to noon	Frequent showers	Cold with high winds
Noon to 2 P.M.	Very rainy	Snow or rain
2 P.M. to 4 P.M.	Changeable	Fair and mild
4 P.M. to 6 P.M.	Fair	Fair
6 P.M. to 10 P.M.	Fair if wind is northwest; rain if wind is south or southwest	Fair and frosty if wind is north or northeast; rain or snow if wind is south or southwest
10 P.M. to midnight	Fair	Fair and frosty

This table was created more than 180 years ago by Dr. Herschell for the Boston Courier; *it first appeared in* The Old Farmer's Almanac *in 1834.*

Safe Ice Thickness*

ICE THICKNESS	PERMISSIBLE LOAD	ICE THICKNESS	PERMISSIBLE LOAD
3 inches	Single person on foot	12 inches	Heavy truck (8-ton gross)
4 inches	Group in single file	15 inches	10 tons
7½ inches	Passenger car (2-ton gross)	20 inches	25 tons
8 inches	Light truck (2½-ton gross)	30 inches	70 tons
10 inches	Medium truck (3½-ton gross)	36 inches	110 tons

*Solid, clear, blue/black pond and lake ice
Slush ice has only half the strength of blue ice. The strength value of river ice is 15 percent less.

R
E
F
E
R
E
N
C
E

Heat Index °F (°C)

TEMP. °F (°C)	RELATIVE HUMIDITY (%)								
	40	45	50	55	60	65	70	75	80
100 (38)	109 (43)	114 (46)	118 (48)	124 (51)	129 (54)	136 (58)			
98 (37)	105 (41)	109 (43)	113 (45)	117 (47)	123 (51)	128 (53)	134 (57)		
96 (36)	101 (38)	104 (40)	108 (42)	112 (44)	116 (47)	121 (49)	126 (52)	132 (56)	
94 (34)	97 (36)	100 (38)	103 (39)	106 (41)	110 (43)	114 (46)	119 (48)	124 (51)	129 (54)
92 (33)	94 (34)	96 (36)	99 (37)	101 (38)	105 (41)	108 (42)	112 (44)	116 (47)	121 (49)
90 (32)	91 (33)	93 (34)	95 (35)	97 (36)	100 (38)	103 (39)	106 (41)	109 (43)	113 (45)
88 (31)	88 (31)	89 (32)	91 (33)	93 (34)	95 (35)	98 (37)	100 (38)	103 (39)	106 (41)
86 (30)	85 (29)	87 (31)	88 (31)	89 (32)	91 (33)	93 (34)	95 (35)	97 (36)	100 (38)
84 (29)	83 (28)	84 (29)	85 (29)	86 (30)	88 (31)	89 (32)	90 (32)	92 (33)	94 (34)
82 (28)	81 (27)	82 (28)	83 (28)	84 (29)	84 (29)	85 (29)	86 (30)	88 (31)	89 (32)
80 (27)	80 (27)	80 (27)	81 (27)	81 (27)	82 (28)	82 (28)	83 (28)	84 (29)	84 (29)

EXAMPLE: *When the temperature is 88°F (31°C) and the relative humidity is 60 percent, the heat index, or how hot it feels, is 95°F (35°C).*

The UV Index for Measuring Ultraviolet Radiation Risk

The U.S. National Weather Service's daily forecasts of ultraviolet levels use these numbers for various exposure levels:

UV Index Number	Exposure Level	Time to Burn	Actions to Take
0, 1, 2	Minimal	60 minutes	Apply SPF 15 sunscreen
3, 4	Low	45 minutes	Apply SPF 15 sunscreen; wear a hat
5, 6	Moderate	30 minutes	Apply SPF 15 sunscreen; wear a hat
7, 8, 9	High	15–25 minutes	Apply SPF 15 to 30 sunscreen; wear a hat and sunglasses; limit midday exposure
10 or higher	Very high	10 minutes	Apply SPF 30 sunscreen; wear a hat, sunglasses, and protective clothing; limit midday exposure

"Time to Burn" and "Actions to Take" apply to people with fair skin that sometimes tans but usually burns. People with lighter skin need to be more cautious. People with darker skin may be able to tolerate more exposure.

R
E
F
E
R
E
N
C
E

85	90	95	100
135 (57)			
126 (52)	131 (55)		
117 (47)	122 (50)	127 (53)	132 (56)
110 (43)	113 (45)	117 (47)	121 (49)
102 (39)	105 (41)	108 (42)	112 (44)
96 (36)	98 (37)	100 (38)	103 (39)
90 (32)	91 (33)	93 (34)	95 (35)
85 (29)	86 (30)	86 (30)	87 (31)

What Are Cooling/Heating Degree Days?

Each degree of a day's average temperature above 65°F is considered one cooling degree day, an attempt to measure the need for air-conditioning. If the average of the day's high and low temperatures is 75°, that's ten cooling degree days.

Similarly, each degree of a day's average temperature below 65° is considered one heating degree and is an attempt to measure the need for fuel consumption. For example, a day with temperatures ranging from 60° to 40° results in an average of 50°, or 15 degrees less than 65°. Hence, that day would be credited as 15 heating degree days.

How to Measure Hail

The **Torro Hailstorm Intensity Scale** was introduced by Jonathan Webb of Oxford, England, in 1986 as a means of categorizing hailstorms. The name derives from the private and mostly British research body named the TORnado and storm Research Organisation.

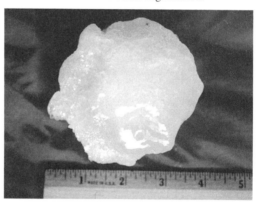

INTENSITY/DESCRIPTION OF HAIL DAMAGE

H0 True hail of pea size causes no damage

H1 Leaves and flower petals are punctured and torn

H2 Leaves are stripped from trees and plants

H3 Panes of glass are broken; auto bodies are dented

H4 Some house windows are broken; small tree branches are broken off; birds are killed

H5 Many windows are smashed; small animals are injured; large tree branches are broken off

H6 Shingle roofs are breached; metal roofs are scored; wooden window frames are broken away

H7 Roofs are shattered to expose rafters; autos are seriously damaged

H8 Shingle and tile roofs are destroyed; small tree trunks are split; people are seriously injured

H9 Concrete roofs are broken; large tree trunks are split and knocked down; people are at risk of fatal injuries

H10 Brick houses are damaged; people are at risk of fatal injuries

R
E
F
E
R
E
N
C
E

How to Measure Wind Speed

The **Beaufort Wind Force Scale** is a common way of estimating wind speed. It was developed in 1805 by Admiral Sir Francis Beaufort of the British Navy to measure wind at sea. We can also use it to measure wind on land.

Admiral Beaufort arranged the numbers 0 to 12 to indicate the strength of the wind from calm, force 0, to hurricane, force 12. Here's a scale adapted to land.

"Used Mostly at Sea but of Help to All Who Are Interested in the Weather"

Beaufort Force	Description	When You See or Feel This Effect	Wind Speed (mph)	(km/h)
0	Calm	Smoke goes straight up	less than 1	less than 2
1	Light air	Wind direction is shown by smoke drift but not by wind vane	1–3	2–5
2	Light breeze	Wind is felt on the face; leaves rustle; wind vanes move	4–7	6–11
3	Gentle breeze	Leaves and small twigs move steadily; wind extends small flags straight out	8–12	12–19
4	Moderate breeze	Wind raises dust and loose paper; small branches move	13–18	20–29
5	Fresh breeze	Small trees sway; waves form on lakes	19–24	30–39
6	Strong breeze	Large branches move; wires whistle; umbrellas are difficult to use	25–31	40–50
7	Moderate gale	Whole trees are in motion; walking against the wind is difficult	32–38	51–61
8	Fresh gale	Twigs break from trees; walking against the wind is very difficult	39–46	62–74
9	Strong gale	Buildings suffer minimal damage; roof shingles are removed	47–54	75–87
10	Whole gale	Trees are uprooted	55–63	88–101
11	Violent storm	Widespread damage	64–72	102–116
12	Hurricane	Widespread destruction	73+	117+

RETIRED ATLANTIC HURRICANE NAMES

These storms have been some of the most destructive and costly.

NAME	YEAR	NAME	YEAR	NAME	YEAR
Charley	2004	Wilma	2005	Paloma	2008
Ivan	2004	Dean	2007	Igor	2010
Dennis	2005	Felix	2007	Tomas	2010
Katrina	2005	Noel	2007	Irene	2011
Rita	2005	Gustav	2008	Sandy	2012
Stan	2005	Ike	2008	Ingrid	2013

Atlantic Tropical (and Subtropical) Storm Names for 2015		
Ana	Ida	Rose
Bill	Joaquin	Sam
Claudette	Kate	Teresa
Danny	Larry	Victor
Erika	Mindy	Wanda
Fred	Nicholas	
Grace	Odette	
Henri	Peter	

Eastern North-Pacific Tropical (and Subtropical) Storm Names for 2015		
Andres	Ignacio	Rick
Blanca	Jimena	Sandra
Carlos	Kevin	Terry
Dolores	Linda	Vivian
Enrique	Marty	Waldo
Felicia	Nora	Xina
Guillermo	Olaf	York
Hilda	Patricia	Zelda

How to Measure Hurricane Strength

The **Saffir-Simpson Hurricane Wind Scale** assigns a rating from 1 to 5 based on a hurricane's intensity. It is used to give an estimate of the potential property damage from a hurricane landfall. Wind speed is the determining factor in the scale, as storm surge values are highly dependent on the slope of the continental shelf in the landfall region. Wind speeds are measured at a height of 33 feet (10 meters) using a 1-minute average.

CATEGORY ONE. Average wind: 74–95 mph. Significant damage to mobile homes. Some damage to roofing and siding of well-built frame homes. Large tree branches snap and shallow-rooted trees may topple. Power outages may last a few to several days.

CATEGORY TWO. Average wind: 96–110 mph. Mobile homes may be destroyed. Major roof and siding damage to frame homes. Many shallow-rooted trees snap or topple, blocking roads. Widespread power outages could last from several days to weeks. Potable water may be scarce.

CATEGORY THREE. Average wind: 111–129 mph. Most mobile homes destroyed. Frame homes may sustain major roof damage. Many trees snap or topple, blocking numerous roads. Electricity and water may be unavailable for several days to weeks.

CATEGORY FOUR. Average wind: 130–156 mph. Mobile homes destroyed. Frame homes severely damaged or destroyed. Windborne debris may penetrate protected windows. Most trees snap or topple. Residential areas isolated by fallen trees and power poles. Most of the area uninhabitable for weeks to months.

CATEGORY FIVE. Average wind: 157+ mph. Most homes destroyed. Nearly all windows blown out of high-rises. Most of the area uninhabitable for weeks to months.

How to Measure a Tornado

The original **Fujita Scale** (or F Scale) was developed by Dr. Theodore Fujita to classify tornadoes based on wind damage. All tornadoes, and other severe local windstorms, were assigned a number according to the most intense damage caused by the storm. An enhanced F (EF) scale was implemented in the United States on February 1, 2007. The EF scale uses 3-second gust estimates based on a more detailed system for assessing damage, taking into account different building materials.

F SCALE		EF SCALE (U.S.)
F0 • 40–72 mph (64–116 km/h)	light damage	EF0 • 65–85 mph (105–137 km/h)
F1 • 73–112 mph (117–180 km/h)	moderate damage	EF1 • 86–110 mph (138–178 km/h)
F2 • 113–157 mph (181–253 km/h)	considerable damage	EF2 • 111–135 mph (179–218 km/h)
F3 • 158–207 mph (254–332 km/h)	severe damage	EF3 • 136–165 mph (219–266 km/h)
F4 • 208–260 mph (333–419 km/h)	devastating damage	EF4 • 166–200 mph (267–322 km/h)
F5 • 261–318 mph (420–512 km/h)	incredible damage	EF5 • over 200 mph (over 322 km/h)

Wind/Barometer Table

Barometer (Reduced to Sea Level)	Wind Direction	Character of Weather Indicated
30.00 to 30.20, and steady	westerly	Fair, with slight changes in temperature, for one to two days
30.00 to 30.20, and rising rapidly	westerly	Fair, followed within two days by warmer and rain
30.00 to 30.20, and falling rapidly	south to east	Warmer, and rain within 24 hours
30.20 or above, and falling rapidly	south to east	Warmer, and rain within 36 hours
30.20 or above, and falling rapidly	west to north	Cold and clear, quickly followed by warmer and rain
30.20 or above, and steady	variable	No early change
30.00 or below, and falling slowly	south to east	Rain within 18 hours that will continue a day or two
30.00 or below, and falling rapidly	southeast to northeast	Rain, with high wind, followed within two days by clearing, colder
30.00 or below, and rising	south to west	Clearing and colder within 12 hours
29.80 or below, and falling rapidly	south to east	Severe storm of wind and rain imminent; in winter, snow or cold wave within 24 hours
29.80 or below, and falling rapidly	east to north	Severe northeast gales and heavy rain or snow, followed in winter by cold wave
29.80 or below, and rising rapidly	going to west	Clearing and colder

NOTE: *A barometer should be adjusted to show equivalent sea-level pressure for the altitude at which it is to be used. A change of 100 feet in elevation will cause a decrease of 1/10 inch in the reading.*

Windchill Table

As wind speed increases, your body loses heat more rapidly, making the air feel colder than it really is. The combination of cold temperature and high wind can create a cooling effect so severe that exposed flesh can freeze.

							TEMPERATURE (°F)								
Calm	**35**	**30**	**25**	**20**	**15**	**10**	**5**	**0**	**−5**	**−10**	**−15**	**−20**	**−25**	**−30**	**−35**
5	31	25	19	13	7	1	−5	−11	−16	−22	−28	−34	−40	−46	−52
10	27	21	15	9	3	−4	−10	−16	−22	−28	−35	−41	−47	−53	−59
15	25	19	13	6	0	−7	−13	−19	−26	−32	−39	−45	−51	−58	−64
20	24	17	11	4	−2	−9	−15	−22	−29	−35	−42	−48	−55	−61	−68
25	23	16	9	3	−4	−11	−17	−24	−31	−37	−44	−51	−58	−64	−71
30	22	15	8	1	−5	−12	−19	−26	−33	−39	−46	−53	−60	−67	−73
35	21	14	7	0	−7	−14	−21	−27	−34	−41	−48	−55	−62	−69	−76
40	20	13	6	−1	−8	−15	−22	−29	−36	−43	−50	−57	−64	−71	−78
45	19	12	5	−2	−9	−16	−23	−30	−37	−44	−51	−58	−65	−72	−79
50	19	12	4	−3	−10	−17	−24	−31	−38	−45	−52	−60	−67	−74	−81
55	18	11	4	−3	−11	−18	−25	−32	−39	−46	−54	−61	−68	−75	−82
60	17	10	3	−4	−11	−19	−26	−33	−40	−48	−55	−62	−69	−76	−84

WIND SPEED (mph)

Frostbite occurs in   30 minutes   10 minutes   5 minutes

EXAMPLE: *When the temperature is 15°F and the wind speed is 30 miles per hour, the windchill, or how cold it feels, is −5°F. For a Celsius version of this table, visit Almanac.com/WindchillCelsius.*   –courtesy National Weather Service

How to Measure Earthquakes

In 1979, seismologists developed a measurement of earthquake size called **Moment Magnitude**. It is more accurate than the previously used Richter scale, which is precise only for earthquakes of a certain size and at a certain distance from a seismometer. All earthquakes can now be compared on the same scale.

MAGNITUDE	EFFECT
Less than 3	Micro
3–3.9	Minor
4–4.9	Light
5–5.9	Moderate
6–6.9	Strong
7–7.9	Major
8 or more	Great

A Gardener's Worst Phobias

Name of Fear	Object Feared
Alliumphobia	Garlic
Anthophobia	Flowers
Apiphobia	Bees
Arachnophobia	Spiders
Batonophobia	Plants
Bufonophobia	Toads
Dendrophobia	Trees
Entomophobia	Insects
Lachanophobia	Vegetables
Melissophobia	Bees
Mottephobia	Moths
Myrmecophobia	Ants
Ornithophobia	Birds
Ranidaphobia	Frogs
Rupophobia	Dirt
Scoleciphobia	Worms
Spheksophobia	Wasps

Herbs to Plant in Lawns

Choose plants that suit your soil and your climate. All of these can withstand mowing and considerable foot traffic.

Ajuga or bugleweed *(Ajuga reptans)*
Corsican mint *(Mentha requienii)*
Dwarf cinquefoil *(Potentilla tabernaemontani)*
English pennyroyal *(Mentha pulegium)*
Green Irish moss *(Sagina subulata)*
Pearly everlasting *(Anaphalis margaritacea)*
Roman chamomile *(Chamaemelum nobile)*
Rupturewort *(Herniaria glabra)*
Speedwell *(Veronica officinalis)*
Stonecrop *(Sedum ternatum)*
Sweet violets *(Viola odorata* or *V. tricolor)*
Thyme *(Thymus serpyllum)*
White clover *(Trifolium repens)*
Wild strawberries *(Fragaria virginiana)*
Wintergreen or partridgeberry *(Mitchella repens)*

Lawn-Growing Tips

■ Test your soil: The pH balance should be 7.0 or more; 6.2 to 6.7 puts your lawn at risk for fungal diseases. If the pH is too low, correct it with liming, best done in the fall.

■ The best time to apply fertilizer is just before it rains.

■ If you put lime and fertilizer on your lawn, spread half of it as you walk north to south, the other half as you walk east to west to cut down on missed areas.

■ Any feeding of lawns in the fall should be done with a low-nitrogen, slow-acting fertilizer.

■ In areas of your lawn where tree roots compete with the grass, apply some extra fertilizer to benefit both.

■ Moss and sorrel in lawns usually means poor soil, poor aeration or drainage, or excessive acidity.

■ Control weeds by promoting healthy lawn growth with natural fertilizers in spring and early fall.

■ Raise the level of your lawn-mower blades during the hot summer days. Taller grass resists drought better than short.

■ You can reduce mowing time by redesigning your lawn, reducing sharp corners and adding sweeping curves.

■ During a drought, let the grass grow longer between mowings and reduce fertilizer.

■ Water your lawn early in the morning or in the evening.

Flowers and Herbs That Attract Butterflies

Allium	*Allium*
Aster	*Aster*
Bee balm	*Monarda*
Butterfly bush	*Buddleia*
Catmint	*Nepeta*
Clove pink	*Dianthus*
Cornflower	*Centaurea*
Creeping thyme	*Thymus serpyllum*
Daylily	*Hemerocallis*
Dill	*Anethum graveolens*
False indigo	*Baptisia*
Fleabane	*Erigeron*
Floss flower	*Ageratum*
Globe thistle	*Echinops*
Goldenrod	*Solidago*
Helen's flower	*Helenium*
Hollyhock	*Alcea*
Honeysuckle	*Lonicera*
Lavender	*Lavandula*
Lilac	*Syringa*
Lupine	*Lupinus*
Lychnis	*Lychnis*
Mallow	*Malva*
Mealycup sage	*Salvia farinacea*
Milkweed	*Asclepias*
Mint	*Mentha*
Oregano	*Origanum vulgare*
Pansy	*Viola*
Parsley	*Petroselinum crispum*
Phlox	*Phlox*
Privet	*Ligustrum*
Purple coneflower	*Echinacea purpurea*
Rock cress	*Arabis*
Sea holly	*Eryngium*
Shasta daisy	*Chrysanthemum*
Snapdragon	*Antirrhinum*
Stonecrop	*Sedum*
Sweet alyssum	*Lobularia*
Sweet marjoram	*Origanum majorana*
Sweet rocket	*Hesperis*
Tickseed	*Coreopsis*
Verbena	*Verbena*
Zinnia	*Zinnia*

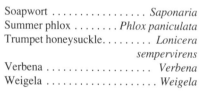

Flowers* That Attract Hummingbirds

Beard tongue	*Penstemon*
Bee balm	*Monarda*
Butterfly bush	*Buddleia*
Catmint	*Nepeta*
Clove pink	*Dianthus*
Columbine	*Aquilegia*
Coral bells	*Heuchera*
Daylily	*Hemerocallis*
Desert candle	*Yucca*
Flag iris	*Iris*
Flowering tobacco	*Nicotiana alata*
Foxglove	*Digitalis*
Larkspur	*Delphinium*
Lily	*Lilium*
Lupine	*Lupinus*
Petunia	*Petunia*
Pincushion flower	*Scabiosa*
Red-hot poker	*Kniphofia*
Scarlet sage	*Salvia splendens*
Soapwort	*Saponaria*
Summer phlox	*Phlox paniculata*
Trumpet honeysuckle	*Lonicera sempervirens*
Verbena	*Verbena*
Weigela	*Weigela*

*NOTE: Choose varieties in red and orange shades, if available.

R
E
F
E
R
E
N
C
E

pH Preferences of Trees, Shrubs, Flowers, and Vegetables

An accurate soil test will indicate your soil pH and will specify the amount of lime or sulfur that is needed to bring it up or down to the appropriate level. A pH of 6.5 is just about right for most home gardens, since most plants thrive in the 6.0 to 7.0 (slightly acidic to neutral) range. Some plants (azaleas, blueberries) prefer more strongly acidic soil in the 4.0 to 6.0 range, while a few (asparagus, plums) do best in soil that is neutral to slightly alkaline. Acidic, or sour, soil (below 7.0) is counteracted by applying finely ground limestone, and alkaline, or sweet, soil (above 7.0) is treated with ground sulfur.

Common Name	Optimum pH Range	Common Name	Optimum pH Range	Common Name	Optimum pH Range
Trees and Shrubs		Walnut, black	6.0–8.0	Nasturtium	5.5–7.5
Apple	5.0–6.5	Willow	6.0–8.0	Pansy	5.5–6.5
Ash	6.0–7.5			Peony	6.0–7.5
Azalea	4.5–6.0	**Flowers**		Petunia	6.0–7.5
Basswood	6.0–7.5	Alyssum	6.0–7.5	Phlox, summer	6.0–8.0
Beautybush	6.0–7.5	Aster, New		Poppy, oriental	6.0–7.5
Birch	5.0–6.5	England	6.0–8.0	Rose, hybrid tea	5.5–7.0
Blackberry	5.0–6.0	Baby's breath	6.0–7.0	Rose, rugosa	6.0–7.0
Blueberry	4.0–5.0	Bachelor's button	6.0–7.5	Snapdragon	5.5–7.0
Boxwood	6.0–7.5	Bee balm	6.0–7.5	Sunflower	6.0–7.5
Cherry, sour	6.0–7.0	Begonia	5.5–7.0	Tulip	6.0–7.0
Chestnut	5.0–6.5	Black-eyed Susan	5.5–7.0	Zinnia	5.5–7.0
Crab apple	6.0–7.5	Bleeding heart	6.0–7.5		
Dogwood	5.0–7.0	Canna	6.0–8.0	**Vegetables**	
Elder, box	6.0–8.0	Carnation	6.0–7.0	Asparagus	6.0–8.0
Fir, balsam	5.0–6.0	Chrysanthemum	6.0–7.5	Bean, pole	6.0–7.5
Fir, Douglas	6.0–7.0	Clematis	5.5–7.0	Beet	6.0–7.5
Hemlock	5.0–6.0	Coleus	6.0–7.0	Broccoli	6.0–7.0
Hydrangea, blue-flowered	4.0–5.0	Coneflower, purple	5.0–7.5	Brussels sprout	6.0–7.5
Hydrangea, pink-flowered	6.0–7.0	Cosmos	5.0–8.0	Carrot	5.5–7.0
Juniper	5.0–6.0	Crocus	6.0–8.0	Cauliflower	5.5–7.5
Laurel, mountain	4.5–6.0	Daffodil	6.0–6.5	Celery	5.8–7.0
Lemon	6.0–7.5	Dahlia	6.0–7.5	Chive	6.0–7.0
Lilac	6.0–7.5	Daisy, Shasta	6.0–8.0	Cucumber	5.5–7.0
Maple, sugar	6.0–7.5	Daylily	6.0–8.0	Garlic	5.5–8.0
Oak, white	5.0–6.5	Delphinium	6.0–7.5	Kale	6.0–7.5
Orange	6.0–7.5	Foxglove	6.0–7.5	Lettuce	6.0–7.0
Peach	6.0–7.0	Geranium	6.0–8.0	Pea, sweet	6.0–7.5
Pear	6.0–7.5	Gladiolus	5.0–7.0	Pepper, sweet	5.5–7.0
Pecan	6.4–8.0	Hibiscus	6.0–8.0	Potato	4.8–6.5
Pine, red	5.0–6.0	Hollyhock	6.0–8.0	Pumpkin	5.5–7.5
Pine, white	4.5–6.0	Hyacinth	6.5–7.5	Radish	6.0–7.0
Plum	6.0–8.0	Iris, blue flag	5.0–7.5	Spinach	6.0–7.5
Raspberry, red	5.5–7.0	Lily-of-the-valley	4.5–6.0	Squash, crookneck	6.0–7.5
Rhododendron	4.5–6.0	Lupine	5.0–6.5	Squash, Hubbard	5.5–7.0
Spruce	5.0–6.0	Marigold	5.5–7.5	Tomato	5.5–7.5
		Morning glory	6.0–7.5		
		Narcissus, trumpet	5.5–6.5		

Produce Weights and Measures

VEGETABLES

Asparagus: 1 pound = 3 cups chopped

Beans (string): 1 pound = 4 cups chopped

Beets: 1 pound (5 medium) = 2½ cups chopped

Broccoli: 1 pound = 6 cups chopped

Cabbage: 1 pound = 4½ cups shredded

Carrots: 1 pound = 3½ cups sliced or grated

Celery: 1 pound = 4 cups chopped

Cucumbers: 1 pound (2 medium) = 4 cups sliced

Eggplant: 1 pound = 4 cups chopped = 2 cups cooked

Garlic: 1 clove = 1 teaspoon chopped

Leeks: 1 pound = 4 cups chopped = 2 cups cooked

Mushrooms: 1 pound = 5 to 6 cups sliced = 2 cups cooked

Onions: 1 pound = 4 cups sliced = 2 cups cooked

Parsnips: 1 pound = 1½ cups cooked, puréed

Peas: 1 pound whole = 1 to 1½ cups shelled

Potatoes: 1 pound (3 medium) sliced = 2 cups mashed

Pumpkin: 1 pound = 4 cups chopped = 2 cups cooked and drained

Spinach: 1 pound = ¾ to 1 cup cooked

Squashes (summer): 1 pound = 4 cups grated = 2 cups sliced and cooked

Squashes (winter): 2 pounds = 2½ cups cooked, puréed

Sweet potatoes: 1 pound = 4 cups grated = 1 cup cooked, puréed

Swiss chard: 1 pound = 5 to 6 cups packed leaves = 1 to 1½ cups cooked

Tomatoes: 1 pound (3 or 4 medium) = 1½ cups seeded pulp

Turnips: 1 pound = 4 cups chopped = 2 cups cooked, mashed

FRUIT

Apples: 1 pound (3 or 4 medium) = 3 cups sliced

Bananas: 1 pound (3 or 4 medium) = 1¾ cups mashed

Berries: 1 quart = 3½ cups

Dates: 1 pound = 2½ cups pitted

Lemon: 1 whole = 1 to 3 tablespoons juice; 1 to 1½ teaspoons grated rind

Lime: 1 whole = 1½ to 2 tablespoons juice

Orange: 1 medium = 6 to 8 tablespoons juice; 2 to 3 tablespoons grated rind

Peaches: 1 pound (4 medium) = 3 cups sliced

Pears: 1 pound (4 medium) = 2 cups sliced

Rhubarb: 1 pound = 2 cups cooked

R
E
F
E
R
E
N
C
E

Sowing Vegetable Seeds

Sow or plant in cool weather	Beets, broccoli, brussels sprouts, cabbage, lettuce, onions, parsley, peas, radishes, spinach, Swiss chard, turnips
Sow or plant in warm weather	Beans, carrots, corn, cucumbers, eggplant, melons, okra, peppers, squashes, tomatoes
Sow or plant for one crop per season	Corn, eggplant, leeks, melons, peppers, potatoes, spinach (New Zealand), squashes, tomatoes
Resow for additional crops	Beans, beets, cabbage, carrots, kohlrabi, lettuce, radishes, rutabagas, spinach, turnips

A Beginner's Vegetable Garden

The vegetables suggested below are common, easy-to-grow crops. Make 11 rows, 10 feet long, with at least 18 inches between them. Ideally, the rows should run north and south to take full advantage of the sun. This garden, planted as suggested, can feed a family of four for one summer, with a little extra for canning and freezing or giving away.

ROW
1 Zucchini (4 plants)
2 Tomatoes (5 plants, staked)
3 Peppers (6 plants)
4 Cabbage

ROW
5 Bush beans
6 Lettuce
7 Beets
8 Carrots
9 Chard
10 Radishes
11 Marigolds (to discourage rabbits!)

Traditional Planting Times

■ Plant **corn** when elm leaves are the size of a squirrel's ear, when oak leaves are the size of a mouse's ear, when apple blossoms begin to fall, or when the dogwoods are in full bloom.

■ Plant **lettuce, spinach, peas,** and other cool-weather vegetables when the lilacs show their first leaves or when daffodils begin to bloom.

■ Plant **tomatoes** and **peppers** when dogwoods are in peak bloom or when daylilies start to bloom.

■ Plant **cucumbers** and **squashes** when lilac flowers fade.

■ Plant **perennials** when maple leaves begin to unfurl.

■ Plant **morning glories** when maple trees have full-size leaves.

■ Plant **pansies, snapdragons,** and other hardy annuals after the aspen and chokecherry trees leaf out.

■ Plant **beets** and **carrots** when dandelions are blooming.

In the Garden

When to . . .

	. . . FERTILIZE	. . . WATER
Beans	After heavy bloom and set of pods	Regularly, from start of pod to set
Beets	At time of planting	Only during drought conditions
Broccoli	3 weeks after transplanting	Only during drought conditions
Brussels sprouts	3 weeks after transplanting	At transplanting
Cabbage	3 weeks after transplanting	2 to 3 weeks before harvest
Carrots	In the fall for the following spring	Only during drought conditions
Cauliflower	3 weeks after transplanting	Once, 3 weeks before harvest
Celery	At time of transplanting	Once a week
Corn	When 8 to 10 inches tall, and when first silk appears	When tassels appear and cobs start to swell
Cucumbers	1 week after bloom, and 3 weeks later	Frequently, especially when fruits form
Lettuce	2 to 3 weeks after transplanting	Once a week
Melons	1 week after bloom, and again 3 weeks later	Once a week
Onion sets	When bulbs begin to swell, and when plants are 1 foot tall	Only during drought conditions
Parsnips	1 year before planting	Only during drought conditions
Peas	After heavy bloom and set of pods	Regularly, from start of pod to set
Peppers	After first fruit-set	Once a week
Potato tubers	At bloom time or time of second hilling	Regularly, when tubers start to form
Pumpkins	Just before vines start to run, when plants are about 1 foot tall	Only during drought conditions
Radishes	Before spring planting	Once a week
Spinach	When plants are one-third grown	Once a week
Squashes, summer	Just before vines start to run, when plants are about 1 foot tall	Only during drought conditions
Squashes, winter	Just before vines start to run, when plants are about 1 foot tall	Only during drought conditions
Tomatoes	2 weeks before, and after first picking	Twice a week

How to Grow Herbs

HERB	START SEEDS INDOORS (weeks before last spring frost)	START SEEDS OUTDOORS (weeks before/after last spring frost)	HEIGHT/ SPREAD (inches)	SOIL	LIGHT**
Basil*	6–8	Anytime after	12–24/12	Rich, moist	○
Borage*	Not recommended	Anytime after	12–36/12	Rich, well-drained, dry	○
Chervil	Not recommended	3–4 before	12–24/8	Rich, moist	◐
Chives	8–10	3–4 before	12–18/18	Rich, moist	○
Cilantro/ coriander	Not recommended	Anytime after	12–36/6	Light	○◐
Dill	Not recommended	4–5 before	36–48/12	Rich	○
Fennel	4–6	Anytime after	48–80/18	Rich	○
Lavender, English*	8–12	1–2 before	18–36/24	Moderately fertile, well-drained	○
Lavender, French	Not recommended	Not recommended	18–36/24	Moderately fertile, well-drained	○
Lemon balm*	6–10	2–3 before	12–24/18	Rich, well-drained	○◐
Lovage*	6–8	2–3 before	36–72/36	Fertile, sandy	○◐
Mint	Not recommended	Not recommended	12–24/18	Rich, moist	◐
Oregano*	6–10	Anytime after	12–24/18	Poor	○
Parsley*	10–12	3–4 before	18–24/6–8	Medium-rich	◐
Rosemary*	8–10	Anytime after	48–72/48	Not too acid	○
Sage	6–10	1–2 before	12–48/30	Well-drained	○
Sorrel	6–10	2–3 after	20–48/12–14	Rich, organic	○
Summer savory	4–6	Anytime after	4–15/6	Medium rich	○
Sweet cicely	6–8	2–3 after	36–72/36	Moderately fertile, well-drained	○◐
Tarragon, French	Not recommended	Not recommended	24–36/12	Well-drained	○◐
Thyme, common*	6–10	2–3 before	2–12/7–12	Fertile, well-drained	○◐

*Recommend minimum soil temperature of 70°F to germinate

** ○ full sun   ◐ partial shade

Annual

Annual, biennial

Annual, biennial

Perennial

Annual

Annual

Annual

Perennial

Tender perennial

Perennial

Perennial

Perennial

Tender perennial

Biennial

Tender perennial

Perennial

Perennial

Annual

Perennial

Perennial

Perennial

Drying Herbs

Before drying, remove any dead or diseased leaves or stems. Wash under cool water, shake off excess water, and put on a towel to dry completely. Air drying preserves an herb's essential oils; use for sturdy herbs. A microwave dries herbs more quickly, so mold is less likely to develop; use for moist, tender herbs.

■ **Hanging Method:** Gather four to six stems of fresh herbs in a bunch and tie with string, leaving a loop for hanging. Or, use a rubber band with a paper clip attached to it. Hang the herbs in a warm, well-ventilated area, out of direct sunlight, until dry. For herbs that have full seed heads, such as dill or coriander, use a paper bag. Punch holes in the bag for ventilation, label it, and put the herb bunch into the bag before you tie a string around the top of the bag. The average drying time is 1 to 3 weeks.

■ **Microwave Method:** This is better for small quantities, such as a cup or two at a time. Arrange a single layer of herbs between two paper towels and put them in the microwave for 1 to 2 minutes on high power. Let the leaves cool. If they are not dry, reheat for 30 seconds and check again. Repeat as needed. Let cool. Do not overcook, or the herbs will lose their flavor.

Storing Herbs and Spices

■ **Fresh herbs:** Dill and parsley will keep for about 2 weeks with stems immersed in a glass of water tented with a plastic bag. Most other fresh herbs (and greens) will keep for short periods unwashed and refrigerated in tightly sealed plastic bags with just enough moisture to prevent wilting. For longer storage, use moisture- and gas-permeable paper and cellophane. Plastic cuts off oxygen to the plants and promotes spoilage.

■ **Spices and dried herbs:** Store in a cool, dry place.

Cooking With Herbs

■ **Bouquet garni** is usually made with bay leaves, thyme, and parsley tied with string or wrapped in cheesecloth. Use to flavor casseroles and soups. Remove after cooking.

■ **Fines herbes** use equal amounts of fresh parsley, tarragon, chives, and chervil chopped fine. Commonly used in French cooking, they make a fine omelet or add zest to soups and sauces. Add to salads and butter sauces, or sprinkle on noodles, soups, and stews.

How to Grow Bulbs

	COMMON NAME	LATIN NAME	HARDINESS ZONE	SOIL	LIGHT*	SPACING (inches)
SPRING-PLANTED BULBS	Allium	*Allium*	3–10	Well-drained/moist	◯	12
	Begonia, tuberous	*Begonia*	10–11	Well-drained/moist	◐●	12–15
	Blazing star/ gayfeather	*Liatris*	7–10	Well-drained	◯	6
	Caladium	*Caladium*	10–11	Well-drained/moist	◐●	8–12
	Calla lily	*Zantedeschia*	8–10	Well-drained/moist	◯◐	8–24
	Canna	*Canna*	8–11	Well-drained/moist	◯	12–24
	Cyclamen	*Cyclamen*	7–9	Well-drained/moist	◐	4
	Dahlia	*Dahlia*	9–11	Well-drained/fertile	◯	12–36
	Daylily	*Hemerocallis*	3–10	Adaptable to most soils	◯◐	12–24
	Freesia	*Freesia*	9–11	Well-drained/moist/sandy	◯◐	2–4
	Garden gloxinia	*Incarvillea*	4–8	Well-drained/moist	◯	12
	Gladiolus	*Gladiolus*	4–11	Well-drained/fertile	◯◐	4–9
	Iris	*Iris*	3–10	Well-drained/sandy	◯	3–6
	Lily, Asiatic/Oriental	*Lilium*	3–8	Well-drained	◯◐	8–12
	Peacock flower	*Tigridia*	8–10	Well-drained	◯	5–6
	Shamrock/sorrel	*Oxalis*	5–9	Well-drained	◯◐	4–6
	Windflower	*Anemone*	3–9	Well-drained/moist	◯◐	3–6
FALL-PLANTED BULBS	Bluebell	*Hyacinthoides*	4–9	Well-drained/fertile	◯◐	4
	Christmas rose/ hellebore	*Helleborus*	4–8	Neutral–alkaline	◯◐	18
	Crocus	*Crocus*	3–8	Well-drained/moist/fertile	◯◐	4
	Daffodil	*Narcissus*	3–10	Well-drained/moist/fertile	◯◐	6
	Fritillary	*Fritillaria*	3–9	Well-drained/sandy	◯◐	3
	Glory of the snow	*Chionodoxa*	3–9	Well-drained/moist	◯◐	3
	Grape hyacinth	*Muscari*	4–10	Well-drained/moist/fertile	◯◐	3–4
	Iris, bearded	*Iris*	3–9	Well-drained	◯◐	4
	Iris, Siberian	*Iris*	4–9	Well-drained	◯◐	4
	Ornamental onion	*Allium*	3–10	Well-drained/moist/fertile	◯	12
	Snowdrop	*Galanthus*	3–9	Well-drained/moist/fertile	◯◐	3
	Snowflake	*Leucojum*	5–9	Well-drained/moist/sandy	◯◐	4
	Spring starflower	*Ipheion uniflorum*	6–9	Well-drained loam	◯◐	3–6
	Star of Bethlehem	*Ornithogalum*	5–10	Well-drained/moist	◯◐	2–5
	Striped squill	*Puschkinia scilloides*	3–9	Well-drained	◯◐	6
	Tulip	*Tulipa*	4–8	Well-drained/fertile	◯◐	3–6
	Winter aconite	*Eranthis*	4–9	Well-drained/moist/fertile	◯◐	3

REFERENCE

DEPTH (inches)	BLOOMING SEASON	HEIGHT (inches)	NOTES
3–4	Spring to summer	6–60	Usually pest-free; a great cut flower
1–2	Summer to fall	8–18	North of Zone 10, lift in fall
4	Summer to fall	8–20	An excellent flower for drying; north of Zone 7, plant in spring, lift in fall
2	Summer	8–24	North of Zone 10, plant in spring, lift in fall
1–4	Summer	24–36	Fragrant; north of Zone 8, plant in spring, lift in fall
Level	Summer	18–60	North of Zone 8, plant in spring, lift in fall
1–2	Spring to fall	3–12	Naturalizes well in warm areas; north of Zone 7, lift in fall
4–6	Late summer	12–60	North of Zone 9, lift in fall
2	Summer	12–36	Mulch in winter in Zones 3 to 6
2	Summer	12–24	Fragrant; can be grown outdoors in warm climates
3–4	Summer	6–20	Does well in woodland settings
3–6	Early summer to early fall	12–80	North of Zone 10, lift in fall
4	Spring to late summer	3–72	Divide and replant rhizomes every two to five years
4–6	Early summer	36	Fragrant; self-sows; requires excellent drainage
4	Summer	18–24	North of Zone 8, lift in fall
2	Summer	2–12	Plant in confined area to control
2	Early summer	3–18	North of Zone 6, lift in fall
3–4	Spring	8–20	Excellent for borders, rock gardens and naturalizing
1–2	Spring	12	Hardy, but requires shelter from strong, cold winds
3	Early spring	5	Naturalizes well in grass
6	Early spring	14–24	Plant under shrubs or in a border
3	Midspring	6–30	Different species can be planted in rock gardens, woodland gardens, or borders
3	Spring	4–10	Self-sows easily; plant in rock gardens, raised beds, or under shrubs
2–3	Late winter to spring	6–12	Use as a border plant or in wildflower and rock gardens; self-sows easily
4	Early spring to early summer	3–48	Naturalizes well; a good cut flower
4	Early spring to midsummer	18–48	An excellent cut flower
3–4	Late spring to early summer	6–60	Usually pest-free; a great cut flower
3	Spring	6–12	Best when clustered and planted in an area that will not dry out in summer
4	Spring	6–18	Naturalizes well
3	Spring	4–6	Fragrant; naturalizes easily
4	Spring to summer	6–24	North of Zone 5, plant in spring, lift in fall
3	Spring	4–6	Naturalizes easily; makes an attractive edging
4–6	Early to late spring	8–30	Excellent for borders, rock gardens, and naturalizing
2–3	Late winter to spring	2–4	Self-sows and naturalizes easily

R
E
F
E
R
E
N
C
E

Substitutions for Common Ingredients

ITEM	QUANTITY	SUBSTITUTION
Baking powder	1 teaspoon	¼ teaspoon baking soda plus ¼ teaspoon cornstarch plus ½ teaspoon cream of tartar
Buttermilk	1 cup	1 tablespoon lemon juice or vinegar plus milk to equal 1 cup; or 1 cup plain yogurt
Chocolate, unsweetened	1 ounce	3 tablespoons cocoa plus 1 tablespoon unsalted butter, shortening, or vegetable oil
Cracker crumbs	¾ cup	1 cup dry bread crumbs; or 1 tablespoon quick-cooking oats (for thickening)
Cream, heavy	1 cup	¾ cup milk plus ⅓ cup melted unsalted butter (this will not whip)
Cream, light	1 cup	⅞ cup milk plus 3 tablespoons melted, unsalted butter
Cream, sour	1 cup	⅞ cup buttermilk or plain yogurt plus 3 tablespoons melted, unsalted butter
Cream, whipping	1 cup	⅔ cup well-chilled evaporated milk, whipped; or 1 cup nonfat dry milk powder whipped with 1 cup ice water
Egg	1 whole	2 yolks plus 1 tablespoon cold water; or 3 tablespoons vegetable oil plus 1 tablespoon water (for baking); or 2 to 3 tablespoons mayonnaise (for cakes)
Egg white	1 white	2 teaspoons meringue powder plus 3 tablespoons water, combined
Flour, all-purpose	1 cup	1 cup plus 3 tablespoons cake flour (not advised for cookies or quick breads); or 1 cup self-rising flour (omit baking powder and salt from recipe)
Flour, cake	1 cup	1 cup minus 3 tablespoons sifted all-purpose flour plus 3 tablespoons cornstarch
Flour, self-rising	1 cup	1 cup all-purpose flour plus 1½ teaspoons baking powder plus ¼ teaspoon salt
Herbs, dried	1 teaspoon	1 tablespoon fresh, minced and packed
Honey	1 cup	1¼ cups sugar plus ½ cup liquid called for in recipe (such as water or oil)
Ketchup	1 cup	1 cup tomato sauce plus ¼ cup sugar plus 3 tablespoons apple-cider vinegar plus ½ teaspoon salt plus pinch of ground cloves combined; or 1 cup chili sauce
Lemon juice	1 teaspoon	½ teaspoon vinegar
Mayonnaise	1 cup	1 cup sour cream or plain yogurt; or 1 cup cottage cheese (puréed)
Milk, skim	1 cup	⅓ cup instant nonfat dry milk plus ¾ cup water

R
E
F
E
R
E
N
C
E

ITEM	QUANTITY	SUBSTITUTION
Milk, to sour	1 cup	1 tablespoon vinegar or lemon juice plus milk to equal 1 cup. Stir and let stand 5 minutes.
Milk, whole	1 cup	½ cup evaporated whole milk plus ½ cup water; or ¾ cup 2 percent milk plus ¼ cup half-and-half
Molasses	1 cup	1 cup honey or dark corn syrup
Mustard, dry	1 teaspoon	1 tablespoon prepared mustard less 1 teaspoon liquid from recipe
Oat bran	1 cup	1 cup wheat bran or rice bran or wheat germ
Oats, old-fashioned (rolled)	1 cup	1 cup steel-cut Irish or Scotch oats
Quinoa	1 cup	1 cup millet or couscous (whole wheat cooks faster) or bulgur
Sugar, dark-brown	1 cup	1 cup light-brown sugar, packed; or 1 cup granulated sugar plus 2 to 3 tablespoons molasses
Sugar, granulated	1 cup	1 cup firmly packed brown sugar; or 1¾ cups confectioners' sugar (makes baked goods less crisp); or 1 cup superfine sugar
Sugar, light-brown	1 cup	1 cup granulated sugar plus 1 to 2 tablespoons molasses; or ½ cup dark-brown sugar plus ½ cup granulated sugar
Sweetened condensed milk	1 can (14 oz.)	1 cup evaporated milk plus 1¼ cups granulated sugar. Combine and heat until sugar dissolves.
Vanilla bean	1-inch bean	1 teaspoon vanilla extract
Vinegar, apple-cider	—	malt, white-wine, or rice vinegar
Vinegar, balsamic	1 tablespoon	1 tablespoon red- or white-wine vinegar plus ½ teaspoon sugar
Vinegar, red-wine	—	white-wine, sherry, champagne, or balsamic vinegar
Vinegar, rice	—	apple-cider, champagne, or white-wine vinegar
Vinegar, white-wine	—	apple-cider, champagne, fruit (raspberry), rice, or red-wine vinegar
Yeast	1 cake (⅗ oz.)	1 package (¼ ounce) or 1 scant tablespoon active dried yeast
Yogurt, plain	1 cup	1 cup sour cream (thicker; less tart) or buttermilk (thinner; use in baking, dressings, sauces)

R
E
F
E
R
E
N
C
E

Types of Fat

One way to minimize your total blood cholesterol is to manage the amount and types of fat in your diet. Aim for monounsaturated and polyunsaturated fats; avoid saturated and trans fats.

■ **Monounsaturated fat** lowers LDL (bad cholesterol) and may raise HDL (good cholesterol) or leave it unchanged; found in almonds, avocados, canola oil, cashews, olive oil, peanut oil, and peanuts.

■ **Polyunsaturated fat** lowers LDL and may lower HDL; includes omega-3 and omega-6 fatty acids; found in corn oil, cottonseed oil, fish such as salmon and tuna, safflower oil, sesame seeds, soybeans, and sunflower oil.

■ **Saturated fat** raises both LDL and HDL; found in chocolate, cocoa butter, coconut oil, dairy products (milk, butter, cheese, ice cream), egg yolks, palm oil, and red meat.

■ **Trans fat** raises LDL and lowers HDL; a type of fat common in many processed foods, such as most margarines (especially stick), vegetable shortening, partially hydrogenated vegetable oil, many commercial fried foods (doughnuts, french fries), and commercial baked goods (cookies, crackers, cakes).

Calorie-Burning Comparisons

If you hustle through your chores to get to the fitness center, relax. You're getting a great workout already. The left-hand column lists "chore" exercises, the middle column shows the number of calories burned per minute per pound of body weight, and the right-hand column lists comparable "recreational" exercises. For example, a 150-pound person forking straw bales burns 9.45 calories per minute, the same workout he or she would get playing basketball.

Chopping with an ax, fast	**0.135**	Skiing, cross country, uphill
Climbing hills, with 44-pound load	**0.066**	Swimming, crawl, fast
Digging trenches	**0.065**	Skiing, cross country, steady walk
Forking straw bales	**0.063**	Basketball
Chopping down trees	**0.060**	Football
Climbing hills, with 9-pound load	**0.058**	Swimming, crawl, slow
Sawing by hand	**0.055**	Skiing, cross country, moderate
Mowing lawns	**0.051**	Horseback riding, trotting
Scrubbing floors	**0.049**	Tennis
Shoveling coal	**0.049**	Aerobic dance, medium
Hoeing	**0.041**	Weight training, circuit training
Stacking firewood	**0.040**	Weight lifting, free weights
Shoveling grain	**0.038**	Golf
Painting houses	**0.035**	Walking, normal pace, asphalt road
Weeding	**0.033**	Table tennis
Shopping for food	**0.028**	Cycling, 5.5 mph
Mopping floors	**0.028**	Fishing
Washing windows	**0.026**	Croquet
Raking	**0.025**	Dancing, ballroom
Driving a tractor	**0.016**	Drawing, standing position

R E F E R E N C E

Freezer Storage Time

(freezer temperature 0°F or colder)

PRODUCT	MONTHS IN FREEZER

Fresh meat

Beef . . . . 6 to 12
Lamb . . . . 6 to 9
Veal . . . . 6 to 9
Pork . . . . 4 to 6
Ground beef, veal, lamb, pork . . . . 3 to 4
Frankfurters . . . . 1 to 2
Sausage, fresh pork . . . . 1 to 2
Ready-to-serve luncheon meats . . . . . Not
recommended

Fresh poultry

Chicken, turkey (whole). 12
Chicken, turkey (pieces) . . . . 6 to 9
Cornish game hen, game birds. . . . 6 to 9
Giblets . . . . 3 to 4

Cooked poultry

Breaded, fried. 4
Pieces, plain 4
Pieces covered with broth, gravy 6

Fresh fruits (prepared for freezing)

All fruits except those
listed below . . . . 10 to 12
Avocados, bananas, plantains 3
Lemons, limes, oranges . . . . 4 to 6

Fresh vegetables (prepared for freezing)

Beans, beets, bok choy, broccoli,
brussels sprouts, cabbage, carrots,
cauliflower, celery, corn, greens,
kohlrabi, leeks, mushrooms, okra,
onions, peas, peppers, soybeans,
spinach, summer squashes . . . .10 to 12
Asparagus, rutabagas, turnips . . . 8 to 10
Artichokes, eggplant . . . . 6 to 8
Tomatoes (overripe or sliced) 2
Bamboo shoots, cucumbers, endive,
lettuce, radishes, watercress . . . . . Not
recommended

Cheese (except those listed below) 6
Cottage cheese, cream cheese, feta, goat,
fresh mozzarella, Neufchâtel, Parmesan,
processed cheese (opened) . . . . . . Not
recommended

PRODUCT	MONTHS IN FREEZER

Dairy products

Margarine (not diet). 12
Butter . . . . 6 to 9
Cream, half-and-half 4
Milk 3
Ice cream . . . . 1 to 2

Freezing Hints

For meals, remember that a quart container holds four servings, and a pint container holds two servings.

To prevent sticking, spread the food to be frozen (berries, hamburgers, cookies, etc.) on a cookie sheet and freeze until solid. Then place in plastic bags and freeze.

Label foods for easy identification. Write the name of the food, number of servings, and date of freezing on containers or bags.

Freeze foods as quickly as possible by placing them directly against the sides of the freezer.

Arrange freezer into sections for each food category.

If power is interrupted, or if the freezer is not operating normally, do not open the freezer door. Food in a loaded freezer will usually stay frozen for 2 days if the freezer door remains closed during that time period.

R
E
F
E
R
E
N
C
E

Plastics

In your quest to go green, use this guide to use and sort plastic. The number, usually found with a triangle symbol on a container, indicates the type of resin used to produce the plastic. Call **1-800-CLEANUP** for recycling information in your state.

Number 1 • *PETE or PET (polyethylene terephthalate)*

IS USED IN . . . . microwavable food trays; salad dressing, soft drink, water, and juice bottles

STATUS . . . . hard to clean; absorbs bacteria and flavors; avoid reusing

IS RECYCLED TO MAKE. . . carpet, furniture, new containers, Polar fleece

PETE

Number 2 • *HDPE (high-density polyethylene)*

IS USED IN . . . . household cleaner and shampoo bottles, milk jugs, yogurt tubs

STATUS . . . . transmits no known chemicals into food

IS RECYCLED TO MAKE. . . detergent bottles, fencing, floor tiles, pens

HDPE

Number 3 • *V or PVC (vinyl)*

IS USED IN . . . . cooking oil bottles, clear food packaging, mouthwash bottles

STATUS . . . . is believed to contain phalates that interfere with hormonal development; avoid

IS RECYCLED TO MAKE. . . cables, mudflaps, paneling, roadway gutters

V

Number 4 • *LDPE (low-density polyethylene)*

IS USED IN . . . . bread and shopping bags, carpet, clothing, furniture

STATUS . . . . transmits no known chemicals into food

IS RECYCLED TO MAKE. . . envelopes, floor tiles, lumber, trash-can liners

LDPE

Number 5 • *PP (polypropylene)*

IS USED IN. . . . . ketchup bottles, medicine and syrup bottles, drinking straws

STATUS . . . . transmits no known chemicals into food

IS RECYCLED TO MAKE. . . battery cables, brooms, ice scrapers, rakes

PP

Number 6 • *PS (polystyrene)*

IS USED IN . . . . disposable cups and plates, egg cartons, take-out containers

STATUS . . . . is believed to leach styrene, a possible human carcinogen, into food; avoid

IS RECYCLED TO MAKE. . . foam packaging, insulation, light switchplates, rulers

PS

Number 7 • *Other (miscellaneous)*

IS USED IN . . . . 3- and 5-gallon water jugs, nylon, some food containers

STATUS . . . . contains bisphenol A, which has been linked to heart disease and obesity; avoid

IS RECYCLED TO MAKE. . . custom-made products

OTHER

How Much Do You Need?

WALLPAPER

Before choosing your wallpaper, keep in mind that wallpaper with little or no pattern to match at the seams and the ceiling will be the easiest to apply, thus resulting in the least amount of wasted wallpaper. If you choose a patterned wallpaper, a small repeating pattern will result in less waste than a large repeating pattern. And a pattern that is aligned horizontally (matching on each column of paper) will waste less than one that drops or alternates its pattern (matching on every other column).

To determine the amount of wall space you're covering:

■ Measure the length of each wall, add these figures together, and multiply by the height of the walls to get the area (square footage) of the room's walls.

■ Calculate the square footage of each door, window, and other opening in the room. Add these figures together and subtract the total from the area of the room's walls.

■ Take that figure and multiply by 1.15, to account for a waste rate of about 15 percent in your wallpaper project. You'll end up with a target amount to purchase when you shop.

■ Wallpaper is sold in single, double, and triple rolls. Coverage can vary, so be sure to refer to the roll's label for the proper square footage. (The average coverage for a double roll, for example, is 56 square feet.) After choosing a paper, divide the coverage figure (from the label) into the total square footage of the walls of the room you're papering. Round the answer up to the nearest whole number. This is the number of rolls you need to buy.

■ Save leftover wallpaper rolls, carefully wrapped to keep clean.

INTERIOR PAINT

Estimate your room size and paint needs before you go to the store. Running out of a custom color halfway through the job could mean disaster. For the sake of the following exercise, assume that you have a 10x15-foot room with an 8-foot ceiling. The room has two doors and two windows.

For Walls

Measure the total distance (perimeter) around the room:

(10 ft. + 15 ft.) x 2 = 50 ft.

Multiply the perimeter by the ceiling height to get the total wall area:

50 ft. x 8 ft. = 400 sq. ft.

Doors are usually 21 square feet (there are two in this exercise):

21 sq. ft. x 2 = 42 sq. ft.

Windows average 15 square feet (there are two in this exercise):

15 sq. ft. x 2 = 30 sq. ft.

Take the total wall area and subtract the area for the doors and windows to get the wall surface to be painted:

400 sq. ft. (wall area)
− 42 sq. ft. (doors)
− 30 sq. ft. (windows)
328 sq. ft.

As a rule of thumb, one gallon of quality paint will usually cover 400 square feet. One quart will cover 100 square feet. Because you need to cover 328 square feet in this example, one gallon will be adequate to give one coat of paint to the walls. (Coverage will be affected by the porosity and texture of the surface. In addition, bright colors may require a minimum of two coats.)

Metric Conversion

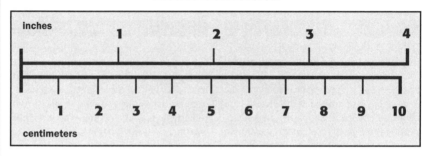

U.S. measure	x this = number	metric equivalent	metric measure	x this = number	U.S. equivalent
inch	2.54	centimeter		0.39	inch
foot	30.48	centimeter		0.033	foot
yard	0.91	meter		1.09	yard
mile	1.61	kilometer		0.62	mile
square inch	6.45	square centimeter		0.15	square inch
square foot	0.09	square meter		10.76	square foot
square yard	0.8	square meter		1.2	square yard
square mile	0.84	square kilometer		0.39	square mile
acre	0.4	hectare		2.47	acre
ounce	28.0	gram		0.035	ounce
pound	0.45	kilogram		2.2	pound
short ton (2,000 pounds)	0.91	metric ton		1.10	short ton
ounce	30.0	milliliter		0.034	ounce
pint	0.47	liter		2.1	pint
quart	0.95	liter		1.06	quart
gallon	3.8	liter		0.26	gallon

If you know the U.S. measurement and want to convert it to metric, multiply it by the number in the left shaded column (example: 1 inch equals 2.54 centimeters). If you know the metric measurement, multiply it by the number in the right shaded column (example: 2 meters equals 2.18 yards).

Where Do You Fit in Your Family Tree?

Technically it's known as consanguinity; that is, the quality or state of being related by blood or descended from a common ancestor. These relationships are shown below for the genealogy of six generations of one family. *–family tree information courtesy Frederick H. Rohles*

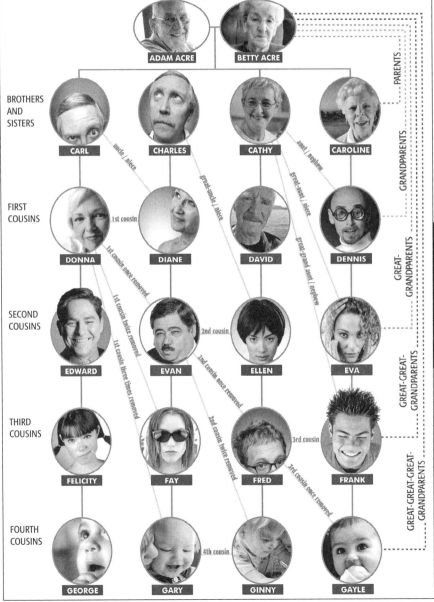

The Golden Rule

(It's true in all faiths.)

Brahmanism:

This is the sum of duty: Do naught unto others which would cause you pain if done to you.

Mahabharata 5:1517

Buddhism:

Hurt not others in ways that you yourself would find hurtful.

Udana-Varga 5:18

Christianity:

All things whatsoever ye would that men should do to you, do ye even so to them; for this is the law and the prophets.

Matthew 7:12

Confucianism:

Surely it is the maxim of loving-kindness: Do not unto others what you would not have them do unto you.

Analects 15:23

Islam:

No one of you is a believer until he desires for his brother that which he desires for himself.

Sunnah

Judaism:

What is hateful to you, do not to your fellow man. That is the entire Law; all the rest is commentary.

Talmud, Shabbat 31a

Taoism:

Regard your neighbor's gain as your own gain and your neighbor's loss as your own loss.

T'ai Shang Kan Ying P'ien

Zoroastrianism:

That nature alone is good which refrains from doing unto another whatsoever is not good for itself.

Dadistan-i-dinik 94:5

—courtesy Elizabeth Pool

Famous Last Words

Waiting, are they? Waiting, are they? Well—let 'em wait.

(To an attending doctor who attempted to comfort him by saying, "General, I fear the angels are waiting for you.")

—Ethan Allen, American Revolutionary general, d. February 12, 1789

A dying man can do nothing easy.

—Benjamin Franklin, American statesman, d. April 17, 1790

Now I shall go to sleep. Good night.

—Lord George Byron, English writer, d. April 19, 1824

Is it the Fourth?

—Thomas Jefferson, 3rd U.S. president, d. July 4, 1826

Thomas Jefferson—still survives . . .

(Actually, Jefferson had died earlier that same day.)

—John Adams, 2nd U.S. president, d. July 4, 1826

Friends, applaud. The comedy is finished.

—Ludwig van Beethoven, German-Austrian composer, d. March 26, 1827

Moose . . . Indian . . .

—Henry David Thoreau, American writer, d. May 6, 1862

Go on, get out—last words are for fools who haven't said enough.

(To his housekeeper, who urged him to tell her his last words so she could write them down for posterity.)

—Karl Marx, German political philosopher, d. March 14, 1883

Is it not meningitis?

—Louisa M. Alcott, American writer, d. March 6, 1888

How were the receipts today at Madison Square Garden?

—P. T. Barnum, American entrepreneur, d. April 7, 1891

Turn up the lights, I don't want to go home in the dark.

—O. Henry (William Sidney Porter), American writer, d. June 4, 1910

Get my swan costume ready.

—Anna Pavlova, Russian ballerina, d. January 23, 1931

Is everybody happy? I want everybody to be happy. I know I'm happy.

—Ethel Barrymore, American actress, d. June 18, 1959

I'm bored with it all.

(Before slipping into a coma. He died 9 days later.)

—Winston Churchill, English statesman, d. January 24, 1965

You be good. You'll be in tomorrow. I love you.

—Alex, highly intelligent African Gray parrot, d. September 6, 2007